ACID Pro 3.0
Keyboard Shortcuts

Here are the keyboard shortcuts you ca...
... universal
...me are specifi...
...n 12 basic groups...

Project File Commands

Option	Description
Ctrl+N	Create new project
Ctrl+Shift+N	Create new project and bypass the New Project dialog box
Crtl+O	Open existing project or media file
Ctrl+S	Save project
Alt+Enter	Open New Project dialog box

Window View Commands

Description	Keys
Alt+1	Hide/display the dockable window that has focus
F6/Shift+F6	Shift focus forward/backward through open ACID windows
F11	Minimize/restore the Window Docking area
Shift+F11	Minimize/restore the Track List
Crtl+F11	Minimize/restore the Track List and Window Docking area simultaneously

WHEN THE TRACK VIEW HAS

Up/down arrow	Zoom time ... small increments
Crtl+up/down arrow	Zoom t... large incr...
Shift+up/down arrow	Zoom tra... n/out in smal...
Crtl+Shift+up/ down arrow	Zoom ... in/out in larg... s
F9	Zoom...

Track View Cursor ... ...t

Description	Keys
Home/End	Go t... g/end of sel... w (if no s...
Ctrl+Home/End or Ctrl+W/E	G... g/end of p...
Page Up/Down	M... ...rid marks
Ctrl+G	Go ... and ...
Shift+G	Go To (using absolute time)
\	Center in view
Numpad 5	Swap on selection
Ctrl+left/right arrow	Move left/right to next marker
Ctrl+Alt+left/ right arrow	Move left/right to event edit points including fade edges

Track View Cursor Placement (continued)

Description	Keys
Left/right arrow	Move left or right by one pixel
Alt+left/right arrow	Move through a video event one frame at a time

Selection Commands

Description	Keys
Shift+click range	Range selection (events) of objects
Ctrl+click	Multiple selection (events) individual objects
Ctrl+A	Select All
Ctrl+Shift+A	Deselect All

Loop Region/Selection Commands

Description	Keys
Shift+Page Up/Down	Select left/right by grid marks
I (in) and O (out)	Make a selection during playback
Ctrl+Shift+Alt+ left/right arrow	Snap selection to event edges
Shift+Alt+left/ right arrow	Expand selection one pixel
Shift+left/right arrow	Make a time selection
Backspace	Restore selections (up to last five)
' (apostrophe)	Double selection length
; (semicolon)	Halve selection length
, (comma)	Shift selection left
. (period)	Shift selection right

Event Commands

Description	Keys
Paint Tool: Ctrl+click	Add a single event containing the entire media file
Erase Tool: Ctrl+click	Erase entire event
Numpad 6	Move selected event(s) right 1 pixel
Numpad 4	Move selected event(s) left 1 pixel
Ctrl+M	Render to new track
S	Split event(s)
F	Create crossfades on selected overlapping events
Ctrl+T	Trim/crop time-selected events only

WITHDRAWN

Teach Yourself
ACID 3.0
in 24 Hours

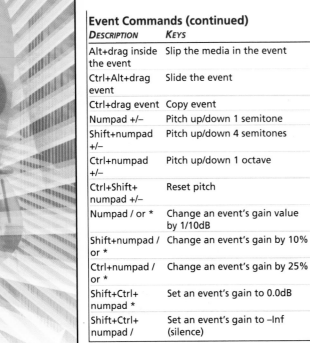

Event Commands (continued)

DESCRIPTION	KEYS
Alt+drag inside the event	Slip the media in the event
Ctrl+Alt+drag event	Slide the event
Ctrl+drag event	Copy event
Numpad +/–	Pitch up/down 1 semitone
Shift+numpad +/–	Pitch up/down 4 semitones
Ctrl+numpad +/–	Pitch up/down 1 octave
Ctrl+Shift+ numpad +/–	Reset pitch
Numpad / or *	Change an event's gain value by 1/10dB
Shift+numpad / or *	Change an event's gain by 10%
Ctrl+numpad / or *	Change an event's gain by 25%
Shift+Ctrl+ numpad *	Set an event's gain to 0.0dB
Shift+Ctrl+ numpad /	Set an event's gain to –Inf (silence)

Playback Commands

DESCRIPTION	KEYS
Spacebar	Start/stop playback
L	Looped playback
Shift+spacebar	Play from start
Ctrl+spacebar or F12	Playback from any window
Ctrl+R	Record
Ctrl+Home/End	Go to start/end
Page Up/Down	Skip backward/forward

Track View Commands

DESCRIPTION	KEYS
Ctrl+L	Ripple Edit mode
Ctrl+D	Draw tool
D/Shift+D	Select next/previous edit tool in list
I or [	Mark in point
O or]	Mark out
Ctrl+M	Render to new track
P	Insert/Show/Hide track-panning envelope
Shift+P	Remove track-panning envelope
V	Insert/Show/Hide track-volume envelope
Shift+V	Remove track-volume envelope
R	Insert region
M	Insert beat marker
H	Insert time marker
C	Insert command marker
T	Add tempo change
K	Add key change

Track View Commands (continued)

DESCRIPTION	KEYS
Shift+T	Add tempo and key change
Alt+drag time marker	Change project tempo

Track List Commands

DESCRIPTION	KEYS
Numpad +/–	Pitch up/down 1 semitone
Ctrl+numpad +/–	Pitch up/down 1 octave
Shift+numpad +/–	Pitch up/down 4 semitones (Windows 2000 only)
Left/right arrow	Decrease/increase fader value
Up/down arrow	Move track selection up/down one track
Shift+up/down arrow	Multi-select tracks
Page Up/Down	Move track selection up/down one "page" of tracks

View Commands

DESCRIPTION	KEYS
Shift+up/down arrow	Increase/decrease track height
Up/down arrow	Zoom in/out time (incremental)
Alt+up arrow	Zoom in time until all video frames display
Ctrl+up/down arrow	Zoom in/out

Chopper Commands

DESCRIPTION	KEYS
/ or A	Insert the Chopper selection
Ctrl+ <	Shift the insertion point left
Ctrl+ >	Shift the insertion point right
N	Link/unlink the length of the increment arrow with the length of the selection
; (semicolon)	Halve the selection length
' (apostrophe)	Double the selection length
< or , (comma)	Shift the selection left by the length of the selection
> or . (period)	Shift the selection right by the length of the selection
Ctrl+Shift+ <	Shift the selection left by the length of the increment arrow
Ctrl+Shift+ >	Shift the selection right by the length of the increment arrow
Ctrl+ ; (semicolon)	Halve the length of the increment arrow
Ctrl+ ' (apostrophe)	Double the length of the increment arrow

Miscellaneous Commands

DESCRIPTION	KEYS
F8	Enable/disable Snapping
Shift+drag	Temporarily disable Snap To
F5	Refresh screen

ACID Pro 3.0 Keyboard Shortcuts

SAMS

Gary Rebholz
Michael Bryant

SAMS
Teach Yourself

WITHDRAWN

Acid 3.0

in 24 Hours

SAMS

201 West 103rd St., Indianapolis, Indiana, 46290 USA

Sams Teach Yourself Acid in 24 Hours

Copyright © 2002 by Sams Publishing

International Standard Book Number: 0-672-32046-0

Library of Congress Catalog Card Number: 00-105838

Printed in the United States of America

First Printing: August 2001

04   03   02   01   4   3   2   1

Trademarks

Warning and Disclaimer

EXECUTIVE EDITOR
Jeff Schultz

DEVELOPMENT EDITOR
Kate Small

MANAGING EDITOR
Charlotte Clapp

PROJECT EDITOR
Carol Bowers

COPY EDITOR
Alice Martina Smith

INDEXER
Sharon Shock

PROOFREADER
Plan-It Publishing

TECHNICAL EDITOR
Sonic Foundry

TEAM COORDINATOR
Amy Patton

MEDIA DEVELOPER
Dan Scherf

INTERIOR DESIGNER
Gary Adair

COVER DESIGNERS
Aren Howell
Alvaro Barros

PAGE LAYOUT
Susan Geiselman
Michelle Mitchell

Contents at a Glance

Contents

PART III   Adding Additional Track Types   123

HOUR 8   Working with MIDI Tracks   125

HOUR 9   Incorporating One-Shot and Beatmapper Tracks   137

Foreword

I have been making music with computers since I purchased my first 512K Macintosh back in the early 1980s. With a one-in and one-out MIDI interface (!) and a single synthesizer, I was one high-tech musical scientist, a regular beat-box Beethoven.

Fast forward a decade-and-a-half and I start to hear rumblings about ACID, Sonic Foundry's click-and-drag miracle music creation tool. It was the talk of the town here in Lotusland: a program that made samples conform to each others' key and tempo, instantaneously! No more laborious tuning and tinkering, time-compressing or time-expanding—somehow, these gifted eggheads had taken all the pain out of linking samples together. It sounded way too easy...could it be illegal?

The only wrinkle was that, to use ACID, I had to leave the Apple world and get a PC for the first time in my life. Hewlett Packard was trying to make inroads in the music production world and sent me a 1Ghz Pavilion to fool around with. An hour later, I had ACID up and running and have never looked back. It is easily the most revolutionary way to make music since Bob Moog started drilling holes in his piano and sticking wires in them.

And the book you are holding in your hands is the way to add rocket fuel to this already sleek racecar, a virtual Cabala of arcane secrets and handy shortcuts to get the most out of ACID. The authors know this program better than most parents know their own kids, so if you own ACID or are considering buying it, don't forget to park this book somewhere between the mouse and the mainframe. It is indispensable.

Imagine having thousands of samples at your fingertips—string passages, drumbeats of every stripe, piano and guitar chord progressions, solo riffs, sound effects and ambient beds—all of them genetically linked and awaiting the entry of your intuition and whimsy! Africa meets the Mississippi Delta meets New Delhi meets Phillip Glass, in B flat or D, at a hip-hoppity 87 beats per minute or a technofied 170. Amazing....

If you promise not to tell, I will wipe a corner of my studio window clean for you to take a peek at how I used ACID for fun and profit a while back. My partner, Don Was, was hired to be the musical director of the Academy Awards in the year 2000 and asked whether I'd like to score the montages of clips from the nominated films—you know, for best Art Direction and such. I, of course, agreed, booting up the old HP and ACID and popping the videotape in the VCR.

Three days later, I had scored eight such segments for the Oscar broadcast. The producers were amazed and delighted that I'd troubled to hit each and every change of mood in the montages, and I had been credited as an orchestrator alongside Burt Bacharach and

Marc Shaiman! Little did they know I had performed this compositional magic with a mouse in one hand and a remote control in the other. And with the new video capabilities in ACID 3.0, I can dispense with the remote altogether. As they have said in a thousand cheesy TV spots, "Thanks, ACID!"

I only wish I had had this book handy. I will next time—believe that!
David Was
Los Angeles, June 2001

About the Authors

Gary Rebholz works as a Training and Development Specialist for Sonic Foundry where, for the past three years, he has created training materials and programs for employees as well as customers. Gary has been involved with training in the graphics and creative arts fields for more than 10 years. He has also been involved with audio production and music since he started a personal vendetta against disco in the late 1970s. This is Gary's third book for Sams Publishing. His other titles are *How to Use Flash 5* (with Denise Tyler), and *How to Use HTML and XHTML*. Gary lives a quiet life in a small rural Wisconsin town when he's not snatching sharp objects out of his toddler's mouth or trying to determine the whereabouts of his teenagers.

Currently the Director of Training and Consulting Services at Sonic Foundry in Madison, Wisconsin, **Michael Bryant** has been helping people unlock the secrets of ACID Pro and other Sonic Foundry products for more than two years. He has been involved in education of one kind or another for more than 25 years. He has taught students at all levels: from sixth grade to college-level classes as well as adult technical education programs. Along with his career in education, he has spent more than 18 years in the audio and video production industry. He first joined the digital audio revolution in the late 80s while operating a recording studio. As soon as he learned about the power and ease with which you can work with audio in the digital domain, he quickly traded in his razor blade for a mouse.

Dedication

Michael's Dedication

To Karen, for your love, inspiration, and support.

Gary's Dedication

To Kevin Rau, M. Scott Young, and Joe Vosen. And to our buddy, Rick Tacey, who would have loved to make music with ACID Pro.

Acknowledgments

A lot of people helped us along the way with this book. First we'd like to thank the ACID 3.0 development team at Sonic Foundry for their hard work on creating such an awesome product. We especially want to thank Chris Moulios, Frank Shotwell, Dennis Adams, Caleb Pourchot, Koriana Kent, Shawn Pourchot, Matt Miller, Peter Haller, Curt Palmer, and Mike Leger who went out of their way to help us understand the ins and outs of the program, tolerated our constant questioning, and offered help above and beyond what we asked for. Jenn Liang and Joel Gilbertson also played important roles in building our understanding of the new features in the software. Thanks to Dave Hollinden, an indispensable source of information on both ACIDplanet and using ACID with Flash. Thanks to Kevin Canney (who wrote the ACID Online help), and Shane Tracy for reviewing chapters and providing valuable feedback. Thanks also to Rebecca Rivest who wrote the ACID manual to which we frequently turned for help and ideas. Thanks to Stephanie Pfeiffer who allowed her staff to take time out of their regular duties to help us. Thanks to Chris Cain and Trish Sarubbi. Thanks to Steve "The Playah" Foldvari for finding Mr. Was. Thanks to Kevin St. Angel and Tim Mair for help with the companion CD. Thanks to Mike Scheibinger and his artists for the great loops used in our examples. Thanks to Brad Reinke for supporting our efforts and for clearing the way to get this project done. Thanks to Rob Uhrina for helping to get the word out.

We also want to thank the people behind the scenes at Sams Publishing, especially Kate Small and Jeff Schultz who showed amazing patience and provide valuable guidance, and Alice Martina Smith, Carol Bowers, and Mark Taber.

Thanks to David Was (still looking for the powers what am) for showing how the pros use ACID Pro, and for his contribution to this project.

Finally, thanks to Mary Waitrovich and Denise Tyler. Their early involvement in this project got us up and running and took us a long way down the road to finishing it.

Gary's Acknowledgements

First I want to thank my co-author, Michael Bryant for sticking with me on the roller coaster. His steady hand and calm approach made this project—and all our projects—manageable and enjoyable and made our goals achievable. Thanks to my brother Tom and all my sisters (Sue, Judy, Jeanne, and Barb) for always showing their faith in my abilities. Thanks to Becky, Jake, Leah, and Kyri (and the two to be born about the time this book hits the press) for making life a true joy.

Michael's Acknowledgements

I want to thank my good friends David Englestad and Dean Barker. Their constant encouragement keeps me on track. Thanks to Tracy Comer and Damon Bourne for keeping the music alive in my life. Thanks to Lester and Margaret Bryant who taught me how to work hard and get the job done. A very special thank you to my co-author Gary Rebholz. No matter how tough it got, he still made it fun. I have learned a great deal from him about writing and about life. It is a joy to work with him and an honor to be his friend. Finally, thanks to my wife and best friend Karen. Your love is the center of my life.

Tell Us What You Think!

As the reader of this book, *you* are our most important critic and commentator. We value your opinion and want to know what we're doing right, what we could do better, what areas you'd like to see us publish in, and any other words of wisdom you're willing to pass our way.

You can e-mail or write me directly to let me know what you did or didn't like about this book—as well as what we can do to make our books stronger.

Please note that I cannot help you with technical problems related to the topic of this book, and that due to the high volume of mail I receive, I might not be able to reply to every message.

When you write, please be sure to include this book's title and author as well as your name and phone or fax number. I will carefully review your comments and share them with the author and editors who worked on the book.

E-mail: M3feedback@samspublishing.com

Mail: Jeff Schultz
        Executive Editor
        Sams Publishing
        201 West 103rd Street
        Indianapolis, IN 46290 USA

Introduction

The ACID Revolution

Sometimes something comes along that is so unique you can only describe it as revolutionary. ACID from Sonic Foundry is truly such a thing. Think we're exaggerating? Think we're just saying that because we work for Sonic Foundry? Judge for yourself. Whether or not you're a musician, ACID will change the way you think about making music. It will also supply hours of musical enjoyment.

What else do you call a software package that is so fresh, so innovative, and so ingenious that even after the release of version 3, no competitor has been able to release a similar product that comes close to the awesome power built into the program? Nothing does what ACID does. Nothing allows people—musicians and non-musicians alike—to create compelling, original music so quickly and easily. Making music is now a simple process of pick, paint, and play. That's ACID. That's a revolution.

Using computers to make music is nothing new. Musicians have been doing it for a long time now. For a number of years, musicians have been loading samples of real audio (called "loops") into sophisticated synthesizers (called "samplers") to re-create the sound of various instruments. Still, any musician who has ever worked with loops in a sampler will tell you that making music this way can be a painstaking process.

Notice that we keep saying *musicians*. That's important because, until the release of ACID 1.0 in 1998, you really had to be a musician to make music on a computer. You had to play an instrument. You had to know at least some music theory. And a musician who uses loops in a sampler needs even more specialized knowledge.

Making music on the computer was a game for a rare breed of musician/techno-whiz-kid. Then, in 1998, along came ACID. ACID not only gave musicians a new and powerful way of working with music, it also opened the music creation doors to people with little or no formal musical background. ACID allows anyone to combine a wide variety of loops into a project and make music.

Right about now, we hear our musician friends out there saying, "Now wait just a minute! The loops that were recorded in the key of F will sound horrible when played with loops recorded in the key of A. And if they've been recorded at different tempos, nothing is going to work. Far from making music, you'll only make very unpleasant noise! You can't just pick a bunch of audio loops, paint them together into a project, play the song back, and expect it to sound decent."

Yes, you can. ACID automatically matches the key and tempo of any loop you add (and all the other loops in your project) to the master project tempo and key. Take a bass loop recorded at a specific tempo in a specific key, paint it into your project along with that guitar loop recorded at a different tempo and key, and play your project. It sounds great. Not only that, you can change the project tempo and key to any setting you want—and all your loops change to match the new project settings. And they still sound great! As you can see, ACID takes the idea of using loops to make music in a totally new direction.

By the way, it's okay if you don't understand this discussion about tempos and keys. You don't have to understand it to use ACID. Still, it certainly can't hurt your ability to create great-sounding music if you know a little bit about music. As you progress through this book, you'll learn how to make music with ACID. If you're not careful, you'll even pick up some music theory along the way.

We've made it clear that you don't have to be a musician to use ACID. But don't think that because you are a musician you can't find a use for the software. Many musicians, from beginners to professionals (like David Was, who wrote the Foreword for this book), make great use of the power in ACID. Singers use ACID to build music beds for demo songs. Guitar players use ACID to build killer drum, percussion, and rhythm arrangements. With the help of ACID, countless musicians add to their recordings instruments that they don't actually own or know how to play. Far from threatening musicians by allowing anyone to make music, ACID empowers musicians to take their music to a higher level or in a totally new direction. The possibilities are endless, and the more you use the program, the more your musical creativity soars.

This book is written for music enthusiasts of all levels. Advanced users will pick up tips and tricks even in the basic sections, and beginners will find even the advanced topics easy to understand. New terms are clearly defined in the hour in which they are used, as well as in the Glossary in the back of the book. There are plenty of examples to work with in every lesson, and the CD-ROM that accompanies this book contains all the loops you need to follow along in ACID. (All the loops are yours to keep and use however you like—for free!) This is meant to be a hands-on book. In the next 24 hours, you'll learn by doing. Open the book, open ACID, and start making music within the first couple hours. Use the techniques we teach here, even as you learn them.

The book is divided into seven parts. Part I, "Understanding the Basics," introduces the basics you need to get started and will have you creating music right away, no matter what your musical skill level. In Part II, "Moving Beyond the Basics," you'll work with complete arrangements and more advanced editing techniques. Part III, "Adding Additional Track Types," introduces new track types and an exciting new tool called the Beatmapper. In Part IV, "Using the Special Construction Tools," you'll mix your project with digital effects and work with some new tips and tricks. Part V, "Recording," shows you how to record your own loops and add vocals to your project. Part VI, "Delivering Your Creations," discusses several ways to deliver your composition, including burning to CD, posting on the World Wide Web, and creating music for your Macromedia Flash movies. Finally, Part VII, "Using the Companion Software," introduces several additional applications included with ACID Pro 3.0—Sound Forge XP, Vegas Audio LE, and the Sonic Foundry Virtual MIDI Router—and how these applications complement ACID.

These 24 hours show you how to create music with ACID. At several points along the way, we'll give you a piece of advice that is so important we want to repeat it now, before you even get started: There is no "one right way" to use ACID 3.0. Your only bounds are defined by the limits of your creativity. You might very well find ways to use this software that haven't been thought of yet. If you do, don't forget to tell your fellow ACID users…and us!

We hope you enjoy reading the book and working through the sample projects in each hour. Now, let's get busy making music with ACID 3.0!

PART I
Understanding the Basics

Hour

Hour 1

Introducing ACID 3.0

So, you want to make some music. In this book, we show you how you can make original, royalty-free music with ACID. *Your* music. But, if you've ever been in a band, you know the realities. Before you can make the music, you have to spend a little time getting ready. Practice that guitar. Set up those amplifiers. Well, this hour is the ACID equivalent to those tasks.

This first hour gets you up and running with ACID. It explores the concept of making music the ACID way, discusses the nuts and bolts of hardware setup and program installation, and gives a quick overview of the essential pieces of the ACID interface.

If you are new to ACID, this hour is critical. Even if you've been using previous versions of ACID, we suggest that you read through this hour. ACID 3.0 introduces so many rich new features that you might need a little help orienting yourself to the new look and feel of certain parts of the program. Yet, even with all the new functionality and the improved user interface features, ACID remains incredibly easy to use.

In this hour, you will:

- Learn how to make music the ACID way
- Gather the hardware you'll need
- Install and register ACID
- Take a quick walk through the program's interface
- Preview the new version 3.0 features

Making Music with ACID

In simple terms, ACID allows you to combine musical *loops* to create music projects on your computer. As long as you own the loops you use in your projects, you own the music you create. You can use that music for whatever purpose you desire. All the loops that come with ACID (there are hundreds) are royalty free. Additionally, you can buy other royalty-free loop library collections from the Sonic Foundry Web site (at www.sonicfoundry.com). There are many other sources for buying loops (though they might not be optimized for use in ACID). We'll even show you how to make your own loops!

A musical *loop* is typically a small file of precisely edited digital audio that can smoothly repeat continuously. For example, the file might be a recording of a drum beat that you play from beginning to end. When the loop reaches the end, it starts over again at the beginning and continues to play seamlessly over and over for as many times as you specify. Loops make it possible for you to create a long drum track (as an example) using a relatively small loop file.

ACID enables you to create original music for that CD of jazz songs you've always wanted to record, or to score original music for your video projects. You can create original dance remixes for your next party. Techno, house, rock, blues, classical, country, ethnic, world, and on and on—you can create it in ACID.

You use a simple three-step process to create music in ACID. Sonic Foundry calls this process "pick, paint, and play," and literally anyone can do it. First, you pick the loop you want to add to your song. Second, you paint it into the project. Third, you play your new song and listen to your craftwork. Of course, there's much, much more to the program than that, but the pick, paint, and play approach makes it easy to dive in and start creating original music.

Setting Up the Hardware

We know you're anxious to get started, but there are a few things we should mention before we get to making the music. First, we need to discuss a few basic hardware issues.

Minimum System Requirements

Because of its new robustness, ACID 3.0 has minimum computer requirements that are a bit stiffer than its ancestors. Here's what you'll need to run the software:

- 300MHz processor (400MHz processor for video editing)
- Windows-compatible sound card
- CD-ROM drive
- Supported CD-Recordable drive (for CD burning only)
- 64MB RAM (128MB recommended)
- 60MB hard-disk space for program installation
- Microsoft Windows 98, Me, or 2000 (Windows 98SE, Me, or 2000 for video scoring and to use Vegas Audio LE)
- DirectX Media 8.0 Runtime (included)
- Internet Explorer 5.0 or later to view online Help

ACID 3.0 does not work with Windows NT because this operating system lacks certain features that are essential to ACID. Be particularly mindful of which version of Windows 98 you have. Although ACID 3.0 works with both versions, only Windows 98SE supports the video scoring features. If you're not planning on working with video (or using Vegas Audio LE), you can successfully run ACID with Windows 98a.

Your Computer Sound Card

To hear sound from your computer, the computer must be equipped with a sound card. Although ACID works with virtually any Windows-compatible sound card, a high-quality sound card enhances your ability to make great-sounding music. The benefits of using a professional-level card (for which you can expect to pay $300 and up) include higher audio fidelity, lower noise levels, multiple inputs and outputs, and MIDI support.

Consumer-level cards continue to improve, and you can find relatively high-quality cards starting at around $150. Your computer equipment retailer can help you find a card that fits your needs and budget.

Your Computer Speakers

High-quality speakers help you create high-quality music. On the other hand, you can still enjoy ACID even if you don't want to spring for expensive speakers. Anything that allows you to hear the output of your computer will let you create music in ACID.

> We believe that you won't regret buying the highest quality sound card and speakers you can afford. As you become more proficient with ACID, you'll most likely want to upgrade to a sound card that results in better quality audio, and in speakers that allow you to better monitor your musical creations. If you know that's where you're headed, consider making the investment in higher-end gear now.

Installing and Registering ACID

If you don't already own ACID 3.0, you can install the demonstration version of ACID Pro from the companion disc to this book. To do so, insert the companion CD into your disc drive. Navigate to the ACID Setup folder and double-click `msisetup.exe`. This launches the ACID Installation Wizard (shown in Figure 1.1). Follow the prompts to accept the license agreement, provide user information, choose a setup type, and specify an install location. Click Next on each screen of the Installation Wizard to move to the next screen. On the final screen of the wizard, click Install to complete the installation process.

FIGURE 1.1

Follow the steps of the Installation-Wizard to install ACID Pro.

You can use the demo version of ACID Pro provided on this book's companion disc to follow along with most of the examples. A couple major restrictions of the demo version are that you can record and play back only two minutes of sound or video. Also, the demo version does not allow you to save, export, burn your work to CD, or publish your project. To upgrade from the demo version to the full version of ACID, choose Upgrade Now from the Help menu and follow the prompts. Or see your local ACID dealer.

As noted in the minimum requirements for ACID, Microsoft DirectX 8.0 is required to run the program. DirectX 8.0 allows programmers to increase the performance of games and multimedia software. If your computer does not currently have DirectX 8.0, the installation process alerts you of that fact and points you to where you can find the program so you can install it.

Because the new generation of games and multimedia software requires higher performance, Microsoft has designed DirectX Media 8.0 to be an extension to the Windows operating system, expecting that software manufacturers will keep up with the technology. After you install it, you cannot uninstall it. The only way to remove it is to completely reinstall your operating system. Although ACID 3.0 supports DirectX Media 8.0, not all software programs do. Some multimedia programs and games might not run properly after you install DirectX 8.0 on your computer. If you have a question about the software currently on your computer, contact the software vendor to verify that it runs properly under DirectX Media 8.0 before you install the extension!

Understanding the Interface

Let's take a quick look at the ACID interface. This orientation will prepare you for Hour 2, "Getting Started" in which you will learn the basics of assembling your first ACID project.

For anyone familiar with other Sonic Foundry applications, particularly Vegas Audio and Vegas Video, the new ACID looks very familiar. Sonic Foundry has ported many of the best features of the Vegas products over to ACID. Still, if you've used ACID 1.0 or 2.0, the look of ACID 3.0 is familiar enough that you'll quickly catch on to the new features of the user interface.

The Menu Bar

The ACID menu bar, shown in Figure 1.2, presents many of the same menus and options available in other Windows programs.

FIGURE 1.2

The ACID Pro menu bar and toolbar enable you to access ACID Pro features.

The File menu contains commands related to creating, saving, and closing files. The Edit menu contains familiar entries such as Cut, Copy, and Paste, as well as editing features and tools specific to ACID. The View menu allows you to show and hide various elements of the ACID interface and to change your desired Time ruler format.

The Insert menu provides options for inserting markers into your project. We'll use a considerable amount of ink talking about the various markers and their usefulness. You also use the Insert menu when you want to insert time into your project and add envelopes to a track.

> We're introducing a number of terms here with which you might be unfamiliar, such as Time ruler, markers, tracks, and envelopes. Rather than defining all the terms here and overloading you with definitions that can't yet be tied to practical use, we'll define these terms when we discuss them in later hours.

The Tools menu allows you to access many of the special functions of ACID, including rendering audio from one track to a new track, extracting songs from CDs, burning new CDs, and linking directly to your chosen audio and MIDI editors.

The Options menu lets you define much of the practical behavior of ACID, such as whether or not objects snap to the timeline grid and markers, or whether your envelopes are locked to the events on the ACID Track View. The Options menu also offers commands to customize the toolbar (discussed in the following section) and reset your ACID preferences.

Finally, the Help menu gives you access to the ACID Online Help file, the Sonic Foundry and ACIDplanet.com Web sites, and (if you have installed the demo version) the option to instantly upgrade to the full version of ACID.

The Toolbar

Many buttons on the ACID toolbar exist as shortcuts for performing the functions that can be found in the ACID menus. The first half of the toolbar contains standard buttons for creating new projects, opening existing projects, saving, and so forth. It also holds the Publish To button, which we'll talk more about in Hour 19, "Publishing to ACIDplanet.com."

The last half of the toolbar contains buttons specific to ACID. The last button in the toolbar, the What's This help button, allows you to click on an element in the ACID interface for a quick description of that element and its function.

The Time Displays

As shown in Figure 1.3, two displays (Time at Cursor, and Measure and Beat at Cursor) show the time at the current cursor position in their respective formats. Double-click either of the displays, type a new position, and press the Tab key to move the cursor to the exact position specified.

FIGURE 1.3

The time displays make it easy to move to a specific location in your project.

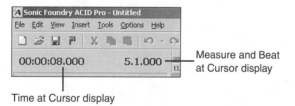

Measure and Beat at Cursor display

Time at Cursor display

The Track List

The Track List area (see Figure 1.4) contains nothing when you start a new project. After you add a track to your project, a Track Header for that track appears in the Track List area. The Track Header provides a variety of buttons, faders, and sliders you use to work with the audio on the track.

Two controls at the bottom of the Track List area control the project *tempo* and *key*. Use the Tempo slider to change the tempo of your music to a setting within the default range of 70 to 200 beats per minute (bpm). To widen the tempo range, choose Options, Preferences from the menu bar; on the Editing tab of the Preferences dialog box, use the Project Tempo Range fields to set the endpoints of the range to as little as 40bpm or as much as 300bpm.

ACID automatically adjusts the original tempo of a loop to match the tempo of the project. You can add loops originally recorded at a fast tempo to a project that contains loops originally recorded at a slow tempo, and all the loops will play at the specified project tempo. Click the Project Key button (it looks like a tuning fork) to set the key of your project. ACID automatically transposes each loop based on its "root note" to match the key you specify for the project.

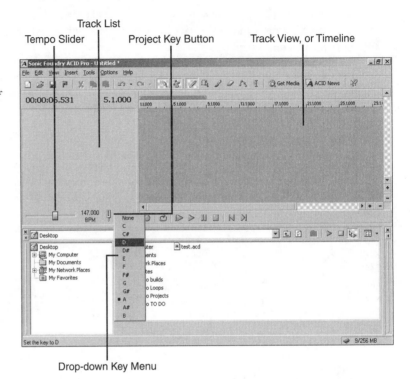

FIGURE 1.4

Use the Tempo slider to adjust the speed of your composition; use the Project Key button to change the key of your music.

NEW TERM   For those nonmusicians in the group, the *tempo* of your project simply means the speed at which the song plays. Measured in beats per minute, the project tempo setting tells ACID how fast to play the loops you add to your project.

NEW TERM   The notes used in a song are usually based on a specific arrangement of notes that sound good together, called a *musical scale*. The *key* of a song specifies the musical scale used as the basis of the music.

The Track View Area

In the Track View area (sometimes referred to as the timeline), you do most of the work required to write your ACID music. We'll spend a great deal of time in the Track View area in the next 23 hours!

The Window Docking Area

The Window Docking area serves as a storage center for various windows (see Figure 1.5). You can dock windows in this area or tear windows away to allow them to float freely. There are several windows you can dock in this area in addition to the windows ACID docks here by default (the Explorer and Mixer windows).

When you have several windows docked in the Window Docking area, a tab for each window appears at the bottom of the area. Click any of these tabs to bring the window associated with that tab to the front of the screen.

Drag here
to undock   Explorer window   Resize the panels here   Mixer window

FIGURE 1.5
The Window Docking area manages various ACID windows.

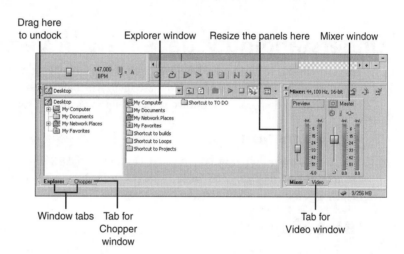

Window tabs   Tab for   Tab for
               Chopper   Video window
               window

Notice also that the Window Docking area has (by default) two panels, separated by a thick border. Click and drag the border to resize the adjacent panels. Click the Maximize/Restore button in the top-left corner of each panel (just under the familiar Close button that closes the window and removes it from the Window Docking area) to cause the window to occupy the entire Window Docking area. Click the button again to restore the window to its previous size.

Click the Mixer tab if the Mixer window is not already active. As do all docked windows, the Mixer window contains a Move handle (the thin vertical line on the left edge of the window). Use the Move handle to drag and drop the Mixer window in a new location in the Window Docking area. This action creates a new panel unless you drop the window close enough to the existing panel, in which case the window docks to that panel. A panel disappears when you remove the last window from the panel.

To undock a window from the Window Docking area and make it free-floating, click the Move handle and drag the window anywhere outside the Window Docking area. Release the mouse button to make the window a floating window. Drag and drop it back onto the Window Docking area to redock it.

If you've closed a window and want to reopen it, choose the window from the View menu. The window reopens in whatever state it was in when you closed it. For instance, if the window was docked in the Window Docking area when you closed it, the window will reopen, docked in the same place. You can also select the name of an open window from the View menu to close it.

Understanding What's New in Version 3.0

If you've used ACID version 1.0 or 2.0, you've already noticed a few changes to the user interface in ACID 3.0. In addition to these interface changes, there are many other new features in version 3.0. The following sections provide a brief summary of these features.

CD Extraction

ACID 3.0 allows you to insert a music CD into your CD-ROM drive and extract songs from it to your hard drive. Hour 9, "Incorporating One-Shot and Beatmapper Tracks," teaches you how to use this feature.

Beatmapper

The Beatmapper Wizard, shown in Figure 1.6, finds the beats in an audio file. It places markers where it estimates that the beats fall and allows you to fine-tune the placement of those markers if it guesses wrong. This information enables these files (called Beatmapper files) to react to tempo changes just as normal loops do. Refer to Hour 9 for details on the Beatmapper feature.

Chopper

The Chopper makes it easy to add specific portions of a file to your project. The Chopper is especially valuable when used in conjunction with long Beatmapper files. We devote Hour 11, "Editing with the Chopper," to this feature.

The King of the Remix

Extract it, run it through the Beatmapper, Chop it. These three new features make ACID the undisputed king of the dance remix!

FIGURE 1.6

The Beatmapper Wizard calculates the beats in a long file so that you can use that file in your ACID projects.

Video

ACID 3.0 now supports video. You can bring in a video file, watch the video in the Video window, and create music that you can instantly and easily time with the video. Learn how to work with video tracks in Hour 10, "Scoring to a Video."

MIDI Support

You can now add MIDI sequences to ACID. You can combine MIDI sequences with audio files in ACID to really open up the possibilities. Hour 8, "Working with MIDI Tracks," shows you how to work with MIDI tracks.

New FX

Although audio effects (referred to as FX in ACID) are not new to ACID, there have been major changes in the way they are handled. ACID now gives you virtually unlimited FX capabilities. In addition, ACID now includes all the Sonic Foundry XFX series (1, 2, and 3) of DirectX plug-ins previously sold separately. See Hour 12, "Using Audio FX," for a complete discussion of the new handling of FX.

New Mixer

Another example of an impressive improvement on an old feature that makes it virtually new is the Mixer. This powerful tool allows you to create mixes and submixes, add FX at the bus level, and more. Hour 13, "Using the Mixer," provides a thorough discussion of the new ACID Mixer.

Window Docking Area

As mentioned earlier in this hour, ACID 3.0 now features a Window Docking area. This area makes it easy to store, organize, and work with frequently used windows.

Summary

In this hour, we've set the stage. If you're new to ACID, you now understand the concepts of making music with ACID. If you've used previous versions of ACID, you should be anxious to start learning all about the fun and powerful new features of version 3.0. It's time to start making music! In the next hour, "Getting Started," you'll jump in with both feet and start creating your own original music!

Q&A

Q. **Won't the music I make in ACID sound unnatural—like "computer" music?**

A. Not unless you want it to. Many of the loops you use to make music in ACID were recorded by real musicians with real instruments in real recording studios. All the feel of a human performance are captured in these loops. On the other hand, some loops were recorded with synthesizers, drum machines, and so on. These loops may have a more "mechanical" feel to them, and are perfect for certain musical styles. Of course, when you add MIDI to your project, you could introduce an even more "machine-like" feel. With ACID, you can mix real sounds in with MIDI sounds to minimize the "computer" music effect if that's what you want.

Q. **Won't I be tied into purchasing additional loops from Sonic Foundry?**

A. No! You can use any `.wav`, `.aiff`, or `.mp3` file (among several other formats) in your ACID project. You can get loop files from countless sources, including the Internet.

Q. **Do I have to pay Sonic Foundry more money for each use of the songs that I create?**

A. Absolutely not! As long as you have permission from the owner of the copyrights for the loops you use (loops from Sonic Foundry come with that permission), you own the music you create. It is yours. As soon as you create it, *you* own the copyright to that song, and you can use it, or do whatever you like with it.

Workshop

This first hour's workshop tests your basic knowledge of making music with ACID and invites you to spend some time snooping around the ACID interface to become more familiar with it.

Quiz

1. What section of the ACID screen allows you to control the mix of your individual tracks?

2. How many different instruments can I add to my ACID project?

3. Which of the new features of ACID make it an incredibly useful tool for creating remixes?

Quiz Answers

1. The main mixing for an individual track is done using the controls and buttons in the track's Track Header, found in the Track List area.

2. The number of tracks (and therefore the number of instruments) you can add to your projects is limited only by your computer's processing power (especially the amount of RAM you have).

3. The new CD Extraction, Beatmapper, and Chopper features are perfect for making remixes.

Activities

1. Start ACID and poke around the screen a little bit. Click the buttons. Select menu choices. See whether you can even add some loops to the project (we'll show you how in Hour 2). Spend a few minutes finding out where things are and what some of the buttons do. Keep in mind that some operations are unavailable until you have added loops to the project. Learn your way around the screen so that you're ready for Hour 2.

Hour 2

Getting Started

- Opening Your ACID Project
- Getting Familiar with Your Project
- Task: Understanding the Transport Controls
- Previewing Loops
- Adding Loops to Your Project
- Arranging Loops on the Timeline
- Task: Creating an Arrangement
- Adjusting the Master Project Settings

We spent the first hour learning key ACID concepts, finding our way around the screen, and glimpsing the new features in ACID 3.0. Continuing with the band metaphor, you've finished setting up the gear; now it's time to get some serious work done. Let's start making music!

This hour starts by showing you how to preview loops and add them to a sample project. You'll learn how some of the fundamental controls and concepts work. You'll also learn about some of the buttons and tools in ACID while you're creating your first arrangement. Finally, you'll learn how to adjust the project's tempo and key settings.

By the time you're done with this hour, you'll know enough of the basics that you can begin creating your own original music.

In this hour, you will:

- Find the loops you want to use in your project
- Add loops to the project
- Construct an arrangement by adding events to the Track View area
- Define the tempo and key for your project

Opening Your ACID Project

As you know by now, ACID can make sure that all your loops play in the same key at the same tempo, but you have to decide for yourself whether a certain loop sounds good with another loop, or if it fits well into your project. To do this most effectively, take advantage of the ACID Explorer window to preview the loops. As you will see, you can even preview a loop as your project plays so that you can hear exactly how the loop fits in with what you've already written.

The examples in this hour are based on a sample project located on the companion CD that accompanies this book. The `PreviewLoops.acd` project, shown in Figure 2.1, contains just one track—a basic 8-bar blues drum beat.

FIGURE 2.1

The `PreviewLoops.acd` *project file is located on the companion CD.*

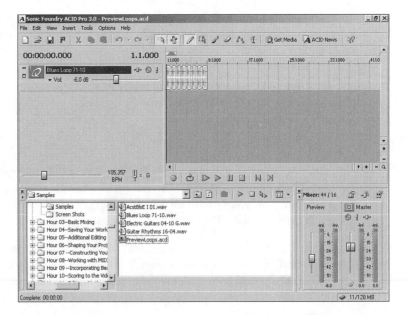

This drum beat loop (Blues Loop 71-10.wav) comes from the *Drum Tools* loop library collection from Sonic Foundry. Throughout this book, we'll use loops from a wide variety of the Sonic Foundry loop libraries. The projects located on the companion CD will give you a taste of the types of loops available for use in your ACID projects.

You already know how to find files on your computer, so you already know most of what you need to know to navigate to the loops you want to preview. You could use Windows Explorer to open the folder containing your loop files. You could then double-click the loop you're considering and listen to it in the Windows Media Player (or whatever player you use).

In addition to taking a lot of time, this approach has another major limitation: If you listen to your loops this way, you can't tell how they're really going to sound in your project because the media player won't play the loop you're previewing along with the loops you've already added to your ACID project (let alone match the pitch and tempo of your loops). ACID has no such limitations. In the ACID Explorer window, you can use the same navigational techniques you use in Windows Explorer to navigate to the folder where you store your loops.

You'll find three guitar loops in the Hour 2 Samples folder. The first, Guitar Rhythms 16-04.wav, comes from the *'On the Jazz Tip* library. The second, AcstBlsE I 01.wav comes from the *Paul Black's Whiskey Cigarettes and Gumbo* collection. The *Classic Country* library brings us the third guitar loop, Electric Guitars 04-10 G.wav. Each of these loop libraries is available from Sonic Foundry.

Notice that several of the buttons at the top of the Explorer window look familiar. These are the same navigation and organizational buttons that you find throughout the Windows operating system (see Figure 2.2).

All the buttons in ACID contain ToolTips that identify them. When you're not sure what a button does, hover the mouse over it until the ToolTip appears to identify the button. If you're still not sure, click the What's This Help button (in the main ACID toolbar), and then click the button in question to see a short description of its function.

Up One Level ┐ ┌ Refresh ┌ Add to
          My Favorites

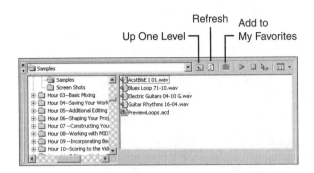

FIGURE 2.2

Become familiar with the Explorer window buttons.

The buttons in the Explorer window allow you to perform file management tasks from within ACID. If you decide that you need a new folder in which to store loops, click the New Folder button to create such a folder. If you decide that you no longer need a file or folder, select it in the Explorer window and press the keyboard Delete key to remove it. Alternatively, right-click the file, and choose Delete from the shortcut menu.

The Refresh button comes in handy when you've made a change within the folder you currently have open in the Explorer window, but the change was made outside of ACID (that is, using the Windows operating system tools). In such cases, ACID does not reflect the change in the open window. Click the Refresh button to update the list of files in ACID to match the current state of the folder.

When you make a change to your file structure in ACID, the change has the same effect as making the change with Windows Explorer. For example, if you choose to delete a file from within ACID, you delete it from your hard drive, just as if you had been in Windows Explorer when you deleted the file.

The Add to My Favorites button is an exception to the preceding caution. The Favorites folder exists as a virtual folder inside ACID. In the Favorites folder, you can place links to other places on your computer system that you often want to find quickly. Note that the Favorites folder does not really exist on your computer. This folder works perfectly for creating links to your various loop storage locations.

Notice the Views button at the far right of the Explorer window. Click the arrow on the right side of this button to display a drop-down menu as shown in Figure 2.3. The first option in the menu, Tree View, shows the file structure that leads to the selected file. Click the left side of the View button to quickly toggle Tree view on and off.

FIGURE 2.3

The Views button gives you a number of view options for the Explorer window.

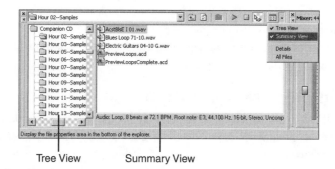

Tree View   Summary View

The next option in the View drop-down menu, Summary View, allows you to choose whether you want ACID to display information about the file you select. For example, with the Summary view enabled, select the AcstBlsE I 01.wav file. A summary appears at the bottom of the Explorer window that includes valuable information about how the loop was recorded.

The Details option in the Views drop-down menu allows you to view even more details related to your files.

With the All Files option disabled, ACID shows only the files it can import into your ACID project. With this option enabled, all files in the displayed folder show up in your list.

Notice that when you open a loop file in ACID, you create another file behind the scenes. The new file has the same name as the original loop file, but with an .sfk extension. ACID creates this file so that it can show the waveforms in your project. You can safely delete these files because ACID recreates them when it needs them. However, these files are very small; forcing ACID to recreate them can slow down the load time when you reopen a project.

Navigate to the Samples folder for Hour 2 on the CD that accompanies this book. The folder contains all the loops you need for this discussion. To prepare for the next set of instructions, open PreviewLoops.acd now.

Getting Familiar with Your Project

Before we start adding more loops to this project, let's take a few minutes to talk about what's already here. The `PreviewLoops.acd` project is a very simple one. In fact, at the moment it contains just one track—a simple blues drum shuffle. Even though it is simple, it already contains a number of critical elements that you will see and use over and over again when building your compositions.

Using the Track List Area

Recall from Hour 1 that the Track List area is the section on the left of the ACID screen just below the time displays. Notice the colored icon with the looping arrow in it. This is the track icon, and it is part of the Track Header. Each track has its own Track Header, and every time you add a track to your project, a new Track Header is added to the Track List area.

The track icon in the Track Header gives you information about the type of track this is. The looping arrow indicates that this is a loop track, which is the most common type of track in ACID projects. A loop track holds a loop of audio that can play over and over and still keep perfect time with the beat of the song.

There are a number of additional controls in the Track Header, and we'll talk in great detail about all of them throughout various hours of this book. All the controls are defined in Hour 3, "Basic Mixing."

At the bottom of the Track List area is the tempo slider, which shows that the current tempo for this project is 105.357bpm and that the current key is G. You'll learn how to work with and adjust these settings in later hours.

Using the Track View Area

As we mentioned in Hour 1, the Track View area (to the right of the Track List) is where you'll spend most of your time working. You add *events* to the Track View area (also called the timeline) that allow you to build the arrangement of your composition. These events hold references to the media file that this track holds. For example, in this simple project, track 1 (the only track in the project) holds a media file called `Blues Loop 71-10`.

NEW TERM

Events

Events represent occurrences of the media files associated with the tracks in which they reside. They appear in the timeline as boxes with waveforms (or

MIDI information on MIDI tracks, which we will talk more about in Hour 8, "Working with MIDI Tracks"). In the case of media files that are loops (as is the file in the drum track in our example), the notches in the top and bottom of the event show where one repetition of the loop ends and the next repetition begins. For example, the event in track 1 holds eight repetitions of the drum loop associated with the track. You can create events of any desired length. In this way, a short loop can be made to play throughout an entire song.

There is one event in the timeline for this track. Look at the Beat ruler (just above the timeline); you can see that the event starts at the beginning of the song (measure 1, beat 1), and ends at measure 9, beat 1. In other words, this event lasts for eight measures. You can also see by the Time ruler (toward the bottom of the timeline) that the event lasts for around 18 seconds.

As you'll see in later hours, you can change the length of the event to be anything you want. You can also move the event to a new position. Finally, you can add more than one event to the same track. Every event you add to a track holds the media file associated with that track. You'll learn how to use all this information to create arrangements for your songs.

Task: Understanding the Transport Controls

There are several other important features of the timeline. We'll talk about all of them before we're finished, but for now, let's look at the Transport bar (see Figure 2.4). The Transport bar (at the very bottom of the timeline) contains all of the buttons you need to play your project and navigate through it. In this task, you'll learn what all the buttons in the Transport bar do.

1. The first button on the left is the Record Button. The Record button enables you to add original recordings to your ACID project. Don't click the Record button just yet; you'll get very familiar with the Record button during Hour 15, "Recording and Creating Your own Loops," and Hour 16, "Adding Vocals."

2. Next to the Record button is the Loop Playback button, which sets ACID into Loop Playback mode. In Loop Playback mode, you define a region (called the loop region) that plays over and over again until you manually stop playback. Notice the gray bar with yellow triangles at each end just above the Beat ruler in the timeline. This is the Loop Region Indicator. When you click the Loop Playback button to engage it, the Loop Region Indicator turns blue.

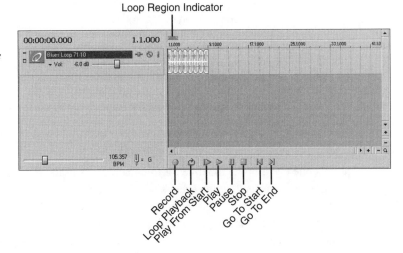

FIGURE 2.4

Use the controls on the Transport bar to play and navigate through your project.

3. To alter the length of the loop region, click and drag the yellow triangle at the right of the Loop Region Indicator. Drag it to the left to make the loop region shorter; drag it to the right to make the loop region longer. For now, set the Loop Region Indicator to include the entire event on track 1.

4. Click the Play From Start button to begin playback of this project. Regardless of where your timeline cursor is, when you click the Play From Start button, playback starts at the very beginning of the project. Watch the timeline cursor move through the song as you listen to the drum track. When the cursor reaches the end of the loop region, it returns to the beginning of the loop region, and continues playing.

5. Wait until the timeline cursor is somewhere around measure 5, and click the Stop button to stop playback. The project stops playing, and your timeline cursor jumps back to the position it was resting at before you clicked the Play From Start button (in this case, that's most likely the beginning of your project).

6. Click the Play From Start button to restart playback. When the cursor reaches measure 5, click the Pause button. The Pause button acts much the same as the Stop button, with one major difference. When you end playback with the Pause button, the cursor does not jump back to its original position as it did when you clicked the Stop button in step 5. Instead, it stops and remains right where it is.

7. Click the Play button. Playback resumes at the current position of the timeline cursor. Note the difference between this behavior and the behavior of the Play From Start button in step 4.

8. Click the Pause button again. Now click the Go To Start button. The cursor returns to the very beginning of the project. The Go To End button moves the cursor instantly to the end of the project. Leave this project open; you'll use it later in this hour.

> Hover the mouse pointer over each of the buttons in the Transport bar to see a ToolTip that lists a keyboard shortcut for that button. The one we use most often is the shortcut for starting and stopping playback. The spacebar on your keyboard functions alternatively as the Play button and the Stop button. Another helpful shortcut uses the Enter key in place of the Pause button.

Previewing Loops

Okay, now that you've got a project going, let's preview some loops to add to it. If you're not already there, use the ACID Explorer window to navigate to the CD-ROM that accompanies this book. Open the Samples folder for Hour 2 and click the AcstBlsE I 01.wav file once to select it.

Now you have two options. You might have noticed that we neglected to talk about three of the buttons in the Explorer window. (You thought we forgot, didn't you?) These buttons, shown in Figure 2.5, allow you to control the playback of the file you have selected.

FIGURE 2.5

Control the playback of your previews within the Explorer window with these buttons.

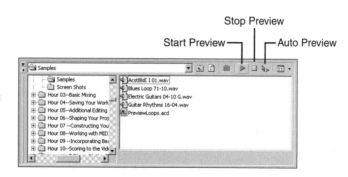

Click the Start Preview button to begin playback of the selected file. This button allows you to hear the file so that you can decide whether or not you like it. Click the Stop Preview button to discontinue the preview playback.

The Auto Preview button enables you to quickly preview multiple files. Click this button to engage Auto Preview mode. Now, as soon as you click on any file, the currently previewing file stops, and the newly selected file begins to preview—you don't have to click the Stop or Start Preview button.

> Click in a blank area of the Explorer window, or anywhere outside the Explorer window, to stop previewing without clicking the Stop Preview button.

It's great to be able to preview the file before adding it to your project, but it would be even better to listen to the rest of the project at the same time so that you can hear what the loop you're previewing sounds like with the rest of your project. It's easy to do. Use the buttons in the Transport bar to begin playback of your project, then preview your loops as described in this section. ACID previews the file at the project tempo and in the project key so that you can hear exactly what it sounds like along with your existing project.

> You'll find Loop Playback mode (introduced in the previous task) to be an extremely useful tool when you're previewing files. In fact, this is the perfect way to preview loops because you can take all the time you need, and your project never stops playing! Perfect for you, that is—after a while, your roommate might form a different opinion.

Preview the other guitar loops in the project so that you can get a feel for how each works with the drum track. When you're done previewing loops, click the Stop button on the Transport bar to stop playback.

Adding Loops to Your Project

This is the moment we've all been waiting for. It's time to add some loops to your project. After you have a loop or two in your project, we'll spend some time talking about how to arrange and build your composition.

When you've decided which loop you want to add to your project's Track View area, it's easy to add it. You can pick your favorite of two methods. The first method is to click and drag the loop (for this exercise, use the Electric Guitars 04-10 G.wav loop) up to the Track View or the Track List area. Notice that a small plus sign appears below the cursor. This icon indicates that you can release the mouse button and add the loop to your project. Release the mouse button. This action instantly creates a new track below the last track (in this case, the only track) in the Track List area as shown in Figure 2.6.

Figure 2.6

There are two methods to add the Electric Guitars 04-10 G.wav *loop to your project.*

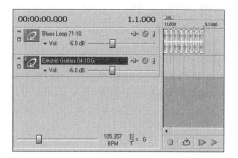

You now have two tracks in your project: the original drum track and the guitar track you just added. Congratulations: You're writing your first ACID song! In the Explorer window, double-click the AcstBlsE I 01.wav file to add that guitar track to the project. Double-clicking a loop is the second method to add a new track to your project.

Here's a tip with a built-in caution. You can add a new track to your project in a location other than the bottom track. To do so, click and drag the new loop to the Track List area. Position the mouse over the track *icon* (the colored square below which you want to insert the new track). Release the mouse; the new track appears directly under the track onto which the loop was dropped.

Now here's the caution part. Although you haven't gotten far enough along in your ACID education to understand why, take our word on this one. Be very careful not to drop the new loop onto the *name* of an existing track! You won't get the result you expect. We explain the result you will get (a highly desirable result in the right situation, and a very neat hidden ACID trick) in Hour 14, "Uncovering Tips and Techniques."

Arranging Loops on the Timeline

Now that you've got a few tracks in your project, let's start making music. Each track you add represents a single file you're using in your project. If you've followed along with this hour thus far, you have three tracks: Track 1 holds the drum beat (Blues Loop 71-10.wav), Tracks 2 and 3 contain two different guitar loops (Electric Guitars 04-10 G.wav and AcstBlsE I 01.wav).

Even though you've added the loops and created the tracks to hold them, when you play your ACID project at this point, you only hear the drum loop. What gives?

ACID gives you complete control over the arrangement of your music. Therefore, although ACID creates a track for you when you add a file, it waits for you to specify the exact placement of the file in the song. For instance, should the first guitar come in at the first measure, and the second guitar wait until the third measure? Or should the first guitar play for one measure, drop out for a measure, come back in on the third, and continue this alternating pattern while the second guitar plays in an opposite pattern? Well, it's all up to you...it's your song! ACID waits for you to specify the order of things; in short, you have to create a musical arrangement, and you do so by drawing events into the new tracks.

A number of tools help you create your arrangements. Here we discuss some of the basic tools. Later hours explore the rest of the tools.

Look at the Track View, or timeline. Notice that the drum track contains a single event (with eight loop repetitions). The other two tracks do not yet contain events.

To add an event to the first guitar track, click the button on the Toolbar that looks like a pencil to activate the Draw tool. Now click and drag to draw an event into the timeline of the first empty guitar track (see Figure 2.7). Notice that you can draw events only into the track in which you initially clicked. A track can hold as many events as you want; repeatedly click and drag the Draw tool to add more events to the first guitar track. Now click the Play button and listen while the guitar track plays along with the drums!

FIGURE 2.7

Use the Draw tool to draw events into a single track.

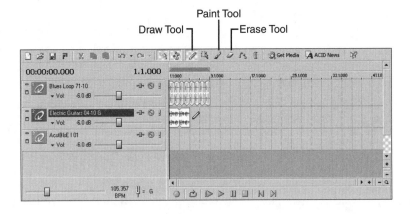

You also can create events using the Paint tool. The Paint tool works much the same as the Draw tool, except that you can paint across tracks with it. In other words, with one click-and-drag motion, you can add events to all three tracks.

If you decide that an event you added lasts too long, use the Erase tool to erase a portion of the event. Click the Erase tool and then click on the portion of the event that you want to erase.

Task: Creating an Arrangement

In this task, you'll create an arrangement using the three tracks already added to your song.

1. Click the Draw tool to select it and then click at the beginning of track 2. Drag to the grid mark that corresponds with 5.1 on the Beat ruler above track 1. Release the mouse button. Track 2 now contains an event that stretches for four bars.

2. Select the Paint tool. In track 2, click at the beginning of bar 7 (at location 7.1 in the Time ruler) and drag to the beginning of bar 9 (at location 9.1 on the Time ruler). Continue to hold down the mouse button.

3. Still holding the mouse button, drag down to track 3 and over to the left until you've painted back to the beginning of bar 3 (at location 3.1 on the Time ruler). Notice how the Paint tool allows you to paint across tracks.

4. Select the Erase tool. Click on the drum event in track 1 to erase the first two bars of that track (the event now starts at the beginning of bar 3). Also erase bars 5 and 6 of the drum track.

5. You've just created your first arrangement! Your screen should look like the project shown in Figure 2.8. You can see that track 1 contains two events. The first starts at measure 3, beat 1 and ends at measure 5, beat 1. The second event in track 1 starts at measure 7, beat 1 and ends at measure 9, beat 1. Track 2 also contains two events. Notice that the first event in track 2 holds two repetitions of the loop, while the second event holds just one repetition. Track 3 contains just one event containing three repetitions of the file. Click the Play From Start button to hear the song. If you are still in Loop Playback mode, you'll have to click the Stop button to end playback.

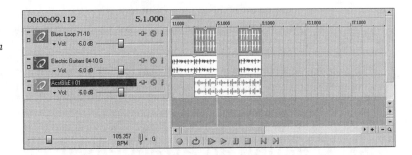

FIGURE 2.8
Your project should look like this one when you're done creating the arrangement.

Adjusting the Master Project Settings

Now that you've got a bit of a song going, what happens if you decide that it is too slow or too fast? What if your singer can't reach the high notes in this particular key? Remember that we told you ACID changes the pitch and tempo of every loop in your project to match the project settings? Well, as if that weren't enough, ACID also allows you to *change* the project tempo and key settings. The following sections show you how to adjust the project tempo and key.

Adjusting Project Tempo

ACID sets the project default tempo to 120 beats per minute (bpm). Regardless of the tempo at which the loops were originally recorded, they all play at 120bpm when brought into your project. If you want your song to play faster, click and drag the Tempo Slider (located at the bottom of the Track List area) to the right. To slow the song down, click and drag to the left. If you have an exact tempo in mind, double-click the BPM label or value to select the value. Type the desired value and press the Tab key. Your project (and all the loops in it) now lock to the new project tempo.

Adjusting Project Key

In the same way, ACID adjusts, or transposes, all your loops to match the project key. You can change the project key from the default key of A to any specified key. To do so, click the Project Key button (the one that looks like a tuning fork at the bottom of the Track List area). From the drop-down menu that appears, choose the desired key for your song. ACID now plays all the loops in your project back in the new key.

> ### Don't Transpose Me
>
> "Hey, you can't fool me! You guys said that when you change the project key, the key for all the loops changes to match. Well apparently that's not entirely true, because my drum track sounds exactly the same in the key of F# as it does in the key of A. What are you trying to pull?"
>
> Give yourself a gold quarter-note if you found yourself asking that question! Yes, everything you say is true (ACID can be a wily rascal!), but it works that way by design. Think about a band. When the guitar, bass, and keyboard players start a song in the key of A, the drummer plays in the key of...well, the key of the drums. When the others switch to the key of E, the drummer still plays...you guessed it, in the key of the drums.
>
> ACID recognizes that some instruments don't play in a specific key. That is, many instruments (especially percussion instruments such as drums) are frequently not "pitched" instruments. ACID lets you decide for yourself whether or not a loop should act as a pitched instrument. Hour 14 explains this fully and describes exactly how to specify a loop as nonpitched or nontransposing.

Summary

How about that? Only two hours into the book, and already you're making music. In this hour, you learned how to use the ACID Explorer window to find projects and loops on your computer system and to preview loops to hear how they fit with the project. You also learned how to add new loops to your project, construct an arrangement, and use the Transport buttons to hear your creation. Finally, you changed the project settings for tempo and pitch so that you can get just the right feel for your song. All that's great, but you know what? The best is yet to come! In the next hour, we'll talk about some basic mixing concepts. But before you get there, take a few minutes for some questions and answers, and work through a few exercises to help solidify what you've learned here.

Q&A

Q. Why can't I just browse to my loops using Windows Explorer and place the loops into my ACID project from there?

A. Although you certainly could use this approach, you miss out on one of the great features of ACID—the ability to hear what a loop sounds like along with the rest of your project before you even add it to your project.

Q. How come when I draw or paint events into the Track View, they always jump to those dotted gray lines?

A. Those dotted gray lines are called *grid lines*. Events jump (or snap) to the grid lines because of the Snap To feature in ACID. You'll learn how to use this feature (and how to override it when you don't want it) in Hour 6, "Shaping Your Project."

Q. The Project Tempo slider only goes down to 70bpm and up to 200bpm. Is that the extent of the tempo range I have available?

A. No. The default range represents the range in which most loops seem to work best. You can expand the range so that it stretches from 40bpm to 300bpm. You can also contract the range. To make a change in tempo range, choose Options, Preferences; in the Preferences dialog box that opens, click the Editing tab. Type a number of beats per minute or use the arrow buttons and sliders to set your new tempo range. Click OK when you've made your changes.

Workshop

Before you move on to the activity that follows, take a couple of minutes to test your knowledge of the material in this hour.

Quiz

1. Which tool allows you to paint events to multiple tracks with one movement?

2. Imagine that you add or delete a file from a folder using Windows Explorer, and that folder happens to be open in the ACID Explorer window, also. How can you make sure that the ACID Explorer window recognizes the addition or deletion you performed in Windows Explorer?

3. If you think a song is playing too fast, how can you slow it down?

Quiz Answers

1. The word *paint* is the clue. To quickly paint events to more than one track, use the Paint tool.

2. Click the Explorer window's Refresh button to update the Explorer window. The window will then show any files or folders that had been added or deleted outside of ACID while the folder was open in the ACID Explorer window.

3. Use the Project Tempo slider to adjust the tempo of your song. Click and drag it to the left to slow the song down.

Activities

1. Use the three guitar loops and the drum loop in the Samples folder for Hour 2 (on the CD-ROM that accompanies this book) to create a few new arrangements of your own.

2

Hour 3

Basic Mixing

- Exploring Track Headers
- Task: Place Track 9 Between Tracks 2 and 3
- Task: Color-Coding Your Tracks
- Resizing Your Tracks
- Zooming Horizontally
- Task: Adjusting Track Time and Height
- Controlling Volume
- Panning in the Stereo Field

As you learned in Hour 2, "Getting Started," it's easy to add files to your project and build a composition. Now you have to create a good *mix* of the elements in your tracks. In this hour, we take a closer look at Track Headers and the controls found there. We'll also talk about some techniques to use during the mix process. When you're done with this hour, you'll be ready to move on to Hour 4, where you'll learn to save your project.

NEW TERM

Mix

To mix simply means to blend all the parts and pieces of your project together to make a song. Audio mixing is sort of the same as mixing a cake. When you make a cake, you have eggs, sugar, flour, chocolate chips, and so forth. If you take all the right ingredients and toss them into a bowl without any thought, what you end up with will be something, but it might not be a very good cake. In the same way, in your ACID project, you have drums, guitars, basses, and so on. Throw them together without much thought, and you'll have *something*, but it might not be very pleasant music. Mix the ingredients properly, and you'll enjoy a cake worth eating while listening to music worth hearing!

In this hour, you will:

- Arrange the tracks in a logical order
- Color-code the tracks for visual grouping
- Adjust track height and width
- Adjust the track volume and the master volume
- Pan tracks to create a stereo mix
- Use the Solo and Mute buttons when mixing

Exploring Track Headers

Open the `Mixereze.acd` project in the Samples folder for Hour 3 on the companion CD-ROM for this book. Notice that the project contains nine tracks. Each track has its own Track Header, and all the Track Headers appear in the Track List area on the left side of the ACID window. Click the Play From Start button and listen to it all the way through to get familiar with the project. At first glance, you see a number of buttons and controls in each Track Header. The following few sections go "under the hood" to discuss the functionality of Track Headers. There's a lot here, so let's get to it!

All the loops in the `Mixereze.acd` project can be found in the *ACID DJ* loop collection available from Sonic Foundry. This collection is full of jazz, house, techno dance, and techno industrial loops, all optimized for use in ACID.

Changing Track Order

As mentioned in the previous hour, when you add a new loop to your project, a new Track Header appears under the last existing Track Header in the Track List area.

Sometimes, you might want your tracks to be in a different order. For instance, you might want to keep all your drum tracks together. In the current `Mixereze.acd` project, that's not the case.

To change the order of your tracks, click the track icon of the track you want to move, and drag it up or down. Notice the dark line that appears between the Track Headers, following the movement of your mouse. This line represents the top of the track you are moving. When you release the mouse button, you drop the track at the location of this line and move the other tracks down. The following task steps you through the process.

Task: Place Track 9 Between Tracks 2 and 3

The steps in this task teach you how to reorder tracks.

1. Tracks 1 and 2 are both drum/percussion tracks. Click the track icon for track 9 (this track is also a drum track), and drag it up until you see a dark line appear between tracks 2 and 3.

2. Release the mouse button and notice that the track that was track 9 (`BD Crash 1`) is now track 3. All the other tracks below it have moved down and have been renumbered so that track 9 is now the `Quintessential Belz 2` track.

3. Repeat this process to move `Housebass22-02` directly underneath the other bass track, `Housebass 22-08`. Your project should now look like the one shown in Figure 3.1. Keep this project open; you'll work with it more in the next task.

FIGURE 3.1

Drag and drop a Track Header to quickly reorder the tracks in your ACID project.

Color-Coding Tracks

In the previous task, you learned how to change the order of tracks in your project. Another way to organize your projects involves changing the color of a track or multiple tracks. This gives you a quick visual reference of how your tracks are grouped. For instance, in the case of our example, it might be very helpful if both of our bass tracks were the same color but were a different color from the drum tracks.

> We strongly suggest that you get into the habit of reordering and color-coding your tracks. Further, we suggest that you pick a color scheme and stick with it from project to project. For instance, always make all your drum tracks red, and rearrange your project so that all the drum tracks sit one after another in the Track List. This way, you will quickly get oriented when you open old projects.

To change the color of a track, right-click the track icon in the Track Header. From the shortcut menu, choose Color; from the cascading menu that opens, choose the color square that matches the desired color you want to assign to the track.

> ### Windows Selection Techniques
>
> Before you continue with your ACID lessons, take a moment to step away from ACID. Let's talk about some Windows selection tricks. Some of you know this already, but for those who don't, Windows allows you to make selections in a number of different ways. For instance, you can select more than one thing at a time by combining the Ctrl key with a couple of clicks. Click something to select it. Then press and hold the Ctrl key and click another thing to select it in addition to the first object. Continue holding the Ctrl key and clicking additional items to add those items to the selection. Ctrl+click an already-selected item, and you remove it from the selection group. Here's another trick: Click an item. Press and hold the Shift key and click another item. Notice that the first item, the last item, and every item in between become part of the selection. Keep those Windows selection techniques in mind...they're about to come in very handy.

Because you want both bass tracks to be the same color, use one of the selection techniques discussed in the Coffee Break to select both tracks at the same time. Now change the color of one of them; note that the color of both selected tracks change.

In fact, as you'll see throughout this book, many of the manipulations you make to one Track Header affect all other selected Track Headers as well. These selection tricks work in the ACID Explorer window too, so you can easily add more than one loop to your project at the same time, or put a group of loops into a newly created folder.

Task: Color-Coding Your Tracks

In this task, you'll change the color of your track icons so that you can easily identify useful groupings of related tracks.

1. In the `Mixereze.acd` project that you began working on in the previous task, recall that you rearranged your tracks so that tracks 1 through 3 are all drum/percussion tracks. Click the track icon for track 1 to select that track. Press and hold the Shift key and click the track icon for track 3. Notice that tracks 1 through 3 are selected.

2. Right-click any of the selected Track Headers and choose Color from the shortcut menu (as shown in Figure 3.2). From the popup list of color choices, select red to make all the selected track icons red.

3. Repeat steps 1 and 2 to change the color of the two bass tracks to green.

FIGURE 3.2

Color-coding the tracks creates a handy visual grouping of similar track types.

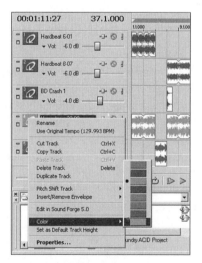

Maximizing/Minimizing Tracks

Sometimes when you're working with a track, you'll want to see more or less detail about the track. You can resize a track in several ways, two of which we'll talk about in this section. These two buttons are located (one above the other) just to the left of the track icon for each track. Click the Maximize Track Height button (the lower of the two buttons) to make the track fill the entire height of the Track List and Track View areas. This action pushes all other tracks out of the visible area. When you maximize a track, the Restore Track Height button replaces the Maximize Track Height button. Click the Restore Track Height button to set the track back to the height it had before you maximized it.

The Minimize Track Height button (the upper button of the pair) minimizes the track to its smallest possible height. Minimize the tracks you consider to be complete in your project so that they don't eat up valuable screen real estate while you work on other tracks. After you minimize a track, click the Restore Track Height button (now the only button available) to set the track back to the height it had before you minimized it.

> ACID contains a number of useful shortcuts. From the menu bar, choose Help, Keyboard Shortcuts for a listing of many of them. Here's one of our favorite tricks: To minimize all the tracks in your project at once, press the tilde key (usually that's the key to the left of the number 1 key at the top of your keyboard; it looks like this: ~). Press the tilde key a second time to restore all tracks to their previous height.

Cutting, Copying, Pasting, and Deleting a Track

ACID follows the basic Windows conventions for cut, copy, paste, and delete. Click the track icon of a track to select the track. To cut the track from your project and place it on the Clipboard, press Ctrl+X. To copy the track to the Clipboard, press Ctrl+C. To paste a track you have previously cut or copied, press Ctrl+V. Finally, to delete a track (without placing it on the Clipboard), press the Delete key on your keyboard. You can also find commands to perform these functions in the Edit menu and in the right-click shortcut menu for each track. The toolbar also contains buttons for the cut, copy, and paste operations.

Naming Your Tracks

ACID automatically names your tracks for you when you add files to your project. The newly created track assumes the name of the file that it contains. But you can change the name of the track. To do so, double-click the track's name. Just as in Windows, this action selects the name and puts a box around it; you can now type whatever new name you want for the track. When you're finished typing, press the Tab or Enter key, or simply click away from the name (the track icon is a good target) to apply the new name to the track. Alternatively, right-click the track icon and choose Rename from the shortcut menu.

ACID calls the field that holds the track's name the "Scribble strip." As you'll learn in later hours, many other objects in the ACID window also have a Scribble strip.

Resizing Your Tracks

We've already talked about how you can resize your tracks in the Track List area by using the Minimize and Maximize Track Height buttons. You can use several other techniques to adjust your Track List configuration. The following sections show you how to adjust the height and the width of your Track Headers.

Resizing Tracks by Dragging

Maximizing and minimizing Track Headers has limitations. The track ends up big, small, or the default size. Using other techniques, ACID lets you adjust the size of the Track Headers to whatever you desire.

To change the height of the Track Header, position the cursor directly over the Track Header's bottom edge, as shown in Figure 3.3. The cursor changes to a double line/ double arrow. Click and drag the edge up or down to resize the Track Header. Taller tracks show complete controls and information in the Track Header and the events on the track grow to match the track height.

FIGURE 3.3

Drag the bottom edge of a Track Header up or down to change the track's height.

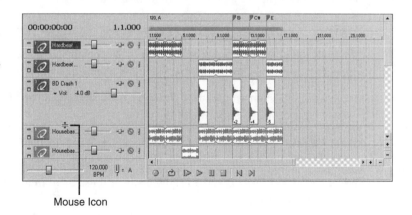

Mouse Icon

This click-and-drag-the-edge method of resizing an area of the screen is available in many places in the ACID interface. If you feel the urge to resize an item on the ACID screen, point to its edges. If you see the double line/double arrow cursor, drag to resize the item.

If you've read the tip regarding resizing items in ACID, you might have already figured out that changing the width of the Track List works much the same way as changing the height of a Track Header. Point to the right edge, click, and drag to your heart's content.

When you change the height of a Track Header, you affect only that track. But when you change the width of the Track List, you change the width of all the Track Headers.

Resizing Track Height with Zoom Control

The Vertical Zoom control enables you to change the height of all Track Headers simultaneously. At the bottom of the vertical scrollbar at the right side of the timeline, notice the two buttons and a spin control that make up the Vertical Zoom control.

Click the Zoom In Track Height button to increase track height. When the Track Height is large enough that one Track Header occupies the entire visible Track List, this button ceases to have any effect. Likewise, click the Zoom Out Track Height button to decrease track height. When the tracks reach their minimum size, the button ceases to have any effect. Notice that both buttons affect all tracks, and that all tracks assume the same size. Click and hold either button to steadily increase or decrease the size of all tracks.

A Zoom spin control is located between the two buttons. Click and drag this spin control for fine adjustments either up or down to your track height.

Using Keyboard Shortcuts to Change Track Height

Normally we don't devote an entire section to keyboard shortcuts, but you'll use these so often that we want to make sure that you know them early on in your work with ACID.

To increase the height of all Track Headers, press Shift+up arrow. To increase the height in finer increments, press Shift+Alt+up arrow.

To decrease the height of all Track Headers, press Shift+down arrow. To decrease the height in finer increments, press Shift+Alt+down arrow.

When you master these keyboard shortcuts, you'll use them frequently to change the height of your tracks.

Setting the Default Track Height

Now that you know how to adjust your track heights, you might have settled on a favorite. Sooner or later, you'll find a height that you find to be adequate for most of the work you do. When you find this magical height, you can make it the default for all tracks you add to this project and to any future projects.

To make a track's height the default for all new tracks, right-click the track icon and choose Set As Default Track Height from the shortcut menu.

Zooming Horizontally

As you're editing an event, it helps if you zoom in for a closer look before you make your changes. The Zoom In/Out Time feature allows you to view more or less time in the Track View area. In fact, you can zoom out to see several hours at a glance if your project is that long. On the other hand, you can zoom in almost to the sample level. Now that's microscopic!

ACID provides several methods you can use to zoom in time. Notice the set of controls at the end of the horizontal scrollbar, just down and to the left of the Vertical Zoom control. This control, called the Time Zoom control, is similar to the Vertical Zoom control. Click the Zoom In Time button to show less time and more waveform details in the timeline. Click the Zoom Out Time button to show more time and less detail.

You can also use the keyboard equivalent for these buttons. To zoom in, press the up arrow on your keyboard. To zoom out, press the down arrow on your keyboard. Press and hold the Ctrl key and tap the up-arrow key to zoom in very close in one jump. Press and hold the Ctrl key and tap the down-arrow key to instantly zoom all the way out.

Click and drag the Spin control (located between the two buttons) to the left to zoom in; drag it to the right to zoom out. You can also click and drag either edge of the horizontal scrollbar. Position the mouse pointer over one of the edges of the scrollbar. Notice that the pointer changes to a double arrow. Click and drag to make the scrollbar shorter; notice that you're zooming in to the timeline and can see more detail. Naturally, as you make the scrollbar longer, you zoom out. Double-click the scrollbar to zoom all the way out (see Figure 3.4).

The Zoom tool, shown in Figure 3.4, is a flexible tool that lets you zoom in a number of ways:

- Select the Zoom tool and click and drag in the timeline to select an area of the Track View that you want to zoom in to. ACID zooms in on the area you select until that area fills the entire Track View. After completing the zoom, the mouse pointer reverts to the previously active tool.
- Double-click the Zoom tool to switch to *Zoom Overview mode.*
- Triple-click the Zoom tool to switch to Zoom Overview mode and change the cursor to the Zoom tool. This handy shortcut enables you to zoom all the way out and then quickly select an area into which to zoom.

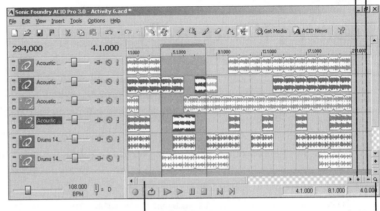

FIGURE 3.4

Click the Zoom tool for more zooming options.

The Zoom out Time button

The Zoom in Time button

Double-click to Zoom all the way out

The Zoom Tool

NEW TERM

Zoom Overview Mode

Zoom Overview mode minimizes all tracks and zooms out to show the entire project timeline in the Track View area.

When you zoom using the Zoom In Time or Zoom Out Time button, ACID uses your project cursor as the zoom anchor. In other words, the project cursor determines the point into which you are zooming. When you've zoomed in so far that you can no longer see the entire timeline, ACID centers the project cursor in the visible timeline. Keep this in mind because if you have your project cursor in a spot other than where you're trying to work, you might find yourself scratching your head and mumbling, "Where am I?" after you zoom in.

Task: Adjusting Track Time and Height

In this task, you'll have a chance to zoom around a large project.

1. Open the file called BigProject.acd which can be found in the Hour 3 Samples folder on the CD-ROM that accompanies this book.

You don't have to bother playing this project (although you can if you insist). It is 30 minutes long, contains 36 tracks, and gets old fast. Use this project as a tool to explore the zooming functions.

2. Use the vertical scrollbar to scroll down through all 36 tracks. Use the horizontal scrollbar to scroll to the right. Click at the end of the very last event in the project to move the project cursor there. In the Time Display, you can see that the project is 919 measures long and takes 30 minutes, 34 seconds, and 4 ticks to play. Now try this shortcut: Hold down the Ctrl key and press the Home key. Presto! The project cursor jumps back to the beginning of the timeline.

Press the Home key to move the project cursor to the left edge of the Track View. Press the End key to move the project cursor to the right edge of the Track View. Press Ctrl+Home to send the project cursor to the beginning of the project (even if that location is not currently visible); press Ctrl+End to jump to the end of the project.

3. If you can't see track 1, use the vertical scrollbar to adjust the timeline view so that you can see it. Triple-click the Zoom tool. You are now zoomed out as far you'll ever get. You can see the entire length of the project, all the way to measure 919. But you still can't see all the tracks. How many you see depends on the size of your monitor, your Windows Properties settings, and the depth of the Track View area. Still, you can see quite a bit of the project to get an overall picture of what's going on.

4. To fill the screen with the timeline so that you can see more of your project, press Alt+tilde (~) to hide the Window Docking area and expand the Track View to show more tracks. Press Ctrl+Alt+tilde to hide both the Window Docking area and the Track List, filling both vacancies with more of the timeline. Press the key combinations again to restore ACID to its normal configuration.

5. Move the mouse over the Track View area and notice that it is shaped like a magnifying glass. Starting at bar 1, click and drag down to track 5 and over to around bar 120. (You don't have to be exact here; just get as close as you can.) As you drag, notice that a dotted rectangle starts to draw. Release the mouse button and notice that you are now zoomed in to the portion of the project outlined by the rectangle. Also notice that the mouse cursor changed back to the Draw tool.

6. Place the cursor somewhere around bar 30 and click the Zoom In Time button three times. Notice that each time you click the button, you zoom in at the cursor position.

7. Press the up arrow on your keyboard three times. Notice that this does the same thing as step 6—it zooms in, using the cursor position as the zoom anchor point.

8. Click the Zoom Out Time button a few times and then press the down arrow on your keyboard a few times. Notice that both these actions have the same effect—you zoom out of the cursor position.

9. Click the Zoom In Track Height button a few times. Notice that you now see fewer tracks. Press Ctrl+Shift+up arrow to get the same results.

10. Click the Zoom Out Track Height button a few times and then press Ctrl+Shift+down arrow. Both actions reduce the track height so that you can fit more tracks into the view.

11. Double-click the horizontal scrollbar. You're back out to the big picture again. Now point to the right edge of the horizontal scrollbar and drag to the left. Notice that, as you drag, you zoom in to the project with the left edge of the timeline as the anchor point.

12. Double-click the horizontal scrollbar and press the tilde key to get back to the big picture.

Controlling Volume

The task you'll perform most often when mixing the tracks in your project is adjusting the volume of each track relative to the overall mix (the volumes of all tracks combined). You can control the overall volume of the project using the Master, described later in this hour. The following sections explore these two types of volume control.

Adjusting Track Volume

Use the volume fader located in the Track Header to control the volume of a track. You can also control a track's volume with a track volume envelope. Because this hour focuses on basic mixing techniques, we'll talk about the volume fader techniques here and save the more advanced topic of track envelopes for Hour 5, "Additional Editing Techniques."

Start by adjusting the height and width of the Track Header you want to work with (use any track in the Mixereze.acd project). Adjust the size of the track until you can see the multipurpose fader label, which contains information about the track's volume.

The multipurpose fader label is a very important little object. As it turns out, the track fader not only controls track volume, but when you click it, you'll see that it also controls panning (see Figure 3.5). In later hours, you'll see that the track fader can also control bus routing and effects. It's called the multipurpose fader because it has—you guessed it—multiple purposes. The label also contains further information concerning the current state of the fader. For instance, as you move the fader to adjust the volume, the label displays the current setting in *dB* (decibels).

FIGURE 3.5

Click the multipurpose fader label to switch the function of the fader control.

3

dB

The unit dB, or decibel, is a way of describing volume—or more precisely, the relative intensity of sound. Think of 0dB as 100% of the original signal (volume). In digital audio, you can't have more than 100% (0dB) without creating distortion in your audio. As a simple analogy, think about a glass of water. The brim of the glass is 0dB. Up to that point, the water stays in the glass. You can add more water (volume) to the glass, but the excess spills all over the table and creates a mess. When you add too much volume to your tracks, the excess "spills over" and creates a mess of your project (distortion). This explains why most often you see negative values for volume settings on meters and faders in ACID. In digital audio, no sound (zero volume) is referred to as "–Inf" (–infinity).

One Man's Fader is Another Man's Slider...Or Is It?

As you work on your ACID projects, you'll see other controls that look and work just like the volume fader. Some of these controls are called faders, and others are called sliders. What's the difference between a slider and a fader? Simple. If it changes volume, it's a fader. This term comes from the early days of analog audio consoles, when you pulled down the volume control to gradually "fade out" the audio. If the control changes anything else, it's called a slider.

Click the Loop Playback button and then click the Play button so that you can listen to the changes you are about to make. To adjust the volume of the desired track, click and drag the volume fader to the left to decrease the volume or to the right to increase the volume. If you click either side of the fader, the volume decreases or increases by one whole number for each click. Use the left and right arrow keys on your keyboard to adjust the volume of the selected track or tracks in 0.10dB increments. And here's a trick: Double-click the fader to quickly set it to 0.0dB. Continue adjusting the volume until you like how this track fits into your mix.

Using the Master Control

To mix your tracks properly, you need to see the Master control (frequently called, simply, the Master). To view the Master, the Mixer window must be open (by default, the Mixer is open in the right section of the Window Docking area). If another window is covering the Mixer in the Window Docking area, click the tab labeled Mixer at the bottom of the Window Docking area to bring it to the front. If you don't see the Mixer tab, choose View, Mixer from the menu bar. Adjust the size of the Mixer window by dragging the top and side edges until you can see all the controls on the Master (see Figure 3.6). In addition to the Output Fader and the Output Meters that we'll talk about here, the Master contains the following buttons:

- Mute
- Solo
- Master FX
- Device Selection (in some cases)

FIGURE 3.6

The ACID Master enables you to control the overall volume of your project.

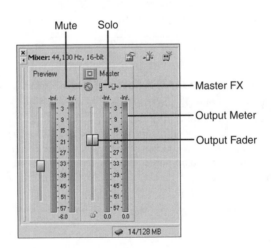

The Mixer window contains powerful advanced mixing tools. By default, it contains two controls: the Preview control and the Master control (Master). We talk a little about the Master in this section, but save a detailed discussion of the Mixer window and additional controls for Hour 13, "Using the Mixer."

The Master meters represent the mix of all the tracks in your project. Let's go back to our water-glass analogy. Think of the Master as an infinitely expandable waiter's tray. You can add as many glasses (tracks) to the tray as you want, and it always expands to hold more so that all the water can be delivered together. Only when one of the glasses overflows (that is, when one of the tracks exceeds 0dB) do you have a mess (distortion).

While you're adjusting your track volumes, keep an eye on the Master and be careful to keep the meters mostly in the yellow (between –6dB and –3dB). If you get the signal too "hot" (that means too loud), the Master meters peak above 0dB and display red. The top of each meter shows numbers representing the peak (loudest volume). When your volume is too high, a red rectangle encloses the peak value, and you're probably distorting the signal (water is overflowing from one of the glasses).

You need to find which one of your tracks is causing the Master to peak above 0dB. To do this, click the Solo button (discussed in the section "Solo and Mute" later in this hour) on track 1, and play the project. If the Master peaks above 0dB, track 1 is too loud. If track 1 is not the culprit, unsolo track 1, and solo track 2. Repeat the process until you find the track that is causing the problem. When you find it, lower the track volume for that track. If you feel that lowering the volume of the offending track will adversely affect your overall mix, click in the middle of the Master fader and drag it to a lower setting. Watch the numbers at the bottom of the meters to see the current fader settings.

Make sure that you understand the function of the meter labels. The numbers at the top of the meters are the highest peak values. If the labels at the top of the Master meters are –Inf, it means that you have not yet sent any signal to the meters. The numbers at the bottom of the meters represent the current setting of the Master fader. If the labels are 0.0, it means that you are neither boosting nor attenuating (cutting) the signal level being delivered to the Master from the timeline.

3

Panning in the Stereo Field

Another aspect of mixing is *panning*. You can use the multipurpose fader to pan the audio of a track so that it comes out the left speaker only, the right speaker only, or anywhere in between. Making use of the pan feature adds interest to the mix; in some cases, panning adds realism to the project.

NEW TERM

Panning

Recording engineers call the process of placing the audio across the stereo field panning. In ACID (as with most traditional mixing boards), when you adjust the panning, the total amount of signal always stays constant. In other words, if you pan all the way to the left ("hard left"), the left channel contains all the audio signal. This is important because it explains why panning a track sometimes causes the Master to peak above 0dB even though the evenly panned track caused no problems.

Click the multipurpose fader label on the last track and choose Pan from the drop-down menu. Notice that all the tracks now show the pan setting. Click and drag the pan fader all the way to the left to direct the audio to the left speaker. Drag it all the way to the right to place it in the right speaker. As you drag the fader, notice that the information on the multipurpose fader label updates as well. For instance, drag the slider to the left until you see the readout display 80%. This means that 80% of the signal will come out the left speaker and 20% will be directed to the right speaker. Double-click the slider to reset the fader to the center position.

A Handy Indicator

See the rectangular slot that guides each fader? Let's call it the fader slot. You might have noticed earlier that when you adjust the volume fader, the area in the fader slot to the left (or bottom in a fader that moves up and down) of the fader is darker than the area to the right (or top.) This shading simply indicates the current distance between –Inf and the current fader position. Although some of us find that to be a neat, but not particularly useful feature, the pan fader is a different story.

In Figure 3.7, notice that, when you adjust the panning of a track, the dark area of the fader slot grows from the center instead of the left edge as it does with volume faders. This serves as a good visual reminder of just how far off center you have panned that particular track, and allows you to quickly scan your Track List to see where all the tracks fall within the stereo field.

FIGURE 3.7

The gray shading beneath the pan faders give you a quick visual of the panning for each track.

For the pan feature to work, you must be sure that your hardware is set up correctly. For instance, if you pan the audio right and you hear it in the left speaker, you might want to check that your speakers are properly connected and placed. If you are using an outboard mixer, check whether the pan control on the mixer is set correctly.

Solo and Mute

When mixing, there will be times you need to concentrate on a single track, for example when you are adding an effect. It might be difficult to hear the results with all the other tracks playing as well. This is a perfect opportunity to use the Solo button. When you click the Solo button on a Track Header, you simultaneously mute all other tracks. Click the Solo button again to hear the full mix again. The Solo button is a great way to concentrate on just one track, and then quickly compare how it sounds mixed in with the rest of the tracks.

You can solo more than one track at a time. For instance, if you have three tracks of horns, you might want to first hear how they are blending with each other before you hear how they sound in the full mix. Select all three of the horn tracks and click the Solo button for any of the tracks in the group; all the tracks in the group are soloed. Click any of the Solo buttons again, and you're back to the full mix. Pretty slick.

The Mute button simply takes the selected track temporarily out of the mix. Just as you can with the Solo button, you can mute more than one track at a time. If you want to hear what the mix would sound like without a particular track, click the Mute button. Click it again to un-mute the track.

Another function the Mute button provides relates to the Render As process. If you render an ACID project to a mixed file (as discussed during Hour 17, "Creating Mixed Audio and Video Files"), any tracks that are muted will not be included in the final mixed file. This is a good way to create an alternate mix without having to delete the unwanted tracks.

There is a lot more to mixing than simply adjusting track volume and panning. Effects, track envelopes, and event envelopes all play a part in the final mix. All these topics are covered in detail later in the book.

Summary

In this hour, you've learned about the basic mixing tools in ACID. You learned how to group the tracks visually using position and color in the Track List. You also learned how to use Windows multiple selection techniques to affect more than one track at a time. You learned how to use the multipurpose fader label to switch between volume and pan. You know how to rearrange, resize, move, and delete tracks to better organize your project for more efficient mixing.

Mixing style is a very personal thing. No two people approach it exactly the same way. We hope the ideas we have presented here will be of some help to you and that the tricks you learned in this hour will be incorporated into your mixing style.

Q&A

Q. Why is the hottest point on the volume meters labeled 0?

A. The label 0dB on the Master bus represents the concept that the Master bus control is not increasing (a positive number) or decreasing (a negative number) the signal at this point. Because in digital audio 0dB also represents the loudest possible signal (translated as the highest possible number in digital terms) you can attain before risking distortion, there are no numbers above 0 on the ACID Master meters.

Q. I keep moving the pan fader to hard left or hard right but the audio still comes out both speakers. What could be the problem?

A. If you are sending the signal to an external mixer before it goes to your amp and speakers, you must set the pan correctly on the mixer as well. For instance, if you are sending the left output of your sound card to channel 1 and the right output to channel 2 on your mixer, pan channel 1 hard left and channel 2 hard right. Now the pan function in ACID should work correctly.

Q. Sometimes when I try to use the keyboard shortcut for Play (the spacebar), it doesn't work. Why not?

A. For this shortcut to work, the Track List or Track View area must have the focus. For instance, if you click the Master to give it focus, the spacebar will not start playback. Click anywhere in the Track List or Track View area and then press the spacebar. Now playback begins. If you want to learn one more keyboard shortcut, you press Ctrl+spacebar to start and stop playback no matter which window has focus. In fact, if you get in the habit of always using this new shortcut, you'll never have to worry about focus. You can play your project no matter which area of ACID currently has focus.

Workshop

Use the quiz questions and activities to put the information from this hour to good use. This will help these techniques and concepts become a part of your long-term memory.

Quiz

1. What is the difference between a fader and a slider?

2. What do we call the process of placing audio in the stereo field?

3. Which key do you use to quickly minimize all track heights at once?

Quiz Answers

1. The control is called a fader if it affects volume. If it adjusts any other parameter, the control is called a slider.

2. The process of placing audio at a specific point in the stereo field is called panning.

3. Press the tilde key (~) to minimize all tracks. Press it again to restore all the track heights.

Activities

1. Reopen the `mixereze.acd` project. Set a loop region the length of the project and click the Play Looped button. Use the Solo buttons to get familiar with each track in the project. Next, rearrange and color-code the tracks in a logical order and color scheme to facilitate submixing. While keeping an eye on the Master bus, create a mix using the techniques you learned in this hour.

Hour 4

Saving Your Work

- Saving an ACID Project
- Exporting Loops
- Rendering Your Project
- Publishing Your Songs to the Internet

Now that you know how to create ACID projects, you're undoubtedly going to want to save them so that you can show them off to your friends. In this hour, we'll discuss the different saving options available in ACID.

In this hour, you will:

- Save and archive your ACID project files
- Save your music as a deliverable mixed audio file
- Export the individual tracks of your project
- Make your songs available for everyone to hear on the Internet

Saving an ACID Project

The most important save operation you can make is to save your ACID project. Doing so allows you to walk away for a while, grab a bite to eat, call your agent to tell her about the new hit you're writing, and then come back and pick up where you left off. Just as with any software, good policy dictates that you save your work early and often.

Saving for the First Time

ACID offers a number of ways to perform the basic save operation. First, you can choose File, Save from the menu bar. Second, you can click the Save button on the toolbar. Finally (and if this is not already automatic for you from working on other Windows applications, it certainly should be!), you can use the keyboard shortcut Ctrl+S.

The very first time you choose any of these options, the Save As dialog box opens. The Save As dialog box allows you to navigate to where you want to store your project file, give your project a name, and choose a file type into which to save your work. When you've done all these things, click Save to complete the operation.

> The Save As dialog box gives you two options in the Save As Type drop-down list. Both of these options are variations on an ACID Project File. The first option—ACID Project File (*.acd)—is the basic project file. The second option—ACID Project With Embedded Media (*.acd-zip)—is designed specifically for archiving your projects along with all the media files you used to construct the project. We'll talk more about the second option later.
>
> If you want to save your project in a different file format without first saving it as an ACID project, choose File, Render As from the menu bar. We'll discuss the Render As dialog box in a few minutes.

After you save the project the first time, choosing save again simply saves the file to the same location, with the same name, in the same file type as you initially chose—the same way the process works in any other Windows application.

Copying the Media

Figure 4.1 shows the Save As dialog box. In the bottom-left corner of the dialog box, you'll find the Copy All Media with Project check box. When you enable this box and click Save, ACID copies all the media—that is, the loops and the video file you've used in the project (more on working with video in Hour 10, "Scoring to a Video")—to the same location you chose for the project file. This option makes it easy to organize your files and transport them to another machine so that you can collaborate with a song-writing partner or work on your project at the office (instead of entering those sales figures into the spreadsheet the boss wants by 4:30).

FIGURE 4.1

The Save As dialog box lets you copy the project file and all the media used in the project to the same directory in one operation.

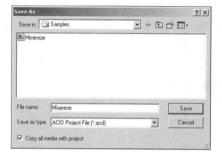

Why would you want to save your media to the same location as your project file? Normally when you work up a tune in ACID, you draw from a wide variety of loop resources. For example, in Hour 2, "Getting Started," we built a short four-track song that used loops. These loops originally came from four different Sonic Foundry loop library CD-ROMs. The fact that the loops came from different CDs poses no problem while you work on your project the first time. Because ACID loads the loops into RAM, they remain available to you throughout your session. (By the way, that's also why you want as much RAM as you can afford. More RAM equals more tracks.)

But what happens when you close ACID (presumably so that you can prove to your family that you really are still alive) and then come back to work on it later? Because the loops no longer reside in RAM (they were cleared out when you closed the project), ACID has to find them again. If you store the loops on your hard drive, ACID can find them (as long as you did not change their location).

If ACID can't find the loop files during the start-up sequence, ACID presents the dialog box shown in Figure 4.2. This dialog box lets you know which files ACID cannot locate.

FIGURE 4.2

When ACID can't find the loops you've used in your project, this dialog box alerts you to that fact and gives you options for solving the problem.

The dialog box asks you what you want to do and gives you four options:

- **Search for missing file.** This option runs an automatic search of your system in case you can't remember where you stored the file.
- **Specify a new location or replacement file.** This option allows you to either navigate to the new location of the file or replace the file with a different loop.
- **Ignore missing file and leave it offline.** If you select this option, your project will open, but the missing file will be left out of the project.
- **Ignore all missing files and leave them offline.** Choose this option if you know that several files will not be found, and you want to ignore all of them instead of responding to this dialog box for each of the missing files.

All of this gets rather cumbersome, especially if you have used loops from a large number of different CD-ROMs that you have to constantly swap in and out until ACID finds all of the files. It's a lot easier to avoid the problem in the first place by enabling the Copy All Media with Project check box in the Save As dialog box so that the next time you start the project, all media files will be right where ACID can find them quickly!

Opening the Save As Dialog Box

You can access the Save As dialog box at any time if you want to save the project with a new name or in a new location. To open the Save As dialog box, choose File, Save As.

You might want to use the Save As option when you are about to make major changes to a project, but you don't want to lose the project in its present state (in case the new changes don't work out). In this case, choose File, Save As, give the project a different name, and work on that copy, leaving the original version of the project available if you decide to go back later. Don't worry, ACID project files (files with the extension .acd) are quite small, so keeping a copy won't eat up precious storage space.

Saving Your Project as an ACID Archive

The ACID archive format (a file with the extension .acd-zip) allows you to save an archived copy of your project along with the loops you used in the project in one compact file. Because the archive contains the loop files as well as the project file, an .acd-zip file is much larger than an .acd file. In Figure 4.3, notice that when you choose the ACID archive format from the Save As Type drop-down list, the Copy All Media with Project check box is selected and grayed out. This indicates that when you choose this format, you have no choice but to copy the media with the project file. That, after all, is the whole idea behind the archive format!

FIGURE 4.3

The ACID archive format (`.acd-zip`*) copies the project file and all media to the same compressed file.*

Even though the archive file contains all the pieces and parts of your project, it preserves the integrity of the separate tracks. Therefore, you can still open an `.acd-zip` file in ACID and change your arrangement just as you can with a regular `.acd` file.

Exporting Loops

The Export Loops command under the File menu enables you to save a "family" of related loops. You might want to do this when you use a number of loops together outside of ACID.

The most common example is using a family of loops to create a music sound track for your Macromedia Flash animations. Because Flash cannot match the pitch and tempo of various loops the way ACID can, you'll need to bring the loops into ACID first, then run the Export command. When you export, ACID saves new copies of the loops in the project tempo and key. This means that even though the loops might not have matched when you first brought them into ACID, ACID matches them and saves them as a family of related loops that will work well together in any application. We'll get into this concept in much more detail in Hour 20, "Creating Music for Flash Movies," when we talk about using ACID to create original music for your Flash animations.

Rendering Your Project

When you're ready to share your music with others, you'll want to save your project in a format that enables people to hear the project even if they don't have ACID installed on their computer. ACID calls this process "rendering a file." For these times, you'll want to render your work in a *mixed file format*. ACID gives you a number of options for doing so.

New Term

Mixed File Format

In this type of file, all the separate tracks in your ACID project are mixed down to a two-channel (stereo) or one-channel (mono) file. The settings you chose back in Hour 3, "Basic Mixing," when you learned about the ACID mixing tools define the mix that ACID saves. Different mixed file formats work best in different situations. Hour 17, "Creating Mixed Audio and Video Files," contains a complete discussion of mixed file formats.

To render your ACID project, choose File, Render As from the menu bar. This command opens the Render As dialog box. The Render As dialog box allows you to choose the location where you want to store the rendered file, and allows you to name the file. Let's explore the other options in a little more detail.

Choosing a File Format

The Save As Type drop-down list in the Render As dialog box gives you many render options, as shown in Figure 4.4. Most PCs have the Windows Media Player installed. The Windows Media player plays all these formats (unless otherwise noted in the descriptions that follow).

FIGURE 4.4

ACID enables you to save your mixed files in many different file formats.

The file format options offered by the Render As dialog box include the following:

- Macintosh AIFF (*.aif)—A high-quality, uncompressed audio format most often used for playback on Macintosh computers.
- MP3 Audio (*.mp3)—A "lossy" compression format that allows you to store audio in a much smaller file size (that's the compression part) at the loss of some sound quality (that's the "lossy" part). This format is common for delivery of music over

the Internet. Because developers (like Sonic Foundry) are charged for the use of MP3 technology, they must in turn charge their customers for MP3 capabilities. Therefore, ACID allows a limited number of MP3 encodes. You can purchase the rights to unlimited encodes from Sonic Foundry.

- OggVorbis (*.ogg)—Another lossy compression format. This relatively new format has been designed as a free alternative to the MP3 format.

- QuickTime (*.mov)—The standard audio/video format used on Macintosh computers. These files can also be played on a PC using the Windows operating system.

- RealMedia (*.rm)—A highly compressed format developed by RealNetworks to facilitate streaming of audio/video over the Internet.

- Sonic Foundry Audio (*.sfa)—A Sonic Foundry proprietary, uncompressed format designed specifically for use with other Sonic Foundry products.

- Sonic Foundry Perfect Clarity Audio (*.pca)—A Sonic Foundry proprietary format that is compressed (although not as much as MP3 or OggVorbis files) and completely lossless (capable of the highest audio quality). This brand-new format might be incompatible with other applications, but is an excellent choice for use in Sonic Foundry products.

- Sonic Foundry Wave64 (*.w64)—This format is the same as the WAV format except that it allows for larger file sizes (over 2 gig). This format might not work with some non-Sonic Foundry applications.

- Video for Windows (*.avi)—The standard audio/video format used on Windows-based computers.

- Wave (Microsoft)(*.wav)—The high-quality, uncompressed format most often used for playback on Windows-based computers.

- Wave (Scott Studios)(*.wav)—The same as a standard .wav file (described in the preceding entry) except that it offers the ability to embed additional nonaudio data. Designed specifically for broadcast use.

- Windows Media Audio 7 (*.wma)—The Microsoft highly compressed format used for streaming audio over the Internet.

- Windows Media Video 7 (*.wmv)—The Microsoft highly compressed format used for streaming video over the Internet.

As mentioned, we'll talk in detail about many of these format options in later hours, but right now you might be saying, "I just want to play my new song for my friends! What do I choose?" If you want to play your project

> from a computer, choose either `.aif` (Macintosh) or `.wav` (Windows). If you want to e-mail the music file to your buddy across town or across the continent, `.mp3` and `.ogg` are good choices because of their smaller file sizes.

Choosing a Template

Each of the various file formats listed in the preceding section provide you with a number of template choices for defining the properties of your file. Templates allow you to quickly set up your file to render in some of the most common configurations for the given file type. For example, when saving a WAV file, you'll most likely use the default template, which results in CD-quality sound. But you might also want to render the file in mono instead of stereo, so you'd choose a template that allows you to do so.

For some of the formats, there are no template choices; for other formats, there are several template options. We'll take a closer look at some of these template choices in Hour 17, "Creating Mixed Audio and Video Files." Choose a template name from the Template drop-down list in the Render As dialog box to apply it to your rendered file.

To create a custom template, click the Custom button in the Render As dialog box. This opens the Custom Settings dialog box. The Custom Settings dialog box is different for each file format. It provides you with a number of options for customizing the properties of the file you are saving. Hour 17 also looks more closely at these custom settings.

Saving the Loop Region

The Render Loop Region Only check box, shown in Figure 4.5, allows you to decide whether you want ACID to save the entire project or just the portion of the project within the loop region (remember the loop region from Hour 2?). It might seem unlikely to you right now, but we guarantee that you'll find multiple uses for this feature as you work more and more with ACID. It comes in handy, particularly when you're running experiments on music and video that you want to deliver over the Internet.

Exporting Tracks for Use with Other Software

The Save Each Track as a Separate File option on the Render As dialog box enables you to save each track of your project as an individual mixed file. All the volume adjustments, panning, FX, arrangement, and so forth that have been assigned to the track will be saved along with the track. In Hour 20, "Creating Music for Flash Movies," we show you how to use this feature when preparing music to incorporate into your Macromedia Flash animations. You can also use this option to create tracks that you can then import into your multitrack recording software such as Vegas Audio from Sonic Foundry or Pro Tools from DigiDesign.

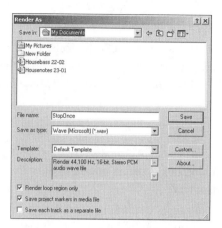

FIGURE 4.5

The Render As dialog box allows you to render only the portion of your project within the loop region or to save each track separately.

Because several files will be created (depending on the number of tracks in your project), ACID does not ask you to name the files. Instead, ACID names them for you. The name of each track contains the track number, followed by the name of the media file that the track holds. For instance, if track 4 of your project contains a guitar loop called `crunchguitar.wav`, ACID names the file created from that the track `Track 04 crunchguitar.ext` (where `.ext` is `.wav`, `.mp3`, or whatever format you're rendering to).

Publishing Your Songs to the Internet

The popularity of the Internet as a music delivery vehicle continues to grow at an astounding pace. ACID makes it very easy for you to let the world hear your music. You can publish your music directly to ACIDplanet.com by clicking the Publish To button in the toolbar or choosing File, Publish from the menu bar. This process creates a streaming media mixed file (with the extension `.rm` or `.wma`) and walks you through the process of publishing your song. Hour 19, "Publishing to ACIDplanet.com," describes the process of publishing to *ACIDplanet.com*. In the future, ACID will likely support publishing to other sites in addition to ACIDplanet.com.

NEW TERM

ACIDplanet.com

ACIDplanet.com is a growing community of people who love to make music with ACID. On this site, you can publish your songs, listen to the creations of others in an amazingly wide variety of styles and genres, chat with other ACID musicians, learn the latest news in the ACID world, participate in contests, download loops and complete ACID projects, and more. There's always something to hear on ACIDplanet.com.

Summary

In this hour, you learned how to save your ACID projects. You also learned a little bit about the Save As and Render As options, discovered how to archive your finished projects, and learned about mixed file formats. The following questions and activities help cement your new knowledge.

Q&A

Q. In the Render As dialog box, I see an option to Save Project Markers in Media File. What does this mean?

A. We'll discuss the various types of markers in ACID in later hours. For now, just be aware that you can place location markers in your project and save those markers as part of the mixed file. These markers can then be used to navigate to particular locations in the mixed file.

Q. I hear so much about MP3 files. What is so special about this file format?

A. MP3 files gained popularity because they are very small files yet they sound great. When you download music from the Internet or e-mail a music file to a friend, small file size is an important factor. The MP3 format can produce a good-sounding file at 1/5 to 1/10 the size of the same file saved at CD-quality. New file formats (such as .ogg, .pca, and .wma) now offer similar advantages.

Workshop

Before moving on to Hour 5, "Additional Editing Techniques," test your knowledge of saving ACID files with the quiz and explore your new skills with the activities.

Quiz

1. When should you save your work?

2. What two choices do you have for saving your project file and all the associated media in the same directory in one save operation?

3. After you've saved your project for the first time, what is the difference between the Save command and the Save As command?

Quiz Answers

1. Save your work early in the project-creation process. Then save your work any time you have done something you don't want to lose. Save your work every time you make a change to the project. In other words, save early and save often. Don't

forget that the Ctrl+S shortcut may be your best friend when working in any Windows software application!

2. Your first option is to enable the Copy All Media with Project check box in the Save As dialog box. Alternatively, you can choose the ACID Archive format from the Save As Type drop-down list to save all the files with a single extension (.acd-zip).

3. Every time you choose the Save command (after the first time), ACID saves the file with the same name in the same location without asking any questions. The Save As command opens the Save As dialog box, which allows you to change the name, the save location, and the file format.

Activities

1. In the Windows Explorer window, create a new folder on your hard drive called Save_Test. Open the Mixereze.acd project that you used in the previous hour (you can find it in the Hour 3 Samples folder on the CD-ROM that accompanies this book). Choose File, Save As from the menu bar. Navigate to the Save_Test folder, name the file save_all_test, choose ACID Project File (.acd) from the Save As Type drop-down list, and enable the Copy All Media with Project check box. Click Save to finish the procedure. Switch back to Windows Explorer and navigate to the Save_Test folder to observe its contents. What do you find?

2. Create another folder called Save_Test_2 on your computer's hard drive. Follow the procedure described in Activity 1 but choose the .acd-zip file format to save the project. Navigate to the Save_Test_2 folder in Windows Explorer and observe the contents. Now what do you find?

4

PART II
Moving Beyond the Basics

Hour

HOUR 5

Additional Editing Techniques

- Duplicating a Track
- Task: Duplicating a Track
- Changing the Pitch of a Track
- Task: Creating a Harmony Track
- Adjusting the Start Offset of an Event
- Task: Creating Effects with Offset
- Changing the Pitch of an Event
- Task: Shifting the Pitch of an Event to Create Harmony
- Automating Your Mix with Envelopes
- Task: Customizing a Track Volume Envelope
- Task: Applying a Pan Envelope

With the basic editing techniques you have learned in the last few hours, you can start making exciting music with ACID. But as your creativity catches fire, you'll want to know about the more advanced techniques you can use to take your project to the next level. In this hour, we'll look at some of those techniques and walk you through some examples of how to use them.

In this hour, you will:

- Create stereo effects and harmony using track duplication
- Adjust the pitch of an entire track separately from the project key
- Alter an event by adjusting the start offset
- Change the sound of an event by adjusting its pitch
- Automate your mix using envelopes

Duplicating a Track

To duplicate a track, right-click the track icon of the track you want to duplicate and choose Duplicate from the shortcut menu. Bingo! ACID creates an exact duplicate of the track. The new track uses the same loop as the original track. Even better, it duplicates the placement of events and all the settings of the Track Header.

Why would you want more of exactly the same thing? You can do several interesting things with the new track that makes this time-saving command useful. For example, on the duplicate track, you might change the pitch to create a harmony part, or adjust the offset to create *slap-back, echo, and flange effects*.

 New Term

Slap-Back, Echo, and Flange Effects

A slap-back effect occurs when a sound is followed very quickly (but not so quickly as to be indistinguishable from the original sound) by a single repetition of that sound.

An echo effect occurs when a sound is followed by several distinct repetitions of that sound. Each repetition is typically a little quieter than the one before it until you can no longer hear it.

A flange effect occurs when a sound is followed extremely closely by a repetition of the sound. The repetition is so close that it is indistinguishable from the original sound, yet delayed enough as to cause an effect that has a sweeping, wind-like quality. This is a very difficult effect to describe—work through this hour to hear it.

Task: Duplicating a Track

In this task, you'll experiment with a couple of the reasons for duplicating a track and get a feel for the techniques used. You'll also start forming your own ideas for using these techniques in your ACID compositions.

1. In a new ACID project, add the file Rock-Pop 01 Flute 02.wav from the Hour 5 Samples folder on the CD-ROM that accompanies this book.

2. Draw an event from bar 1 to bar 3, a second event from bar 4 to bar 6, and one more event from bar 7 to bar 9.

3. Right-click the track icon and choose Duplicate Track as shown in Figure 5.1.

FIGURE 5.1

Right-click a track icon to find the Duplicate Track command.

4. Notice that you now have a duplicate of the original track and all its events and pan settings. The duplicate track is named (oddly enough) Copy of Rock-Pop 01. A duplicate track is always named the same as the original track with the words "Copy of" tacked on to the beginning. Of course, you can always change the name of the track to whatever you want as you learned in Hour 3, "Basic Mixing."

5. Save your project (or at least leave it open) so that you can pick up at this point in the next task.

> The loop you're using for this task comes from the *Orchestral Series 4: Rock & Pop* loop collection from Sonic Foundry. This collection consists of four discs with orchestral styles in the classical, modern, cinematic, and rock/pop styles.

5

Changing the Pitch of a Track

ACID gives you the ability to change the pitch of any track. Changing the pitch of a track is different than changing the project key (as you learned in Hour 2, "Getting Started"). When you change the pitch, you affect an individual track and not the entire project. You can adjust the pitch in increments of an *octave*, four *semitones* (also commonly referred to as a "third"), one semitone, and *cents*.

NEW TERM

> **Octaves, Semitones, and Cents**
> Music is divided into octaves, semitones, and cents. An octave is the full "do, re, mi, fa, sol, la, ti, do" scale. There are 12 semitones in an octave. On a piano, if you play a white key and then the black key right next to it, you have changed the pitch one semitone. There are 100 cents in a semitone.

Changing the pitch not only gives you the ability to create harmony parts but also to correct for pitch problems in case you record a loop that is slightly out of tune with the other tracks. (See Hours 15, "Recording and Creating Your Own Loops," and 16, "Adding Vocals," to learn how to record your own loops in ACID.)

When you change the pitch of a track, you change the pitch of all the events in that track. To change the pitch of a track or group of tracks, select one or more tracks and then press the plus (+) key or the minus (–) key on your numeric keypad. The + key raises the pitch one semitone each time you press it. The – key lowers the pitch one semitone. Hold the Shift key while you press + or – to adjust the pitch by four semitones. Hold the Ctrl key and press + or – to adjust the pitch an octave higher or lower.

If you don't have a numeric keypad on your keyboard (many smaller PCs and laptops don't), right-click the Track Header of the track whose pitch you want to adjust and choose Pitch Shift Track, Up Semitone or Down Semitone. Again, hold the Shift key when you click the command to adjust the pitch by four semitones, and hold the Ctrl key to adjust the pitch by a full octave.

To "tweak" the pitch in increments of cents, adjust the track pitch using the Track Properties dialog box. Right-click the Track Header and choose Properties from the shortcut menu. Alternatively, double-click the track icon. Both of these actions open the Track Properties dialog box. On the General tab of the Track Properties dialog box, double-click the Pitch Shift (Semitones) field to highlight the current value, and then type your desired value. Press the Tab key to finalize the change. Click the up arrow to raise the pitch or click the down arrow to lower it. As another alternative, click and drag the spin control (between the two arrows) to change the value.

Task: Creating a Harmony Track

In this task, you'll change the pitch of the duplicate track you made in the previous task in order to create harmony.

1. Start by picking up where you left off with the ACID project you began in the last task. To make the results of your harmony adjustments easier to hear, click the multipurpose fader label for track 1 and choose Pan from the drop-down menu. Pan track 1 hard left. Pan track 2 hard right. Play the project. Because the same sound is coming from both speakers equally, the flute sounds like it is coming from directly in between the speakers.

2. Right-click track 2 and choose Properties from the shortcut menu. The Track Properties dialog box opens.

3. Change the value in the Pitch Shift (Semitones) field to 4. Press the Tab or Enter key on your keyboard to accept the setting you typed into the Pitch Shift (Semitones) field. The track icon for track 2 now displays the value +4 (see Figure 5.2). Click the Close button in the upper-right corner of the Track Properties dialog box to close the box.

FIGURE 5.2

When you change the pitch of a track, the track icon displays the Pitch Shift value.

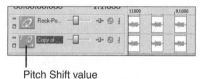

Pitch Shift value

4. Click the Loop Playback button. Drag the yellow triangles on the Loop Region Indicator bar to create a loop region from the start of the project to bar 3.

5. Click the Play From Start button. You can now hear the original track playing back in your left speaker at the project pitch (that is, the project key), and the duplicate track playing back in the right speaker four semitones higher—instant harmony track! Use the Solo buttons to listen to the tracks individually if you want to hear what the adjusted track sounds like alone.

Adjusting the Start Offset of an Event

When you draw an event into a project, that event starts the playback of the media file it contains from the beginning of the media file. Sometimes it's helpful to have the event start playback from another position in the media file. To accomplish this, adjust the *start offset* of the event.

5

NEW TERM

Start Offset

By default, an event plays the media file it contains starting at the very beginning of the media file. You can tell the event to start playing the media file at a point other than the very beginning. In this case, you are off-setting the start of the media file so that it no longer matches the beginning of the event. In other words, you create a start offset. For example, if you are using a four-beat loop, the loop normally starts with beat 1. You can change the start offset of the event so that the loop starts playing on any other beat (or even anywhere between beats).

To adjust the start offset of an event with your mouse, press and hold the Alt key on your keyboard and hover the mouse pointer over the middle of an event. When the cursor changes to a box with a double horizontal arrow in it, you have entered Adjust Offset mode. Still holding the Alt key, click and drag the waveform in the event to either the left or the right. Notice that the waveform slides as you move the mouse, but that the event does not slide. Also notice the notches in the top and bottom of the event. These notches mark the beginning of the loop file and give you a visual idea of the length of the start offset.

For an alternative method of changing the start offset, right-click the event and choose Properties from the shortcut menu. Alternatively, double-click the event. In the Event Properties dialog box that opens, double-click the Start Offset (Samples) field to select the current start offset value. Type any number from 0 up to the total number of samples in the loop to specify a new start offset value. Press the Tab key to finalize the change.

> If you're not familiar with the term *sample*, don't worry. We'll talk about that in detail in Hour 17, "Creating Mixed Audio and Video Files."

Now that you know how to change the start offset of an event, here are a few reasons you might want to do so:

- Perhaps, when you recorded the loop, it was not quite in rhythm with the other loops. Maybe the loop comes in late or early. Adjust the start offset to align it with the other loops.

> Don't confuse moving an event with changing the start offset of the file within the event. We'll talk more about moving events in later hours, but

for now you should know that if you click and drag an event (without holding down the Alt key), you can reposition it on the timeline. This action does not affect the start offset we are discussing here; it merely moves the event and the file it holds to a new position. When you change the start offset, you change the relationship between the start of the event and the start of the file in the event. The position of the event on the timeline does not change.

- To create interesting rhythms, adjust the start offset so that an accent that normally appears on a certain beat now occurs on a different beat.

- To create flange, slap-back, and echo effects, duplicate a track and adjust the start offset of one of the tracks.

We're sure that you'll discover your own ways to take advantage of the start offset feature. In the meantime, let's make practical use of the knowledge by trying a few experiments.

Task: Creating Effects with Offset

In this task, you'll use the Duplicate Track feature in conjunction with changing the start offset to create interesting effects. Follow these steps to create flange and slap-back effects:

1. Start a new ACID project. Add the file 070gsl02.wav and draw in an eight-bar event. Create a loop region over the event, set the project to Loop Playback mode, and click the Play button to listen to this drum beat.

2. Click the Stop button to stop playback. Right-click the track icon for this track and choose Duplicate Track from the shortcut menu.

3. Press the Tab key on your keyboard to switch the focus from the Track Header area to the timeline.

4. It often helps to zoom far into your project so that you can see the details of the waveforms in the events. Press the up arrow on your keyboard about a dozen times so that you are really zoomed in to the project. Note that you can also zoom in using the Zoom In Time controls at the bottom-right corner of the Track View area (zooming techniques were discussed in Hour 3).

5. Point to the event in track 2. Press and hold the Alt key and drag the mouse slightly to the right. Notice that the waveform within the event moves, but that the event

5

itself stays in its original position. Be careful not to drag too far—with the Adjust Offset feature, a little goes a long way! Notice that the waveforms in tracks 1 and 2 no longer line up exactly (see Figure 5.3).

FIGURE 5.3

To achieve this effect, zoom in and move the waveform in one track slightly to the right or left. Notice that the waveforms are slightly offset.

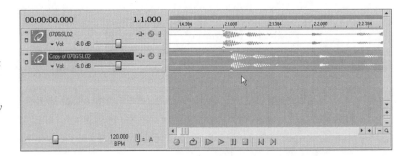

6. Click the Play From Start button. The drum track sounds as if it is routing through a flanger.

7. Repeat step 5, sliding the waveform even farther to the right. Then click the Play From Start button to listen again to the project. Experiment with different positions for the second waveform until you get the feel of how sliding the waveform of the event on the second track affects the overall mix. See whether you can create a slap-back effect. You can also use the Mute button on Track 2 (or the Solo button on Track 1) to toggle between listening to just one track, or to both tracks together to get a feel for how changing the start offset in track 2 affects the final mix.

8. Right-click the event in track 2 and choose Properties from the shortcut menu. Notice that the Start Offset field now represents the start offset you created by moving the waveform in step 5. As the project plays, drag the waveform further left (or right) using the Alt+drag method described in the preceding section. As you slide the waveform, the number in the Start Offset field changes. You can also hear the overall sound change as the two tracks get more and more out of phase.

9. Double-click the Start Offset field to select the current value. Type **750** and press the Tab key (or click in another field) to accept the number you typed into the field. Notice that the waveform in the event moves as soon as the number is accepted. You've created a flange effect on the drums. Close the Event Properties dialog box and click the Stop button.

10. Click in the timeline to give that area the focus. Press the down arrow as many times as it takes to see the whole project. Add eight bars of Guitar 34-10.wav to the project. Click the Play button to hear how the guitar sounds along with the drum tracks.

11. Duplicate the guitar track and offset the second track by 419,815 samples. This setting creates a slap-back echo effect.

12. Pan the first guitar track hard left; pan the second guitar track hard right. Then click Play From Start. Experiment with different offsets to increase or decrease the amount of delay.

All the files used in this task can be found in the *ACID DJ* loop collection from Sonic Foundry.

Changing the Pitch of an Event

Earlier, you learned how to change the key of the project and how to change the pitch of a track. You can also change the pitch of a single event. Combine this with the ability to split events into sections as small as a pixel (a technique we'll discuss in Hour 6, "Shaping Your Project"), and you can really get creative with your loops. There are three ways to change the pitch of an event:

- Right-click the event and choose Pitch Shift, Up Semitone or Down Semitone from the shortcut menu.

- Right-click the event and choose Properties. In the Event Properties dialog box, the Pitch Shift field works exactly like it does in the Track Properties dialog box (which is explored earlier in this hour). Using the Event Properties dialog box, you can adjust the pitch in cents and semitone increments. Use the arrows or the slider, or type a value to shift the pitch.

- Select the event and use the + or – key on the numeric keypad to raise or lower the pitch by one semitone each time you press the key.

Hold the Shift key and press the + or – key on the numeric keypad to change the pitch in four-semitone increments; hold the Ctrl key and press the + or – key to change the pitch by a full octave.

5

Change the pitch of an event to create harmony, to modify a melody, or to create special effects. Sometimes you can achieve interesting effects by changing the pitch of a *one-shot*.

One-Shot

Unlike the loop files you've been using so far, one-shot files are not designed to loop repeatedly as you draw a longer and longer event. Things that you typically want to come in only once every now and then (such as crash cymbals, sound effects, and sound bites) make good candidates for one-shot files. When you add a long file to your project (a sound file that is more than approximately 30 seconds long), ACID gives you the option of adding the file as a one-shot or as a Beatmapper file (another new file type that you'll learn about later). Unlike when you change the pitch of a loop, if you change the pitch of a one-shot file, you also affect its duration. Hour 9, "Incorporating One-Shot and Beatmapper Tracks," discusses one-shot files in much more detail.

Task: Shifting the Pitch of an Event to Create Harmony

In this task, you'll duplicate a track and change the pitch of various events on the duplicate track.

1. Start a new ACID project, change the project key to F, and add eight bars of `Drumbeat 50-06.wav`.

2. Add `Sax 09-11.wav`. Draw four events, each one-bar long, into bars 1 through 4. Then duplicate the saxophone track.

A handy shortcut for duplicating a track is to copy and paste it. Click the Track Header of the track you want to duplicate, press Ctrl+C to copy the track, and press Ctrl+V to quickly paste the copy back into the project. This action has exactly the same result as choosing Duplicate Track from the Track Header shortcut menu.

3. Click the second event in track 3 to select it, and press the + key four times (or hold the Shift key and press the + key once) to raise the pitch four semitones.

4. Select the third event and raise it five semitones; select the fourth event and raise it seven semitones.

If you zoom in on the events, you'll notice that not only do you see a number representing the number of semitones you have raised the event, but you also see a letter in parentheses indicating the current pitch of the event relative to the project key. For instance, the second event has an (A). Because the project key is F (assuming that you followed the instructions in step 1), and you raised the event four semitones—F to F#, F# to G, G to G#, and G# to A—the pitch of the event is now A.

It's a good idea to zoom in when working with event pitches so that you can make use of this additional information (see Figure 5.4).

FIGURE 5.4

Zoom in on the event so that you can see additional pitch information.

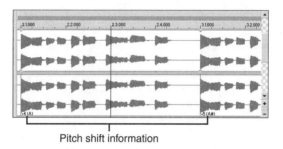

Pitch shift information

5. Pan track 2 hard left; pan track 3 hard right so that you can better hear the results of this experiment.

6. Click the Play From Start button and listen to the harmony part you have just created.

7. Mute both of the saxophone tracks.

8. Add `One Shots Cymbals 75-09.wav` to your project and draw in three new events at bars 2, 3, and 4.

9. Select the event at bar 3 and press the + key 10 times. Notice that the duration of the waveform for the one-shot file becomes shorter with each press of the + key. Notice also that the event itself does not become shorter, only the waveforms within the event.

10. Select the event at bar 4 and press the – key 10 times. Notice that the duration increases, as indicated by the waveform growing toward the right edge of the event.

11. Click the Play From Start button and listen to the difference between the cymbal crash at its original pitch (in the first event), and the other cymbal crash events that have had their pitch shifted.

All the loops in this task came from the *On the Jazz Tip* loop library from Sonic Foundry.

Automating Your Mix with Envelopes

Hour 3 explored the basics of mixing in ACID. Although you can get a good mix using those techniques, adding *envelopes* to your bag of tricks takes mixing to a whole new level.

Envelopes

Envelopes let you automate a great deal of the mixing process by changing certain parameters over time. In ACID, you can use envelopes to create fades by adjusting the volume; you also can use envelopes to create the illusion that a sound sweeps from one speaker to the other by changing the panning. As we'll discuss in Hour 13, "Using the Mixer," you can also control FX and buses with envelopes.

Most envelops in ACID exist at the track level. However, ASR envelopes exist at the event level. In the following sections, you'll learn to use ASR envelopes on individual events, as well as volume and pan envelopes on tracks.

ASR Envelopes

Every event has its own ASR envelope that stays with the event no matter where you move it. The ASR envelope allows you to make adjustments to the volume of its event independent of the volume of any other event in the project. ASR stands for Attack, Sustain, Release—the three distinct portions of these envelopes. Adjust the attack portion of the envelope to create a fade in at the beginning of an event. Use the sustain portion to define the volume level of the event from the end of the attack to the beginning of the release. Use the release portion of the envelope to create a fade out. Both the attack and release portions have three different fade types to choose from: slow, linear, and fast.

To adjust the attack portion of the envelope, point the mouse to the upper-left corner of the event. The arrow changes shape to look like a double-headed horizontal arrow attached to a quarter piece of pie (see Figure 5.5).

FIGURE 5.5

To adjust the attack, point the mouse to the upper-left corner of the event, click, and drag right.

Click and drag to the right to create a fade in. The sloping blue line that appears is the envelope. Position the cursor over the point at which the envelope ends and right-click; from the shortcut menu that appears, choose from the slow, linear, or fast fade options shown in Figure 5.6.

FIGURE 5.6

Right-click the envelope to choose from slow, linear, or fast fade options.

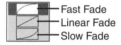

To adjust the release (or fade out) portion of the ASR envelope, point the mouse to the upper-right corner of the event and click and drag to the left. Right-click the envelope to pick the fade type, just as you did with the attack portion of the envelope.

To adjust the sustain, point the mouse anywhere along the top of the event. As you can see in Figure 5.7, the mouse changes to a hand with a pointing finger. Attached to the hand is a double-pointing vertical arrow. You'll also see a floating ToolTip box indicating the current Gain (volume) level in decibels (dB). Drag down to lower the sustain volume. After you've adjusted the sustain portion of the envelope, you'll see the blue envelope line. To make further adjustments to the sustain portion, click and drag the envelope line up or down.

FIGURE 5.7

Point to the top of the event until the mouse changes to the shape of a pointing hand; click and drag to adjust the sustain.

Track Volume Envelopes

Whereas an ASR envelope controls only the volume of the event to which it belongs, a track volume envelope controls the volume of all the events in the track. The envelope can be locked to and moved with the events, or it can be unlocked and independent of the movement of the events.

To create a track volume envelope, right-click the track icon (or anywhere on the track that does not contain an event). From the shortcut menu, choose Insert/Remove Envelope, Volume. A red envelope line appears through the middle of the selected track.

> You also can choose Insert, Envelopes, Volume to add a volume envelope to the selected track.

When you point the mouse at the envelope line, the mouse cursor changes to the same pointing-hand shape you saw when adjusting the sustain portion of an ASR envelope. Drag this red envelope line up and down to adjust the volume of the entire track. But we can adjust the volume of the entire track with the track volume fader, so what's the advantage of the track volume envelope? The big advantage is that you can add points to the envelope that can be set at different levels.

To add a point, right-click the envelope where you want the point and choose Add Point from the shortcut menu. Alternatively, double-click the envelope where you want to place the point. Click and drag a point to adjust its position horizontally as well as vertically. Right-click the envelope between any two points to define the fade from the first point to the second point as a linear, slow, or fast fade.

As mentioned earlier (and discussed in detail during Hour 7, "Constructing Your Musical Arrangement"), you can move events. Even though this is a track envelope, ACID locks it (and all other track envelopes) to events on the timeline by default. If you move an event, any envelope points that fall within that event also move. Envelope points that fall outside of the moved event do not move. Choose Options, Lock Envelopes to Events from the menu bar, or click the Lock Envelopes to Events button in the toolbar to toggle this feature off and on.

Task: Customizing a Track Volume Envelope

In this task, you'll adjust the volume of a track over time with an envelope.

1. Start a new project and add eight bars of Drumbeat 50-06.

2. Right-click the track icon and choose Insert/Remove Envelope, Volume to insert a track volume envelope.

3. Double-click the envelope at bars 3, 5, 7, and 9 to place points at those locations.

4. Drag the point at bar 3 down to –Inf.

5. Right-click the envelope line between bars 3 and 5 and choose Slow Fade from the shortcut menu.

6. Click and drag the envelope section between bars 5 and 7 to around 3dB.

7. Drag the point at bar 9 down to –Inf.

8. Right-click to the line between bars 7 and 9 and choose Fast Fade. Your project should now look like the one in Figure 5.8.

FIGURE 5.8

Track volume envelopes allow you to make detailed changes to the track volume.

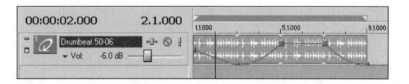

9. Click the Play From Start button and listen to the effect of the envelope on the track volume. Leave this project open; you'll use it in the next task.

The volume envelope acts as a post-volume fader. This means that any adjustment made by the envelope is added to or subtracted from the volume level you set with the volume fader in the Track Header. For instance, assume the volume fader is set at –6.0dB. If you add an envelope to that track, and set the envelope at 6dB (by dragging the envelope all the way to the top of the track), the file plays back at its normal volume because the 6dB envelope boost cancels out the –6dB volume fader cut.

This information is important; if you set your volume fader at or above 0dB and then add an envelope at a positive dB value, you can quickly create a signal that is too hot and that might cause unwanted distortion. On the other hand, if you set the volume fader to –Inf and set the envelope to a positive dB value, you still hear nothing because the volume fader isn't sending any signal to the envelope. The envelope in this case is boosting "no signal." Boosting nothing still gives you nothing!

Track Pan Envelopes

Just as you can use a volume envelope to control a track's volume, you can automate the panning of a track with a pan envelope. Because you can add as many points as you like along the envelope, you can create an envelope that continuously sweeps the audio back and forth across the stereo field if you want. Pan envelopes work the same way as volume envelopes. To use a pan envelope, right-click the track icon of the desired track and choose Insert/Remove Envelope, Pan from the shortcut menu. Apply pan envelopes to as many tracks as you want.

Task: Applying a Pan Envelope

This task demonstrates the use of pan envelopes to cause a crash cymbal to "bounce" back and forth between your two speakers.

1. With the project from the last task still open, add `One Shots Cymbal 75-09.wav` to the project.

2. Drawn in an event at bar 3, beat 1. Draw another event starting at bar 2, beat 3, and ending when it touches the beginning of the first event you added (you might need to zoom in to find the correct beat). Draw one more event starting at bar 2, beat 1, and ending when it reaches the next event.

3. Right-click the Track Header for track 2. Choose Insert, Envelopes, Pan. Notice the purple pan envelope running down the center of track 2.

4. Place a point on the envelope at the beginning of the first crash cymbal event; place another point near the end of the event. Place two similar points in each of the other two events.

5. Click and drag the portion of the pan envelope over the first event all the way to the bottom of the event. Read the information in the floating ToolTip as you drag; notice that this action pans the event 100% right.

6. Pan the next event 100% left by dragging its portion of the envelope all the way to the top of the event.

7. Pan the third event 100% right.

8. Just to spice things up (and to review the lesson in an earlier task), raise the pitch of the second crash cymbal 3 semitones and lower the pitch of the third cymbal 3 semitones. (Reminder: The + and – keys allow you to quickly change the pitch of the selected event.) The track should look like the one in Figure 5.9.

Setting volume and pan envelopes does not change the appearance of the waveform in an event affected by the envelope. The waveform always retains its original shape. This serves as a valuable reference because it helps you visualize what the file sounds like in its original state. The envelope line is your visual cue as to how you have changed the volume or panning.

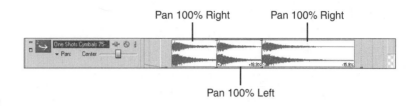

Pan 100% Right   Pan 100% Right

Pan 100% Left

FIGURE 5.10

*Pan envelopes allow
you to automate the
movement of tracks
across the stereo field.*

9. Click the Play From Start button and listen to the volume of the drums change as
   the cymbals move from right to left to right.

Track Assignable FX and Bus Envelopes

You also can control the amount of signal being sent to assignable FX and buses with
envelopes. FX and bus envelopes work just like volume and pan envelopes do. However,
these choices do not show up in the Insert/Remove Envelope menu unless you have created at least one assignable FX or have added at least one additional bus to the project.
Don't worry if you aren't familiar with the terms "assignable FX" and "bus"; because we
cover assignable FX in Hour 11, "Editing with the Chopper," and buses in Hour 13,
"Using the Mixer," we'll hold off until then to explore using these envelopes.

Envelope Options

Now let's talk about some envelope behavior. First, note that the Envelope Edit tool
restricts your editing to envelopes. With this tool, you can't select events, so you don't
have to worry about inadvertently changing them. You might want to click the Envelope
Edit tool now, but you don't have to. You can work with your envelopes using the Draw
tool, too.

Notice that you can move either a point on the envelope line (in any direction) or the
envelope line itself (up and down only). When you move the line, you move only the
segment between the beginning or end of the line and a point, or between two points.
The points at the end of the line segment you are moving also move up or down according to where you place the line.

As you know, you right-click any envelope point to open the shortcut menu. Let's run
through the options you find in the shortcut menu. You might find it difficult to hit an
exact volume or pan value with the click-and-drag method. The first three options in the
shortcut menu give you some common preset levels. The Set To options let you choose
common preset levels or type in an exact value for the point. The Delete option should be
obvious, and we've already talked about the fade type options.

5

The Select All option allows you to select all the points on the line. Now when you click and drag one point, all the other points move with it so that you maintain the relationship between all points. Notice that after you choose the Select All option, it changes to Select None, another obvious choice.

Finally, be careful with the Reset All option because it doesn't just reset all the points to 0dB (or center for pan envelopes) as you might initially think. Rather, it resets the envelope to its default state. In other words, the envelope returns to 0dB or center, and all the points you added are removed.

One more note: You might have noticed that, in its default state, a track envelope has one point at the beginning that you can't delete or move horizontally. Any adjustments you make to this point affect the entire envelope.

Hiding and Removing Envelopes

There might be times when you have more than one type of envelope on a single track. Even though they are different colors, it can be hard to work with all the envelopes visible at the same time. With the track or tracks selected, choose View, Show Envelopes from the menu bar and then choose the name of the envelope you want to hide. The envelope still affects the track, even though you cannot see it. To make that envelope visible again, choose View, Show Envelopes and choose the envelope type again.

> In the View, Show Envelopes menu, an envelope with a check mark by it can be seen in the Track View area. If the envelope does not have a check mark by it, that envelope is currently hidden from view.

To remove a track envelope, right-click the track icon (or a blank spot in the track on the timeline), choose Insert/Remove Envelopes from the shortcut menu, and choose the envelope you want to remove from the cascading menu. Alternatively, select the track that holds the envelope you want to remove and choose Insert, Envelopes. Then choose the envelope you want to remove from the cascading menu. These commands remove the envelope so that it no longer has any effect on the track. If you turn the envelope on again, any points you had added previously will be lost.

Summary

In this hour, you learned to duplicate a track and change the pitch of the duplicate tracks (or the events within it) to create harmony and stereo effects. You also learned how to adjust the start offset of an event so that it starts playback from a spot other than the beginning. You also explored the envelopes feature and how they can automate volume and panning.

In the next hour, you'll learn all about editing events to create even more interesting effects and arrangements. But first, spend a few minutes testing the knowledge you gained during this hour.

Q&A

Q. I'm trying to move an envelope point to the middle of a measure, but each time I drag it, the point jumps to either the beginning or the end of the line— I can't get it in the middle. What am I doing wrong?

A. If you have snapping enabled (Options, Snapping, Enable), envelope points follow the snap-to settings. To override this setting, you can either turn off snapping or simply hold the Shift key while you drag the point. Holding the Shift key temporarily overrides snapping.

Q. If I have applied both a track volume envelope and an event ASR envelope, which will control the volume?

A. Earlier you learned that a track volume envelope acts on the settings of the volume fader. In the same way, the ASR envelope acts on the settings of the track volume envelope. Even if you have the track volume envelope at 100%, an event ASR fade still fades the volume to –Inf. In short, event properties take precedent over track properties.

Workshop

This workshop will help you review the material presented in the last hour and give you an opportunity to use the techniques you've learned.

Quiz

1. How do you add points to an envelope so that you can adjust the parameters?

2. How do you change the start offset of an event using the mouse?

3. What does ASR stand for, and what does an ASR envelope do?

Quiz Answers

1. Right-click an envelope and choose Add Point from the shortcut menu, or double-click an envelope to add a point to an envelope line.

2. Hold the Alt key, click within the event, and drag the waveform left or right to adjust the start offset.

3. Every event has an ASR envelope. These envelopes have three segments that can be adjusted independently: attack, sustain, and release. You create a fade in using the attack parameter, you control overall volume of the event with the sustain parameter, and you create a fade out using the release parameter.

Activities

1. Open the project called Hour5 Activity.acd, found in the Hour 5 Samples folder on the CD-ROM that accompanies this book. Apply a volume envelope to the Interaction 03 and Event Horizon Beat 17 tracks so that they fade in over four bars and fade out over four bars. Duplicate the Interaction 01 track and raise the pitch of the duplicate track seven semitones. Add a pan envelope to the Interaction 06 track and set it up so that each event pans across the stereo field as it plays. Save your work and open the file Hour5 Activity Complete.acd. Compare this project to the one you just created. Were you able to get all the envelopes to work?

Hour **6**

Shaping Your Project

- Making Selections on the Timeline
- Trimming Edges
- Working with Snapping
- Task: Editing Edges With and Without Snapping Enabled
- Splitting Events
- Task: Splitting Events
- Working with Beat Markers
- Using Undo/Redo History

As you create more and more music with ACID, you'll expect more and more from the software. That's all right. In fact, it's encouraged by the talented group of developers who created and are constantly improving this amazing music creation tool. In this hour, you'll get down to the details of event editing, and still keep track of the big picture as you develop your ACID masterpiece.

In this hour, you will:

- Select the events you want to edit
- Trim an event to create the precise phrase you're after
- Split an event to customize the loop right on the Track View timeline
- Use markers to organize the arrangement and easily navigate from one section to another
- Use the Undo/Redo history list so that you can experiment without losing your work

Making Selections on the Timeline

Luckily, you don't have to live with the first arrangement you create. You'll constantly be changing things until you get it "just right." You can do a lot to change existing events, but before you can do much of anything, you have to select the event or events you want to manipulate. There are three selection possibilities in ACID: You can select individual events, you can select a time range, or you can select individual events within a time range. Let's take a closer look at each of these options.

Selecting Events

To select an event, click it with the Draw tool. Notice that the background of the event changes from white to light blue, and that the waveform within the event changes from the Track Header color to white (see Figure 6.1). These visual indications tell you which event or events are selected.

Not Selected

FIGURE 6.1

A selected event changes color to indicate that it is selected.

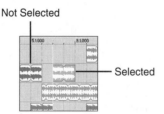

Selected

You can select more than one event using the techniques discussed in the coffee break called "Windows Selection Techniques," in Hour 3, "Basic Mixing." You can also select multiple events with the Selection tool. To use this tool, click and drag to create a selection box. Any event touched by the box becomes selected.

The Selection tool has three possible states. In the default state, you define the exact dimensions of the selection box. To get to the second state, click and hold the left mouse button. Now click the right mouse button. The selection box stretches from the top of the project to the bottom—you can only resize the box horizontally. Use this technique to quickly select every event that falls within the width of the selection box, regardless of the track on which it is located. Click the right mouse button again to change to the third state, in which the selection box stretches the length of the project. You can only adjust the selection box up and down. Use this technique to quickly select every event on every track touched by the selection box. Remember to switch back to the Draw tool after you have made your selection.

These same three selection-shape options also work with the Zoom tool you learned about in Hour 3. Hold down the left mouse button and click the right mouse button to choose between the three selection-shape options.

Selecting a Time Range

Use the Time Selection tool, shown in Figure 6.2, to make a selection on the timeline. Click the Time Selection tool to select it. Then click in the Marker bar where you want the time selection to start and drag to where you want the selection to end. Release the mouse button.

FIGURE 6.2

The Time Selection Tool is located in the ACID toolbar.

Time Selection Tool

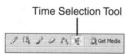

Notice that, as you make the time selection, a blue highlighted area appears on the timeline. Also note that the length of the Loop Region Indicator bar corresponds with the time selection. The fact that the Loop Region Indicator bar and the time selection correspond is handy because it allows you to quickly reestablish a time selection if you lose it. For example, click away from the time selection on the timeline. The selection disappears from the timeline, but the Loop Region Indicator bar is still there. Double-click the Loop Region Indicator bar to instantly reestablish the selection in the timeline. If you resize the Loop Region Indicator bar, you also resize the corresponding selection in the timeline.

You'll find several reasons for establishing a time selection. For example, in a few minutes, we'll show you how to use a time selection to split events.

6

Selecting a Combination of Time and Events

In the preceding section, you learned how to select time. Before that, you learned how to select events. Sometimes, you'll want to combine the two techniques. First, select an event (or several events) on the timeline. With the Time Selection tool, click and drag in the Marker bar to establish a time selection that includes at least one of the events you selected. You now have both time and events selected, as shown in Figure 6.3.

FIGURE 6.3

Only the selected events are affected by the time selection.

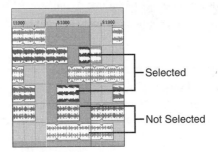

Trimming Edges

Suppose that you want to use only a portion of a loop rather than the whole phrase. Or suppose that you have drawn an event over four bars and now want only two bars of it. Or maybe your event is only six bars long when you really want seven bars. Each of these scenarios calls for editing an event.

One way to make an event shorter is to use the Erase tool discussed in Hour 2, "Getting Started." Similarly, you can use the Paint tool to make the event longer. ACID provides a couple of other techniques for editing events. One of these is the Edge Trim function, which lets you make an event longer or shorter.

Point the mouse at either end of any event. The shape of the mouse pointer changes to a box/double arrow combination to indicate that you're in Edge Trim mode. The little box attached to the pointer represents an event, and the middle of the arrow rests on the edge to be edited. As you can see in Figure 6.4, if you point to the right edge, the box is on the left side of the pointer. Figure 6.5 shows that the opposite is also true.

FIGURE 6.4

An example of the shape of the mouse pointer when you're ready to edge trim the right edge of an event.

FIGURE 6.5

An example of the shape of the mouse pointer when you're ready to edge trim the left edge of an event.

Being aware of which side the box is on comes in handy when you're edge trimming two events that sit right next to each other, as Figure 6.6 shows. Because the arrow is on the left side of the box in Figure 6.6, the left edge of the second event will be edited.

FIGURE 6.6

In this example, there are two events right next to each other. The arrow indicates that the mode is set to edge edit the left side of the second event.

It's important to keep the edits musical. Two features that aid in this process are the grid lines and the Snapping settings. Before we explore edge editing in a task, we'll take a moment to explore these two features.

Working with Snapping

ACID has a Snapping function that works much the same as snapping does in other programs you might already use. With the Snapping function on, events that you add to the ACID Track View jump, or "snap," to specific objects when the events are placed near those objects. ACID has several different snapping options, as described in the following section.

Snapping Options

To toggle the Snapping function on and off, choose Option, Snapping, Enable. Alternatively, click the Enable Snapping button in the ACID toolbar. There are certainly times when being able to move freely is beneficial. Turn snapping off when you want to make fine adjustments to the position of an event without it jumping suddenly to a snap object.

As you no doubt have already noticed, the Track View is divided into sections by grid lines. These grid lines portray musical divisions—measures, beats, and divisions of

6

beats. The placement of these grid lines and what they represent changes as you zoom in and out and when you adjust the Grid Spacing settings (we'll talk more about Grid Spacing shortly). For instance, if the Grid Spacing is set to its default, and you zoom all the way out, each grid line represents a measure. Zoom all the way in, and each grid line represents a 32nd note *triplet*.

Triplet

Here's just a little music theory to explain a triplet. In standard 4/4 musical time, there are 4 beats per measure. A whole note lasts for the whole measure, a half note lasts for half the measure, and a quarter note lasts for a quarter of the measure. That makes sense. A quarter note can further be divided into two 8th notes. An 8th note triplet occurs when a group of three 8th notes are performed in the time of two 8th notes. If that confuses you, don't feel bad. The math doesn't really work out, but the music does.

You can control whether objects snap only to the ACID grid lines or to other objects in addition to the grid. To make objects snap to the grid only, choose Options, Snapping, Grid Only. Now when you move an event, it snaps only to the grid lines in the Track View area.

When you turn the Grid Only option off, events will snap to several other objects in addition to the grid—including the timeline cursor, markers, and the edges of other events.

Grid Spacing

By default, the lines on the grid match the marks on the Time ruler. Choose Options, Grid Spacing to access a cascading menu of grid spacing choices. If you choose the 8th Notes option, you'll notice that some grid lines now appear between the ruler marks. You can set the grid spacing quite close together to enable fine adjustments while still taking advantage of the snap-to functionality to keep you in time with the beat.

Task: Editing Edges with and Without Snapping Enabled

This task will show how edge editing an event is affected by whether snapping is enabled or disabled.

1. Open the project EdgeEditDemo.acd located in Hour 6 Samples folder on the CD-ROM that accompanies this book.

2. Choose Options, Snapping, Enable to turn on the Snapping feature. Choose Options, Grid Spacing, Ruler Marks if that option is not already selected.

3. With the cursor at the beginning of the project, zoom in until you can see four grid lines per measure.

4. Point the mouse at the right edge of the event to enter Edge Trim mode then click and drag to the left. Notice that as you do so, the edge of the event jumps to the next grid line to the left. Try to stop somewhere between gridlines; you can't. In this case, each of these gridlines represents one beat. The Snapping function is enabling you to edit in one-beat increments.

 Even if the Snapping function is active, you can temporarily override the feature. To do so, press and hold the Shift key as you edge edit.

5. Choose Options, Snapping, Enable to turn this function off and edge edit an event again. Notice that now you can stop between the grid lines.

6. Now click and drag the right edge of the event to the right. Notice that you can make the event last for as long as you want. With events on a loop track, no matter how far to the right you drag the edge of the event, the entire event is filled in with recurrences of the loop file.

Splitting Events

Another method of editing an event is to split it into two separate events. There are two ways to split an event: You can split it at the cursor, and you can split it according to a time selection.

Splitting Events at the Cursor

To split an event at the cursor, click the event at the location where you want the split to occur. This action selects the event and places the project cursor at the specified location. Now choose Edit, Split or press the S key on your keyboard. ACID splits the event into two *separate* events—one to the left of the cursor and one to the right (see Figure 6.7).

If you have several tracks in your project, and each track contains events that all occur at the same time, one of two things happens when you choose the Split command. If no events are selected, ACID splits *all events touched by the cursor*. If any events are selected, ACID splits only the selected events that are touched by the cursor; nonselected events are left whole.

6

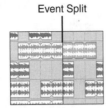

Event Split

FIGURE 6.7

The selected event has been split at the cursor. There are now two separate events.

Actually, a third possibility exists when you make a split. If the project cursor happens to be located such that it does not touch any event, the split operation has no effect at all.

Remember that all the edits in ACID are nondestructive. What does "nondestructive" mean? When you add a loop (or other media file) to your ACID project, you are not physically adding that loop file. You are actually creating a reference to an external loop file. In other words, you're telling ACID, "When the playback cursor reaches this point, go find the loop and play it."

If you decide later that you don't want that loop to play, and you delete it from your project, all you've done is to delete the reference to that loop from your project. You haven't deleted the loop from your system. Therefore you can still use it later.

In the same way, when you split an event, you're not splitting the original loop file. You're merely making two reference calls to the file where before you only had one. And when you edge edit an event, you're not cutting the beginning or end off the file, you're just editing the event in your project that references that file.

Splitting Events at a Time Selection

You can also split selected events in combination with a time selection. Use the Time Selection tool to make a time selection as discussed earlier in this hour. This action creates two split locations, one each at the start and end of the selection (see Figure 6.8). Press S on your keyboard; because you have not selected any events, ACID splits every event in the timeline that touches one of these split locations (the beginning and end of the time range).

Now select a few events and make a time selection that includes part of one or more of the events in the selection and that also includes part of an event that you did not select. Now when you press S on your keyboard, ACID splits the selected events but leaves the unselected event untouched.

Figure 6.8

Both the beginning and the end of the time selection act as split points.

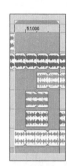

You can also use the Time Selection tool to trim an event. Select an event or events and select a time range that encompasses the portion of the events you want to keep. Choose Edit, Trim to delete the portions of the event (or events) outside the time selection.

Task: Splitting Events

In this task, you'll use the various techniques you've learned for splitting events.

1. Open the project `SplitDemo.acd` located in the Hour 6 Samples folder on the CD-ROM that accompanies this book. Click the three events, one after another. Notice that each track holds one event that will be selected if you click it. Point the mouse to bar 5, but make sure that you are at an empty spot on the timeline (below track 3). Click to place the project cursor at that location.

2. If you followed the instructions in step 1 carefully, no events are selected in the project, and the project cursor is at bar 5. Press the S key on your keyboard.

3. Click the event in track 1 to the left of bar 5. Notice that the original event has been split into two separate events, one on either side of bar 5. In fact, all three tracks now contain two events—one to the left of bar 5, and one to the right of bar 5. Click each event in succession to select it.

4. Click in track 1 at bar 9. This action selects only the second event in track 1. Press the S key to split the event. Track 1 now contains three events. Notice that no other events were split because they were not selected.

5. Click in a blank area of the timeline to deselect all events. Select the Time Selection tool and define a time selection from bar 13 to bar 17.

6. Press the S key. Click any event just to the left of the time range, then click within the time range, and finally click to the right of the time range. Notice that all three original events touched by the time selection have been split at the beginning and end of the range.

6

7. Click the event in track 2 after the time selection range to select it. Define a new time range from bar 21 to bar 25.

8. Press the S key; notice that only the event in track 2 is split.

Working with Beat Markers

There are several kinds of markers you can use in ACID. These markers correspond to the various rulers on the ACID screen and have specialized functions. When you first open ACID, or any time you start a new project, the Beat ruler is visible at the top of the timeline, and the Time ruler is visible at the bottom of the timeline. The Marker ruler is the blank area directly above the Beat ruler. You can place beat markers along the Marker ruler to mark important locations in the project. For instance, you might want to place a marker to identify various sections of your project—verse, chorus, Section A, Section B, and so on. These markers become more important as your project increases in length because they also aid in navigating around your composition.

In this hour, we talk only about beat markers. In Hour 7, "Constructing Your Musical Arrangement," you'll learn how to use tempo and key-change markers to construct an arrangement for your song. In Hour 10, "Scoring to a Video," you'll learn about the time markers you'll use when working with video. In Hour 17, "Creating Mixed Audio and Video Files," you'll learn how to add command markers to your timeline. Because this hour focuses on beat markers, we'll refer to them simply as "markers." When referring to one of the other types of markers, we'll use the full name of that marker.

To add a beat marker to your project, place the cursor at the point where you want to insert the marker and press M on your keyboard. As shown in Figure 6.9, an orange tab appears in the Marker ruler, and a line runs vertically through the project to mark that spot in the composition. The tab and line make up your new marker.

FIGURE 6.9

To drop a marker at the cursor location, press the M key.

Marker #1

Click and drag a marker's tab to move the marker to a new location. Markers follow all the snapping rules described earlier in this hour. (Reminder: Hold the Shift key to temporarily override the Snapping function.)

One wonderful feature of markers is that you can place them "on the fly." This means that you can click the Play button and, as you are listening to the project, press M to add (or as power users say, "drop") a marker wherever the cursor is at the time. The marker drops at the appropriate spot, and the project continues to play. We use this feature constantly, and you will find that it comes in handy time and time again.

To delete a single marker, right-click the marker's tab and choose Delete from the shortcut menu. To delete multiple markers, right-click the Marker bar and choose Markers/Regions, Delete All from the shortcut menu. Alternatively, make a time selection (as discussed earlier this hour) that encompasses the markers you want to delete. Then right-click the Marker bar and choose Markers/Regions, Delete All in Selection to delete just those specific markers.

Renaming Markers

ACID labels the first 10 markers with the numbers 1 through 0. You can add as many markers as you want, but only the first 10 contain a number label. However, ACID lets you add a name label to any marker. To do so, right-click the marker tab, choose Rename from the shortcut menu, and type in a name. When you finish typing, press the Enter or Tab key on your keyboard. The name now appears next to the marker. Another way to name a marker is to double-click just to the right of the marker tab.

Navigating to Markers

You can quickly jump to any of the numbered markers with a keyboard shortcut. To do so, press the number associated with the marker; the project cursor jumps to that marker instantly—even if you're currently playing the project. Another way to navigate to a marker is to hold the Ctrl key and press the right or left arrow. When you do so, the project cursor jumps to the next marker. Yet another technique is to right-click the marker and choose Go To. The cursor jumps to the marker you right-clicked. Markers are a great way to organize a large project and navigate through it.

6

Using Undo/Redo History

As you're edge editing, trimming, and splitting events, you might make a mistake or two. (We know…unthinkable. But it happens.) No problem; ACID has unlimited Undo/Redo capabilities. The Undo feature allows you to restore the project to any state it has passed through since it was opened. In fact, the feature records a history of all your actions in case you want to undo or redo several edits at a time. You can even undo a redo, or redo an undo!

To undo your last edit, click the Undo button in the toolbar or choose Edit, Undo. As soon as you undo an edit, the Redo feature becomes available. To Redo the edit, click the Redo button or choose Edit, Redo.

To undo or redo several edits, click repeatedly on the appropriate button, or click the arrow next to the Undo or Redo button. A history of all edits appears in a drop-down list. Select an edit from the list to undo (or redo) that edit and all the edits above it in the list. Figure 6.10 shows the Undo history for a project.

FIGURE 6.10

Click the arrow next to the Undo or Redo button to access the Undo or Redo history list. Choose an action from the list to undo or redo that action and all subsequent actions.

Summary

The techniques you learned in this hour will come in handy when you get down to detail editing as well as when you're working with bigger sections of a project. You learned how to select time, events, and a combination of both. You learned some great editing techniques such as splitting, edge editing, and trimming an event. You also learned to drop markers, name them, and use them for navigation. In the next hour we'll put these markers to work in creating an arrangement. For now, take a few moments to go over the questions and work through the activities that follow.

Q&A

Q. I'd like to be able to make a time selection using the Time Selection tool by dragging across the event I'm working with. But whenever I try, instead of selecting a range of time, the event moves. I know I can click and drag in the Marker ruler (the blank space just above the Beat ruler) to select a range of time, but I'd rather work in the event. Is there a way to do this without moving the event?

A. We understand the problem. Sometimes when you're trying to make a precise time selection, it is much easier to work in the event so that you can use the waveform as a guide. The trick is to hold both the Ctrl and Shift keys while you click and drag across the event to select the time range. And remember, you heard it here first!

Q. **I know that when I make a time selection and then press S to create a split, any event that is touched by the beginning or end of the time selection is split at those points. But what happens if the time selection includes an entire event? In other words, what if the time selection starts before the event and ends after it; will the event be affected?**

A. No, the event is left unchanged. The only way an event is affected is if the beginning or end of the time selection intersects with the event.

Q. **Is there a quick way to select the range of time between two markers?**

A. We're glad you asked! Of course there is. In fact, there are a few ways. First, double-click in the Marker ruler as close as you can to the midpoint between the two markers (don't worry, you don't have to be exactly in the middle). Another way is to use the keyboard shortcuts to navigate to the next marker (Ctrl+left arrow or Ctrl+right arrow), but in addition to holding the Ctrl key, also hold the Shift key. The third way is to click the Time Selection tool and then double-click a blank area of the timeline between the two markers. Don't double-click an existing track (this action selects the time between two events or the time between the beginning of the project and the first event—also a useful trick).

Workshop

Here's a quick test to help you review this hour's material. When you're done, take some time to work through the activity to see how well you've learned these editing concepts.

Quiz

1. How do you split an event?

2. How do you drop a marker?

Quiz Answers

1. Place the cursor where you want to split the event and press the S key.

2. Place the cursor where you want to place a marker and press the M key.

Activities

For this activity, you'll have to launch ACID twice so that you can have two projects open at the same time. (That's right, you can have more than one instance of ACID running at once. Just start ACID twice, and you can load two different ACID projects at the same time.) In the first ACID window, open the project called Activity6.acd from the companion CD-ROM to this book. Click the Play button, but prepare yourself—right now, the project sounds like a train wreck.

In the other ACID window, open `Activity6 complete.acd`. It's your job to use the selection techniques as well as edge editing, splitting, trimming, and delete techniques to make the first project sound (and look) like the second. Play the second file to hear what your results should sound like. You can compare one to the other as you're working.

Here are some helpful hints:

- Use the Edit, Trim command to edit tracks 6 and 4.
- Use a time selection to edit tracks 1 and 5 at the same time.
- Edit tracks 2 and 3 using a combination of split and edge trim.
- Use what you learned about track envelopes back in Hour 5, "Additional Editing Techniques," to create the fade-out ending.

 All the loops used for this activity come from the *Classic Country* loop collection from Sonic Foundry.

HOUR 7

Constructing Your Musical Arrangement

Up to this point, we have been focusing on events and tracks without much real thought given to how they relate to the project. In this hour, we'll look at how to work with events and tracks to build a composition. We'll explore some of the features of ACID that help you quickly build a full arrangement from sections of tracks and events. We'll also explore how tempo and key changes can add interest to your arrangement.

In this hour, you will:

- Create a musical progression using key-change markers
- Use tempo markers to create tempo variations
- Rearrange sections using the Cut, Copy, and Paste commands
- Create regions using location and region markers
- Construct a composition using regions

Using Key-Change Markers

You've already learned how to set the project key using the Project Key button in the Track List. When you change the project key, that change affects all the tracks in the project.

ACID also allows you to change the project key in real time during the course of the project. You accomplish this by placing key-change markers along the timeline and specifying a new key at those points. As the cursor passes over these markers, the master project key changes in real time. Any events and tracks that have been individually pitch-shifted are shifted again based on the new key. Refer back to Hour 5, "Additional Editing Techniques," if you need a refresher course on how to change the pitch of individual tracks and events.

Let's spend a few minutes discussing exactly how to add key change markers. You'll soon begin to see how these techniques can be used to create a *musical progression* for your project.

Musical Progression

When two or more specifically related notes are played at the same time, the result is called a chord. As a song moves along, or progresses, it typically moves through a series of related chords (sometimes actually played, sometimes merely implied). The movement of a song from one chord to the next is referred to as a musical progression, or a chord progression (or most often, just progression).

The progression of a song plays a huge role in how interesting the song sounds. ACID allows you to transpose events (using key-change markers) to simulate a chord progression. If your ACID project never changes key, you are writing a song that essentially has no progression. And a song without a progression can get very boring, very fast.

To create key changes in your project, place the cursor where you want the key change to occur and press the K key on your keyboard. Alternatively, choose Insert, Tempo/Key Change from the menu bar. This command opens the Tempo/Key Change dialog box (see Figure 7.1). Here you can specify whether you want a key change, a tempo change, or both.

FIGURE 7.1

Add real-time tempo and key changes to your project.

If you use the keyboard shortcut K to open the Tempo/Key Change dialog box, the Key Change option is checked, and the current key is highlighted. Later in this hour, you'll press the T key to add a Tempo change. In that case, the Tempo Change (BPM) option is checked, the current tempo is highlighted. If you use the Insert, Tempo/Key Change menu command to add the marker, both dialog-box options are checked and contain the current values.

In the Tempo/Key Change dialog box, choose the new key from the Key Change drop-down list and click OK to dismiss the dialog box. The Tempo and Key Marker bar opens above the Marker bar, and the key-change marker appears at the location of the project cursor. To edit the new marker, right-click the marker tab and choose Edit from the shortcut menu. This action reopens the Tempo/Key Change dialog box where you can make your desired changes.

To change the key-change marker without reopening the Tempo/Key Change dialog box, double-click just to the right of the marker tab. This action opens a text field containing the highlighted current key. Type the new key. It doesn't matter whether you use uppercase or lowercase letters because as soon as you press Enter to accept the key change, ACID converts the letter to uppercase. Use the # key to signify sharps, for instance A#. There is no method to specify flats, so instead use the corresponding sharp (also known as the enharmonic). For example use A# in place of B♭.

Click and drag the key-change marker to move the key change to a new location. If the Snapping feature is engaged, the markers adhere to the snapping rules discussed in Hour 6, "Shaping Your Project." As usual, hold down the Shift key as you drag a marker to temporarily disable the Snapping feature. If you right-click the marker, you can choose the appropriate option from the shortcut menu (that is, you can change its type, edit it, delete it, or move your cursor to it).

In some cases, the key change may end up putting a particular track in an octave that, although it's not technically wrong, may not be desirable. The following task lets you experiment with this situation.

Task: Combining Key Changes with Event Pitch Shift

In this task, you combine an event-level pitch shift with a key change. Before you begin, open the KeyChangeDemo.acd project from the Hour 7 Samples folder on the CD-ROM that accompanies this book and follow these steps.

1. Play the project and notice that it remains in one key (the project key) for the entire project. Imagine this being a typical 3-minute long song. By the time you reach the end, you would definitely have heard enough!

2. To change the project key to D at bar 5, position the cursor at bar 5 and press the K key. Type **D** in the Key Change text box (or choose **D** from the Key Change drop-down list) and click OK.

3. Let's try an alternative method. Move the cursor to bar 9 and choose Insert, Tempo/Key Change. Change the key to E. Make sure that you deselect the Tempo Change (BPM) check box so that you don't inadvertently add a tempo change, too.

4. Change the key back to A at bar 13.

5. Play the project and notice the key changes you just added. Your song is already more interesting, isn't it?

6. Solo track 3, the Tenor Sax track (click the Solo button in the Track Header for track 3 to accomplish this goal). Play the file and notice that, when the key changes to D, ACID plays the D above the original A, but when it changes to the key of E, the track drops down an octave and plays the E below the A. Even though it doesn't sound bad, you might not want this drop in octave. Shift the pitch of the third event (which starts at bar 9 where the project changes to the key of E) up an octave to solve this problem. To raise the pitch of the event one octave, select the third event in track 3, hold the Ctrl key, and press the + key.

7. Un-solo track 3, play the project again, and notice that this time when the key changes to E, the sax changes key and stays in the same octave. Just as if our sax player had recorded it that way!

 The loops in the preceding project come from the *Essential Sounds I* loop collection, available from Sonic Foundry.

Adding Tempo Changes

You can also place tempo-change markers in your project to change the tempo in real time along the timeline. To add a tempo-change marker, place the cursor where you want the tempo change to occur and press T on your keyboard. In the Tempo/Key Change dialog box, the Tempo Change (BPM) check box is enabled and the field contains the current project tempo. Type a new tempo into the Tempo Change (BPM) field, or use the spin-control arrows to set a new tempo for this marker. When you're finished, click OK. A tempo marker appears in the Key and Tempo ruler, and a text box shows the current tempo.

Here's a neat way to create a convincing *ritard* or a natural-sounding *accelerando* in ACID Pro. Place tempo markers on every quarter note or eighth note of a phrase, and enter a progressively slower (or faster) tempo for each. This is a great way to add interesting tempo effects in your composition.

Ritard

A ritard, more formally known as ritardando, is a gradual diminishing of speed. If you place a tempo marker on every quarter note in a two-bar phrase and decrease the tempo each time by 5bpm, you've created a ritardando.

Accelerando

An accelerando is just the opposite of a ritard—it is a gradual increase in speed. To create this effect, add tempo markers that increase the bpm over time.

Task: Experiment with Tempo Changes

Work through this task to try your hand at creating tempo changes.

1. Open the `TempoChangeDemo.acd` project from the Hour 7 Samples folder on the CD-ROM that accompanies this book.

2. Play the project and notice that it stays in the same tempo and the same key throughout.

3. Place the cursor at the beginning of the project and press T on your keyboard to insert a tempo marker. Notice that the tempo is currently set at 88bpm. (You don't normally have to place a tempo marker at the beginning of a project. We do it here for illustration purposes.) Click OK without changing the tempo.

4. Move the cursor to bar 9, press T, and change the tempo to 110bpm.

5. Change the tempo at bar 10 to 120bpm, at bar 11 to 125bpm, and at bar 12 to 130bpm so that your project looks like the one in Figure 7.2. You've just created your first accelerando! Play the project to hear the changes you've made so far.

7

FIGURE 7.2

Change the tempo to create a convincing accelerando.

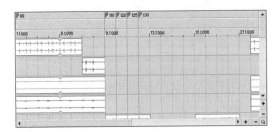

6. Now change both the tempo and the key with just one marker. Place the cursor at bar 21 and press Shift+T. This keyboard shortcut has the same affect as choosing Insert, Tempo/Key Change in that it opens the Tempo/Key Change dialog box with both the Key Change and the Tempo Change (BPM) check boxes enabled. Type G for the key, and 98.225 for the tempo. Click OK. (We admit that the .225 might be overkill here, but when we start working with video in Hour 10, you'll see how that level of precision is critical to doing the job right.)

7. Play the project and notice the big difference that adding tempo and key changes make in the overall production.

All the loops used in the preceding task are from the *Latin* loop collection, available from Sonic Foundry. This collection is a spicy mix of Latin rhythms and instruments put together by members of Carlos Santana's band.

Rearranging Events

As the composition begins to take shape, you'll find that you frequently need to move events that might not be in exactly the right spot. You might also find it desirable to repeat a single event or an entire section of the project. Sometimes these events and sections may be elaborate, and therefore time-consuming to re-create. Thankfully, ACID Pro allows you to freely move all events. You can also copy events and paste them back into your project at different points.

Moving Events Using the Mouse

You can only move an event to a new location on the track in which it currently resides. To do so, use the Draw tool to click and drag the event to its new location. The event might snap to grid marks and markers (depending on the snapping mode you are in); you can always hold down the Shift key to override the Snapping feature.

Need to make a quick copy of an event? Hold down the Ctrl key while you drag it. Just like that, you have a copy of the event at the new location.

Be very careful when using the quick-copy trick mentioned in the preceding tip. Here's what frequently happens: You have just finished editing an event, and it remains selected in the timeline. Now you see another event that you want a copy of, so you hold the Ctrl key, click, and drag the event.

What you expect to happen is that you make a copy of the event you clicked on. What really happens is that—because you first held the Ctrl key, and then clicked the new event—*the first event is still selected*. So you end up making copies of both the selected events.

The correct procedure is this: Click the new event to select it *and simultaneously deselect the first event*. Then hold down the Ctrl key and click and drag the desired event to make a new copy of only that event.

Using Cut, Copy, Paste, and Delete

You can also cut, copy, paste, and delete events; the process for doing so is the same as the one you use for words in a word processing document. Select an event and choose the appropriate command from the Edit menu. Or click the appropriate button in the toolbar. Or right-click the event and choose the desired operation from the shortcut menu. As a final option, use the standard keyboard shortcuts for cut (Ctrl+X), copy (Ctrl+C), paste (Ctrl+V), or delete (the Delete key).

Using the Paste Repeat Command

The Paste Repeat command allows you to paste multiple versions of the contents of your Windows Clipboard into your project with one command. For instance, draw a new event into a project. Now copy the event. Copying the event places it on the Windows Clipboard.

Place the cursor at a bar further into the project. The cursor defines the point at which the pasted event will appear. Choose Edit, Paste Repeat. In the Number of Times to Paste field in the Paste Repeat dialog box (shown in Figure 7.3), type a number representing the number of times you want to repeat the event. Choose the End to End radio button to paste the events one after another with no space in between. Alternatively, select the Even Spacing radio button to paste the events, separated by the time increments specified in the Space Every: fields.

7

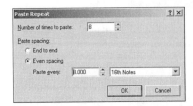

FIGURE 7.3

Paste an element multiple times in one operation.

You can use this technique on multiple events as well. Select each event you want to copy and paste and click the Copy button in the toolbar. Use the Paste Repeat dialog box to specify the number of times you want to paste the copied events.

When you copy multiple events onto the Windows Clipboard, you also copy their relationship to one another. When you paste them back into your project, the pasted events maintain that original relationship. For example, imagine that you copy two events from two separate tracks, the first event starting at bar 5 and the second starting at bar 7. Now you move the cursor to bar 10 and click the Paste button. The first event is pasted at bar 10 and the second at bar 12, thus maintaining the relationship between the copied events.

Using the Paste Insert Command

The normal Paste command pastes only the contents of the Windows Clipboard into your project at the cursor position. If you position your cursor within an existing event, ACID pastes the new event right over the existing event. The Paste Insert command also pastes the time occupied by the event into the project, and it does so across all tracks.

For example, if the event on the Clipboard lasts for 3 seconds, the Paste Insert command first inserts 3 seconds of time into the ACID timeline *on all tracks*. Figure 7.4 shows an example of a project after using the Paste Insert command. Everything that occurs later in the timeline is shifted to the right 3 seconds. The Paste Insert command then pastes the contents of the Clipboard into the selected track to fill the newly added time. If the cursor sits within an existing event when you choose this option, ACID splits the event at the cursor position. The portion of the event to the right of the cursor is shifted over to make room for the event being pasted.

Pasted event

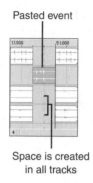

FIGURE 7.4

The Paste Insert command creates space in the project.

Space is created
in all tracks

Editing in Ripple Edit Mode

Another way to affect the time of your project is to use Ripple Edit mode when you cut, delete, and paste. When you perform the cut, delete, or paste operations in this mode, ACID moves existing events. In other words, your edits have a "ripple effect" on any existing events.

Let's talk about the cut and delete operations together, because the ripple effect works the same with both. If ripple edits are to work, you must define a time selection. You already know that when you make a time selection (with no events selected) and choose delete or cut, you remove every event that falls within the time selection. You are literally left with a big hole in your project because the delete operation affects only the events and not the time associated with them.

In Ripple Edit mode, ACID Pro removes not only the events, but also the time they occupy. All events that occur later in the timeline slide to the left to fill the space vacated by the removed events.

The key to successfully using Ripple Edit mode for cutting and deleting events is to first make a time selection. If you don't, the project will not ripple as expected. But there's another aspect to be mindful of. If you select an event, create a time selection encompassing that event, and then cut or delete in Ripple Edit mode, only the track containing the selected event ripples. If you make a time selection, but do not select individual events, all tracks ripple.

7

When pasting, you normally paste only the events on the Clipboard, but not the time associated with the events. In other words, if you paste the new event on top of an existing event, the new event literally replaces the old one.

In Ripple Edit mode, you paste the event as well as the time associated with the event. So if you paste over the top of an existing event, ACID Pro first splits the existing event, then moves the second half of that event (along with any other events that occur later) to the right. This shift makes room for the new event. ACID then drops the new event into the freshly created space.

> Pasting in Ripple Edit mode sounds just like using the Paste Insert command, but there is an important difference. The Paste Insert command creates space on *every track* in the project; pasting in Ripple Edit mode creates space only on the track or tracks into which you are pasting an event or events.

Locking Envelopes with Events

There are times when you have worked hard to create some effect on a particular event using the track envelopes in Hour 5, and then realize that the event should be moved earlier or later in time. Wouldn't it be a pain to have to recreate all those envelopes? You want to be able to move the event and have the track envelopes move with it.

Well, you can. If you add an envelope point within an event, ACID locks the envelope points to the event. This way, when you move an event, any envelope point that you placed within that event moves with the event. Envelope points that fall outside the event remain unaffected.

Of course, there are also times when you want to move events but leave the envelopes in place. Choose Options, Lock Envelopes to Events from the menu bar to turn this feature off. Choose the option again to turn the feature back on. (You can also use the Lock Envelopes to Events button—located just to the left of the Draw Tool button in the ACID toolbar—to toggle this feature off and on.) The following task shows another handy feature that this option enables.

Task: Copying and Pasting an Envelope with the Event

In this task, you'll create a pan envelope and copy and paste an event to see how the envelope's points are copied and pasted along with the event.

1. Start a new project and add 4 bars of `Krafty Loop 2-elec perc.wav`, located in the Hour 7 Samples folder on the CD-ROM that accompanies this book.

2. Add a pan envelope and place points at the beginning of every bar.

3. Pan the first point hard right, pan the next point hard left, and continue alternating like this for the rest of the points. The event should look like the one in Figure 7.5.

FIGURE 7.5

The pan envelope alternates between the left and right speakers.

4. Make sure that the Lock Envelopes To Events option is engaged in the Options menu. Now click the event to select it and then click the Copy button in the toolbar.

5. Position the cursor at the end of the event and choose Edit, Paste Repeat. In the Number of Times to Paste field, type **3** and enable the End to End radio button. Click OK. Notice that not only the event but also the points you added to the envelope are copied and pasted.

6. Click the Play From Start button and listen to the percussion move back and forth across the stereo field.

This method of creating a small event with an elaborate pan (or volume) envelope, and then copying and pasting it across the timeline keeps you from having to create numerous points on the envelope to get the same job done. If you decide that the multiple events created using this method are difficult to manage, you can join them into one event. To do so, select all the events you want to join (note that joining works only with events on the same track). Press J on your keyboard. ACID transforms the selected events into one event. This trick works great for events that contain the entire media file and that are butted up next to each other. Be careful when joining events you have edited (for example, events you've edge-trimmed) or events that have space between them. Essentially, joining two events has the same effect as deleting the second event and lengthening the first event so that it ends where the second event ended previously. This might not always be the result you want.

Using Region Markers

7

In Hour 6, "Shaping Your Project," you learned how to place markers in the Beat ruler. Now we'll take this one step further and create regions that we'll use to help construct our musical arrangement.

Creating Regions

To create a region, first make a time selection or set the loop region to span the area where you want to define the region. Press R on your keyboard to mark the range as a region. Two green markers appear in the Marker ruler to mark the beginning and end of the region.

Right-click the second of the two markers; a menu appears with commands that enable you to go to that marker, go to the start of the region, select the region, or delete the region. Right-click the first of the two markers; the menu commands enable you to go to that marker, go to the end of the region, select the region, rename it, or delete it. It's very useful to label your regions by using the Rename option, especially when you're working with a large project.

To adjust the length of a region, simply drag either marker. You can even overlap regions. For instance, you could drag the start region marker for region 3 in front of the end region marker for region 2. There are no rules as to how you section off your project. Think in terms of how these regions can help you organize and possibly reuse sections of your composition.

Task: Creating Regions

In this task, you'll define specific sections of your project. You'll then create regions to mark those sections so that you can find them quickly later.

1. Open the `RegionsDemo.acd` project from the Hour 7 Samples folder, located on the CD-ROM that accompanies this book.

2. Play the project and listen for how you might divide it into logical musical sections.

3. Using the Time Selection tool, make a time selection over the first two bars.

4. Press R on your keyboard to create a region. Right-click the first region marker and name the region `Intro`.

5. Repeat steps 3 and 4 to create the following regions:

   Bars 3 to 5: `Drum Fill`

   Bars 5 to 11: `Section A`

   Bars 11 to 17: `Section B`

   When you're done, your project should look like the one in Figure 7.6. Leave this project open; in the next task, you'll pick up where you left off.

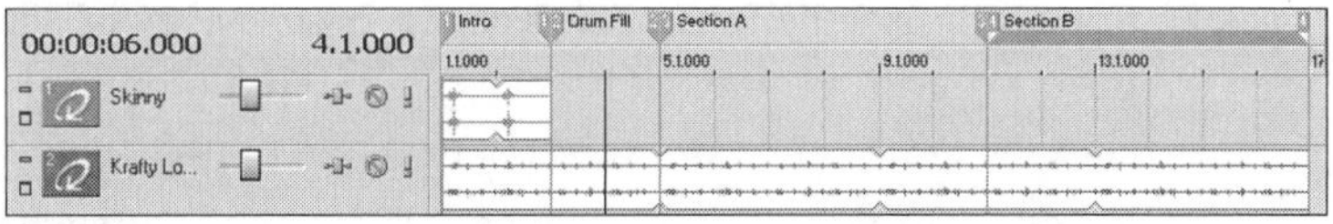

FIGURE 7.6

Turn time selections into descriptively labeled regions.

Copying and Pasting Project Regions

Marking an important section of your composition with a region (as you did in the previous task) enables you to quickly find it and copy and paste it to another point in the project. For example, you might have created a great chorus section that you want to repeat later. To do so, choose the Time Selection tool and double-click a region marker (or double-click between a pair of region markers). This action selects the time range defined by the region. Now copy and paste the selection to another spot in your project.

Using Regions to Construct an Arrangement

One method of composition widely used in ACID is to construct an arrangement using regions as the building blocks for the larger work. Many popular songs use a form such as this: Intro, Verse 1, Chorus, Verse 2, Chorus, Verse 3, Bridge, Chorus, Tag. Notice that the Chorus block is repeated several times (possibly with slight variations). In some songs, perhaps the Verse and the Bridge blocks repeat as well.

In classical music, you may have heard of the Rondo form, which has a recurring theme and takes a form similar to this: A B A C A D A. Notice that the piece keeps returning to the A section, which ties the piece together. Using ACID, there's no need to re-create all these sections independently. Simply create regions defining them, and then copy and paste as needed. You can then make adjustments to the newly pasted sections to add interest to the composition.

Task: Copying and Pasting Regions

Experiment with the concept of using regions to create an arrangement by working through this task.

1. Start with the project you began in the previous task.

2. Make sure that you don't have any events selected. Double-click with the Time Selection tool to select the events in the section of your project marked by Region 2, Drum Fill, and click the Copy button.

3. Place the cursor at bar 17 and click the Paste button. All the events that you copied in the previous step (the events that make up the drum fill) are pasted at bar 17.

4. Click in a blank area of the project to deselect all events. Then copy and paste Section A at bar 19.

7

5. Copy and paste the Drum Fill at bar 25, paste a copy of Section B at bar 27, and paste a copy of the Intro at bars 33 and 35. (Hint: for this last copy operation, just click the Paste button twice, or use the Paste Repeat command.)

6. Paste a copy of the Drum Fill at bars 35 and 37. You might say, "but we already pasted something at bar 35 in the previous step." Remember, you're using the regions merely as reminders that mark out important sections of your composition. You're not copying the regions, you're copying the events in your project that are marked by the region. Therefore, whatever you paste in your project follows the normal rules for cut, copy, and paste (discussed earlier in this hour) regardless of whether or not the events are identified by a region. So the Drum Fill has just been pasted into empty tracks at bar 35.

7. Copy the Intro, place the cursor at bar 25, and choose Edit, Paste Insert. This command pastes a copy of the Intro into bar 25 and moves the rest of the project later in time.

8. Choose Options, Ripple Edits to turn on the Ripple Edits feature. Click in the project to deselect any events. Use the Time Selection tool to select a range from bar 27 to 29 and press Delete. All the events in the time selection are deleted along with the time they occupy. All the events in the rest of the project move to the left, earlier in time, to fill the newly vacated space. Now you're really working with regions and sections!

9. Now for the spice. Change the key of the project to B at bar 19, to C# at bar 23, and back to A at bar 27. Your project should look like the one in Figure 7.7.

FIGURE 7.7

Use regions to help organize your project and construct arrange- ments quickly.

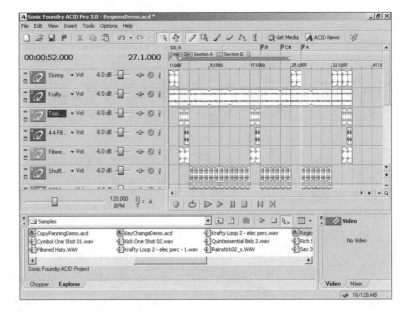

10. Play the project and notice how quickly we created an expanded project—with plenty of variation—using regions.

Summary

In this hour, you learned how to use markers to change tempo, change key, and create regions. You also learned some time-saving ways to use region markers to construct a musical arrangement. Use the questions and activities that follow to put this new knowledge to work.

Q&A

Q. What's the point of ripple editing and Paste Insert?

A. There are many reasons to use Ripple Edit mode and the Paste Insert command. Here are some simple examples. Imagine that you have a song in which two verses follow one another with no chorus in between. When you're all done, you decide that you'd really like a chorus between them after all. Without Paste Insert, you'd have a lot of work on your hands. But with Paste Insert, you can copy another chorus from the song, position the insertion point, and Paste Insert. You're done. The rest of the song "moves aside" to make room for the new chorus. Now imagine that you come back a couple days later and realize that you were right in the first place—you want to take the chorus back out. Simple. Make a time selection over it, engage Ripple Edit mode, and delete. Done.

Q. How many regions can I add to my project?

A. How many do you want? There is no limit to the number of regions ACID allows you to add to a project. However, too many regions could begin to cause more confusion than they're worth. You have to make a personal call on that.

Q. When simulating progressions using key-change markers, how do I know which key to change to next?

A. Many people have spent a lifetime researching the answer to that innocent-sounding little question! Although there are certainly rules and common musical structures that dictate what key you should go to from the key you're currently in, it is ultimately a matter of personal taste. If you think it sounds good, and you're happy with it, who's to say you're wrong?

7

Workshop

Here are a few questions to test your new knowledge, and an activity to sharpen your new skills.

Quiz

1. How do you specify the key of E flat in ACID Pro?

2. What's the easiest way to paste 25 copies of an event one after another in the timeline?

3. How can you make the points on a track envelope move with the event with which they're associated?

Quiz Answers

1. Because there is no symbol in ACID that you can type to indicate a flat key, you must use the corresponding sharp key. For instance, half way between D and E is E flat. But that key is also D sharp (#). If you want to change to the key of E flat, use its other name, D#.

2. Use the Paste Repeat command from the Edit menu to open the Paste repeat dialog box.

3. Click the Lock Envelopes To Events button in the ACID toolbar to put ACID into Lock Envelopes To Events mode. Click the button again to exit that mode.

Activities

You now know enough to construct a fairly complex ACID composition. Start a new project and use the techniques you've learned for adding tracks, editing events, and changing keys to construct an arrangement that you'll use as the verse to your song. Make sure that you create some sort of musical progression. Create a region over the verse to identify it as **Verse 1**. Next, construct a chorus, and create a region over it called **Chorus**.

Use the techniques for copying and pasting you learned about in this hour to copy the first region (Verse 1), paste it after the Chorus, and rename it Verse 2. Add another Chorus, and maybe some more verses. Experiment with the Ripple Edits feature and the Paste Insert command to add a chorus in the middle of the song or to remove one of the existing verses. Have fun...you're writing music now!

PART III

Adding Additional Track Types

Hour

HOUR 8

Working with MIDI Tracks

Using ACID 3.0, you can add MIDI tracks to your project. This is exciting news to MIDI enthusiasts. You can add an entire MIDI composition, or any portion of a composition, to your project and use it along with regular loop files to build your ACID music. All the editing techniques you use with your regular audio loops also work on MIDI tracks, making this a truly flexible and valuable feature. ACID MIDI tracks support `.mid`, `.smf`, and `.rmi` files.

In this hour, you will:

- Add a MIDI file to your project
- Become familiar with MIDI
- Use three different methods to play back MIDI files
- Filter MIDI information
- Record a MIDI track

Understanding MIDI

A little background on MIDI will be helpful to understanding what it is, and why it is important to ACID. As the use of synthesizers (synth for short) grew in the 60s and 70s, it became clear that there was a need to establish a standard for transmitting and receiving musical performance information between various models, brands, and types of electronic musical instruments. MIDI was born of this need.

MIDI is not sound. Rather, it is a recording of performance information. You can liken MIDI to an old player piano. These marvels of the late 1800s relied on "piano rolls," which were literally rolls of paper with holes punched in them. The holes were really playback instructions for the piano. A stream of air was directed at the piano role, and the air would pass through the holes. Each hole corresponded to a key on the piano, so that when the air passed through a particular hole, it triggered the corresponding key on the piano. Using these instructions, the piano would play "by itself."

That's basically how MIDI works, too. When you connect your *MIDI controller* to a MIDI recording device (usually a software program called a sequencer because it allows you to build a "sequence" of MIDI events) and begin to play, the recording device records what note you play, when you play it (note on) and when you stop playing it (note off), among other things (in short, all the information that makes up the MIDI sequence). By itself, the MIDI information is useless. Listening to MIDI information is about as exciting as listening to a piano roll. Neither the piano roll nor the MIDI information is any good unless you "feed" it to an instrument that can follow the instructions and thus make music.

New Term	**MIDI Controller**
	Most people think of a MIDI controller as keyboard, but it can also be a wind instrument or a guitar, to name a couple other choices. In fact, new ways to generate MIDI information are being invented all the time.
	These days, MIDI is being used to control more than just musical instruments. You'll find MIDI controlling theatrical lighting and recording consoles among other things. The devices that generate this information are also considered MIDI controllers.

You need to play the recorded MIDI information back into a synthesizer, which re-creates the performance and lets you hear it as if it were being played live—sort of the modern day version of the player piano. This information can then be stored for later retrieval in the form of a standard MIDI file.

How Many Instruments Can You Play?

One of the things that makes MIDI so useful is that you can record your MIDI information using a MIDI controller with which you are familiar (typically a keyboard). You can set your synthesizer up so that it follows the instructions while playing the sound of a different instrument (a French horn, for example). In this way, you can create entire arrangements of music including an amazing array of exotic instruments that you've never even touched before!

8

ACID acts as a MIDI recording device and arrangement tool, but does not take the place of a traditional MIDI sequencer. In other words, you can record a MIDI file directly into ACID by connecting your MIDI keyboard and playing live. Alternatively, you can build more complex MIDI files in your sequencer and bring them into ACID (using the ACID Explorer window) to incorporate them into an overall arrangement that includes not only the MIDI files, but also the other types of media files that we talk about throughout this book. The two most common types of standard MIDI files you can use in ACID are Type 0 and Type 1. Even though there is a technical difference between these two MIDI types (as you will learn in a moment), ACID treats both types exactly the same and creates one MIDI track for a MIDI file of either type.

If you're familiar with MIDI, the distinction between recording via MIDI into ACID and building a MIDI composition in your sequencer should be clear. Although ACID will record a MIDI track, ACID is not intended to take the place (or perform all the functions) of your MIDI sequencer.

If you're a newcomer to MIDI, this distinction might be confusing. There is not enough time in this hour for a detailed discussion of the difference between the MIDI capabilities in ACID and those of a sequencer. If you want to become more involved in creating MIDI compositions, you should research MIDI and sequencers. Still, we provide enough information here to allow even beginners to use MIDI files in their ACID projects.

Type 0 Files

The Type 0 MIDI format is intended for material that does not have to be edited. The Type 0 format stores the MIDI information as a single, multi-channel track. This is a perfect format for ACID, which you'll use to arrange and play back the sequence. Because MIDI can "broadcast" 16 different channels simultaneously, a single track of a Type 0 MIDI file is capable of controlling 16 different MIDI instruments at once.

Type 1 Files

Type 1 is a MIDI format used by sequencers, MIDI editors, and notation programs. It keeps all the original MIDI tracks separated, yet in one file. A typical Type 1 track might contain MIDI information for a bass sound, a horn sound, or any other sound your synthesizer can make. However, it can also contain multiple tracks/channels of information (just as a Type 0 MIDI file can).

Adding a MIDI file

You can open a standard MIDI file and arrange it in your ACID project in just the same way you open a .wav file and arrange it in your project. Select the file in the ACID Explorer window and drag it into the Track View. This action creates a new MIDI track. Use the Draw tool or the Paint tool to create MIDI events in the Track View timeline just as you would create any other audio events.

As you'll see later in this hour, you can also record your own MIDI files with ACID. If you have the appropriate MIDI hardware—a MIDI controller that sends MIDI information, and a MIDI interface card in your PC—you can use ACID to record a MIDI track.

It's easy to recognize a MIDI track in ACID by the icon in the Track Header. Figure 8.1 shows that the MIDI icon looks like the connector on the end of a MIDI cable. Special plugs called DIN plugs connect all MIDI devices. A DIN plug has five pins or five holes depending on whether the plug is on the cable (five pins) or on the MIDI device (five holes).

FIGURE 8.1

The icon representing a MIDI track looks like a MIDI connector.

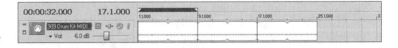

Considering Three Different MIDI Scenarios

ACID makes use of the MIDI information in one of three ways. ACID does one of the following:

- Routes the MIDI information out a MIDI port to an external synthesizer
- Routes the MIDI information to the synthesizer built into the computer sound card
- Routes the MIDI information to a .dls file (Soft Synth)

The following sections help clarify the advantages and disadvantages of each of these options.

Using External MIDI Hardware

To send MIDI track information from ACID to an external MIDI instrument, you have to install a MIDI interface into your PC. Some sound cards have MIDI capabilities while others do not. Consult the documentation for your sound card if you are unsure.

Use a cable, called (of all things) a MIDI cable, to connect a MIDI device to the PC. To route MIDI information from ACID to that device, add a MIDI file to a new ACID project. Click the Device Selection button in the Track Header. All available MIDI devices are displayed, as shown in Figure 8.2. From the drop-down list, choose the MIDI port that is connected to the external MIDI device you want to use.

FIGURE 8.2

Click the Device Selection button to choose a playback device for your MIDI file.

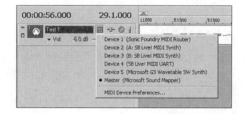

If you do not see the device you want to use, choose MIDI Device Preferences from the drop-down list. This option opens the MIDI tab in the Preferences dialog box. Enable the check box associated with the device you want to use.

The Preferences dialog box also enables you to select a *MIDI Thru device*. This option is handy if you are using a MIDI controller that does not produce sound and you want to pass the MIDI information on to a synth so that you can hear what you are playing. Use the MIDI Thru device for recording: From the drop-down list, choose the device connected to the synth. Click OK when you're done making choices.

MIDI Thru Device

Most MIDI devices have three MIDI ports: In, Out, and Thru. Often, several devices are "daisy-chained" together. For example, the MIDI signal runs from the MIDI Out of the first device to the MIDI In of the second device. Then it runs from the MIDI Thru of the second device to the MIDI In of the third device. So, you might ask, why not connect them using the MIDI Out of the second device? The MIDI Out port sends MIDI information *generated by that device*. The MIDI Thru port simply forwards the MIDI signal coming into the device from its MIDI In port. The MIDI Thru signal is not processed, it's simply passed through, which cuts down on latency.

Make sure that the MIDI instrument is set to receive MIDI information and that you have selected the sounds you want to use. Click the Play button, and ACID "plays" the instrument—with the aid of the MIDI information, of course!

Using a Sound Card Synthesizer

If the sound card on your PC has a built-in MIDI synthesizer, you can route MIDI tracks to it. Click the Device Selection button in the MIDI Track Header and pick the sound card synthesizer from the drop-down list. No special cables are needed because the MIDI information is routed internally, and the audio is heard through the speakers connected to the sound card. Check the documentation that comes with your sound card for information on setting the MIDI channel and assigning instruments.

The Good News and the Bad News

The good news is that the two options explored in the preceding sections give you a lot of flexibility in how you use MIDI information. There are hundreds of MIDI instruments from which to choose, and the number of sounds that can be produced is limitless.

The bad news (and it's not really all that bad) is that when you're done with your project, you can't just save your project to a mixed file format and instantly hear the finished mixed composition. Any MIDI file being played by an external MIDI instrument (and here we include the synthesizer that is on the sound card) will not be part of the mix. Why? Because another computer (the one inside the MIDI instrument) is generating that audio, not your PC. Only the audio that is being generated/rendered by your PC will be included in the mixed file.

So what do you do? Simply mix the audio coming from the PC with the audio coming from your synthesizers. You'll need an outboard mixer to accomplish this goal. Send the audio outputs of your PC sound card and the audio outputs of your synthesizers to a mixer, and mix them to a tape or back into your PC by recording the signal to a new track in ACID. See Hour 15, "Recording and Creating Your Own Loops," to learn how to set ACID and your computer up for recording.

DLS to the Rescue

The third way ACID can use MIDI information solves the problem just described and looks into the future of making music with a PC. This method makes use of a relatively new file type called *DLS* Level 2. Instead of routing the MIDI information to a piece of hardware (such as a synthesizer on a sound card or an external synthesizer), you route the information to a .dls file. This process turns ACID into a *Soft Synth*. In other words, ACID uses the computer's processing power and software to do the job that is normally done by a dedicated hardware device—a synthesizer. The audio generated by a MIDI file (via DLS) can be combined with the other audio in your ACID projects all within your

8

PC. When you use DLS, you can mix a MIDI file into your project in exactly the same way as you mix regular audio files. We'll give you a brief explanation of what DLS is and how to use it in the next few minutes. See the resources listed in the activity at the end of this hour to find out more about DLS.

NEW TERM

DLS

DLS stands for **D**own**L**oadable **S**ound file format. This standard was developed with the input from several organizations and companies including the Motion Pictures Expert Group (MPEG), MIDI Manufactures Association, Creative Technology Ltd, Microsoft, and the MIT Media Laboratory. This standardized file format, along with Microsoft's DX8 (which contains the DirectMusic Synthesizer), turns ACID into a Soft Synth.

NEW TERM

Soft Synth

A Soft Synth is a computer program that emulates all the functions commonly found in a hardware synthesizer. Basically, the Soft Synth program turns your computer into a synthesizer. You can control it by sending MIDI information to it from a MIDI controller (such as a MIDI keyboard), a sequencer, or a MIDI playback program such as ACID.

The Windows operating system comes with a DLS file (or *sound set*) called GS Sound Set (16-Bit). By default, ACID uses this sound set to play back your MIDI files. You can reroute your MIDI to other playback devices as just described, or you can choose to use a different DLS sound set. One place you can find DLS files is at http://www.sonicimplants.com. You might also want to visit http://www.fmjsoft.com/ for information about a program called Awave that allows you to create your own DLS files.

DLS evolved because General MIDI (GM)—although a step in the right direction—still does not provide the consistency needed by electronic music composers.

Because different synthesizers have unique sounds, the same MIDI file may sound different on two different synths. In fact, what plays as a piano on one synth might sound like a harpsichord (or any other instrument) on another synth. This is one of the main reasons that MIDI has gotten such a bad rap from people who don't understand how it works and have heard MIDI files that "sound stupid." DLS solves this problem.

DLS files enable composers to combine a recorded waveform (small .wav files) with information about how the .wav file should be played back (articulation information). In this way, the composer can completely define the sound of an instrument.

The DLS file can be sent along with the MIDI file, downloaded onto any device that supports the DLS standard, and used in place of a standard MIDI synthesizer to provide the "voice" of the MIDI file. In this way, the listener hears exactly what the composer created.

Assigning a Track to the Desired DLS

Using DLS files with a MIDI track is a two-step process. First, you select the MIDI track you want to use with a DLS file. Click the Device Selection button in the Track Header and choose Master from the drop-down list.

Next, right-click the track icon, choose Properties from the shortcut menu, and click the Voices tab in the track Properties dialog box. From this dialog box, you can load and apply a new DLS file for use with the sequence.

Click the Load button to open the Synth Configuration dialog box. From here, you can navigate to the folder on your system that contains the DLS file you want to use. After you have loaded the DLS file, click the channel drop-down list and browse to a bank and program. Any selected DLS voice set is merged into the GS Sound Set (16-Bit); it does not replace it. Typically, the sounds that were just loaded are found under Bank 0.

Using the MIDI Filter

A single MIDI track in ACID can contain up to 16 channels of MIDI data. If you don't want or need all this information, you can filter some of it out. Right-click the Track Header and choose Properties from the shortcut menu. Click the Voices tab in the Track Properties dialog box. As shown in Figure 8.3, the Voices tab contains controls and information for the MIDI channel: Program, Mute, Solo, Volume, and Pan for each of the 16 possible MIDI channels. Check the information on the Voices tab of the Properties dialog box to see which instrument is associated with a particular channel. Mute any of the MIDI channels you want to remove.

The Volume and Pan controls found in the Voices tab enable you to build a mix of the various MIDI voices in the selected track.

FIGURE 8.3

The Voices tab of the Track Properties dialog box enables you to control each of the 16 MIDI channels.

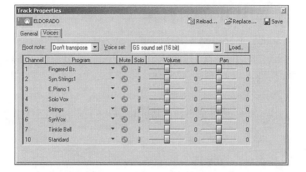

Task: Adding a MIDI Track

In this task, you'll add a couple of MIDI tracks to an ACID project, and then assign the appropriate DLS files to the tracks.

1. Open a new ACID project and add eight bars of 909 Drum Kit MIDI 01 and eight bars of Synth Bass 08 MIDI 01.mid (located in the Hour 8 Samples folder on the CD-ROM that accompanies this book).

2. Click the Device Selection button and select Master for both tracks. Click the Play From Start button. These MIDI files might not sound right at this point (they might not even sound like drums and bass!) because they have to be played with specific DLS files which you have not yet assigned to them.

3. Right-click the Track Header icon for track 1 and choose Properties; click the Voices tab in the Track Properties dialog box.

4. Click the Load button and navigate to the Hour 8 Samples folder on the CD-ROM.

5. Select 909 Drum Kit.dls and click Open. Leave the Track Properties dialog box open.

6. Double-click the Track Header icon for track 2. Notice that the Track Properties dialog box changes to show the properties for track 2. Repeat Steps 4 and 5 to load the Synth Bass 01.dls file for track 2. Click the Close button in the Track Properties dialog box to close it.

7. Click the Play From Start button and listen to the MIDI tracks associated with the DLS files.

These MIDI and DLS files were created by loop developer Leo Cavallo and can be found at www.sonicfoundry.com.

Recording MIDI Tracks

You can also record your own MIDI tracks into ACID. Make sure that your MIDI controller is connected to the MIDI In of your sound card. Click the Record button in the ACID Transport toolbar to open the Record dialog box shown in Figure 8.4.

FIGURE 8.4

The ACID Record dialog box.

The ACID Record dialog box offers the choice to record audio or MIDI. Click the MIDI radio button, name the file, and choose a folder into which to store the recorded MIDI file. Enable the Start of Project radio button to start recording from the first measure; alternatively, enable the Position radio button and then type a specific measure location to start elsewhere in the project. From the Record Device drop-down list, select the appropriate MIDI port. You'll know you're properly connected when you play your MIDI instrument and the ACID record meters react to the signal.

When you're ready to play, click Start. The Start button changes to the Stop button. Play your keyboard (or other MIDI controller). ACID records your performance information as MIDI. Click Stop to end the recording. A new MIDI track is automatically added to the current project. The new track can now be edited using the same tools and techniques you use to edit audio tracks.

> Hour 15, "Recording and Creating Your Own Loops," offers a more detailed discussion of the ACID Record dialog box.

Summary

In this hour, you learned that adding MIDI loops to your ACID project is as easy as adding audio loops. You also learned how to customize the MIDI loops by muting MIDI instruments/channels you don't need. You learned three different ways to play back the

8

MIDI files, and learned about a new file type called DLS. Finally, you learned how to record your own MIDI files.

Take a few minutes to review this information by working through the questions and answers and activities that follow.

Q&A

Q. Why do you make the distinction between "audio" and MIDI? When I play the MIDI file on my computer, I hear it on my speakers. Therefore, it must be audio.

A. When you play a MIDI file on your computer, you are not hearing MIDI. What you are hearing is audio that is created by a synthesizer that is receiving instructions on what to play. Those instructions are communicated to the synth by the MIDI file. It's much like hearing a concert pianist: When she plays, you don't hear the score she's reading, you hear the music that is created when she translates the instructions that the score provides into finger movements on the keyboard.

Q. How can I use just a portion of my MIDI file in my ACID project?

A. The best way to isolate portions of your MIDI files is to open them in the Chopper. There you can work with the MIDI file in exactly the same manner as you work with your audio files. Hour 11, "Editing with the Chopper," contains more information about this useful tool.

Workshop

Take the following quiz to review the material presented in this hour. Then spend some time with the suggested activities to learn more about DLS and to gain hands-on experience with MIDI recording.

Quiz

1. List three ways you can play a MIDI file in ACID.

2. What does DLS stand for?

3. How do you filter out MIDI channels you don't want to play?

Quiz Answers

1. You can send the data from a MIDI track to an external synthesizer, to the synthesizer on the PC sound card, or to a DLS file. To make your choice, click the Device Selection button in the Track Header and make your choice from the list.

2. DLS stands for DownLoadable Sound file format.

3. Open the Track Properties dialog box and click the Voices tab. Click the Mute button for any track you want to remove from the mix.

Activities

1. Spend some time on the following Web pages to learn more about DLS files:

    - `http://www.midi.org/about-midi/dls/dls2spec.htm`   This pages details the DLS specifications.

    - `http://www.midi.org/newsviews/sasbf.htm`   This page contains an article about who is involved in the DLS movement.

    - `http://www.midi.org/newsviews/sasbf.htm`   This page contains links to information about DLS.

2. Connect your MIDI controller to your sound card and record a MIDI track.

HOUR 9

Incorporating One-Shot and Beatmapper Tracks

So far, we've spent a lot of time talking about adding loops to your ACID projects. But there are other ways to treat the audio files you add. One of these approaches is to treat the file as a one-shot. This track type was briefly introduced back in Hour 5, "Additional Editing Techniques." Another option is to use the file to create a Beatmapper track.

As you make your way through this hour, you will:

- Learn the difference between a one-shot and a file containing Beatmapper information
- Add audio from a CD into your ACID project
- Use the Beatmapper Wizard
- Explore ideas for using Beatmapper files

Adding Longer Files to Your Project

When you add a file to your project, ACID calculates its duration. Up to now, the files you've added to the sample projects have been less than 10 seconds long. Let's talk about what happens when you add longer files to ACID Pro.

Files that last for less than 30 seconds automatically create loop tracks when you add them to your project. This is what you've seen in most of the examples so far in this book. The main exception is one-shot files. One-shot files create one-shot tracks.

You can decide for yourself what type of track should be created to hold the files you add to your project. Using the right mouse button, click and drag the file from the Explorer window into the Track View area. When you release the mouse button, a short-cut menu offers the following four choices:

- Add as Autodetected Type—ACID chooses a track type for the file based on a number of factors including the file's length.
- Add as Loop Track—ACID adds the file as a loop so that it repeats as many times as necessary to fill an event drawn into the track.
- Add as One-Shot Track—ACID adds the file as a one-shot that occurs only once in each event drawn into the track.
- Add as Beatmapped Track—ACID adds the file as a Beatmapper file which is typically used for long files, and allows you to detect the beats so that the file can react to tempo changes.

When you add a file that is over 30 seconds long, ACID launches the Beatmapper Wizard. On the first wizard screen, shown in Figure 9.1, you have two choices: You can treat the file as a Beatmapper file or as a regular (non-Beatmapper) one-shot file. We'll explain what a Beatmapper file is in a few minutes.

FIGURE 9.1

The first screen of the Beatmapper Wizard lets you choose whether to create a one-shot or a Beatmapper file.

You can increase or decrease the 30-second threshold that determines whether or not the Beatmapper Wizard will run automatically when you add a file to your project. Choose Options, Preferences, and click the Audio tab of the dialog box. In the Open Files as Loops if Between (Seconds) fields, change the lower and upper limits to the desired values.

Extracting Audio from a CD

ACID 3.0 enables you to extract audio directly from an audio CD. Because most of the tracks you extract from audio CDs will likely be over 30 seconds long (and will thus launch the Beatmapper Wizard when you add them to your projects), it makes sense to talk about the process of extracting songs from an audio CD here.

Insert an audio CD into your computer's CD-ROM drive and browse to the CD using the ACID Explorer window. Select the track you want to use in your ACID project and drag it onto the Track View. The Save As dialog box opens. Specify the location to which you want to save the file you are extracting and give the file a name. Click Save to continue. A progress bar appears, showing that ACID is extracting the track from the audio CD to a .wav file (see Figure 9.2).

Progress bar

FIGURE 9.2

Use the ACID Save As dialog box to extract audio from a CD.

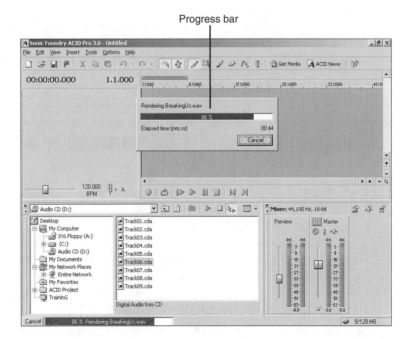

An alternative method to the drag-and-drop approach to ripping tracks from audio CDs is to choose the Tools, Extract Audio from CD command. The Extract Audio from CD dialog box opens, as shown in Figure 9.3. Click a track to select it and then click OK to begin extracting the selected track from the audio CD.

FIGURE 9.3

Use the Extract Audio from CD dialog box to extract audio from an audio CD.

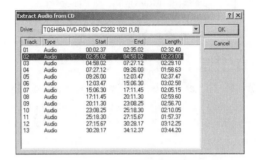

When the extraction process is complete, the Beatmapper Wizard automatically opens. Follow the steps of the wizard (as explained in the following section). When you finish, a new Beatmapper track appears in your project.

Use either of these methods to extract multiple tracks from the same audio CD in one operation. With the first method, select multiple tracks and drag them all to the timeline at once. In the second method, select multiple tracks and click OK. ACID extracts the first track and runs the Beatmapper Wizard for that track. When you're done with the wizard for the first track, ACID extracts the next track and runs the Beatmapper Wizard again for that track, and so on.

Choosing Between Beatmapper and One-Shot Tracks

As mentioned earlier, the first screen of the Beatmapper Wizard gives you the choice of treating the file as a one-shot or as a Beatmapper file. In most cases, you'll probably want to treat your long files as Beatmapper files so that you can tempo match them to the rest of your project without affecting the pitch of the files. Still, there might be times when you want to add a long file as a one-shot. The following sections explore these two options, starting with the easier case—one-shots.

Choosing the One-Shot Option

To a new ACID project, add the oneShot.pca file, which is located in the Hour 9 Samples folder on the CD-ROM that accompanies this book. This song is over 30 seconds long, so the Beatmapper Wizard launches automatically. If you know that you want to preserve the original tempo of this song, you should add it to your project as a one-shot.

To define the file as a one-shot, choose No in response to the question, "Would you like to use the Beatmapper Wizard on this file?" As soon as you do so, the Next button changes to a Finish button—you have no more choices to make. Click Finish. As usual, ACID Pro creates a new track. But instead of the normal loop track icon, this new track is marked with the one-shot track icon, as shown in Figure 9.4.

FIGURE 9.4

A one-shot file has a different track icon than the usual loop track icon.

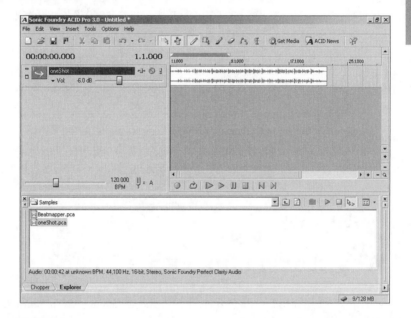

With the Draw tool, draw an event into the new track. As you draw, notice that you don't see the familiar indentations at the top and bottom of the event. That's because one-shots do not loop continually. In fact, if you keep drawing until you reach the end of the file, the waveform simply stops when there is no more audio signal present. This is what distinguishes a one-shot from a loop. As its name implies, a one-shot is a one-time phenomenon. If you want to repeat the audio information contained in the one-shot, you must draw a new event in the one-shot track.

Other than that, one-shot events behave very much like loop events. You can edge-edit them, split them, move them, copy them, change their start offsets, adjust their pitch, and so on.

One big difference between one-shots and regular loop files is that one-shots ignore the project key and tempo settings. This makes sense in most cases, because one-shots are typically used for percussive impact, such as cymbals, drum hits, and other non-pitched sounds. The key and tempo of a single hit won't matter, and you don't normally want them to follow the project settings.

But some one-shots (for example, the track created in the discussion here) may actually be pitched instruments or full arrangements. In these cases, you'll have to set the tempo and key of your project to match the one-shot so that any pitched instrument you add to the project is in the same key as the one-shot. If you want to combine two or more long files in the same project and ensure that their tempos match, you'll want to run the Beatmapper Wizard on each of the files as discussed in the following section.

When you change the pitch of a one-shot event or track, you simultaneously affect the speed with which the audio within the event plays. Try it for yourself. Use the + and – keys on your number pad to raise and lower the pitch of the one-shot in track 1. As you raise the pitch, notice that the waveform shortens, indicating that the file plays faster. As you lower the pitch, watch the waveform lengthen, showing that the file plays slower. Listen to the results to hear how changing the pitch also affects the speed at which the file plays back.

Why Would I Do Such a Thing?

Why would you want to add a file to an ACID project as a one-shot, knowing full well that it won't follow the project tempo and key changes? There might be a number of reasons to do this. Here are a couple.

Perhaps you have a live recording of your band, and now you want to add some great drum loops, handclaps, or other percussion to the mix. You'll most likely need ACID to adjust the tempo of the various loops you add to match the tempo and key of the live recording. Bring the live recording into ACID as a one-shot, set the project tempo and key to the tempo and key of the live recording, and add the additional parts.

Or perhaps the file is a recording of a dialog for which you are writing background music. You need to be able to change the pitch and tempo of the music without affecting the recorded speech. Adding the dialog as a one-shot enables you to do this easily.

Choosing the Beatmapper Option

ACID Pro 3.0 introduces a new type of track called a Beatmapper track. These tracks are files that contain Beatmapper information—that is, information about the tempo and beat locations of the music. Unlike one-shot files, Beatmapper files react to tempo changes you build into your project, making it possible for ACID to synchronize the Beatmapped song with files on other tracks. You can dictate whether or not the pitch of a Beatmapper file is affected when the project changes tempo. The Beatmapper is going to be a valuable tool for all of you who are into making remixes of your songs!

In the next section, we'll explore what happens when you choose "Yes" in response to the Beatmapper Wizard's first question, "Would you like to use the Beatmapper Wizard on this file?"

Creating a Beatmapper Track

The Beatmapper Wizard does most of the work of creating a Beatmapper track for you. After you choose the Yes option on the first wizard screen and click Next, the wizard estimates and marks the first *downbeat* in the file. It makes this guess based on the first *transient* it finds in the waveform. Many times, the wizard is right on the money. Other times, you'll have to lend a hand. Click the Play button (located just below the waveform display) to listen to the file. Determine whether the downbeat marker is in the correct place. If it is, click the Next button. If it's not, click the waveform display at the downbeat of one of the first few measures to reposition the marker to the proper location.

NEW TERM

Downbeat

The downbeat is simply the first beat of a measure. It's probably called this because when conductors lead a band or orchestra, they always wave the baton down to signify the first beat of the measure.

Transient

A transient is a point in the waveform that jumps very suddenly from a quiet (or no) signal to a loud signal. For instance, if there is total silence, and someone hits a snare drum, there is an extremely strong transient in the waveform.

After you properly identify a downbeat, click the Next button. ACID begins to beatmap (that is, to map out the other downbeats and measures) the rest of the file. It then estimates a typical measure as shown in Figure 9.5. Click the Play button; the measure begins to loop continually. Listen to the measure and count along with the beat so that you can hear whether or not it is a solid measure.

You can zoom in and out of the waveform display using the same tools and keyboard shortcuts you learned about in Hour 6, "Shaping Your Project." These tools help you to locate the exact beginning of a downbeat. Sometimes it helps to start playback and then press the Enter key on the downbeat. This action stops playback and places the downbeat marker at the current playback cursor position. Then you can zoom in to place the marker more exactly if necessary.

Sometimes it is easier to locate one of the downbeats further into the song. You don't have to locate the very first one. Any of the downbeats in the first few measures give ACID the information it needs to find the beat of the music in the file.

If ACID got it right, click the Next button. If ACID needs some help, click and drag either end of the selection to trim the selection to the proper length. Use the Metronome check box to turn a metronome on and off. The metronome can help you find a measure accurately. Click the Half Loop Region button to cut the size of the selection in half; click the Double Loop Region button to double the size of the selected region.

FIGURE 9.5

In the Beatmapper Wizard, the selected area represents one measure.

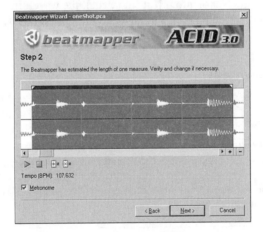

Here are a few keyboard shortcuts that will come in handy as you use the Beatmapper Wizard. While you are listening to the measure in the Beatmapper, look at the edges of the selection area. Notice that one of the edges has a thin flashing line. This line indicates that this edge of the selection currently has focus. Hold down the Shift key and press the right and left arrow keys several times to adjust the focused edge of selection. This shortcut allows you to make very quick adjustments to the selection so that you can get it exact. Press the 5 key on your numeric keypad to shift the focus from one edge of the selection to the other and back.

After you've defined a solid measure, click the Next button. The next screen of the wizard enables you to audition other measures throughout the file to see whether they are also accurately defined. Use the slider to move to other measures and click the Play button to audition those measures. If you hear problems, click and drag the selection in the waveform to reposition it, or click the Back button and return to the previous screen to readjust the measure. When you're satisfied that all measures work properly, click the Next button.

> It can be difficult—if not impossible—to accurately add Beatmapper information to an entire file if the music in that file does not keep time perfectly. In these cases, you might have to run the Beatmapper several times on various portions of the file.

The last step in the wizard enables you to make three important decisions:

- Whether or not to change the ACID project tempo to match the tempo of the file to which you are adding Beatmapper information. If you're working on a project in which you're creating a remix out of more than one song, you'd likely choose this option when running the Beatmapper on the song that will act as the main beat of your remix.

- Whether or not you want the pitch of the Beatmapper track to change when you change the project tempo. You might want the pitch to change when you change the tempo if you want to emulate the "club remix experience." In other words, in a live remix, the DJ spins a record faster or slower to make its beat match the beat of another record. When the record spins faster or slower than normal, the pitch of the music is affected. Choose this option to achieve the same effect in your ACID remix.

- Whether or not to save the Beatmapper information with the file so that you won't have to rerun the Beatmapper wizard on the same file when you use it in another ACID project. There might be times when you want to use the file as a one-shot in another project (for the reasons we discussed in an earlier section) even though you are using it in the current project as a Beatmapper track.

Make your choices and click Finish to close the wizard screens.

ACID creates a new Beatmapper track based on the options you selected in the wizard. You can draw in as many measures of the file as you want to use.

> **No, Not Some Obscure ACID Cult Symbol**
>
> You might recognize the track icon that identifies a Beatmapper track if you've ever played a 45rpm record on a newer turntable that only has a spindle for 33 1/3rpm records. This icon resembles the shape of the plastic insert used to convert the hole in a 45 to something more suitable for the smaller spindle used for 33 1/3rpm records. If you're too young to know what a 45 is, never mind...it's not really important.

Because the Beatmapper track now reacts to changes in the project tempo, you can meld it with other types of tracks in your project. This flexibility makes it possible to create mixes of various songs while maintaining a steady beat. Keep in mind that when you change the tempo of the project, the pitch of the Beatmapper track may change, depending on the behavior you specified in the last step of the Beatmapper Wizard.

Task: Using the Beatmapper Wizard

The following task gives you a bit of hands-on experience at creating your first Beatmapper track.

1. Start a new ACID project. To the timeline, add the file Beatmapper.pca, located in the Hour 9 Samples folder on the CD-ROM that accompanies this book. The Beatmapper Wizard launches.

2. Answer Yes in response to the question, "Would you like to use the Beatmapper Wizard on this file?" and click the Next button.

3. Notice that ACID has estimated the location of the first downbeat. Click the Play button to listen and judge whether or not the estimate is correct. Because it's not, click the Stop button. Click the Play button again, and when you find the down beat of one of the first measures after the introductory "scratch," press Enter on your keyboard to place the downbeat marker there. Click the Play button again. If the first thing you hear is a kick drum, you've got the right transient. You may have to zoom in to get the placement exact, as shown in Figure 9.6. When you're happy with the placement, click the Next button.

4. On the following wizard screen, click the Play button to hear whether or not ACID has defined a nice tight loop. Count along with the beat to verify that the loop is solid. Use the metronome if it helps. It should be extremely close, but if you think that it's not quite there, adjust the time selection until you're happy with the loop. Click the Next button to continue.

FIGURE 9.6

Place the downbeat marker on the first downbeat of the file.

5. On the next screen, Click the Play button and inspect several random measures throughout the piece to verify that they also work as tight loops. Use the slider, or enter a measure number directly into the number field, to inspect a specific measure. When you're happy that the measures are accurately defined throughout the file, click the Next button.

6. Enable all three check boxes on the final screen and click the Finish button. The new Beatmapper track is now in your project.

7. With the Paint tool selected, hold down the Ctrl key and click anywhere in the timeline of the Beatmapper track. This action adds the entire file into the track. Alternatively, use the Draw tool to draw in just a portion of the file. Play the project and adjust the tempo. Notice that the Beatmapper track reacts to your tempo changes. You can now edit the Beatmapper event however you want.

> When you draw an event on the Beatmapper track, the waveform begins to draw at the point in the file at which you identified the downbeat while running the Beatmapper Wizard. Often (as in our example here), this is not the very beginning of the file. Edge-edit the left edge of the event to reveal the hidden information that occurs before the identified downbeat.

Summary

The Beatmapper brings the advantages of tempo matching to long files. In this hour, you learned the differences between a Beatmapped file and a one-shot. You also learned how to extract a track from an audio CD and add it to your ACID project. You then learned how use the Beatmapper Wizard. Now work through the questions and activities to test your new knowledge.

Q&A

Q. If I save a file as a Beatmapped file, will I only be able to use it in ACID?

A. Only ACID recognizes the Beatmapper information, but the file will play normally in other applications.

Q. Can I extract audio from any audio CD that I want?

A. The technology is there to do so, but you are entering that shadowy area of copyright infringement if you don't own the copyrights to the music you extract and use. Be careful.

Q. What if I wish I hadn't made the file a Beatmapper file?

A. Right-click the track icon for the Beatmapper track and choose Properties from the shortcut menu. From the General tab in the Track Properties dialog box, choose One-Shot from the Track Type drop-down list. If you want the file to act as a one-shot in other projects, click the Save button in the upper-right corner of the Properties dialog box. If you don't click the Save button, the file will only ignore the Beatmapper information when the file is used in the current ACID project. Close the Track Properties dialog box. To run the Beatmapper Wizard on the file again, choose Beatmapped from the Track Type drop-down list in the Track Properties dialog box. Click the Stretch tab and then click the Beatmapper Wizard button.

Workshop

See how well you learned the material in this hour. Answer the quiz questions and then tackle the Activities section to exercise your new knowledge.

Quiz

1. What is a downbeat?

2. What is the main difference between a one-shot file and a Beatmapper file?

3. Besides the change in speed that occurs, what noticeable effect does changing the project tempo have on a Beatmapper file?

Quiz Answers

1. The first beat of any measure is referred to as the downbeat of the measure.

2. While neither a one-shot file or a Beatmapper file reacts to a pitch change in your ACID project, a one-shot also does not react to tempo changes, but a Beatmapper file does.

3. Changing the project tempo not only makes a Beatmapper file play faster (or slower), it can also raise (or lower) the pitch of the file depending on the choices you made while running the wizard.

Activities

Find an audio CD that has a song you would like to remix. Insert the disc into your CD-ROM drive and use one of the methods you learned in this hour to extract the song from the CD into ACID. Beatmap the song and then have at it! Remix to your heart's content.

9

Hour 10

Scoring to a Video

Since the day ACID 1.0 was released a couple years back, people said, "It would be great if I could watch a video while scoring custom music to it using ACID!" Now you can. With ACID Pro 3.0, you can watch the video as you write the music, place the sound effects, sync the dialog, and take care of all the other audio-sweetening tasks.

In this hour, we'll explore a number of features that make this process easy and fun. You will:

- Add a video track to your ACID project
- Trim and adjust the video
- Navigate through the video
- Use the Video Preview window
- View the video on an external monitor
- Set and use the Time ruler and time markers
- Render the video to create the final product

Adding Video to the Timeline

Just as you do when adding audio and MIDI files to a project, you drag a video file from the ACID Explorer window to the Track View to add it to your project. ACID accepts either QuickTime or AVI video file formats. Adding a video track automatically also adds a one-shot audio track to hold the audio associated with the video. If the video does not contain any audio, the associated audio track in ACID is silent. You should delete it so that it doesn't take up space in your project.

ACID supports only one video track per project, and that track always appears at the very top of the ACID Track List. If you add another video file, a dialog box asks whether you want to replace the existing video track. Choose Yes or No.

Even though your project supports only one video track, you can still add the audio portions of multiple videos. When you drag a second video into the timeline, the audio portion of the second video is added to the project whether you replace the original video or not.

Adding the audio from more than one video to your project without adding the video itself could come in handy for a lot of reasons. For instance, imagine that you had two cameras shoot an event. The first camera has the better video quality, so you want to use its video while working on audio-sweetening and sound effects. But because of their different placement at the event, both cameras picked up different pieces of valuable audio. It might be very helpful to have both audio tracks to work with in the final mix.

The video track supports either a video or a still image. ACID supports the following video and still image file formats:

- Joint Pictures Expert Group (*.jpg, *.jpeg)
- MPEG 1 (*.mp2)
- Photoshop (*.psd)
- Portable Network Graphic (*.png)
- QuickTime (*.mov, *.qt, *.dv, *.gif)
- TARGA (*.tag, *.targa)
- Video for Windows (*.avi)
- Windows Bitmap (*.bmp, *.dib)

Notice the differences between the Track Header for the video track and the Track Header for the audio track shown in Figure 10.1. For one thing, you can't select the video track, and because it has no controls, you can't make any adjustments to it beyond maximizing and minimizing it. However, you can remove it. To do so, right-click the video event or the Track Header and choose Remove Video from the shortcut menu.

FIGURE 10.1

The ACID video track allows you to preview the video as you compose original audio.

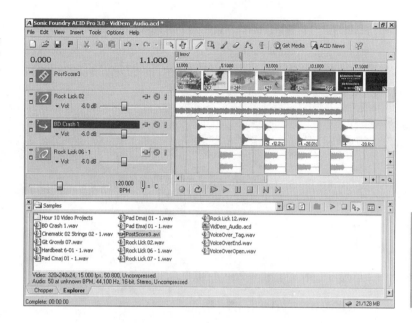

Video Editing Features

ACID is not a video editor. However, you can use it to do a certain amount of simple video editing. Notice that the event shows various video frames. Zoom in using the Zoom In Time controls to see more frames—even to the point where you can see every frame on the timeline. Zooming in helps you make frame-accurate decisions when trimming the video (which we'll talk about in a few seconds).

Moving the Video Event

Most often, you'll adjust your audio tracks in ACID to match the video. But there may be times when you want to adjust the timing of the video so that it better matches the audio. To do so, click and drag the video event to move it to a new position on the timeline.

When you move the video event, the audio originally associated with the video does not move. To resynchronize the audio with the video, right-click the audio event and choose Synchronize with Video from the shortcut menu. Note that this command works only on the audio track that was originally associated with the video.

Edge-Trimming the Video

Click and drag the start or end of the video event to trim the portion you don't need (see Figure 10.2). If you trim too far, click and drag the edge in the opposite direction to reveal more frames. Notice that as you trim, the video does not move inside the event.

FIGURE 10.2

Edge-trim the video to include more or less of it in your final project.

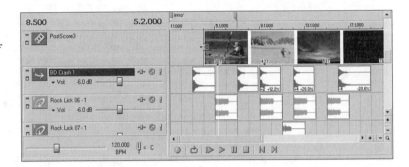

Slipping the Video

You can slip the video within the video event using the same shortcut technique you used to change the start offset of an audio event in Hour 5, "Additional Editing Techniques." Hold the Alt key while you click and drag within the video event (not at the edge). This action slips the video inside the event, but does not change the event itself. You'll notice that video moves inside the event as you drag the cursor.

Slipping (discussed here) and sliding (discussed in the next few minutes) work only when the entire video is not visible in the event. In other words, before trying to slip or slide your video within its event, edge-trim one of the edges of the video event.

Slip-Trimming the Video

To change the start or end time along with the duration of the event without changing the start offset (a technique called "slip-trimming"), hold the Alt key while you click and drag the start or end of the event. When you slip-trim the front of the video event, two things happen simultaneously. First, you change the start time of the event; and second, you trim video from the opposite end of the event. Again, notice that the media moves with the cursor.

Sliding the Event

You can also move the event while leaving the media in place. To slide the event, hold Ctrl+Alt as you drag the event (click in the middle of the event, not at the edges). This action moves the event, but the media stays in place. Sliding the event in this fashion allows you to change the start offset and the position of the event at the same time.

> By the way, these video-editing techniques work great on audio and MIDI events, too.

Task: Trimming the Video Event

In this task, you'll trim the beginning of a video in order to remove color bars and a countdown. You can also use the techniques discussed here to trim the end of the video event.

1. Open the project VidDem_Audio.acd from the Hour 10 Samples folder located on the CD-ROM that accompanies this book.

2. Add the Postscore3.avi video file to the project. Notice that a video and an audio track are added, both of which are called Postscore3. Because the audio track is silent, delete it from your project.

3. Right-click the Time at Cursor display and choose Time at Cursor Format, Absolute Frames from the shortcut menu (see Figure 10.3).

FIGURE 10.3

Choose your desired format from the Time at Cursor display shortcut menu.

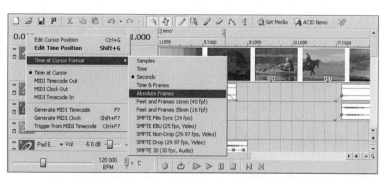

4. Double-click the Time at Cursor display to highlight the current cursor time position. Type **150** and press the Enter key on your keyboard to move the project cursor to frame 150. Press M on your keyboard to place a beat marker at that location.

5. Choose Options, Snapping from the menu bar and make sure that the Snapping feature is enabled. Choose Options, Snapping, Grid Only to deselect that option so that the event will snap to the marker that you created in the last step. Edge-edit the front of the video event all the way to the marker. Notice that the color bars and countdown are no longer visible.

6. Delete the marker you placed in step 4 and move the video event so that it starts at the beginning of the project.

7. Keep this project open. You'll continue with it later in this hour.

Using the Timeline Video Display

When you first add a video file to the project, you see several thumbnails, each containing a frame number and showing the content of the video at that frame. Depending on your zoom level, each of these frames might actually represent multiple frames. For instance, the first thumbnail you see might be frame 160, and the second thumbnail frame might be frame 237. As you zoom in, you see more detail until finally you see each individual frame. (Zoom in until the frame numbers displayed are consecutive.)

Zoom back out so that each thumbnail represents several frames. As you move the cursor to different locations along the timeline, ACID changes the thumbnail to show the frame at the current cursor location in the video event. Press the left and right arrow keys to move the project cursor.

> Your zoom level dictates how far the arrow keys move the cursor. Regardless of your zoom level, you can easily move one frame at a time: Hold the Alt key while you press the right-arrow key. This key combination moves the cursor one frame to the right. Notice that the thumbnail in the event updates to show you the frame at the current cursor position. The frame number updates as well. Use Alt+left arrow to move left through the video one frame at a time.

What does zooming in on the video track and moving through the frames one at a time mean for you? It means that you can synchronize musical events, sound effects, and dialog to an exact frame of the video track. Being able to do frame-accurate editing of audio to video opens up all kinds of possibilities.

Frame Number Formats

By default, the numbers displayed in the video event represent frame numbers. As you know, the frame rate can be described as the number of frames shown per second. For example, when you go to the movies, the film in the projector is shown at 24 frames per second. The human eye interprets this rate as full motion. In video, the frame rate varies from 24 to 30 frames per second (fps).

To turn off the display of the frame numbers, choose Options, Preferences and click the Video tab. From the Show Source Frame Number on Video Thumbnails As drop-down list, choose None.

Working with the Video Window

10

To watch the video you added to a project, you must open the Video window. When open, the Video window displays the frame at the current cursor position (see Figure 10.4). To open the window, choose View, Video. A check mark next to this choice means that the window is already open. If this is the case, look at the tabs along the bottom of the Window Docking area and click the Video tab. If there is no check mark next to the option, choose the Video option to open the Video window.

FIGURE 10.4

The Video window shows the video frame at the current position of the timeline cursor.

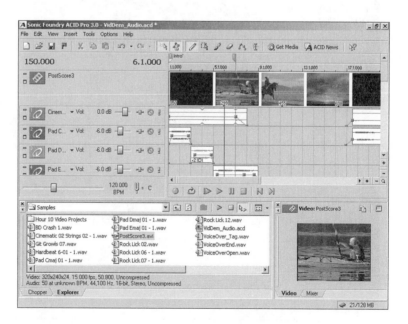

You can adjust the size of the Video window, and thus the size of the video display. If the window is docked, resize the Window Docking area. If the window is undocked, adjust its edges for different preview sizes.

Right-click the Video window, and notice that, by default, the Show Toolbar option has a check mark next to it. Disable this option to hide the toolbar buttons at the top of the Video window. Enable the Show Toolbar option to show the toolbar buttons. Right-click the Video window again and select Show Status Bar to open the status bar at the bottom of the Video window. The status bar holds information about the video's frame size and frame rate. For instance, the video being shown in Figure 10.5 is 320 pixels wide by 240 pixels high and has a frame rate of 15.00fps. To the right of this information, ACID shows the current display size.

FIGURE 10.5

The status bar in the Video window gives you information about the video's frame size, frame rate, and the current display size in the Video window.

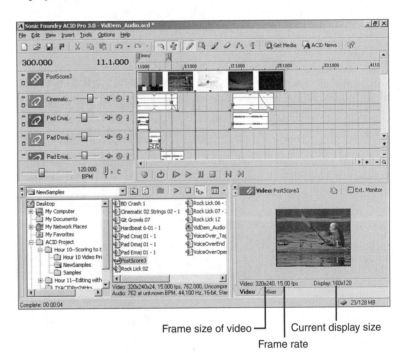

Frame size of video ⎤   Current display size

Frame rate

For the best preview of your video, make sure that the display size matches the frame size. Resize the Video window to make these numbers agree.

If you want the Video window to always show the video at its regular size, right-click the Video window and choose the Display at Media Size option from the shortcut menu. Now, regardless of the size of the Video window, the video always displays at full size. If the Video window is too small to hold the entire video at its full size, you'll see only what can fit.

Click the Copy Frame button to copy the current video frame to the Windows Clipboard. From there, you can paste it into a number of different applications.

Using an External Monitor

Often you'll be editing video that will eventually be copied to a video tape (a process known as printing to tape) and viewed on a TV. In these cases, it is helpful to view the video on a monitor that emulates a TV screen (known as an external monitor) rather than on the computer screen so that you can get a better idea of how the video will really look on a TV. ACID enables you to view the video on an external monitor. To do this, your computer must have an *IEEE 1394/OHCI compliant video card*.

10

NEW TERM

IEEE 1394/OHCI Compliant Video Card

IEEE (pronounced "I-triple-E") stands for the Institute of Electrical and Electronics Engineers. This organization—comprised of engineers, scientists, and students—is best known for developing standards. The IEEE 1394 standard is a very fast external bus standard that supports data transfer rates of up to 400Mbps (400 million bits per second). You may have also heard these cards called FireWire or i-link cards. IEEE 1394 cards can deliver data at a guaranteed fast rate, making them the ideal choice for video.

OHCI stands for Open Host Controller Interface. OHCI allows you to control digital video (DV) devices such as a DV camera or DV deck from your PC.

To set up your system for external video monitoring, make sure that you have properly connected the monitor to the video card in your computer using the appropriate IEEE 1394 cable. Click the Ext. Monitor button in the Video window's toolbar. This action opens the Preferences dialog box with the Video tab active. From the External Monitor Device drop-down list, choose OHCI Compliant IEEE 1394/DV.

From the If Project Format Is Invalid for DV Output, Conform to the Following drop-down list, choose from *NTSC* DV or *PAL* DV settings in either standard or widescreen formats.

NTSC stands for National Television Standards Committee. The NTSC is responsible for setting television and video standards in the United States.

PAL stands for Phase Alternating Line. PAL is the dominant television standard in Europe.

Use the Sync Offset (Frames) slider in the Preferences dialog box to set an offset in case the video you see on your external monitor does not synchronize with the audio associated with that video. When you are done making your choices, click the OK button to dismiss the Preferences dialog box.

Using Time Markers

ACID has a Video bar that remains hidden until you place a *time marker*. Place the cursor at the desired location and press H on your keyboard to drop a time marker. The Time Marker bar appears; this bar holds the new time marker. Right-click the Time ruler to change the time format to any of the following:

- Samples: 1 to inf.
- Time: Hours:Minutes:Seconds.Ticks
- Seconds: 1 to inf.
- Time and Frames: Hours:Minutes:Seconds.Frames
- Absolute Frames: 1 to inf.
- Feet and Frames (16mm 40fpf): Feet+Frames
- Feet and Frames (35mm 16fpf): Feet+Frames
- SMPTE Film Sync (24fps)
- SMPTE EBU (25fps, Video)
- SMPTE Non Drop (29.97fps, Video)
- SMPTE Drop (29.97fps, Video)
- SMPTE 30 (30fps, Video)

The options available when you right-click the Time ruler are the same as those available when you right-click the Time at Cursor display; you can change the format with either method.

> **NEW TERM**
>
> ### Time Marker
>
> A time marker (also known as a hit marker) is used to mark events that you want to emphasize with an audio event. The audio event might be a sound effect—such as the sound of a door closing in synchronization with the video of a door closing. The audio event could also be a musical event—a crash cymbal in synchronization with a splash of water in the video. Time markers are locked to a particular frame in the project timeline and do not move when you change the project tempo.

Right-click the Time ruler and choose Set Time at Cursor from the shortcut menu to set an offset in the Time ruler. In the text box that opens at the cursor, type a new time value in the current time format. The ruler updates to reflect the new offset. For example, place the cursor at frame 200, choose Set Time at Cursor, type **100** for the value, and press Enter. The ruler changes so that now 100 on the ruler is located where 200 was previously.

> ### Working with Offsets
>
> Why would you want to create an offset in the Time ruler? Suppose that you're creating the score for an hour-long TV special. The video is sent to you in 15-minute segments. On the master videotape, the first segment starts at 00:01:05.00. The second segment starts at 00:16:05.00, and so on. If you start a new project for each of the segments (which would be logical), each of these projects would start at 00:00:00.00. You can see that your music will not synchronize very well with the video. Working with the correct offset simplifies your synchronization job, making it likely that your project will be successful.

A good way to get started adding audio to a video project is to add the video and watch it with your finger on the H key on your keyboard. As you're watching, add time markers to the places in the video that you want to emphasize with a musical event, sound effect, or dialog segment. In the case of musical hits, time markers can help you determine the project tempos, which enable you to arrive at that important video event in a musical fashion. In other words, time markers help you create a *tempo map* so that your music is perfectly timed (that is, in sync) with your video.

After you have placed time markers in the video track and established the desired project tempo, you can move through the project to see whether the time markers you placed coincide with logical musical timing. For instance, perhaps you want the beginning of a new scene to coincide with the downbeat of a particular musical phrase. Let ACID automatically determine the tempo at which the project must play to make this all work out.

Tempo Map

A tempo map is a series of tempo markers that tell ACID when to speed up and slow down. As you score to your video, there might be several points at which you want something in the video to match perfectly to a musical event. To ensure that this happens, you must often speed the music up or slow it down. To do this, mark these important spots in the video with time markers, and add tempo markers as discussed in Hour 7, "Constructing Your Musical Arrangement" to adjust the tempo of the song so that musical events synchronize with important video events.

Locate the time marker you want to sync to a musical element such as the downbeat of a measure. Place the project cursor at the target downbeat in the audio track. Right-click the time marker in the video track and select Adjust Tempo to Match Marker to Cursor. ACID automatically calculates and adjusts the tempo so that the video event (such as a scene change) synchronizes with the audio event (the downbeat).

You can press Alt as you drag the time marker to manually adjust the tempo until you have matched the "musical time" (the desired downbeat) to the project time (the time marker).

Continue moving through the project using these techniques to build a tempo map. Frame-accurate synchronization has never been faster or easier!

You might notice that the playback on the Video window seems a little "jerky." This happens when your computer can't handle the high processing demands of video. ACID compensates for inadequate computer power by dropping (skipping) as many frames of the video as necessary to allow perfect playback of the audio. The dropped frames are only for the purposes of playback in ACID. In the rendered version (see the section on rendering your video, later in this hour), playback will be smooth. If you are working with a video compressed using a Digital Video (DV) codec, view the video on an external monitor to significantly lighten the load on your computer processor.

Codec

Codec stands for *coder/decoder* (or *compressor/decompressor*). See the section, "A Word About Codecs," later in this hour for more information.

Task: Using Time Markers

In this task, you'll place time markers at important points in your video and then use tempo markers to create a tempo map so that the music synchronizes with the video. Before you start, right-click the Time ruler and choose Time & Frames from the shortcut menu.

1. Play the video project you started in the earlier task. Drop a time marker at the spot where the scene changes to the kayaker. This is the beginning of the video's action sequence, and the music should change at this point. Right-click the time marker and choose Rename from the shortcut menu. Name the marker Start Action. (Hint: This marker should be at 8 seconds and 1 frame, or 121.0 frames if your Time ruler is still set to show Absolute Frames.)

2. Drop another time marker at the start of the grizzly bear scene. Name the marker 2nd Action Scene. This second marker will help us work with the tempo during the action scenes. (The second time marker should be at 24 seconds, 10 frames.)

3. Drop another time marker at the beginning of the sunrise scene (at 27 seconds, 8 frames) and name it End. This scene is the end of the action sequence, and we'll want the music to change again at this point.

4. Notice that there is a region in the audio track called Intro (identified by the green markers). There are six bars in the intro. We want the intro music to play during the first two scenes—the mountain and the eagle scenes. At the current tempo of 120bpm, the song is too slow and is still playing when the action sequence starts. We need to speed up the audio, but by how much?

5. Place the cursor at bar 7. Right-click the time marker labeled Start Action and choose Adjust Tempo to Match Marker to Cursor as shown in Figure 10.6. Presto! ACID does the math, and sets the tempo at exactly what it needs to be to sync the downbeat of the "action music" with the start of the action video sequence. Notice that your project tempo has been reset to 180bpm. (ACID calculates the tempo down to the 1/1000 of a second. If you did not edit the video exactly the way we did in the earlier task, the tempo you come up with here might be slightly different than ours.)

6. Press the T key on your keyboard to place a tempo marker at bar 7. The Tempo/Key Change dialog box opens. Because the action music sounds best at a tempo around 130bpm, change the tempo setting in the Tempo/Key Change dialog box to 130bpm and click OK. This marker locks the tempo from the beginning up to this point. Notice that the beginning tempo of the piece is unaffected. We can now adjust the tempo further down in the project without affecting the beginning tempo we just set.

10

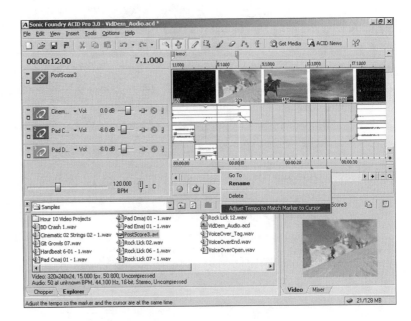

7. The next spot we want to hit is the scene with the grizzly bear. Place the cursor at bar 16 in the audio track. To match the audio to the start of the grizzly bear scene, right-click the time marker you placed in step 2 and choose Adjust Tempo to Match Marker to Cursor. This command makes a subtle change to the tempo so that the crash cymbal syncs to this scene change.

8. Press T to lock in the tempo at this point. Do not change the tempo in the Tempo/ Key Change dialog box. Simply click OK to accept the current tempo. This action dismisses the dialog box and places the marker.

9. Repeat steps 5 and 6 to match the hit at the sunset scene (the marker labeled End) to bar 17 beat 3. This is where the ending music starts.

10. Play the entire project and notice how the audio is now synced to the video. Notice also that the small adjustments we made to the tempo of the project are not notice-able. Keep this file open; you'll use it again in the next task.

Rendering the Final Product

When you finish the project, you can *render* the audio or the audio with the video as a single file. You cannot render just the video. If the audio from a project segment is to be mixed into a larger production or laid back to the master videotape, mix to an audio-only format. It is also useful to render the audio and video together so that the mixed video and audio can be viewed in a media player on a computer or recorded to a DV device.

> **New Term**
>
> **Render**
>
> When you render an ACID project, ACID combines the video track along with all the audio tracks (and any editing you've done along the way) into a "mixed" file that can be played in a program other than ACID. In essence, you can think of rendering your project as saving the project in a different file format. Hour 17, "Creating Mixed Audio and Video Files," discusses rendering your projects in detail.

Choose File, Render As to start the rendering process. The Render As dialog box enables you to pick the storage location for the rendered file, give the file a name, and choose the file type to which you want to render the project. You can choose from several file types. Click the Save As Type drop-down list button to see the complete list of file types:

- .aif (Audio Interchange). Audio-only format used by Macintosh computers.

- .mp3 (MP3 Audio). Audio-only compressed format.

- .mpg (MPEG). Compressed video format popular with broadcasters and authors of DVD.

- .ogg (OggVorbis). Audio-only format that uses VBR (variable bit-rate encoding). Automatically adjust the bit rate based on the source material. A higher bit rate is used during complex passages; a lower bit rate is used during simpler passages.

- .pca (Perfect Clarity Audio). Audio-only compression format developed by Sonic Foundry.

- .mov (QuickTime). Audio/video format developed by Apple.

- .rm (RealMedia). Audio/video streaming format for playback in the RealMedia player.

- .w64 (Sonic Foundry Wave 64). Audio-only format developed by Sonic Foundry. Used for rendering large audio files that exceed 2GB in file size.

- .avi (Video for Windows). Uncompressed audio/video format common on Windows-based computers.

- .wav (Wave). Uncompressed audio-only format common on Windows-based machines.

- .wma (Windows Media Audio). Audio streaming format for playback in the Windows Media Player.

- .wmv (Windows Media Video). Audio/video streaming format for playback in the Windows Media Player.

10

Most of these file formats have several templates available from the Templates drop-down list. These templates offer various choices for bit-depth, sampling rate, and other parameters for encoding in the particular file format.

So, how do you choose? We could write another book on that subject! But answering a few questions helps narrow down the choices.

Do you only need the audio? Do you want a file that contains both the audio and video information? Do you need a compressed format so that you can stream the file over the Internet? What is the intended delivery format—CD, DV Tape, the RealMedia Player, the Windows Media Player? Find the answer to these questions and then refer to the preceding list of file types and their advantages. This approach should help narrow the choices. You should also check Hour 17, "Creating Mixed Audio and Video Files," for details about some of these formats—in particular, the streaming formats.

Task: Rendering to an `.avi` File

Because `.avi` files are the standard for video on a Windows computer, let's walk through the process of rendering a file as an `.avi`.

1. With the file from the previous task still open in ACID, choose File, Render As. The Render As dialog box opens.

2. Choose the My Documents folder on your hard drive from the Save In drop-down list.

3. Name the file Adventure Travel Promo.

4. Choose Video for Windows (`.avi`) from the Save As Type drop-down list.

5. The Project default renders a video that works well for multimedia presentation on your computer. Note that you should compress the video because uncompressed video files have very large file sizes. To compress the file you're creating, click the Custom button.

6. Leave all settings at their defaults except for the Video Format field. In that field, click the drop-down arrow and choose Cinepak Codec by Radius. This is a common *codec* that is present on most Windows machines and will therefore allow you to play your file on various computers. Leave the Quality setting at 100%.

7. Click the Audio tab at the bottom of the Custom Settings window. There's no need to change anything here; just have a look around. Click OK.

8. Click Save to start the render. Because rendering video is very demanding on your computer hardware, the process might take several minutes. Render times vary from PC to PC. When the render is complete, navigate to the My Documents folder and double-click the file to open and play it in the Windows Media Player. This file will look different than the original project you created in ACID because the file has been compressed. However, now you can transfer it to different computers so that you can show off your work!

A Word About Codecs

In the previous exercise, you chose a codec as your video format. A codec codes (or compresses) your file when you save it, and then decodes (decompresses) the file when it is being viewed. Using a codec allows you to save your files with smaller file sizes. Unfortunately, smaller file sizes come at a price. Codecs are typically "lossy," which means that you lose quality as you compress the file. Once lost, the quality cannot be restored. Some codecs damage quality less than others, but generally, the smaller the file size the codec achieves, the greater the loss of quality.

Remember that you need the codec to render the video (that's the compress part); you also need the codec to play the file back (that's the decompress part). If you experience problems playing it back on another computer, check to see that the codec you used is installed on that PC.

To find out which codecs are currently installed on your PC, consult your operating system help files.

Summary

ACID has several features to aid you in your quest to sweeten your video with music, sound effects, and dialog. In this hour, you learned how to add a video track to your ACID project. You also learned about time markers and how these markers—along with tempo markers—can help you build tempo maps that synchronize musical events with the video. You learned how to change the display on the Time ruler and on the video events, and how you can use these displays to your advantage when working on a sound track for your video. You also learned how to render your project in a file format that you can share with your friends. Now imagine what your home videos could be like! Those of you who are pros, imagine how you can integrate ACID into your video production suite to quickly score music to your video projects.

Now take a few minutes to review this hour's material by working through the questions and activities that follow.

10

Q&A

Q. **Why doesn't it sound noticeable when I change the tempo of my project to match the video?**

A. Because normally the tempo changes are so minute that they are virtually unnoticeable. If you try to match a time marker with a musical event that is very far away, the tempo shift could well be noticeable. Strive to find musical events that are as close as possible to the video event, and nobody will be the wiser when the tempo is tweaked slightly!

Q. **Is it really necessary to match the music to the video so precisely?**

A. Well, that's probably as much a matter of personal taste as anything else ACID allows you to do. Most people would say that when the video changes at the same time as a significant audio event, the two senses team up to enhance the overall experience. But if you have a different opinion, go with it. It's your movie!

Workshop

Use the quiz and activity that follow to reinforce the information you learned in this hour. The quiz tests what you have learned, and the activity allows you the opportunity to put your new skills to work.

Quiz

1. How do you open the Time ruler?

2. What are two ways to adjust time markers to match beat markers while simultaneously adjusting the project tempo?

3. You want to save your video in a format that will allow your friends, collaborators, or clients to play it on their Windows computer so that they can check your progress. What render option should you choose?

Quiz Answers

1. Choose View, Time Ruler, Show Time Ruler to display the Time ruler.

2. Place the cursor on the beat marker, then right-click a time marker and choose Adjust Tempo to Match Marker to Cursor. Alternatively, hold the Alt key while you click and drag the time marker into position.

3. A good option is to save the file as an `.avi` file at multimedia frame size settings (the default), using a common codec such as Cinepak from Radius or Indeo Video 5.10. If you think the movie might also be viewed on a Macintosh, save it as a QuickTime file (`.mov`). QuickTime files can be viewed on both Macintosh-based and Windows-based computers.

Activities

1. Load the file `PostScore3.avi` or a video of your own into a new ACID project. Create original music for the video. Save it as an `.avi` file using the Cinepak from Radius video codec.

10

PART IV

Using the Special Construction Tools

Hour

Hour 11

Editing with the Chopper

So far, all the edits you've made to projects in ACID have been made in the timeline. But sometimes this is not the best way to edit. Take, for example, a long Beatmapper file: Adding the entire file as an event on the timeline and then removing the pieces you don't need can be time consuming.

If you've ever tried to create a remix, you know how much work it is to choose the parts you need and then assemble them into a remix. That's where the Chopper can help. The Chopper automates the process of finding just the right piece of an audio or MIDI file so that you can concentrate more on creativity and less on the mechanics.

Here's how the Chopper works: Open the media file (audio or MIDI) in the Chopper, create a time selection that spans a portion of the file, and add the selection as an event to the timeline as many times as you like. Lots of files have more than one usable section hidden inside them. The Chopper makes it easy to find these sections and incorporate them into your project.

In this hour, you will:

- Open media in the Chopper
- Navigate in the Chopper

- Use markers and regions in the Chopper
- Master the Chopper arrow
- Create events with the Chopper

Working with the Chopper

To open a file in the Chopper, first add the file to your project. Choose View, Chopper to make the Chopper visible if it is not already. Click on any Track Header, or anywhere in the Track View area to instantly load the file associated with that track into the Chopper (see Figure 11.1).

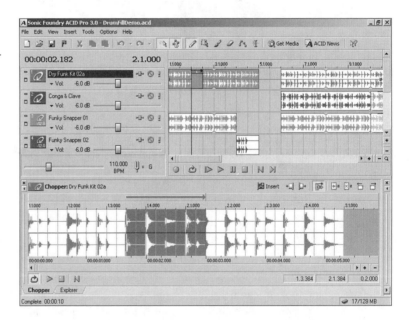

Right-click any event in your timeline and choose Select in Chopper from the shortcut menu. This command opens the entire file in the Chopper and creates a selection in the Chopper window that corresponds to the portion of the file being used in the event. For instance, if the event contains the entire file, then the entire file is selected in the Chopper. But if the event contains only a portion of the file, although the entire file opens in the Chopper, only the portion used in the event is selected in the Chopper window.

Selection and Navigation

A ruler across the top of the Chopper window shows measures and beats; this ruler is invaluable in selecting musical phrases. The zoom functions that work in the Track View work in the Chopper window as well. As you zoom in and out, the ruler displays more or less detail. The snapping options you have set for the main Track View also affect snapping in the Chopper.

Notice that when you make a selection in the Chopper, a colored box (the color matches the track icon of the track that holds the file) and a black arrow appear in the Track View timeline (see Figure 11.2). The colored box indicates the space that will be occupied by the event created when you insert the Chopper selection. The black arrow points to the position to which the project cursor will move. You'll learn more about these elements a little later this hour.

FIGURE 11.2

The colored box and black arrow give you important visual clues about the results of inserting the Chopper selection.

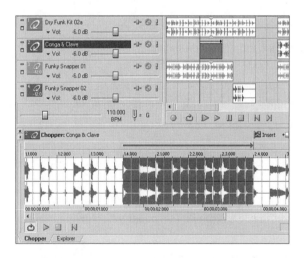

Three text boxes at the bottom-right of the Chopper window supply useful selection information. These fields are (from left to right) Selection Start (or Cursor Position if you have not yet defined a selection in the Chopper), Selection End, and Selection Length. They show the position and length of the selection in `Measures.Beats.Ticks`, as shown in Figure 11.3. Double-click any of the three fields to adjust the selection.

Following is a list of navigation techniques using the mouse and keyboard. Note that these techniques work exactly the same in the Chopper as they do in Track View.

- Press the End key to move the cursor to the end of the current view.
- Press the Home key to move the cursor to the beginning of the current view.
- Press Ctrl+End to navigate to the end of the file.

- Press Ctrl+Home to navigate to the beginning of the file.
- Use the right-arrow and left-arrow keys to move the cursor one pixel to the right or left.
- Use the PageUp and PageDown keys to move left or right one grid mark.

FIGURE 11.3

The Chopper gives you information about the start, end, and length of the current selection.

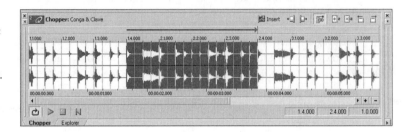

Here is a list of selection techniques using the mouse and keyboard:

- Double-click the waveform displayed in the Chopper window to select the entire file.
- Single-click the waveform displayed in the Chopper window to deselect any current selection and to position the cursor at the click point.
- Click and drag across the waveform to select any range.
- Place the cursor at any point in the waveform, hold the Shift key, and use the right-arrow and left-arrow keys to adjust the selection edge to the right or left, one pixel at a time.
- Hold the Shift key and press PageUp to expand the selection to the next grid mark to the left; press PageDown to expand the selection to the next grid mark to the right.
- Right-click the waveform and choose Selection Length from the shortcut menu. From the cascading menu, choose a selection option. Options include Measure, Note, Half Note, and many others.

Using the Tools

The Chopper window contains a simple transport toolbar in the bottom-left corner (see Figure 11.4). The Loop Playback, Play, Stop, and Go to Start buttons enable you to control the playback of the file currently in the Chopper. These toolbar buttons work exactly the same as the buttons in the timeline transport toolbar.

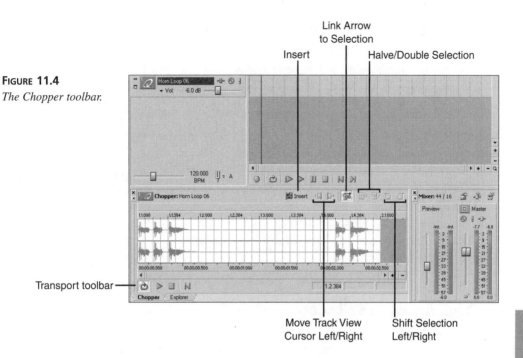

FIGURE **11.4**
The Chopper toolbar.

Link Arrow
to Selection

Insert   Halve/Double Selection

Transport toolbar

Move Track View   Shift Selection
Cursor Left/Right   Left/Right

11

The buttons in the upper-right corner of the Chopper window enable you to navigate through the file, establish and adjust a selection, and add the selected portion of the file to your Track View timeline as one or more events. Notice that most of these buttons are not active until you make a selection in the Chopper. Let's talk a little about the function of each of these buttons.

By the way, we can't stress enough how useful the keyboard commands for the Chopper buttons are. We guarantee that if you take the time to learn them, your productivity with the Chopper will soar. We list these shortcuts in the descriptions that follow.

Make sure that the Chopper window has focus before using any of these keyboard commands. If the Chopper does not have focus, these keyboard commands may have completely different functions!

The Insert Selection Button

Each time you click the Insert Selection button, you insert the selected portion of the file into the timeline over the area indicated by the blue box. The Track View cursor moves to the point indicated by the black arrow just before you insert the selection. By repeatedly clicking the Insert Selection button (or by repeatedly pressing either the A key or the Question Mark/forward-slash key), you can quickly add multiple occurrences of the selection to the timeline.

Move Track View Cursor

The Move Track View Cursor Left/Right buttons enable you to move the blue insertion box and black arrow in the Track View before you insert an event from the Chopper. Click these buttons to move the box/arrow to the left or right in increments equal to the length of the selection you have defined in the Chopper.

The shortcut for the Move Track View Cursor Left is Ctrl+comma (,). The keyboard shortcut for the Move Track View Cursor Right button is Ctrl+period (.).

Link Arrow to Selection

Notice that the arrow above the selection in the Chopper is equal to the length of the selection. This is because, by default, the Link Arrow to Selection button is engaged. Toggle this button to link or unlink the arrow to or from the selection. We'll talk more about this feature later in the hour. The keyboard shortcut for this button is N.

Halve Selection and Double Selection

Use the Halve Selection button to cut the size of your current Chopper selection in half. Click the Double Selection button to double the selection length. The shortcut for the Halve Selection button is the semicolon key (;). The keyboard shortcut for the Double Selection button is the apostrophe key (').

Shift Selection Left/Right

The last two buttons, Move Selection Left and Move Selection Right, are great for moving through the file to search for other possible events while maintaining the selection length. Press the comma key (,) for the Move the Selection Left button; press the period key (.) for the Move the Selection Right button.

To move the selection in the Chopper left and right, you can also press Shift+less-than (<) to move left and Shift+greater-than (>) to move right. It may be easier to use these shortcuts than the buttons or the comma or period keys because these keyboard symbols point in the direction of the selection movement. All methods work, so pick the one you can use most efficiently!

Using Markers and Regions in the Chopper

As you search through the file for usable sections, you'll often find more than one section you want to use. To keep track of these sections, place markers and define regions. You're already familiar with placing markers and regions from your work in the timeline in earlier hours; the techniques are exactly the same in the Chopper. Look back to Hour 6, "Shaping Your Project," and Hour 7, "Constructing Your Musical Arrangement," for details on using markers and regions.

> The regions and markers you place in the Chopper are saved with the project, but not with the media itself. If you close the project and reopen it later, then load the file back into the Chopper, the markers and regions you placed are once again displayed. But if you open the same file in another project, the markers and regions are not available. Remember that ACID is nondestructive: the original media file is never changed.

Using the Chopper Arrow

As you become more adept at remixing with the Chopper, you'll use the Chopper arrow (the arrow above the selection in the Chopper window) to create interesting effects. In the following sections, you'll learn more about the Chopper arrow.

11

Move or Change the Chopper Selection

The Chopper arrow enables you to move the position of the Chopper selection. Click and drag the arrow to a new location in the Chopper; the selection follows the position of the arrow.

Click and drag either end of the arrow to change the length of the arrow. When the Link Arrow to Selection button is engaged (as it is by default), changing the length of the arrow also changes the length of the selection. If the arrow is not linked to the selection, only the arrow length changes. We'll discuss how you can use the arrow length to create interesting effects in the next section.

If the arrow and selection are not linked and are different lengths, right-click the arrow bar and choose Sync with Selection from the shortcut menu to change the arrow length so that it is equal to the selection length. You can also set the arrow length to specific musical measurements from the shortcut menu.

Define the Next Insertion Point

Defining the next insertion point is the most important function of the Chopper arrow. As mentioned, the arrow length controls how far the cursor in the Track View moves when you insert a selection from the Chopper window into the Track View timeline.

By default, the arrow length is linked to the selection length. For instance, if the current Chopper selection is two bars long, the arrow is also two bars long. When you click the Insert Selection button, the Chopper inserts the two-bar phrase into the Track View timeline at the position of the blue box and moves the blue box two bars later in the project to await the next insertion.

With the arrow unlinked from the selection, three different scenarios exist for what happens when you click the Insert Selection button:

- The Chopper arrow could still be the same length as the selection (even though they are no longer linked). Insertions from the Chopper behave the same as if the arrow and selection were linked.

- The Chopper arrow could be longer than the Chopper selection. In this case, multiple insertions create events in the timeline with gaps between them. The gap is determined by the difference between the length of the arrow and the length of the selection.

- The Chopper arrow could be shorter than the Chopper selection. Now multiple insertions create events that overlap. The start of the second event is inserted before the end of the previous event. The overlap is determined by the difference between the length of the arrow and the length of the selection.

Creating a Stutter Effect

To quickly create a stutter effect in your project, set the Chopper arrow to be considerably shorter than your Chopper selection length, and insert the selection multiple times. Each subsequent insertion overlaps the previous one. When you play them back, you have a great stutter effect! Creating stutters has never been this fast or this easy.

Open the file StuterF_Ect.acd in the Hour 11 Samples folder on the CD-ROM that accompanies this book to see what stutters look like in the timeline and to hear what they sound like. Then open the file in track 1 in the Chopper and listen to the complete file. You'll see how you can use the Chopper and a little creativity to come up with interesting variations on your loop collection!

Three Ways to Insert Chopper Selections

So far, we've talked only about using the Insert Selection button, but there are actually two other methods for inserting Chopper events into the Track View: You can also use the Windows Clipboard and the drag-and-drop method. Each method has advantages, and each deals with the Track View cursor in a slightly different manner, as the following sections explain.

Insert Selection Button

As described earlier in this hour, the Insert Selection button moves the blue insertion box based on the length of the Chopper arrow rather than the length of the Chopper selection. This is the method you'll probably use most often.

Copy and Paste

You can also use the Copy and Paste commands to copy the selection from the Chopper to the Windows Clipboard, and then paste the selection into the Track View. After you have copied the selection, use the Paste command to paste the copied material into the timeline no matter which view (Track View or Chopper) has focus. The Track View cursor moves to the end of the newly pasted event regardless of the length of the Chopper arrow. In other words, using the Copy and Paste method yields the same results as using the Insert Selection button when the arrow is the same length as the selection. The Copy and Paste commands are a quick way to override an arrow length that does not match the selection length.

Drag and Drop

Make a selection, point anywhere inside the selected area, and drag and drop it onto the Track View timeline. The event is placed in the proper track (the track that contains the file which is open in the Chopper) wherever you drop it on the timeline. In this case, however, the Track View cursor is unaffected; it remains where you last placed it regardless of selection length, arrow length, or placement of the selection on the Track View. The drag-and-drop approach is a great way to quickly add a section to the timeline without worrying about the position of the blue insertion box.

Getting Creative

The Chopper quickly becomes a permanent member of your editing arsenal. There are lots of ways to make use of this tool. We'll point out a few of the ways we use it, and add some techniques developed by Super Chopper Remix Master Frank Shotwell in his white paper on the topic of the ACID Chopper.

Task: Creating a Melody

In this task, you'll use the Chopper to isolate a single note and add it to your project several times. Then you'll shift the pitch of individual events to compose a new melody.

1. Start a new project and add the file Cinematic 03 Horns 01.wav from the Hour 11 Samples folder located on the CD-ROM that accompanies this book. Open the file in the Chopper and click the Play button in the Chopper Transport bar to hear what the file sounds like in its original, "unchopped" state.

2. In the Chopper window, make sure that the Link Arrow to Selection button is activated. Select the first beat of the file. You'll know you have the right selection when the Selection Start field shows 1.1.00, the Selection End field shows 1.2.0, and the Selection Length field shows 0.1.0 (see Figure 11.5).

FIGURE 11.5

Use the Selection fields to make sure that you select just the first beat of the file in the Chopper.

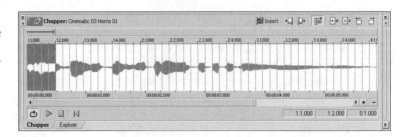

3. Click the Halve Selection button once and insert the selection twice at the beginning of the project.

4. Click the Double Selection button once and insert three events.

5. Click the Link Arrow to Selection button to unlink the arrow. Drag the head of the Chopper arrow out another beat (to Selection Start position 1.3.0) so that the selection is one beat and the arrow is two beats. Insert an event.

6. Link the arrow with the event again, halve the selection, and insert two events.

7. Double the selection and insert four events. (By now you're probably waiting for someone to say "Simon Says." Hang in there; the payoff is coming.)

8. In the Track View timeline, select the events listed below and use the + key on your number pad to pitch-shift them as follows:

   Event 3 up 2 steps (to B)

   Event 5 up 5 steps (to D)

   Event 6 up 4 steps (to C#)

   Event 9 up 2 steps (to B)

   Event 11 up 7 steps (to E)

   Event 12 up 5 Steps (to D)

9. Okay, you're done. Your project should now look like the one in Figure 11.6. Save the project. On your next birthday, open and play the project. (Okay, you can play it now, but you're gonna spoil the surprise.)

FIGURE 11.6

Use the Chopper to add events and create melodies.

> The French horn loop used to create this little party song came from the
> *Orchestral Loop Library* from Sonic Foundry. There are four discs in this loop
> collection covering Classical, Modern, Cinematic, and Pop/Rock styles.

Creating a Drum-Roll Buildup

A drum-roll buildup can really add some excitement to your project. You've heard this
effect before, and it's easy to create with the Chopper. Add a portion of a drum beat to
your project. Halve the selection, and add it twice. Halve it again, and add it four times.
You get the idea. Each time you halve the selection, add it twice as many times as
before. When you're done, you'll have an interesting drum-roll buildup effect. A good
file to try this on is `Break Pattern C.wav` from the Hour 11 Samples folder on the CD-
ROM that accompanies this book. Start by adding the entire file, and work from there.

Task: Creating a Drum Fill

There are lots of occasions for which you need a drum fill, but can't find a loop that
matches the loop you are using for the main drum track. The Chopper solves this problem by helping you create a fill from the existing drum material. Follow these steps to
learn how.

1. Open the project called `DrumFillDemo.acd` from the Hour 12 Samples folder on
   the CD-ROM that accompanies this book.

2. Play the file and notice that there is a big hole in the drum part (the `DryFunk Kit
   02a` track) at measure 5. This is where we need to create a drum fill. Place the cur-
   sor at measure 5 and open the Chopper window.

3. Create a one-eighth note selection anywhere in the Chopper. (Hint: Right-click in
   the Chopper waveform and choose Selection Length, 8th Note from the shortcut
   menu.)

4. Navigate through the file and randomly insert events into the Track View until you
   have filled the hole in the `DryFunk Kit 02a` track in the Track View timeline. If
   you stick with the eight-note length, you must insert eight events. If you'd rather be
   pickier about what you use, audition the selection by playing it in the Chopper
   before adding it to the project.

5. Click Play From Start and listen to your new Chopper-created drum fill.

Later in this same project, at bar 11, another fill has been created using the Chopper. If you want to "reverse engineer" this fill, you can right-click any of the events and choose Select in Chopper to see exactly where in the file that section came from.

Creating a One-Track Remix with the Chopper

Here is an idea that often results in some unexpected and interesting results. Start with a Beatmapper file (see Hour 9, "Incorporating One-Shot and Beatmapper Tracks," if you need a refresher on the Beatmapper). Add this file to a new ACID project and open it in the Chopper. Place the cursor somewhere in the Chopper window, right-click, and choose Selection Length, Half Note from the shortcut menu. Insert the selection twice. Shift the selection to the right and insert the selection twice. From here, start to skip over parts, double or halve the selection, and in general "jam" on the process. Some of these remixes will turn out better than others, but all will produce some interesting results. The process will also give you good ideas and provide starting points for refining the remix into a finished product.

DJ-Style Rapid Crossfade Mix

Perhaps you've seen and heard DJs create a Rapid Crossfade Mix live. First they get both turntables going with their best vinyl. Then, using the crossfader on their mixer, they fade back and forth between the two records. The best DJs can get the beats of the two records to match by slowing one down or speeding it up to match the other. After the beats are matched, switching between records never interrupts the beat.

ACID achieves the same effect and makes the whole process much easier than what the DJ has to go through. You already know that ACID matches the beat for you. It also creates the crossfades automatically. Work through the next task to discover the secret.

Task: Creating a DJ-Style Crossfade Mix

To create this effect, use two Beatmapped songs—one track each for both of the "virtual records." ACID automatically matches the beats, so our task is to set up sections and create the crossfade effect.

Here's another cool hidden ACID feature for you! A fast way to create a
crossfade between events in two different tracks is to overlap the end time
of one event with the beginning of another, select both of them, and press
F on your keyboard. ACID creates a perfectly smooth crossfade equal to the
length of the overlap between the two events. For a fast crossfade, make
the overlap short. Lengthen the overlap for a longer crossfade. Right-click
the fade envelopes and choose from Fast, Linear, and Slow fades.

1. Open the project RapidXfadeDemo.acd from the Hour 12 Samples folder.

2. Click track 1; in the Chopper window, make a random selection that is three beats
   long.

3. Unlink the Chopper arrow from the selection and make the arrow four beats in
   length. (Hint: Right-click the arrow and choose Measure from the shortcut menu.)

4. Insert the Chopper selection at the beginning of the project. This action inserts the
   three-beat selection and moves the cursor to the downbeat of bar 2, leaving a gap at
   bar 1 beat 4.

5. Press the greater-than (>) key on your keyboard. The selection in the Chopper
   moves to the right by the length of the selection. Insert this new selection from the
   Chopper into the project at the cursor location.

6. Press the less-than (<) key to move the selection in the Chopper to the left. Insert
   the new Chopper selection into the project. Continue to move and insert the selection until you have several events in track 1.

7. Position the cursor on beat 3 of the first bar in track 2. Set the arrow and selection
   length as you did in steps 2 and 3: four beats of arrow, three beats of selection.

8. Using the same insert-move-insert routine described in steps 4, 5, and 6, insert several events from the Chopper into track 2. Your events from track 1 now overlap
   those in track 2, and look something like what is shown in Figure 11.7 (you might
   have to adjust the zoom level of your timeline for your screen to look like the one
   in the figure).

9. Click anywhere in the Track View timeline to give it focus. Press Ctrl+A to select
   all the events in both tracks. Press F on your keyboard to create crossfades between
   all overlapping events.

10. Click the Play From Start button to get the party started.

11

FIGURE **11.7**
Two tracks with over-lapping events.

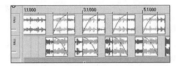

Creating Granular Pseudo-Synthesis

When you take extremely small selections in the Chopper (say, 32nd or 64th notes or smaller), insert them side by side, and play them back, the selections begin to form their own waveform that creates a completely different sound from the original material. Open any audio file in the Chopper and create a very small selection. Insert it into the Track View several times and play it back. Presto! You've created your very own pseudo-synthesizer. For an example of this effect, open the project PseudoSynthDemo.acd in the Hour 12 Samples folder located on the CD-ROM that accompanies this book.

Summary

By now, you should be the best remixer on your block! You have learned how to open a file in the Chopper, navigate through it, select portions of it, and audition sections of it. You learned the functions of the Chopper tools and how to use them. You learned how the Chopper arrow affects the movement of the Track View cursor when you insert sections into the project. You also learned about some special applications that really use the power of the Chopper. Take a few moments to work through the questions and activities that follow to put your knowledge and the Chopper to work.

Q&A

Q. Does the file have to be Beatmapped to use it in the Chopper?

A. No, you can open any audio or MIDI file in the Chopper.

Q. Is there an easy way to tell whether my Chopper arrow is linked to the selection?

A. Here are a couple of quick ways to tell whether the Chopper arrow and selection are linked. The most obvious is an arrow that is a different length than the selection. But the arrow length could be the same as the selection length even if the two are not linked, so look at the arrow color. A blue arrow indicates that the arrow is linked to the selection. A black arrow shows that the two are unlinked.

Q. Is there a keyboard command for toggling focus back and forth between the Chopper and the Track View timeline?

A. You can use the keyboard shortcut Ctrl+Tab to shift the focus between the ACID windows. This shortcut allows you to move between the Track View timeline and all the dockable windows that are currently open. For instance, if you have the Explorer window, the Chopper window, and the Mixer window open (a very common arrangement), pressing Ctrl+Tab cycles through the Track View timeline and each of these open windows. If you have only the Chopper window open, use this keyboard shortcut to toggle between the Chopper and the timeline.

Workshop

In this workshop, we will review some of the concepts you learned in this hour about the Chopper. The activity gives you a chance to try your hand at creating a remix with the Chopper.

Quiz

1. True or False: When you insert a selection into the Track View, the cursor moves later in time based on the length of the Chopper selection.
2. How do you create a stutter effect using the Chopper?
3. How do you create automatic crossfades between overlapping events on different tracks?

Quiz Answers

1. False. The placement of the Track View cursor when a selection is inserted from the Chopper is based on the length of the Chopper arrow.
2. To create a stutter effect, set the arrow length shorter than the selection length. This causes the selections to overlap each time you insert another one. Insert several selections to achieve a stutter effect.
3. Select events that overlap on different tracks and press F on the keyboard to create a crossfade based on the length of the overlap.

Activities

1. Open the file Male Vocal06-01.wav from the Hour 12 Samples folder and use the Chopper to create a stutter effect on the word "Hip."

11

The file `Male Vocal06-01.wav` used in this activity can be found in the *Mac Money-Electro Hip Hop* loop collection. This is one of Gary's favorite libraries and has lots of great loops.

2. Send a couple of your favorite tunes through the Beatmapper, and add them to a new ACID project. Using the techniques described in "Creating a DJ Style Crossfade Mix" above, create your own crossfade mix.

HOUR 12

Using Audio FX

Adding audio effects (FX) to your projects can really liven up your mix. You can use FX—such as reverbs and echoes—to simulate real acoustical spaces or create special effects not found in the "real" world. ACID provides a variety of audio FX, and a great deal of flexibility in how and where you apply them.

In this hour, you will:

- Learn what audio effects (FX) are, and what they're used for
- Discover how ACID enables you to use FX
- Master ACID Track FX
- Create an FX chain
- Work with the Plug-In Chooser
- Learn about DirectX plug-ins

An Introduction to FX

Many of you are already very familiar with how audio FX work. For those who are new to audio FX, we'd like to take a few minutes to give a brief overview of how FX are used to create music.

Pros use a wide variety of audio FX at various stages of a project. Sometimes they add FX at the input (or recording) stage—for example, when the lead guitarist runs his guitar through a distortion pedal. Other FX are added at the mixing stage—for example, when a vocalist records a "dry" (no FX added) vocal signal, and the recording engineer later runs the vocal through a reverb unit. Finally, some FX are added at the mastering stage. An example of this would be running the entire mix through a compressor as the final mastering touch.

An FX chain is a series of different FX (or perhaps the same FX with different parameter settings) through which you run a signal. Let's look back to the lead guitarist for a perfect example of a common FX chain. A guitar player's guitar chord does not usually go directly from the guitar to the amplifier. The signal from the guitar likely passes through a distortion pedal, then maybe through a chorus pedal, a delay unit, and a wha-wha pedal. Then there is often reverb and equalization added in the amplifier. This series of modifications to the original audio signal is called a chain of FX.

FX chains are also created at the other stages of adding FX. For example, at mix-down, you might add delay and then reverb to a dry vocal. At mastering, you'll probably want to shape the recording with equalization (EQ) first, and then run it through the compressor. These are just simple examples, and countless combinations are used to create FX chains.

In ACID, you can add FX at the mix-down stage and at the mastering stage. You cannot add FX at the input stage unless you add them with outboard gear (such as guitar pedals). ACID gives you three ways to add FX to your project. We'll discuss the first method (Track FX) in detail during this hour, and explore the other two methods (Bus FX and Assignable FX) in the next hour when we talk about the ACID Mixer.

Track FX

In ACID, each track contains one or more events that refer to a single file. Track FX are a great way to apply a specialized FX chain to that file without affecting other files in the project. For instance, if track 1 in your project contains a snare drum, it is very handy to use Track FX to add reverb and EQ to that drum. You could then add reverb and EQ with the same or different parameters to track 2, which contains the kick drum. You could also add other FX to track 2 without affecting the file on track 1.

Each track in ACID has a dedicated Track FX chain that you can customize independently of the chains on any other tracks. Any effect applied as a Track FX affects all events in the track. You can chain up to 32 FX on each track. You can also reorder the FX in the chain, change the FX parameters, and add or remove FX at any time.

Preinstalled FX

Before we get started on adding FX to your project, let's take a few minutes to introduce the FX that are automatically installed when you install ACID on your computer.

> We don't have the room in this book to explain the details of what each of the FX we mention in the following sections do. Even if we did, the best way to learn is to experiment. Each of the FX contains a set of presets, so you can start taking advantage of them right away. When you have a good sense of how the various FX alter the audio, use the complete set of controls to customize the FX exactly the way you want. You can then save your settings as a custom preset, and easily recall the settings any time you need them.

The FX installed when you install ACID fall into these three main categories:

- **Audio Enhancing FX**—There are six FX you can use to enhance your audio and to create an ambiance that wasn't originally recorded in the file. These FX are Chorus, Multi-Tap Delay, Pitch Shift, Reverb, Simple Delay/Echo, and Time Compress/Expand. These FX are often called time-based FX because they shape and change the audio over time.

- **Sound Shaping and Mastering FX**—Six other FX are great tools for tweaking your tracks so that they sound their best. These FX are Graphic Dynamics, Graphic EQ, Multi-Band Dynamics, Noise Gate, Paragraphic EQ, and Parametric EQ.

- **Special FX**—An additional six FX are designed specifically to create some exotic and unusual sounds. These are Amplitude Modulation, Distortion, Flange/Wah-Wah, Gapper/Snipper, Smooth/Enhance, and Vibrato.

Constructing FX Chains

Although we're using the Track FX method for this discussion of FX chains, everything that happens within the Audio Plug-In dialog box and the Plug-In Chooser (which you'll learn about in a minute) is the same, no matter which method you use to apply FX to your project.

The Track Header for every track in any project (except for the video track) contains a Track FX button. You'll find this button right between the track name and the Mute button, as shown in Figure 12.1. Click the Track FX button to open the Audio Plug-In dialog box.

12

FIGURE **12.1**
*The Track FX button
allows you to edit a
track's plug-in chain.*

Track FX button

The Audio Plug-In dialog box can open docked in the Window Docking area, but you can tear it out and let it float anywhere on your screen.

What's a Plug-In?

ACID snuck a new term in on us here, so let's take a little break to talk about what a plug-in is. The FX that come with ACID are called "Plug-In Packs." They were not originally—and technically are not now—part of the software code that makes up the ACID program. Plug-ins are special software programs that require a host program (in this case, ACID) to give them full functionality. ACID works fine without the plug-ins, but plug-ins bring extra functionality to the program—in this case, they allow you to add audio FX to your projects.

All the FX available in ACID are plug-ins. That's why the dialog box is called the "Audio Plug-In" dialog box. It also explains why you might see some FX that we don't mention in this hour. For instance, if you previously purchased and installed other plug-ins from Sonic Foundry (such as Noise Reduction or Acoustic Mirror), those plug-ins will also show up as options in ACID. You might even notice third-party FX plug-ins from Cakewalk, Steinberg, or other plug-in developers. Later in this hour, we'll explain how that can be. For now, let's get back to work!

By default, all tracks (with the exception of MIDI tracks) already have the Sonic Foundry Track *EQ* effect assigned to them, as shown in Figure 12.2. The interface for this effect opens in the Audio Plug-In dialog box. Notice the rectangular box toward the top of the dialog box (just below the icon that matches the track icon of the track with which you are working). This is the visual indication of the FX chain for this track. Right now, there is only one FX in the chain (Track EQ), so there is only one box.

Even though every track automatically has the Track EQ plug-in applied at the track level, you don't have to worry that it is altering the sound of your files or taxing the processing resources of your computer. By default, the Track EQ does not affect a track until you change one or more of its parameters.

NEW TERM

EQ

EQ stands for *equalizer*. An EQ effect allows you to boost or cut the volume of an isolated frequency of sound (or frequency range) so that you can "shape" the sound of your audio. For example, the Bass and Treble controls on your home or car stereo are simple EQs. The Bass control affects a frequency range that encompasses the lower frequencies of sound waves, and the Treble control affects the higher frequencies. You can use an EQ to "cut the high end" or "boost bottom end" and so forth. You guys with your license plates rattling—you need to cut the bass frequencies before your taillights fall out!

FIGURE 12.2

The Track EQ effect is assigned to each track by default.

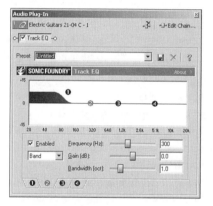

Creating and Using FX Presets

All the Sonic Foundry FX plug-ins have presets with commonly used FX parameters. Choose the presets to quickly get a feel for how the FX alter the sound of the audio.

You don't always get lucky enough to find a preset that fits perfectly for the sound you're trying to achieve. When you can't find the perfect preset, find the one that comes closest and then use the individual parameter controls to tweak the effect until it suits your needs exactly.

Often, when you find an FX setting that you like, you'll want to apply that same setting to other tracks in this or other projects. Instead of readjusting the parameters every time you want to use the same FX, make a new preset. To do this, open the Preset drop-down list and highlight the current name of the preset (if it is not already highlighted). Type in a new name and click the Save Preset button in the FX window toolbar.

12

Task: Experimenting with Your First Track FX Plug-In

1. Open a new project in ACID and add the `Electric Guitars 21-04 C.wav` file from the Hour 12 Samples folder on the CD-ROM that accompanies this book.

2. Draw an event of about 10 bars or so. Create a loop region over the event and set ACID to Loop Playback mode. Now you're ready to experiment with some FX.

3. Play your ACID project; while it's playing, click the Track FX button to open the Audio Plug-In dialog box. Notice that the Track EQ plug-in appears by default.

4. From the Preset drop-down list, choose Boost Bass Frequencies Below 250Hz by 4dB. This preset is kind of like turning the bass control up on your home stereo. Notice that there is now a little more "bottom end" to the guitar.

5. Choose various other presets from the Preset drop-down list. Some of the presets are quite subtle, but you should be able to hear how they affect the sound of the file being played.

6. Now, adjust the controls manually to hear what changes you can make. Click the red circle labeled 1 and drag it up. Notice how this affects the bass (lower) frequencies. Drag the circle all around to hear how it affects the sound. (Note that if a circle is not filled in with red, it is disabled and has no affect on the sound. To enable it, click the circle and select the Enabled check box.) Drag circle 4 around and notice that the effect it has on the sound is different than the effect circle 1 has. You can also use the fader controls to make adjustments to the sound. Notice that the position of the circle affects the settings of the Frequency and Gain sliders, and vice versa.

7. Click the check box to the left of the effect name in the FX chain to bypass the Track EQ (or any other FX in the chain). Notice that when the FX is bypassed (that is, when the check box for that effect does not contain a check mark, as is the case in Figure 12.3), that effect no longer affects the guitar signal.

> As you'll see later, some FX plug-ins are optimized for use as Track FX. Bypassing a non-optimized FX that you're using as a Track FX disables the effect you hear, but not the effect that the plug-in has on your processor. For Track FX, it's best to use only plug-ins that are optimized for use as Track FX.

FX Check box

FIGURE 12.3

Deselect the FX check box to bypass the FX.

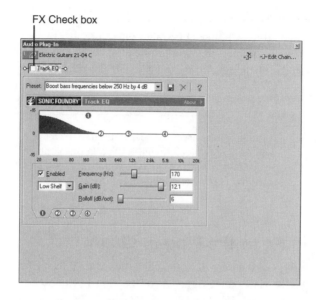

Working with the Plug-In Chooser

The ACID Plug-In Chooser enables you to work with the audio plug-ins on your system and to customize your audio FX chain. With the Plug-In Chooser, you can add, remove, and rearrange the order of FX in the chain.

To open the Plug-In Chooser, first open the Audio Plug-In dialog box and then click the Edit Chain button at the top of the dialog box. The Plug-In Chooser opens as shown in Figure 12.4.

12

FIGURE 12.4

Assemble a plug-in chain in the Plug-In Chooser.

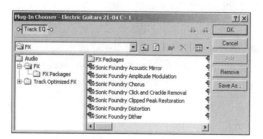

The Plug-In Chooser is laid out like the Windows Explorer window: It has a tree view on the left with which you can navigate through the various FX folders, and a list view on the right that shows the contents of the folder you have selected in the tree view.

In the tree view, you see one folder called FX. In it are listed all the FX on your system. Another folder, Track Optimized FX, lists only those FX that are optimized for use as Track FX. Track-optimized FX work more efficiently than nonoptimized FX; consequently, you can chain more of these FX together before you begin to overload your system.

If you're a software developer interested in creating FX plug-ins that work with ACID, download the PIDK (Plug-In Development Kit) provided on the Sonic Foundry Web site, www.sonicfoundry.com. The PIDK also includes information on optimizing plug-ins for use as Track FX.

Adding FX to the Plug-In Chain

To add plug-ins to the plug-in chain, click the name of the effect you want to add to the chain in the list view on the right side of the Plug-In Chooser window. Then click the Add button. Alternatively, double-click the name of the plug-in you want to add to the chain.

Notice that another box is added to the plug-in chain at the top of the Plug-In Chooser. You can also add several FX at once using standard windows selection techniques. When you click the OK button, the Plug-In Chooser closes, and the plug-in chain at the top of the Audio Plug-In dialog box updates to show the additions you made to the chain while in the Plug-In Chooser.

Reordering FX

Because the order of the FX in the chain is important, you might want to reorder the FX to get the exact results you're after. ACID gives you a number of ways to reorder FX.

As you've seen, all the FX in the chain are listed across the top of the Audio Plug-In dialog box. Point to the name of the FX you want to move, and click and drag it to a new position in the chain. You can use the same drag-and-drop technique in the Plug-In Chooser.

If the chain you've built is too long to fit in either the Audio Plug-In dialog box or the Plug-In Chooser, you'll see two buttons with arrow icons to the right of the chain. These buttons do not reorder the plug-ins! They merely shift the view of the plug-in chain so that you can see parts that might currently be hidden.

Next to these arrow buttons (in the Plug-In Chooser only), are two buttons that allow you to shift the order of your plug-ins in the chain. The order of the plug-ins in the chain can be important. The dry signal enters into FX #1; when it comes out of the plug-in, the signal has been altered. The altered signal then goes into FX #2 and comes out altered again, and so on. You can see that the signal that goes into FX #2 is different than the one that entered FX #1. The difference the order of the FX makes on the signal can be subtle, but it's real nonetheless. Click the Shift Plug-In Left button to move the selected plug-in one position to the left; click the Shift Plug-In Right button to shift the selected plug-in to the right.

> ### You're Dripping All Over the Floor!
>
> Still not convinced about the difference the order of your plug-ins in the chain makes? Try a simple two-night experiment. Tonight take your clothes off, take a shower, get out, dry off, and put your clothes back on. That's a five-step process, or chain of events. And it yields a particular result.
>
> Tomorrow night, execute the same five steps, only change the order of the chain like this: take a shower, get out, take your clothes off, dry off, and put your clothes back on. All the same events in the chain, but what a difference the order makes!

Removing FX

There are a few ways you can remove an FX plug-in from the chain if you decide that you no longer need it. In the Audio Plug-In dialog box, click the plug-in that you want to remove from the chain. Click the Remove Selected Plug-In button (located next to the Edit Chain button). Alternatively, right-click the plug-in and choose Remove from the shortcut menu.

In the Plug-In Chooser, select the effect you want to remove (click its name in the chain, not in the list view) and click the Remove button at the right side of the window. Both of these methods remove the plug-in from the chain, but do not remove the plug-in from your system, so you can always add it back later if you change your mind.

Saving a Plug-In Chain

As you gain more experience with ACID, you'll almost certainly find FX "sounds" that you like. When you do, use the Plug-in Chooser to save the chains you use all the time so that you don't have to re-create them whenever you want them. When you have your customized chain complete, click the Save As button in the Plug-In Chooser. The Save Plug-In Package dialog box opens. Type a name for the package and click OK.

12

If all the plug-ins in your chain are track-optimized plug-ins, you'll find the new package listed in the FX Packages folders under both the FX and Track Optimized FX folders in the tree view of the Plug-In Chooser. If any of the FX in the chain are not track optimized, the new package is added only to the FX Packages folder under the FX folder.

> In the saving process, notice that ACID calls the series of plug-ins a package, not a chain. Why? Because when you save the package, you not only save the chain of FX, you also save all the settings of the individual FX plug-ins in the chain. When you call your package up again later, you can be assured that all your settings are just as you wanted them when you saved the package.

If you decide that you no longer want to keep a package for future use, right-click the package name and choose Delete from the shortcut menu. Alternatively, click the package name and then click the Delete button in the Explorer navigation button area. Finally, you can select the package name and press the Delete key on your computer keyboard to delete it. All three methods delete the package, but not the plug-ins that were in the package. In other words, don't worry that you're throwing away your valuable plug-ins!

Organizing Plug-Ins

You may find it helpful to use names other than the default names that the plug-in developers have given the plug-ins on your system. Or you might decide to change the name of a plug-in package that you created. To do this, right-click the name of the plug-in or package in the Plug-In Chooser window and choose Rename from the shortcut menu. This command selects the name of the plug-in or package so that you can type the new name. Another way to rename a package or plug-in is to click the name of the plug-in or package, wait for a couple of seconds, and then click a second time. You can now type a new name.

As your collection of FX plug-ins grows, you might want to organize them by type of effect, manufacturer, and so on. For example, you might organize all your reverbs or EQs in one easy-to-find location. You can create new folders in the Plug-In Chooser to help you organize the FX.

When you select either the FX folder or the Track Optimized FX folder in the tree view of the Plug-In Chooser, the New Folder button becomes available in the Explorer navigation area. Click this button to create a new folder called (of all things) "New Folder." As soon as you create the new folder, it becomes visible in the tree view. The name is highlighted and ready for you to change to a more appropriate one. Click and drag any FX you want into the newly created folder.

Task: Working with an FX Chain

Let's work on shaping the sound of the guitar we used in the last task. In the process, we'll demonstrate many of the plug-in chain techniques we've talked about so far.

1. If the ACID project you used in the last task is not still open, start a new project and add the Electric Guitars 21-04 C file to it (this file is located in the Hour 12 Samples folder on the CD-ROM that accompanies this book). Draw in a few measures and set the project key to C. Right-click the track icon for the guitar track and choose Use Original Tempo from the shortcut menu. Now set ACID to play the project in Loop Playback mode. You are all set to continually listen to the changes you make during the rest of this task.

2. Begin playback of the file. Click the Track FX button for the guitar track to open the Audio Plug-In dialog box and then click the Edit Chain button to open the Plug-In Chooser. Notice that playback is temporarily suspended when the Plug-In Chooser is open.

3. Click the Track Optimized FX folder icon in the tree view of the Plug-In Chooser to view only the track-optimized FX. Press and hold the Ctrl key and select these effects from the list view: Sonic Foundry Chorus, Sonic Foundry Distortion, and Sonic Foundry Flange/Wah-Wah. Click the Add button to add all three FX to the plug-in chain. Click OK. When playback resumes, notice that the sound of the guitar has already changed.

4. Click and drag the Distortion effect to the left until it is the first FX in the chain. Click the Bypass check boxes for each of the other FX. In fact, we don't need the Track EQ effect at all, so click its name in the chain and then click the Remove Selected Plug-In button at the top of the dialog box. Finally, click the Distortion effect in the chain, and choose Lil' Warmer from the Preset drop-down list. You now have a little bit of distortion on your guitar. Your FX setup should look like the one shown in Figure 12.5.

5. Enable the Bypass check boxes for the other two FX. Click the Chorus box in the plug-in chain. Notice that the bottom portion of the Audio Plug-In dialog box changes to display the controls for the Chorus plug-in. From the Preset drop-down list for the Chorus plug-in, select Chorus 3. In the same way, set the Flange/Wah-Wah preset to Wah-Wah 1. The guitar sounds quite different now!

12

Figure 12.5

The plug-in chain consists of three plug-ins, two of which are currently bypassed.

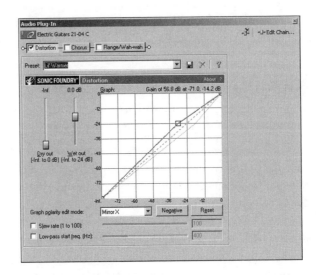

6. Different, but not very nice. The Chorus and Wah-Wah FX don't sound that good with this guitar, so let's experiment a little more. Click the Edit Chain button at the top of the dialog box to open the Plug-In Chooser.

7. Click the Flange/Wah-Wah effect in the FX chain and click the Remove button. Do the same for the Chorus plug-in. Look in the list view of the Plug-In Chooser and notice that even though you removed these FX from the chain, the plug-ins still appear in the list—and on your PC.

8. Add the Sonic Foundry Simple Delay FX to the plug-in chain and click OK. From the Preset drop-down list, choose Echo Chamber and notice how drastic this echo effect is on the guitar. Choose the Grand Canyon preset for a somewhat more subtle echo. Now play with the delay settings until you find a delay that you're happy with.

9. Click the Edit Chain button to return to the Plug-In Chooser window. Click the Save As button. Give this FX package a name and click OK. Notice that the new package exists in the FX Packages folders under both the FX and Track Optimized FX folders in the tree view. You can now choose this same FX package for any track in this or future projects. Click OK to dismiss the Plug-In Chooser.

Using DirectX Plug-In Effects

If you're familiar with other digital audio applications, you've probably been asking yourself, "Hey, what about DirectX plug-ins?" Even if you're not familiar with the term

"DirectX," you might have been asking yourself, "How can ACID support plug-ins that were made by some other company?" Well, for both of those questions, here's the DirectX portion of our discussion on FX.

Defining DirectX

DirectX is an Application Program Interface (API) developed by Microsoft. An API is a set of tools, routines, and protocols used by programmers to build software applications such as DirectX FX.

APIs are the building blocks provided by the operating system developer (in the case of DirectX, the developer is Microsoft) so that third-party developers (such as Sonic Foundry, Cakewalk, Digidesign, and so on) can create applications (among them, audio FX plug-ins) with confidence that they will work with the operating system, the hardware, and any host application that also conforms to the DirectX API. In other words, if someone uses the DirectX tools, protocols, and specifications to build an audio FX plug-in, any application that is a DirectX host application will be able to make use of the plug-in.

ACID is a DirectX host program that can use any properly constructed DirectX audio FX plug-in. Conformity to the DirectX specifications explains why you can use Sonic Foundry's DirectX plug-ins as well as DirectX plug-ins from other software developers.

To allow ACID to recognize your third-party DirectX FX plug-ins, all you typically need to do is install the plug-ins on your system. Because DirectX plug-ins are registered in a specific location of your operating system's registry, the next time you start ACID, ACID finds and recognizes the plug-ins and makes them available in the ACID Plug-In Chooser. However, some plug-ins might not be available in ACID. This is because ACID filters out plug-ins that are known to cause problems for the smooth operation of the program.

12

Advantages of DirectX Plug-Ins

DirectX plug-in support has a couple obvious benefits and one big one that may not be so readily apparent. One obvious benefit is that you can use your DirectX plug-ins in whatever host application you have on your machine that supports DirectX. That means you save money because you don't have to buy one reverb plug-in for ACID and a different one for your other applications.

A not-so-readily-apparent advantage of using DirectX plug-ins is that you can use multiple instances of each plug-in. You can't do that with *outboard* gear, and this saves you tons of money!

> ### Outboard
>
> The term "outboard" refers to a separate piece of hardware equipment (such as a reverb unit or an equalizer) that you connect to your computer, usually through a mixer. Outboard gear is traditionally how FX have been added to audio productions in the past.

For instance, if you rely on an outboard FX processor for your reverb, and you have only one reverb unit, you have to pick one setting and hope it works for all your reverb needs. Alternatively, you can go buy another reverb unit. Neither option is acceptable because the first one is extremely limiting, and the second one can get extremely expensive.

With DirectX in ACID, you have unlimited flexibility even if you don't have an unlimited budget. For example, you can open the reverb plug-in on one track and use one setting (let's say a "small hall" setting). You can then open another instance of the same plug-in on another track and use a different setting (perhaps a "large room" setting). In fact, you could open a separate instance of the reverb plug-in on each of your tracks and give them all completely different settings. You can even use multiple instances of the same reverb plug-in in the same plug-in chain. To accomplish this with outboard gear, you'd have to run out and buy a separate reverb unit for each of your tracks. Of course, this same scenario works for any plug-ins, not just the reverb FX.

Another plus to using DirectX audio plug-ins is that they keep all your audio processing in the digital domain. If you were to run your signal to an outboard processing unit, you would most likely have to convert the signal from digital to analog, run it through the FX processor, and then convert it from analog back to digital so that you can send it back to the computer. These conversions degrade the sound quality.

Sonic Foundry DirectX Plug-Ins

As you've seen, ACID comes with a variety of plug-ins created by Sonic Foundry. These plug-ins are automatically installed when you install ACID, so unless you've read this section, you would not even notice that these FX are not actually a built-in part of ACID! All the Sonic Foundry FX plug-ins discussed in this hour are DirectX compatible. This means that the FX work not only in ACID but in any other DirectX host application installed on your computer.

Third-Party FX

As mentioned earlier, ACID is a DirectX host program. This means that, with ACID, you can use any DirectX plug-ins you purchase from software developers other than Sonic Foundry.

As mentioned in an earlier note, you usually don't have to do anything special to use the DirectX FX plug-ins you buy. You don't even have to know where the plug-ins have been installed on your system. After you have installed these programs, ACID automatically finds them, and displays them as options the next time you start ACID and open the Plug-In Chooser. Simply add the new FX to the chain, and they work right along with the FX that came with ACID.

> Many plug-in manufacturers include their company name as part of the plug-in name so that you can quickly identify their plug-ins (that's why all the names of the Sonic Foundry plug-ins start with *Sonic Foundry*). If you have several third-party plug-ins, you might want to create folders in your Plug-In Chooser (as discussed earlier) to organize your plug-ins by manufacturer.

Summary

Adding FX to your project can really bring the mix to life. There are no limits to how you can manipulate your music using DirectX FX. In this hour, you learned the meaning behind the term DirectX, and how that opens up a world of possibilities for adding audio FX to your projects. You learned how to apply these FX as Track FX. You explored the Plug-In Chooser and learned how to organize, rename, and create FX chains. You also learned how to call up the FX presets and how to create and save your own FX presets for quick recall.

12

Q&A

Q. I see several FX called Sonic Foundry Xpress FX that you didn't mention in this hour. What are they, and where did they come from?

A. The Xpress FX are very much like DirectX FX, except that they work only in Sonic Foundry products. Xpress FX were initially created to work with ACID Music 2.0 (the mid-level version of ACID). Sonic Foundry added these FX to ACID 3.0 so that any projects created in ACID Music 2.0 that used Xpress FX, would open and work properly in ACID 3.0. Xpress FX are generally less feature rich than the pro-level FX, but are no less high-quality in terms of audio fidelity, so feel free to use them in your ACID projects if you like them.

Q. What if I want to add the same FX to multiple tracks in my project? Do I have to apply the same chain to each track individually?

A. Although you *could* do it that way, it probably makes more sense to solve this problem with Assignable FX or Bus FX. In the next hour, you'll learn all about those methods of adding FX.

Q. Can I add FX to some events on my track without altering the sound of other events on the same track?

A. Yes. But not with the Track FX discussed in this hour. This is another situation in which you'll want to use Assignable FX. You can then set up an FX envelope to bring the Assignable FX in on the events you want altered, and drop it back out on the events you want to keep dry. Again, you'll learn more about Assignable FX in the next hour.

Q. How much FX should I use?

A. If the FX sound good to you, and you're happy, it's the perfect amount! It's good to keep in mind however, that often a little bit of FX goes a long way. It might not be a bad idea to start out with subtle amounts of FX until you get a better feel for how they alter the sound.

Workshop

Use this workshop to review what you have learned about DirectX FX and to spice up some ACID music.

Quiz

1. What's the difference between the Audio FX dialog box and the Plug-In Chooser?

2. How many FX can you chain together?

3. What's so special about DirectX plug-ins?

Quiz Answers

1. The Audio FX dialog box allows you to change the parameters of the individual FX plug-ins in your chain. The Plug-In Chooser allows you to manage your plug-ins and build plug-in chains.

2. You can chain up to 32 FX in ACID.

3. DirectX plug-ins can be used in any program that supports them. You can use most any DirectX plug-in on your computer with ACID, even if the plug-in wasn't created by Sonic Foundry. DirectX plug-ins also allow you to use multiple instances of the same plug-in at once.

Activities

1. Now that you know how to create plug-in chains and alter the sound of your tracks using DirectX audio plug-ins, open a new ACID project. Add tracks and build a short song. Apply Track FX to the various tracks and manipulate the FX parameters to see how they affect the mix of your song.

12

Hour **13**

Using the Mixer

A close look at the Mixer reveals the very sophisticated signal-flow capabilities in ACID. The Mixer window gives you the tools you need to polish your project and prepare it for the final stage of production. The Mixer window also provides an interface from which you can access external hardware devices.

In this hour, we'll take a tour of all these features. Along the way, you will:

- Work with multiple buses
- Route a signal to internal and external hardware
- Assign tracks to buses
- Create a sub-mix
- Add Bus FX and Assignable FX
- Automate the mix with bus and FX envelopes

When you start ACID for the first time, the Mixer window appears on the right side of the Window Docking area. It contains the Preview and Master controls. Resize the Mixer, view it, hide it, undock it, and move it just as you can with any other window that resides in the Window Docking area (as introduced first in Hour 1, "Introducing ACID 3.0").

Preview Control

When you audition a file in the ACID Explorer window, the audio signal is routed to (and the volume is controlled by) the Preview control. The two meters represent left and right in the stereo field and show the level of the signal being sent to the default hardware device. The fader allows you to lower and raise the preview volume.

Controlling Preview Volume

Drag the Preview volume fader up and down to adjust the preview volume. The Preview volume determines the initial track volume when you add the file to your project. For instance, set the Preview volume to –6dB and audition the file. Add that file to the project. Notice that the volume for the new track is set to –6dB. Get in the habit of using a setting less than 0dB as your preview volume. This gives you some *headroom* to work with while mixing so that you can avoid *clipping*.

NEW TERM

Headroom

In mixing, the term "headroom" refers to a margin of safety that you maintain for your volume. As you've already learned, if your volume meters peak above 0dB, you might experience distortion in the audio. If you set your volume such that the meters peak at exactly 0dB, you're safe—unless a different portion of your file is louder than the portion you're working on. It's better to set your volume faders so that you peak between –3dB and –6dB. That way, if a portion of your file gets louder than the portion you're working on, you have a margin of safety and shouldn't have to worry about clipping. In other words, you have a bit of headroom.

NEW TERM

Clipping

Clipping is a phenomenon of digital audio that occurs when a signal peaks at above 0dB—the loudest volume it can reach without distorting. In ACID, if the meters go into the red, the signal is clipping.

Would You Dare Smash Hank's Hat?

Need a little help understanding the concepts of headroom and clipping? Let's turn to the great Hank Williams for help. Now Hank might not have known too much about digital audio, but he did know headroom. In Hank's day, he had no trouble finding a car in which he could sit comfortably and still wear his white cowboy hat. A '49 Buick had miles of headroom! If ol' Hank were alive today, he'd have a little more difficulty. In a Toyota, there's not even room for his pompadour hairdo, let alone his hat. There's just no headroom. But suppose that Hank goes mid-size and climbs into a four-door Chrysler. He just fits—hat and all—with a fraction of an inch to spare. Hank cruises along just fine until he hits one of those famous Wisconsin winter potholes. The car lurches; Hank bounces. His hat is smashed and now looks all distorted.

The next time you find yourself pushing your volume peaks too close to 0dB, think of poor Hank. We wouldn't run the risk of clipping any more than we'd dare smash Hank's hat! Give yourself plenty of headroom to avoid clipping.

Because the preview volume dictates the volume of a newly added track, you can use the Preview volume fader to mix the file you are previewing into the project and be assured that when you add the file to your project, the mix you create is preserved.

Meter Options

By default the meters are set to display a range of –60dB to 0dB. The volume labels and *peak hold indicators* also display by default.

NEW TERM

Peak Hold Indicators

The peak hold indicators represent the highest peak levels in the audio output. These thin horizontal lines constantly update on each meter. They indicate the level of the hottest (or loudest) points in your mix.

13

To customize these settings, right-click the meters and choose different settings from the shortcut menu shown in Figure 13.1.

The valley hold indicators work just like the peak hold indicators except that they show the lowest level of the mix over time.

FIGURE 13.1

Make meter display choices from the shortcut menu.

The Reset Clip command resets the numbers at the top of the meters. If the level gets too hot and the meters clip, the boxes containing these numbers turn red and remain so until they are reset.

 You can also click the red boxes at the top of the meters to reset the peak indicator numbers.

Routing the Preview

The preview is routed to the sound playback device (the outputs of your computer's sound card) which you select in the Preferences dialog box. Choose Options, Preferences to open the dialog box and then click the Audio tab. The easiest case is to choose Microsoft Sound Mapper from the Audio Device Type drop-down list. The Sound Mapper selects an appropriate playback device for you; you cannot change the selection in the Default Audio Playback Device drop-down list. If you select something other than Sound Mapper from the Audio Device Type drop-down list (and you have multiple sound cards, or a sound card with multiple outputs), you can select a specific device from the Default Audio Playback Device drop-down list.

If your computer has more than one sound card, or a sound card with multiple outputs, and you select something other than the Sound Mapper as your default audio playback device, you'll see a Device Selection button at the top of the Preview control as shown in Figure 13.2. This button enables you to override the default routing setting and to assign the preview to any device you want.

To hide or show the preview control, right-click anywhere in the Mixer (except on the meters) and choose Show Preview Fader from the shortcut menu.

FIGURE 13.2

Use the Device Selection button to override the default playback device.

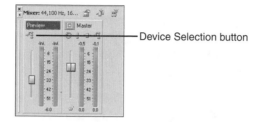

— Device Selection button

Using the Master Control

In the default setup, all audio from your project (with the exception of the preview, as discussed in the preceding section) routes through the Master control. The Master then routes the signal to the default audio device (which you selected in the previous section). The Master control provides the same meter display options as does the Preview control, including the Hold Peak, Hold Valley, and Reset Clip commands.

By default, the *Scribble strip* on the Master control contains the word *Master*.

NEW TERM

Scribble Strip

If you've ever visited a recording studio in the middle of a multitrack recording session, you've probably seen strips of white tape stuck below the faders on each channel of the mixer. These strips of tape allow the engineer to label each channel of the mixer. The ACID Scribble strip serves the same purpose. It allows you to give a descriptive name to the Master (as well as several other elements in ACID) so that you can keep your project organized.

Notice the vertical line running through the middle of the fader. This line indicates that the fader is actually two individual faders. Both the Preview control and the Master control are in stereo. However, you can control the left and right output of the Master separately. Click and drag the line between the two faders to control the faders together; alternatively, click and drag toward the outside edge of a fader to adjust the left or right signal individually. If the two faders are set at different levels, drag the inner edge of either fader to adjust both fader levels proportionately. The Lock Fader Channels toggle button, located at the bottom of the faders area, locks the two faders together so that they always move together. Figure 13.3 shows where this button is located in the Master control area.

13

Figure 13.3

*Move the faders
together or indepen-
dently to control the
volume of the left and
right channels.*

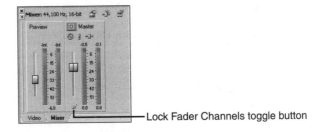

—— Lock Fader Channels toggle button

> As with most faders and sliders in ACID, click and drag with the left mouse
> button to move the Master faders to a new position in large increments.
> With this technique, it can be difficult to hit an exact setting, so how can
> you fine-tune the setting? The trick is to click and drag with the left mouse
> button as usual. As you get close to your target (and while still holding
> down the left mouse button), press and hold the right mouse button (or,
> alternatively, press and hold the Ctrl key). Now the fader moves in much
> finer increments, making it easy to set your faders to an exact level.

Click and drag the left fader all the way down to –Inf. (the very bottom of the scale).
Now double-click the right fader. This action brings the left fader up to match the level
of the right fader. You can always set the faders to the same level by double-clicking one
of them.

The numbers at the bottom of each meter show the current setting of the faders in dB. By
default, the Master faders are set to 0dB. Double-click the line between the faders to
reset them to their default values.

Right-click between the left and right meters on the Master bus to access a shortcut
menu from which you can choose from several different settings for the meters (see
Figure 13.4). We recommend that you select the Show Labels and Hold Peaks options.

The Show Labels option places numbers between the two meters representing the range
of decibels from –Inf. to 0dB. When you choose the Hold Peaks option, you'll notice a
thin horizontal line in the meters that represents the highest peak. This line constantly
updates as the music plays to give you an idea where the peaks are occurring.

From this same shortcut menu, you can choose several different label display formats.
Choose –120 to 0 dB to show more detail; choose –12 to 0 dB to show less detail.
Experiment with the different settings until you find one that works best for you. In our
figures, we use the default setting of –60 to 0 dB.

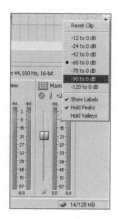

FIGURE 13.4

Right-click between the channels of the Master meter to access the shortcut menu.

The Master signal is automatically routed to the default playback device. However, if you have multiple outputs and have chosen a specific output in the Audio Preferences dialog box, the Device Selection button appears at the top of the Master. This indicates that the Master signal may be routed to any of the available outputs. Click the Device Selection button. All available devices are shown in a drop-down list. Choose one of these to override the default device.

You can also use the Master control to add the same FX to the entire project (that is, to the final mix). For instance, you might want to touch up the EQ or add some compression to the final mix. In these cases, add the FX to the Master control. You can apply an FX chain (with up to 32 FX) to the Master mix. Click the Master FX button to open the Plug-In Chooser. Now (if you read Hour 12, "Using Audio FX") you're on familiar ground.

The other two buttons located above the meters are Master Solo and Master Mute. The Master Solo button solos the output of the Master signal. The Mute button mutes the output of the Master signal. Because you can bypass the Master using multiple buses (which you'll learn about in the next section), muting and soloing the Master can be helpful.

Creating Multiple Buses

ACID supports additional *buses* in the Mixer window. In fact, you can add up to 26 buses, giving you 54 outputs in all (counting the two on the Master control). Each bus is designed like the Master control.

13

NEW TERM

Bus

A bus can be thought of as a way to transmit the audio signal within ACID. The additional buses you set up in ACID can route signals either to the Master (and from there to the outputs of your sound card), or directly to the outputs of your sound card (bypassing the Master). From your sound card, the signal is routed to your speakers or outboard gear.

Here's a simple analogy for how buses work in ACID. Imagine that you and a group of friends all leave your respective homes, meet at a designated spot, get on a chartered bus, and let it carry you to a concert hall where everyone gets out. In the same way, audio signals from various sources in ACID get on an ACID bus and let the bus carry them to the output of your sound card where they all "get out" to your speakers.

Just like the chartered bus has a specific—but changeable—route, you can dictate the route of your ACID buses. This process is called "signal routing." The ACID Master and Preview controls that we've already talked about are both examples of buses. When you use the Device Selection button or the Audio tab in the Preferences dialog box to specify an output device, you are defining the route that those buses follow.

In the following sections, we'll explore some uses for additional buses. As you become more familiar with the bus concept—and become more comfortable with signal routing—you'll undoubtedly find other ways to use buses.

Adding a New Bus

There are a few ways to add additional buses to your ACID project. First, click the Insert Bus button in the top-right corner of the Mixer. Click this button again to add another bus. Alternatively, right-click almost anywhere in the Mixer window (except on the meters) and choose Insert Bus from the shortcut menu.

To add multiple buses in one operation, click the Project Audio Properties button at the top of the Mixer. This action opens the Project Properties dialog box with the Audio tab selected. (Another way to open this dialog box is to choose File, Properties and then click the Audio tab.) Use the arrows or spinner buttons, or simply type a number into the Number of Additional Stereo Buses text box. Enable the Start All New Projects with These Settings check box if you want all your new projects to start with the specified number of buses. Figure 13.5 shows what the Mixer window looks like with four buses added.

FIGURE 13.5

The Mixer now shows four additional buses.

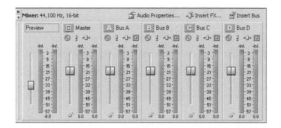

Deleting a Bus

Right-click a bus and choose Delete from the shortcut menu to remove that bus from your project. Alternatively, select the bus and press the Delete key on your keyboard. To remove multiple buses all at once, access the Audio Properties dialog box using one of the methods described in the preceding section and change the number of buses in the project.

In the next section, you'll learn how to route tracks to a specific bus. When you delete a bus, anything that was routed to that bus is rerouted to the Master.

Routing Your Project with Buses

There are a number of possible uses for buses. In the next few minutes, we'll give you some practical ideas on how you can put buses to use in your projects right now.

> If you've used either Vegas Audio or Vegas Video from Sonic Foundry, the ACID buses will look very familiar to you. ACID takes the bus architecture introduced in the Vegas Video and Vegas Audio multi-track recording software and improves on it.

Assigning a Track to a Bus

Before you add any additional buses to an ACID project, remember that each Track Header contains the Track FX, Mute, and Solo buttons along with all the other controls you learned about in Hour 3, "Basic Mixing." As soon as you add a new bus to your project, a new button appears in each Track Header. This button—called the Bus Assignment button—allows you to route each track's audio signal to whichever bus you choose. By default, all tracks are routed to the Master; notice that the icon for the Bus

13

Assignment button matches the icon for the Master in the Mixer window. The icon makes it easy to quickly see where the track is routed.

To change the routing for the audio on a track (after adding one or more additional buses), click the Bus Assignment button in the Track Header and choose the desired bus from the drop-down list. The icon for the Bus Assignment button changes to match the bus you choose. For example, if you assign track 1 to Bus A, the Bus Assignment button for track 1 will be an A. You can route as many tracks as you want to any bus you choose.

Routing

When you clicked the Bus Assignment button in the previous section, you probably noticed that the choices in the drop-down list included more than just the bus names. ACID also includes information about where the bus you choose is currently routed. This information appears in parentheses and might include the words *Microsoft Sound Mapper* or the name of your sound card. Wherever that bus is currently routed appears in the list.

You can change the routing of any bus. You've already learned how to change the routing of the Master; rerouting a bus is just as simple as routing the Master. Each bus has a Device Selection button. By default, every new bus routes to the Master, so the icon for the Device Selection button matches the icon for the Master. To reroute a bus, click the bus's Device Selection button. The drop-down list shows all the audio devices available on your system. Click a device to route the bus to that device. Figure 13.6 shows how the icon for the Device Selection button changes when you select a device other than the Master.

FIGURE 13.6

The Device Selection icon reflects a change in bus routing.

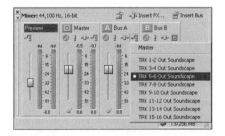

 Theoretically, if you had 28 stereo sound cards or a sound card with 54 outputs, you could route 28 ACID tracks each to its own separate output (making 54 mono tracks). This is like having an outboard mixing console with 54 buses. Have you priced one of those lately? The ACID bus system gives you lots of flexibility with which to approach the mix.

Mixing Scenarios

All the buses and the routing flexibility they provide open the doors wide for a number of interesting mixing scenarios. In the following sections, we'll give you a few ideas to get you started.

Creating Submixes

Use extra buses to create submixes that control the level of several tacks simultaneously. Suppose that you have five tracks of horn loops. Add an additional bus (Bus A) to your project and assign all the horn tracks to that one bus.

Click the Solo button on Bus A so that you hear only the tracks assigned to that bus (the horns "submix"). Start playback and create a nice mix of the horn tracks. Every now and then, unsolo Bus A to hear how the horn submix sounds with the overall mix. You can also add FX to the bus by clicking the Bus FX button. In this way, you can add the same FX to an entire submix. You can also use volume envelopes on the tracks you are routing to the bus to automate the bus mix.

Notice that ACID gives you the opportunity to add a track envelope to any of the buses you've added to your project. Make sure that you choose the volume envelope, and not the bus envelope, to accomplish the automation we talk about here. Later in this hour, we'll talk about another way to use the ACID buses, and then those bus envelopes will come into play. But in the case we describe here, the bus envelopes have no effect on the track.

13

After you have the horn submix just right, blend that submix in with the rest of the tracks. The beauty of creating this submix on a separate bus is that you can control the volume of the submixed tracks as a single unit with the Bus A fader. The bus makes it much easier to mix the horns as a whole section into the overall mix.

Task: Creating Your First Submix

In this task, you'll create a submix to control several drum tracks in your project.

1. Open `SubMixDemo.acd` from the Hour 13 Samples folder on the CD-ROM that accompanies this book. Zoom in horizontally on the project as far as you can and still see the entire project. Put ACID into Looped Playback mode and click the Play From Start button.

2. This 11-track project contains seven drum tracks. The project has not been mixed, and every track is at –6dB. Click the Insert Bus button to add a new bus.

3. Select the first seven tracks. Click the Bus Assignment button for any of the selected tracks and choose Bus A from the list. You've just created your first submix!

4. Click the Solo button on Bus A. You can now hear only the drum tracks. Create a nice mix of the individual drum tracks. If at any time you want to hear the other instruments, click the Solo button on Bus A to unsolo the bus. Keep working in this manner until you are happy with your drum mix.

5. Now mix your project as a whole: Unsolo the drum mix and mix the other tracks to taste using their individual volume and pan faders. If you decide the drums are too loud, click and drag the Bus A faders to adjust the volume of the drum mix while preserving the submix.

Using an External Mixer

Some people like to use an external mixer when creating a final mix. This is easy to accomplish with ACID as long as you have either multiple sound cards or a sound card with multiple outputs.

Submix the tracks as described in the preceding task. If you have enough outputs, route each submix and individual track to its own bus. Then route the buses to your various sound card outputs. Connect the outputs of the sound cards to the channel inputs on the mixing console. Start playback and use the mixer's faders to create the final mix.

Of course, in this scenario, you not only need a mixer, but also something to mix down to—a DAT, cassette, or reel-to-reel tape recorder. Another option is to route the outputs of the mixer back to the stereo inputs of your sound card and record the final mix back into ACID. We'll cover recording in Hour 15, "Recording and Creating Your Own Loops."

Using Outboard Effects

You can use all your outboard effects processors (such as reverbs, compressors, delays, and so forth) when working in ACID. The setup for doing so is similar to that for routing to an external mixer, as described in the previous section.

Route any tracks you want to treat with the outboard effect to an ACID bus. Then route the bus to a stereo pair of outputs on your sound card. Connect those outputs to the inputs of the outboard effects processor. Finally, connect the outputs of the effects processor to a stereo pair of inputs on the sound card (you may want to pass through a mixer first, but you don't have to). Now record the signal coming back into the sound card to a new ACID track (in Hour 15, we'll teach you how to set up recording in ACID).

When you add FX using outboard gear, there are a few ways you can approach mixing the *wet* and *dry* signal of the processor. We suggest that you set your wet/dry mix on the processor to 100% wet, 0% dry. This way, you'll record a 100% wet track into ACID. You can then mix that wet track with the dry original track for complete control over the wet/dry mix.

> **Wet and Dry**
>
> A signal is considered *dry* if it has no FX applied to it. After you apply an FX to a signal, it is considered a *wet* signal.

> Running a signal out of your computer, through outboard gear, and back into your computer can cause a problem known as "latency." Basically, latency means that the signal coming back to ACID might no longer be in sync with the original signal.
>
> Much depends on the FX you add with the outboard gear. For example, if you're running through a reverb unit, no one is going to notice a small amount of latency because of the delay and long decay nature of reverb. With other FX however, the latency might be noticeable.
>
> To solve the problem, zoom way into your project and compare the waveform of the dry track to that of the wet track. Hopefully, you'll be able to see in the waveforms where the tracks should line up. Move the event that holds the wet signal until it lines up properly with the dry waveform. If you can't do this visually, you may be able to do it by ear.

13

Accessing Buses Through the Multipurpose Fader

We've given you one way to route tracks to a specific bus. Now we'll talk about an alternative method for track routing. We'll warn you, this discussion can get confusing, and you might have to read through this a couple of times to understand all of it. It might help to keep in mind that the method we are about to talk about is completely independent of the method we just finished exploring. The good news is that when you master these concepts, you'll find out just how incredibly rich and flexible the ACID bus architecture really is.

You can use the multipurpose fader found in every Track Header as an alternative way to send a signal to a bus. With this method, you do not use the volume fader nor the Bus Assignment button we discussed earlier. To route a track using the multipurpose fader, first drop the volume for the track all the way down to –Inf. Click the multipurpose fader label for the track you are routing. From the drop-down list, choose the desired bus. Notice that the multipurpose faders for all tracks in your project change to the fader for the bus you choose. This allows you to quickly scan your Track Headers and see which tracks are routed to the chosen bus. Now set the fader for the target bus to the level you want (see Figure 13.7). Notice that only the fader you click and drag is adjusted (unless you have multiple tracks selected).

> When you set the multipurpose fader for a track to a specific bus and then raise the level of that bus fader, you route the track's signal directly to the bus. This has the same effect as setting the track's Bus Assignment button to the bus and raising the volume fader. The two methods are totally independent of one another. In fact, you'll see later that you can use both methods on one track at the same time to achieve different goals.

Adding a Track Envelope for a Bus

Earlier you noticed that when you have additional buses in your project, each bus shows up in the Insert/Remove Track Envelopes drop-down list. When you're using the multipurpose fader method we're describing here, you'll need to add a bus envelope if you want to automate the volume of the track signal you are sending to the bus. Remember that you've set the track's volume to –Inf. The signal from the track is now totally controlled by the bus fader. Therefore, to automate that signal, you must add a bus envelope.

FIGURE **13.7**

*Raise the Bus A fader
to send the signal from
the track to Bus A.*

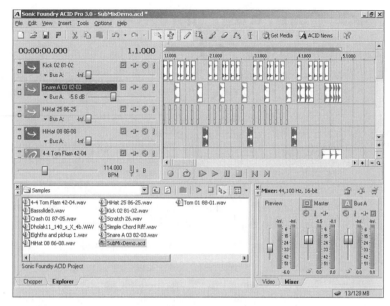

Pre-Fader and Post-Fader Routing

Although we prefer to use the Bus Assignment button for most instances of routing, the multipurpose fader brings a new dimension to the topic of routing. Using the multipurpose button method, you can set the fader feeding the bus to be either a pre-volume or post-volume fader. To do so, choose the bus from the multipurpose drop-down list. Right-click the fader and choose Pre Volume or Post Volume from the shortcut menu.

By default, bus faders are pre-volume faders. This means that they act independently from the track's volume fader. In other words, when you route track 1 to Bus A using the multipurpose fader method, you can turn the volume fader all the way down to –Inf and still route the signal to the bus using the multipurpose fader.

On the other hand, when the multipurpose fader routing Track 1 to Bus A is set to be a post-volume fader, it *is* affected by the setting of the volume fader. If you turn the volume fader all the way down, no signal will be routed to Bus A, no matter how high you've set the multipurpose fader for Bus A.

13

Task: Switching Between Pre-Volume and Post-Volume Faders

This task demonstrates how to set your bus faders to pre-volume or post-volume, and how the fader acts differently depending on the choice you make.

1. Open the `SubMixDemo.acd` project from the Hour 13 Samples folder on the CD-ROM that accompanies this book.

2. Zoom in as far as you can and still see all the events across the timeline. Change the volume of the drum tracks (tracks 1 through 7) to –Inf. (Reminder: When you have multiple tracks selected and make an adjustment to one of them, all the selected tracks react to the adjustment.) Click the Play button to hear that all the drums have been removed from the final mix.

3. Click the Insert Bus button in the Mixer to add a new bus.

4. Change the multipurpose fader label for any one of the drum tracks to Bus A. Notice that when you change the multipurpose fader label for one track, it changes for all of the tracks in your project.

5. Adjust the Bus A slider for the drum tracks to –6dB. Now all the drum tracks are routed to Bus A. Through Bus A they are routed (by default) to the Master, and you can now hear them in your final mix once again. This is true even though, in Step 2, you turned the volume fader all the way down. By default, these bus faders are in pre-volume fader mode so the volume fader has no affect on the bus signal.

6. Select all the drum tracks. Right-click the Bus A fader for any of the selected tracks and, from the shortcut menu, choose Post-Volume. This command changes the Bus A fader for all the selected tracks to post-volume fader; instantly, the drum submix falls out of the main mix. The reason is that in post-volume mode, the level being sent from the Bus A fader is affected by the Volume fader level of the track, which is currently set at –Inf.

7. Click the multipurpose fader button and choose Vol from the shortcut menu. This command sets all the multipurpose faders back to volume. Now raise the volume of the tracks and notice that, as you do, the Bus A meter shows that it is receiving signal. The volume fader now affects the signal sent to Bus A. Note that with this setup, when you raise the volume, you are sending the same signal from the track to the Master (with the volume settings) and to Bus A (with the Bus A settings.) Because Bus A is routed to the Master, you are, in effect, sending the same signal to the Master from two sources.

Multiple Buses: Putting It All Together

Here's a scenario in which you might make use of both of the bus-routing techniques in ACID as well as the pre/post capabilities of the multipurpose fader method.

Suppose that you've created a project in ACID and now want to set up a recording session with a vocalist friend to add vocals. We'll conveniently assume that you've already read Hour 16, "Adding Vocals," and have ACID set up to record the vocals.

You've already mixed your music, although you might want to tweak it here and there. Using the bus assignment method, you've got a great drum submix routed to Bus A, a horns submix routed to Bus B, and your strings mix (including the acoustic guitar) routed to Bus C. All these mixes are routed to the Master along with all the other tracks. Now suppose that you have a sound card with multiple outputs. You have the signal from the Master routed to outputs 1 and 2; this is the mix that you and the vocalist hear over the headphones.

Everything's set up perfectly, but what are you going to do if the only thing your vocalist wants to hear in her headphones is the acoustic guitar track? You spent a lot of time on the mix, and don't want to ruin it now only to have to re-create it later. The solution is to send the vocalist a custom mix while you listen to (and preserve) the main mix.

To do this, add another bus to your project (Bus D), and route this bus to outputs 3 and 4 of your sound card. Route outputs 3 and 4 to your vocalists' headphones. Because you've already used the bus assignment method to create your submixes, and because the guitar is routed to one of those submixes, use the multipurpose fader method to send an alternate mix to Bus D. In this case, you need only send the acoustic guitar track to Bus D. Now you can tweak the master mix all you want while she's singing, and it won't affect her a bit because she's listening to a completely separate mix.

Now, suppose that, in the bridge section of your song, everything quiets down. To accomplish this in the mix, you have a volume envelope on the acoustic guitar track that brings the volume down during the bridge and then back up for the following section. But because your vocalist is no longer listening to the main mix, she doesn't experience these dynamics in her headphones, and forgets to quiet down her singing.

You could add a track envelope for Bus D to the acoustic guitar track that matches the volume envelope. But an easier method is to click the multipurpose fader button on the acoustic guitar track and choose Bus D from the menu. Then right-click the fader and set it to Post-Volume. Now the level routed to Bus D from this track reacts to the changes in the volume of the track, and your singer knows when to hold back a little bit.

13

Now let's take this to the extreme. Suppose that you have a 20-member choir, and each choir member wants a separate headphone mix. A logistical nightmare to be sure (how many outputs does your sound card have, and how big is your bedroom studio?), but it's no problem for ACID! Just set up 20 additional buses and customize the mix for every fickle artist in the bunch! How's that for flexibility?

Assignable FX

Assignable FX allow you to build FX chains and then assign them to as many tracks in your project as you desire. You can create up to 32 Assignable FX, and each can have a chain of up to 32 FX. Assignable FX differ from Track FX in that they run *parallel* with the track rather than *inline*. Assignable FX make it easy to control the dry signal separate from the wet signal to achieve the prefect blend.

NEW TERM

Parallel and Inline FX

A parallel FX is delivered to the Master bus along its own path, separately from the dry signal coming from the original track. This approach allows you to have separate control over the wet and dry signals. The two signals are combined at the bus. An inline FX is combined with the dry signal at the track level and is then delivered to the bus. In this setup, volume changes you make to the dry signal affect the volume of the wet signal, too.

Changes to signal level being sent to an Assignable FX can be automated with track envelopes so that you can increase and decrease the FX over time.

Adding Assignable FX

To add an Assignable FX, click the Insert FX button in the Mixer. Alternatively, right-click anywhere in the Mixer window and choose Insert Assignable FX from the shortcut menu. A third way to start is to choose Insert, Assignable FX from the ACID menu bar. Each of these actions opens the Plug-In Chooser.

To access the Plug-In Chooser at any time, click the Assignable FX button at the top of the Assignable FX control.

Assignable FX Controls

The Assignable FX control is similar to Master and Bus controls, but Assignable FX have two sets of faders and meters. The faders and meters on the left control and indicate the audio level coming in to the FX chain; the faders and meters on the right control and indicate the level being sent to the selected device. Figure 13.8 shows the Mixer with two Assignable FX controls.

> An easy way to notice the difference between a bus and an Assignable FX is that buses are labeled with letters while Assignable FX are labeled with numbers.

FIGURE 13.8

Two Assignable FX have been added to the Mixer.

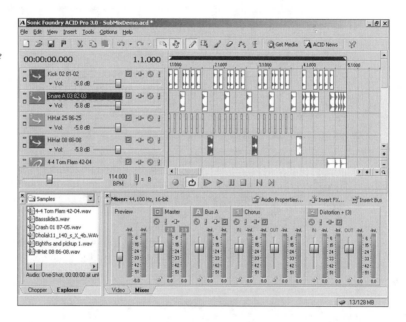

By default, Assignable FX are routed directly to the Master. Click the Bus Assignment button (which looks just like the Bus Assignment button in the Track Header) to change the routing to any of your additional buses. The button icon changes to reflect the routing you establish.

Routing

To route signal from any track to an Assignable FX, click the multipurpose fader label for the track and choose the appropriate Assignable FX from the drop-down list. Adjust the fader level until you are happy with the amount of FX. Do this for every track you want routed to the Assignable FX.

To control the wet/dry mix, we prefer to set every FX in the Assignable FX chain to 0% dry. Then we control the dry signal with the track's volume fader; we control the wet

13

signal with the track's Assignable FX fader. Another approach is to set the track volume to –Inf and create the wet/dry mix using the parameters of the individual FX in the chain. Then we can control the level of the wet/dry mix with the Assignable FX control's fader.

Keep in mind that, by default, Assignable FX are post-volume fader. One way we like to work is to set the Assignable FX fader to pre-volume while we adjust the wet/dry mix (reminder: right-click the fader). This way, the adjustments we make to the dry portion (using the volume fader) don't affect the level of the wet portion (the Assignable FX fader). When the mix is right, we change back to post-volume so that, if we decide we need less volume, we can change the volume slider without altering the wet/dry mix.

FX Envelopes

To automate Assignable FX with envelopes, assign a track to an Assignable FX. Then right-click the Track Header and choose Insert/Remove Envelope from the shortcut menu. All Assignable FX are listed as FX 1, FX 2, and so on. Choose the FX chain you want to automate, and an envelope appears down the length of the track.

We've shown you how to add a number of envelopes to your tracks throughout this book. Even though each envelope is a different color, it can be confusing to remember which is which. To make it easier keep them straight, choose View, Show Envelopes. In the cascading menu, click an envelope type to show or hide that type of envelope. This command does not remove the effects of the envelopes; it just hides them.

Task: Adding an Assignable FX

In this task, we'll add reverb to a track by routing that track's signal to an Assignable FX.

1. Open the SubMixDemo.acd project from the Hour 13 Samples folder on the CD-ROM that accompanies this book. Play the project in Looped Playback mode, paying special attention to the dry sound of the snare drum. Click the Insert FX button in the Mixer window to add an Assignable FX.

2. In the Plug-In Chooser, select the Sonic Foundry Reverb effect and click the Add button to add this FX to the project. Click OK to close the Plug-In Chooser.

3. In the Reverb dialog box, choose Untitled from the Preset drop-down list, choose Warm Space from the Reverberation Mode drop-down list, set the Dry Out field to –Inf, and set the Reverb Out field to –6dB as shown in Figure 13.9. Leave the other settings as they are and close the Audio Plug-In dialog box.

FIGURE **13.9**

FIGURE **13.9**

Add Sonic Foundry Reverb to the plug-in chain and adjust the parameters to match those shown here.

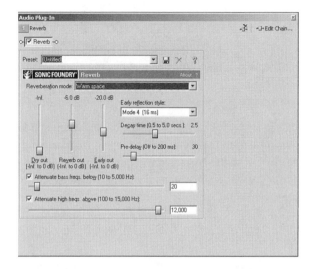

3. Click the multipurpose fader in track 2 (the snare drum track) and choose FX 1 from the drop-down list.

4 Increase the FX volume fader to –12dB to send signal from track 2 to the Assignable FX. Listen to the project. Again pay special attention to the sound of the snare drum, and notice that it now contains reverb.

5. With the project still playing, click the Mute button for Assignable FX 1. This action mutes the reverb. Click the button again to unmute the reverb. You can toggle back and forth between the two options to see how you like the sound.

6. Now add the reverb effect to any other track in your project by raising the FX 1 fader on the desired tracks. Notice how quickly and easily you can apply the same FX to multiple tracks with Assignable FX.

FX Strategies

13

You now know that you can add Track FX, Master FX, Bus FX, and Assignable FX to your project. You can even use a bus to route your signal to an outboard FX module. Having all these options for adding FX to your project gives you a lot of flexibility in how you make use of your DirectX FX. When trying to decide how to use them, think in terms of how pros use FX in a traditional mixing console.

Most mixing consoles have EQ on every channel. In ACID, every track has the EQ plug-in applied by default. Many mixing consoles also have a compressor on each channel. You could easily chain the Sonic Foundry Track Compressor to each Track FX.

If you are going to use the same reverb setting for all your horn tracks, and a slightly different reverb setting for your string tracks, add two buses and route the horns to one and the strings to the other. Add the Reverb FX to each bus, and then pick the setting you desire for each. Now you have a nice submix of the horns and stings, each with a unique reverb setting.

A good way to control track volume and FX volume separately is to set up Assignable FX. Now you can control the track volume with the volume fader, control the amount of each track's signal sent to the FX with the FX fader, and control how much of the FX is returned to the mix with the Assignable FX output fader. This arrangement is like using the FX sends and returns on an outboard mixing console. In ACID, it's like having 32 FX sends on your console.

Summary

In this hour, you learned about the different controls available in the Mixer. You learned about the various tools on each of the controls. You used multiple buses, and you discovered that you can interface ACID to external gear through these buses. You also created submixes and automated the mixing process with Bus and Assignable FX envelopes.

Take a few minutes to work through the questions and activities in the sections that follow.

Q&A

Q. Do I have to use all this fancy routing capability?

A. It's strictly up to you. You might find that you don't always need to add another bus to your projects. But just like anything else, if you take the time to learn the tools, all kinds of options open up to you.

Q. What are auxiliary ("aux") sends, and why doesn't ACID have any?

A. On a traditional outboard mixer, the aux sends allow you to send the signal from a track along a different path than the main output. This is how you would traditionally patch in a reverb unit on a mixer channel. The outboard mixer also has "aux returns" to bring that signal back into the mix. Although ACID doesn't have anything officially labeled "aux send" or "aux return," its buses serve the purpose nicely. A bus that sends signal to an outboard signal processor acts as an aux send. When you record the wet signal back to a new track, that new track acts as the aux return. Because you have 26 possible additional buses, you have 26 possible aux sends!

Q. Do I have to use FX in my projects?

A. Absolutely not! For thousands (if not millions) of years, the only FX that were used were ones that the singer could create with her voice, or the amount of leaves and mud the drummer stuffed into the hollow log. There are times when leaving out an "expected" FX makes a strong statement and is just the right "FX" in and of itself. Don't feel that you have to just because almost everyone else does. Individuality matters!

Workshop

This workshop tests your knowledge of the various controls found in the ACID Mixer.

Quiz

1. How do you add four buses to the Mixer window in a single step?

2. How do you reset the meters after the signal has been clipped?

3. If you route a signal to an external FX processor, how can you make use of the wet signal?

Quiz Answers

1. To add multiple buses to the Mixer window, click the Project Audio Properties button in the Mixer. Type the number of buses you want to add in the Number of Additional Stereo Buses text box and click OK.

2. Click the clipped peak indicator at the top of a meter to reset the meter after clipping has occurred.

3. After you have routed the signal from a bus to an external FX processor, connect the outputs of the processor to the inputs of the PC sound card and record the wet signal to a new track. Then blend the new track into the project.

Activities

1. Open an ACID project (use the file you used in the tasks in this hour, or any of your other projects) and add an additional bus to the Mixer window. Assign all the drum or percussion tracks in the project to the new bus. Use this submix to blend these tracks into the rest of the project. Add an Assignable FX control to the Mixer and create an FX chain containing reverb and delay FX. Assign two different tracks to this FX chain.

13

Hour 14

Uncovering Tips and Techniques

This hour presents a number of useful (and not-so-well-known) tips and techniques that can help you get the most out of ACID. The information is not in any specific order, but all these tips and techniques will come in handy.

In this hour, you will:

- Create a track offset
- Use the Split command to create a drum fill
- Create custom loops
- Work with stretch properties
- Save individual tracks
- Customize the track icons
- Use form, tension, and release in your project

Using Duplicate Tracks

The Duplicate Track and Event Offset features help you create several interesting effects. To duplicate a track, right-click the Track Header icon of the track you want to duplicate and choose Duplicate Track from the shortcut menu. The Duplicate Track command creates an exact copy of the selected track or tracks.

Replacing a File

Sometimes it can be helpful to make a duplicate of a track and then replace the media file that the new track uses. Maybe you want to add a subkick to strengthen the bottom end of an existing kick drum track. Rather than redrawing all the events, mix settings, and envelopes in a new track that uses the subkick file, duplicate the original kick drum track and replace the file in the new track with the subkick one-shot. To replace the file on a track, right-click the track icon and choose Properties from the shortcut menu. Click the Replace button at the top of the Track Properties dialog box (see Figure 14.1), browse to the file you want to use as a replacement, and click Open.

FIGURE 14.1

Click the Replace button in the Track Properties dialog box to replace the media file in a track with a new file.

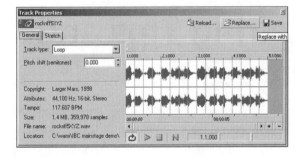

The technique described here of using the Track Properties dialog box to swap files in a track works just fine. But power users accomplish the task another way. Click and drag the new file from the ACID Explorer window directly onto the Scribble strip (the track name) of the track that holds the file you want to replace. When you release the mouse, the swap is instantly complete. This is a fairly hidden trick because ACID provides no visual indication that you are about to replace the file. You just have to know where to drop the new one. Now you know!

Task: Replacing the File in a Duplicate Track

This task shows one useful reason to duplicate tracks and replace media files.

1. Open and play `TrackReplaceDemo.acd` from the Hour 14 Samples folder located on the CD-ROM that accompanies this book.

2. Right-click the track 1 icon and choose Duplicate Track from the shortcut menu.

3. Drag `Kick 02 81-02.wav` from the Explorer window and drop it on the Scribble strip of the new track 2 (the duplicate of track 1). This action replaces the file. You now have two kick drum tracks with different kick drum sounds but identical patterns.

4. Duplicate the Snare track. Click the copy of the snare track to make sure that it is the only track selected, and duplicate *that* track. You now have three snare tracks.

5. Replace the files in the two new snare tracks—one with `HiHat 01 86-01.wav` and the other with `Rim Shot 04 85-04.wav`.

6. Play the project and listen to the difference the doubled and tripled tracks make.

Changing the Offset of an Event

Another technique is to duplicate a track and then slightly offset (change the start time of the loop for) the duplicate track. Smaller offsets create chorus and phasing effects; larger offsets produce slap-back and echo effects.

Task: Creating Effects

Follow these steps to create phase and slap-back effects.

1. Add eight bars of `070gs102.wav` (located in the Hour 14 Samples folder on the CD-ROM that accompanies this book) to a new project.

2. Right-click the Track Header for the track and choose Duplicate Track from the shortcut menu.

3. Press the Tab key on your keyboard to switch focus from the Track Header area to the timeline (that's another tip!). Press the up arrow on your keyboard about a half-dozen times so that you are really zoomed in to the project.

4. Point to the middle of the event in track 2. Hold down the Alt key and notice that the mouse pointer changes to a double arrow inside a rectangle. As you learned in Hour 10, "Scoring to a Video," this icon indicates that you are in Slip mode. Click and drag the waveform to the right (barely nudge it; with this effect, a little goes a long way!)

14

5. Click the Play From Start button. The drum track now sounds as if it is routing through a phaser or flanger.

> Use the technique in this task to accomplish a flange sound. Increasing the difference between the two events creates a slap-back effect, where the second track echoes the first. Of course, if you go too far, your project might sound like noise!

6. Right-click the event in track 2 and choose Properties from the shortcut menu to open the Event Properties dialog box shown in Figure 14.2. The number in the Start Offset (Samples) field represents the number of samples by which you have offset (changed the start point of) the file.

FIGURE 14.2

The Event Properties dialog box.

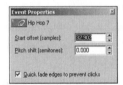

7. Play your project in Loop Playback mode. As the project plays, slip the file further left (or right), using the Alt+drag combination described in step 4. As you slip the file inside the event, notice that the number in the Start Offset (Samples) field in the Event Properties dialog box changes.

8. Double-click the Start Offset (Samples) field to select the current value. Type 750 to set a new offset and press the Tab key.

9. Click in the timeline to give it focus, and press the down arrow as many times as it takes to see the whole project. Add eight bars of `Guitar 34-10.wav` (also located in the Hour 14 Samples folder on the CD-ROM that accompanies this book).

10. Duplicate the guitar track and offset the second track by 3500 samples. Make sure that you open the Event Properties dialog box for the correct track!

11. Pan the first guitar track hard left; pan the second guitar track hard right.

12. Click the Play From Start button if you're not already playing the project. You've created a slap-back echo effect. Experiment with different offsets to increase or decrease the amount of delay.

All the files used in this example are found in the *ACID DJ* loop collection from Sonic Foundry.

Using the Split Command to Create a Drum Fill

Sometimes you need a drum fill, but can't find a loop that does the job. In Hour 11, "Editing with the Chopper," you learned how to solve this problem using the Chopper. Another approach is to use the Split command, along with the Start Offset feature you just explored, to create a drum fill from the existing track. Simply split an event into smaller usable chunks and then change the offset of the various "chunks" to create a completely new rhythm.

Task: Creating a Drum Fill

This task shows you how to use the Split and Event Offset commands to create a drum fill.

1. Add eight bars of `Aranoff 1.wav` (located in the Hour 14 Samples folder on the CD-ROM that accompanies this book) to a new project.

2. Place the cursor at bar 5 and press the S key to split the event. Split the event again at bar 6. You now have a separate event at bar 5 that spans one measure. Click this event to select it.

3. Zoom in on bar 5 until you see 16th note hash marks on the beat ruler (see Figure 14.3).

FIGURE 14.3

Zoom in until you see four hash marks (each representing a 16th note) between each quarter note on the Beat ruler.

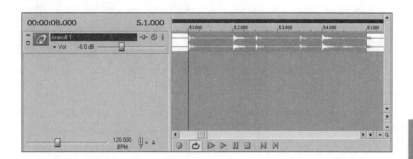

4. Change the Start Offset of the event to 28746. Notice that the second bass drum note (the note that originally occurred on the sixth 16th note hash mark, or the "and" of two (as in counting the beat, "one-and, two-and, three-and, four-and") now occurs at the beginning of the measure.

14

5. Double-click the Measure and Beat at Cursor display (right above the Track Header area). Type **5.2.384** in the Measure and Beat at Cursor field and press the Tab key. This action moves the cursor in the timeline to that exact spot in your project (another tip!) Split the event. Place the cursor at position 5.3.000 and split the event again. These two splits create a small event. Delete that event.

6. Select the second event in bar 5 (which starts at position 5.3.000.) Open the Properties dialog box for that event and change the offset to 57796.

7. Split the event again at position 5.3.384, and again at position 5.4.000. Delete the event between the two splits you just created.

> To quickly highlight the value in the Measure and Beat at Cursor field, type Ctrl+G. To highlight the value in the Time at Cursor field, press Shift+G.

8. Set the offset of the event that starts at position 5.4.000 to 126416 to move the kick to the very beginning of the event. Create two more splits at positions 5.4.192 and 5.4.384. Delete the new event between these two splits.

9. Copy the event at position 5.4.000 and paste it at position 5.4.192.

10. Zoom back out so that you can see the whole project again (see Figure 14.4). Play your new drum fill to hear what you've created. Save your project—you'll work with it more in the next task.

FIGURE 14.4

Your drum track should look like this after you've completed the edits in this task.

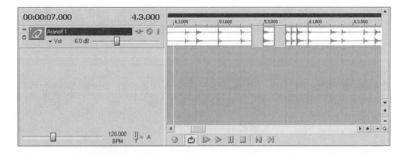

Using the Measure.Beat.Tick numbers to locate to all these edit points is probably not how you are typically going to do this. The Alt+drag operation we talked about earlier is the preferred method for slipping the file in the event until you have the offset you want because it is faster. But giving you the exact edit point in these steps guaranteed that we'd all end up in the same place. Besides, it's nice to know that you can jump to an exact spot in your project with the techniques you learned here.

Although this task uses exact locations to create the drum fill, try placing events in a more "human" fashion: Put the events where they look like they should go. This approach introduces slight timing errors. In other words, instead of placing a snare hit exactly at position 5.4.192, we might be off by just a hair. Much like a real drummer would be off every now and then. That can make your music sound less robotic and more natural.

Masking Drum Fills

Now that you know how to split and offset events, and can navigate to precise locations on the timeline, you can create hundreds of different rhythms and fills. However, sometimes when you split an event, it might be obvious to the listener, so you may have to add another track—perhaps some percussion—to mask the splits.

Task: Masking a Drum Fill

In this task, you'll use cymbals to mask the splits in the fill you created in the previous task.

1. Add Crash 55-03.wav to the project you started in the preceding task and draw in an event at position 5.1.000. Make two duplicates of the track. Move the event in track 3 to position 5.2.000; move the event in track 4 to position 5.3.000.

2. Select the event in track 3 and adjust the pitch one half step down. (Hint: Press the – key on the number pad.) This pitch-shift makes it sound like a slightly different cymbal.

3. Select both track 2 and track 4. Change the panning of tracks 2 and 4 to hard left (100% L); pan track 3 hard right (100% R). Adjust the volume for all three cymbal tracks to approximately –9.0dB. (Hint: Select all three tracks and use the volume slider for one to control all of them.)

4. Click the Play From Start button and check out your new drum fill.

 Notice that when you select more than one track, any adjustment you make to any one of the selected tracks is applied to the other selected tracks. This is another of our favorite shortcuts.

14

When you move a slider, it's often difficult to choose an exact setting because small slider movements translate to large value changes. To solve this problem, get close to the value with the mouse and then use the arrow keys to "nudge" the slider closer to the value you want. Alternatively, get close with the mouse, then, while still holding down the left mouse button, hold down the right mouse button (or press the Ctrl key). Now the slider moves in small increments, allowing you to make finer adjustments to the slider control.

More Fun with Offsets

Another fun way to use offsets is to spice up percussion tracks. Changing the offset of a percussion track can sometimes really alter the flavor and rhythm of the loop. Set the offset so that the loop starts somewhere other than the downbeat. Having the loop start on what used to be beat three or beat two and a half changes how the rhythm sounds against the rest of the tracks. The fastest way to accomplish this trick is to use the Alt+drag method to slip the file within the event. Slip it, listen to the results, then adjust to taste.

Task: Changing Percussion Track Rhythms Using Offsets

In this task, you'll use event offsets to create interesting new rhythms from an existing drum loop.

1. Add 16 bars each of Beat 005.wav, Percussion 01.wav, and Percussion 02.wav to a new project. All three of these loops can be found in the Hour 14 Samples folder on the CD-ROM that accompanies this book. Click the Play From Start button to hear what these loops sound like together.

2. Mute the Percussion 02 track, which contains the conga part. Click the Play From Start button and listen to how the Percussion 01 track works with the Beat 005 track.

3. Change the offset of the event in the Percussion 01 track to 10485. As shown in Figure 14.5, because of the offset, what used to be the second 8th note of the phrase is now the downbeat.

4. Play the project and notice the subtle difference in the Percussion 01 track.

FIGURE 14.5

The offset has changed the event so that now the second eighth note is actually the down-beat.

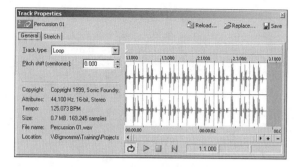

> You may have to change between the offset defined in step 3 to an offset of zero a few times before you recognize the difference. A fast way to do this is to use the Undo and Redo buttons to get a quick "before and after" sampling.

5. Unmute the `Percussion 02` track and click the Play From Start button. Listen to how this track fits with the project.

6. Open the Properties dialog box for the `Percussion 02` event and change the value in the Start Offset (Samples) field to 42322. Now, what used to be the second half of the second beat becomes the downbeat.

7. Click the Play From Start button and listen to the difference that changing the offset for these two percussion tracks has made.

8. Use the Alt+Drag method you learned for slipping the media file within an event to try some different offsets and notice how the accents move around the beat to create interesting results.

> By the way, all the loops used in this example are found in the *ACID Hip Hop* library from Sonic Foundry. This library is filled with great hip-hop sounds.

Using Markers as a Rhythm-Mapping Tool

Sometimes you want a specific melody line but you can't find a loop that plays exactly what you need. Of course, you could record your own (we show you how in Hour 15, "Recording and Creating Your Own Loops"), but what if you need a sax line and you don't play sax? Use markers, along with the split and pitch-change functions you have already learned about, to solve this problem.

14

Use markers to "map out" the rhythm of the desired sax part. To do this, play the project; when you reach the place where you want the new rhythm/melody to be created, tap the rhythm you want on the M key of your keyboard. This action places a marker each time you tap the M key. The markers now mark the spots where you'll place new events.

Then use the Split command to create a single-note event from the sax loop. Use copy and paste techniques to place a copy of the event at each of the markers. Now pitch-shift each of the events to create the desired melody.

Another way to isolate a single note and add it to your project is to use the Chopper. Hour 11, "Editing with the Chopper," gives an example of how to accomplish this same basic principal using the Chopper.

Task: Creating a New Sax Part

In this task, you'll take a sax line and change the pitch of a single note to create an alternative melody. Then you'll create a brand-new melody out of a small piece of a loop.

1. Add eight bars each of Hip Hop 7.wav and Albert 1.wav to a new project. Add six bars of Sax Section 4.wav starting at the very beginning of the project.

2. Click the Play From Start button and notice that the sax part plays the same thing three times, just as you would expect.

3. Place your cursor in the middle of the second sax phrase. Zoom in far enough so that you can distinguish the individual notes in the sax waveform. Place your cursor just in front of the last note in the second phrase of the sax loop. This is just before beat 3 in measure 4 (position 4.2.672) as shown in Figure 14.6.

FIGURE 14.6

Place your cursor just before the last note of the second loop of the sax event.

Use the left-arrow and right-arrow keys to move the cursor in very small increments. It often helps to solo a track when you're trying to find an exact cursor placement.

If you zoom very far into your project, you might see a very short fade out of or fade in to the events in your project. These fades are so short that you can't actually hear them, so why are they there at all? Without getting too technical, you might often hear an audible click in your audio at the beginning and end of events that are edge trimmed so that they don't hold the entire media file. ACID adds the small fades to mask such clicks out so that you don't have to worry about them. You can adjust the length of these fades (or prevent ACID from adding them altogether). To do so, choose Options, Preferences to open the Preferences dialog box and click the Audio tab. To disable the fades, disable the check box for Quick Fade Edges of Audio Events. To change the length of the fades, enter a new value in the Quick Fade Time (ms) field.

4. Press the S key to split the event. Split it again at bar 5 (position 5.1.000).

5. Select the new event between the two splits and lower the pitch two half steps.

6. Click the Play From Start button and notice the subtle difference made by changing one note.

7. Place the cursor on the downbeat of measure 8 (position 8.1.000) and press the M key to place a beat marker there. Zoom in so that the ruler marks show 16th notes (four ruler marks per beat.) Place additional markers at positions 8.1.384, 8.2.000, 8.2.384, and 8.2.576. These markers plot the rhythm locations for placing the events.

An alternative method for placing markers is to count along with the song and tap in the rhythm by pressing the M key in time to the music. This is a real easy way to mark a rhythm, and is the way we *always* do it in practice!

8. Select the sax event, place the cursor just in front of the last note in the last sax phrase (position 6.2.672), and split the event. Select the event containing just the last note, and copy that event to the Windows Clipboard.

9. Choose Options, Snapping, Enable to make sure that the Snapping option is enabled. Choose Options, Grid Spacing, 16th Notes.

10. Hold down the Ctrl key and press the right-arrow key to move the cursor to the next marker (Marker 1). Paste the event on the Clipboard there. Press the number 2 key at the top of your keyboard to move the cursor to Marker 2. Paste another event there. In the same way, paste a copy of the sax note at each remaining marker.

14

In step 10, you use two ways to navigate quickly to a marker in your project. Ctrl+left-arrow and Ctrl+right-arrow takes you to the previous/next marker. Type the number of a marker to jump directly to it. Remember that the number pad does not work for jumping to a marker. You must use the numbers at the top of the standard keyboard.

11. Zoom in if necessary so that you can work with each of the copied events. Click the second event and raise the pitch up from A to C#. Change the pitch of the third event to D, change the pitch of the fourth event to C#, and change the pitch of the fifth event to D. Your project should look like the one in Figure 14.7.

12. Click the Play From Start button and listen to the new sax part you have created.

FIGURE 14.7

The finished project contains several one-note events that have been pitch shifted to create a melody.

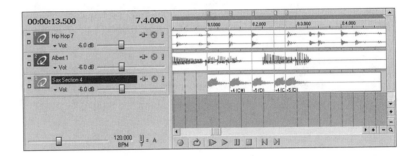

Creating Custom Loops

Sometimes the exact loop you're looking for just can't be found. At times like this, create a new loop using one-shots. For instance, create one or two bars using several tracks, including bass drum, snare, hi-hat, toms, and percussion. Then save that project as a .wav file for use as a loop in another project.

Load the file CustomeLoopDemo.acd to take a look at an example of this process. This is a great way to "build" a loop. Start by auditioning one-shots. Find the sounds you like, place them in a project, and create the rhythm you want. If you're creating a melody loop, use the pitch-shift techniques you have learned to build the melody, as well. Keep the project short—one phrase, one or two bars long. Remember, the idea is to take a small amount of material and loop it to make a longer piece of music.

Now that you have all the events and tracks set up, work on the mix. Add effects, adjust track and event volumes, and set up the panning. Get it sounding exactly the way you want the loop to sound. Create a loop region over the phrase you just created. Choose

File, Render As and enable the Render Loop Region Only option. Choose the `.wav`, `.aif`, `.pca`, or `.mp3` file type from the Save As Type drop-down list.

Now you can add the newly rendered file to your ACID project. As you paint it into the track, notice that your customized loop works just like a loop from one of the loop libraries.

Changing Properties Settings

Change the settings in the Properties dialog box for a loop-based track to create interesting effects. For instance, double-click a Track Header to open the Track Properties dialog box (another shortcut!), and click the Stretch tab. Now change the value in the Number of Beats field to adjust the speed at which the loop plays back. Change the number to half its normal value to make the loop play back twice as fast. Double the number to play the loop back at half speed.

Another trick is to set a loop that normally does not transpose to a specific root note so that it changes keys with the project. Change the root note for transposing in the Root Note field of the Stretch tab in the Track Properties dialog box as shown in Figure 14.8. This effect can be interesting when used on percussion tracks such as ethnic drums.

FIGURE 14.8

Choose a root note for transposing the loop.

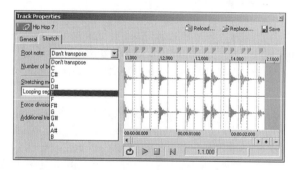

Exporting Individual Tracks and Loops

There are times when, instead of saving the entire project as a `.wav` file, you might want to save each of the tracks—including all the effects, envelopes, and offsets you have made—as individual files. You could then use these files in another application, for instance, in a multitrack recording application such as Vegas Audio from Sonic Foundry or Pro Tools from Digidesign. Or perhaps you want to save a loop at a different tempo. ACID provides several methods for saving tracks as individual files.

14

Saving All Tracks in One Operation

Make sure that all the tracks you want as separate files are unmuted and choose File, Render As. Enable the Save Each Track as a Separate File check box at the bottom of the Render As dialog box (see Figure 14.9). Then select a file format and click Save. ACID saves each unmuted track as a separate file, complete with key changes, tempo changes, pitch shifts, effects, volume envelopes, and panning.

FIGURE 14.9

Enable the Save Each Track as a Separate File check box to make individual files out of each track in your project.

ACID uses the following naming convention to automatically name each individual file: "Track," followed by the track number, followed by the original filename. For example, the first track of the original file named bass loop.wav would be named Track 01 bass loop.wav.

If you want to render only a portion of the project, create a loop region over that portion and enable the Render Loop Region Only check box in the Render As dialog box. Mute any track you don't want to render. Because ACID saves the files exactly as they are mixed in the project, make sure that you're happy with the mix before you render the tracks out as separate files. If the track is causing a clipping problem, the rendered file will also cause a clipping problem.

Exporting Loops

You also can export the loops from your project at their time-stretched or key-changed states. To do so, select File, Export Loops. Rather than saving the entire track, the Export operation saves only the loop, but at the project tempo and key. ACID creates a new loop for each track. This technique also works for all unmuted tracks, and names the tracks using the original filename appended by the project tempo and key. For example, the original track named bass loop.wav that has been pitch-shifted to the key of A and assigned a new tempo of 120bmp would be named bass loop 120.00 BPM A.wav.

If you have a project with multiple key or tempo changes, the File, Export Loops function creates multiple files (loops) for each track; you'll end up with one file for each key and tempo change in the track. This approach is great for building a family of loops to use with animations you create using Macromedia Flash. For those Flash users out there who are getting excited about the possibilities for using ACID to make great music for your animations, Hour 20, "Creating Music for Flash Movies," is completely devoted to showing you how to make high-quality, royalty-free music for your Flash animations.

Adding the Contents of a Long File

When you add a large file to a new track in ACID, it can be annoying to paint in the entire file using the normal click-and-drag method. There's an easier way. Add the file to your project and then open the Chopper window. Double-click the waveform in the Chopper window to select the entire file and click the Insert button. Job done.

Want an even faster method? Create the new track. Click the Paint tool, hold down the Ctrl key, and click in the track. Presto! This shortcut works for all track types.

Customizing Track Icons

This trick will keep your buddies guessing for a long time. Most people don't know that .wav files can contain an embedded bitmap image. When you add a .wav file containing an embedded bitmap image to your ACID project, ACID displays the image as a 32-by-32 pixel icon on the Track Header (the image replaces the normal track icon). Sonic Foundry Sound Forge XP Studio, included with ACID Pro (and the subject of Hours 21, "Introducing Sound Forge XP Studio," and 22, "Improving and Editing Recordings"), allows you to embed bitmaps in .wav files.

Open the file in Sound Forge XP Studio. Choose File, Properties and click the Summary tab. Click the Picture button and browse to and select a .bmp image file. Click OK to dismiss the Properties dialog box, then save the file as a .wav file. This process embeds the image in the .wav file. Open the file in an ACID project, and the bitmap displays as the track icon. (We won't tell your friends if you don't!)

Making a Great Composition

What makes a good composition a great composition? If you ask ten different people, you get ten different answers. But you can follow certain guidelines—specifically, those in the following sections.

14

Tension and Release

Tension and release is a common theme that relates to complexity verses simplicity. Because ACID allows you to have unlimited tracks, you can create very dense and complex sections. Surround these complex sections with simpler sections to create tension and release.

You can also use the key-changing ability of ACID throughout the composition to build tension and release. Try moving up by whole steps, with the key changes growing closer and closer together, then return to the original key.

Varying the tempo is another approach for creating tension and release. Set several tempo changes in small increments close together (every 64th note, if you want to work that hard) to create *accelerando* and *ritard*.

Volume changes also create tension and release. Both ACID Pro and ACID Music allow you to control the volume of your tracks over time with volume envelopes. Increase the volume going into more complex sections or as you build through key changes. Bring the volume back down as you move into simpler sections.

Combining tempo, key, and volume changes, along with varying the degrees of complexity in your project aid you in your quest to build tension and release into your compositions.

Form

Form is another common theme. Whether or not you notice it, most music has form. In some cases, this is very obvious, while in other cases, the use of form is very subtle. A "popular song" might take this form: Intro, verse, chorus, verse, bridge, chorus, close. Another composition might take the form of ABACADA, where each letter represents a section. Sometimes, one section repeats throughout the composition to provide continuity, while other sections provide contrast.

Most people would say that a phrase or section is more musical if it is built with 4, 8, or 16 bars. This is a guideline, not a law. When you think of the form your composition should take, try to build the form with musical phrases in mind.

Know the Rules, Break the Rules

Now that you know these musical guidelines, we encourage you to step beyond them whenever it serves your musical purpose. Still, remember that the use of tension and release along with musical form have, over the years, proven to be excellent tools in the quest to turn a good composition into a great composition. A wise man once said, "It's been working for over 500 years; I'm thinkin' it'll work for one more song!"

Summary

In this hour, you learned several advanced techniques that will help you become an ACID power user and that will take your ACID compositions to a new level. You learned different ways to create track offsets, and you explored creative uses for track markers. Get familiar with the snapping and grid settings to make your work with ACID more efficient.

You learned how to use markers as guides when creating rhythms and new loops. You explored various aspects of the Track Properties and Event Properties dialog boxes, and you learned how to use these settings to perfect your loops and create special effects. The tips for making the most of your ACID compositions should help you achieve your musical goals.

Q&A

Q. If I cut my drum loop up to create a new rhythm or drum fill like we did in this hour, are you sure that no one will be able to tell there is an edit there?

A. There's an old carpenter's saying: "The measure of a good carpenter is not the number of mistakes he/she makes, but how well he/she covers 'em up." The saying applies here. When you create the drum fill you want, the edits are often obvious. But if you cover them up with tasteful additions to the project (such as cymbals), who's gonna know?

Q. If I export my tracks as .wav files and then bring those files into my multi-track recording software, will the stretching properties cause any problems?

A. No. The information that is added by adjusting the stretch properties only has an effect on how the file behaves in ACID.

Workshop

See how you do on the following quiz questions. Then experiment with your new knowledge in the activities.

Quiz

1. How do you use the mouse to create an offset?
2. How do you place a beat marker in ACID?
3. How do you set a loop so that it does not change keys along with the project?

14

Quiz Answers

1. Hold down the Alt key and click and drag the waveform to change the event offset.

2. To place a beat marker, click at the location where you want the marker and press M on the keyboard.

3. To set a loop so that it does not change keys along with a project key change, double-click the track icon for the track that holds the loop. This action opens the Properties dialog box for that track. Click the Stretch tab and choose Don't Transpose from the Root Note drop-down list.

Activities

1. There are way too many helpful tips and techniques for us to list them all in this short hour. Sonic Foundry has compiled a number of wonderful suggestions for you to look at any time. Make sure that your Internet connection is active and click the ACID News button on the ACID toolbar. Take a few minutes to snoop around the site. See what's new and pick up some valuable tips, tricks, and techniques.

Part V
Recording

Hour

Hour 15

Recording and Creating Your Own Loops

Up until now, you have been using prerecorded, edited, and ACIDized files to build music. Now it's time to create your own loops using the ACID record function.

In this hour, you will:

- Prepare your hardware and software for recording
- Set the proper recording level
- Record a loop
- Edit your loop
- ACIDize your loop

Configuring Your Equipment

You can record from almost any source—such as a keyboard, guitar, or microphone—that is connected to your mixer or plugged directly into the computer sound card. But first, you must configure your recording equipment.

Connecting Directly to the Sound Card

Two types of audio inputs exist on your computer sound card. The line input (line-in) connections on your computer accept *line-level devices;* the microphone inputs (mic-in) support *mic-level devices.* You can use either the line-in or mic-in inputs for recording, but you have to know when to use each.

NEW TERM

Line-Level Devices and Mic-Level Devices

Line-level devices (such as a CD player, electronic keyboard, or the output of a mixing console) produce stronger signals than mic-level devices (microphones). If you plug a line-level device into the mic-in input, the signal may distort. If you plug a microphone into the line-in, the signal may be too weak to be adequately recorded by the computer.

For the easiest recording setup, plug directly into the computer sound card. For instance, plug the line outputs of your electronic keyboard into the line inputs of the computer sound card.

Most keyboards have two mono quarter-inch outputs—one for the left channel, and one for the right. If your sound card also has quarter-inch inputs, simply run a cord with quarter-inch connectors on both ends from each of your keyboard outputs to two of your sound card inputs. However, some sound cards have a single stereo mini-plug. If this is the case with your sound card, run cords with quarter-inch connectors on both ends from the outputs of your keyboard to an adapter that converts two mono quarter-inch connections to a single stereo mini-plug. Any electronics supply store and many computer equipment stores will be able to help you find the adapter you need.

When using a microphone, plug the microphone into the mic-in input of the sound card. Most quality microphones use XLR connectors (also known as cannon connectors). You may have to use an adapter or run the signal through a mixer first. We'll talk about recording through an outboard mixer in a few minutes.

Some microphones require electric current from an outside source. Sometimes this current is supplied by a battery in the microphone itself. Other times, the microphone relies on the mixing console to supply the current (known as phantom power). Most computer sound cards don't supply phantom power. Check to see whether your microphone requires phantom power before you proceed. If it does, make sure that you have the proper source of phantom power.

Recording Through a Mixer

Use a mixing console (mixer) for the most flexibility and control over the recording process. Connect the line outputs of the keyboard to the line inputs of the mixer. Watch the mixer's volume meters, and set the mixer levels properly. Route the main outputs of the mixer to your amplifier and speakers so that you can monitor your work. Route the auxiliary sends/outputs (aux sends) for the connection to your computer sound card. This arrangement allows you to use the aux send controls to adjust the signal level sent to ACID independent of the main mix to which you are listening.

What a manufacturer considers "proper levels" varies from mixer to mixer. Consult your mixer's documentation to determine the proper level settings for your gear.

To record with a microphone, use the same setup just described, but plug the microphone into the mixer channel's mic input rather than its line input. Even though you plug into the mic-in of your mixer when recording with a microphone, remember that the mixer always outputs a line-level signal. Always connect the output of the mixer to the line-in on your sound card—even if you're recording with a microphone!

Preparing ACID for Recording

This section shows you how to prepare ACID for the recording process.

Some sound cards use their own software to control playback and record functions on your computer. Because there is no way for us to cover all the possibilities, this discussion focuses only on the simplest case: where the sound card does not have its own software, and you must use the Windows Recording Control to adjust input levels to the card. If your sound card uses dedicated software, consult the sound card's user manual to learn how to configure the sound card for recording.

The Windows Recording Control you determines the signal level sent to ACID during recording. Choose Start, Programs, Accessories, Entertainment, Volume Control to open the Windows Volume Control.

Choose Options, Properties in the Windows Volume Control to open the Properties dialog box (see Figure 15.1). In the Properties dialog box, choose your sound card from the Mixer Device drop-down list. (Select the desired sound card if you have more than one sound card, or the desired input if you have a sound card with multiple inputs.) Click the Recording button in the Adjust Volume For section.

FIGURE 15.1

Select the Recording radio button in the Properties dialog box of the Windows Volume Control.

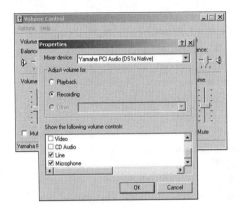

Now select both Line and Microphone from the Show the Following Volume Controls scrolling list. Make sure that you deselect all the other options so that their controls don't take up valuable space on your screen. Click OK. The Recording Control opens with faders for both Line and Microphone. Leave the Recording Control open as you move on to the next section because you'll use this window in conjunction with ACID to record your material.

Setting Recording and Monitoring Levels

It is important to establish the proper recording levels so that you get the best possible results. A signal that is too low may introduce a high signal-to-noise ratio, which is the amount of noise in your recording compared to the amount of desired signal. A signal that is too hot can introduce clipping. Clipping is just as undesirable at the input (recording) stage as it is at the output (playback) stage.

To set your recording and monitoring levels, click the Record button in the ACID Transport bar. The Record dialog box opens as shown in Figure 15.2. We'll go over the details of the Record dialog box in a few minutes. For now, let's establish a good recording level.

FIGURE 15.2

The Record dialog box allows you to customize the recording process.

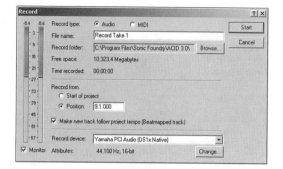

15

Let's assume that you're recording an audio source (your microphone, keyboard, and so on). Click the Audio option at the top of the dialog box (we talked about recording a MIDI track back in Hour 8, "Working with MIDI Tracks"). Enable the Monitor check box (in the bottom-left corner of the dialog box) to activate the record level meters. This feature allows you to monitor your record levels before (and during) the recording process.

Choose your sound card from the Record Device drop-down list. Alternatively, you can choose Microsoft Sound Mapper to let ACID choose the device for you. If you have multiple sound cards, or multiple inputs on your sound card, choose the same device here as you chose in the Windows Recording Control earlier.

Position the Windows Recording Control window and the ACID Record dialog box on the screen so that you can see both simultaneously, as shown in Figure 15.3. You have to be able to see the meters in the ACID Record dialog box while you adjust the level using the fader in the Windows Recording Control. In the Windows Recording Control, enable the check box under the fader for the input type you are using. For instance, if you're recording a vocal through a microphone, enable the check box under the Microphone fader to activate it.

Finally, to set the proper record level, play the keyboard or play/sing/speak into the microphone and adjust the level with the appropriate fader (the Microphone or Line fader) in the Windows Recording Control while monitoring the meters in the ACID Record dialog box.

Shoot for an average level of –6dB on the ACID record meters. Do not let the levels reach or exceed 0dB on the meters because this may cause clipping and distortion.

FIGURE 15.3

Make sure that you can see both the ACID Record dialog box and the Windows Recording Control.

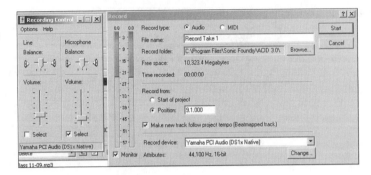

Using the Record Dialog Box

In the ACID Record dialog box, you must make a number of decisions before you begin recording. This section discusses the options available to you.

First you must enter a filename. ACID gives the file you record a default name (Record Take *n* where *n* is a number) unless you enter a custom name into the File Name field. To enter a custom name, highlight the default name and type a more descriptive name in its place. When you finish recording, this name shows up in the Track Header for the track that ACID creates to hold your recorded file.

Then you must select a folder in which to store the file you're recording. By default, ACID picks the drive and folder in which the ACID program is installed to store the files you record. The location is listed in the Record Folder field. To specify a different record location, click the Browse button and navigate to the desired drive and folder.

Then you must set recording options. The Record From option lets you start recording at any point in the project. ACID normally begins recording at the current location of your timeline cursor. To record from the start of your project—regardless of the current cursor position—select Start of Project. If you want to start at another point, select the Position radio button and type the measure and beat at which you want to start recording.

> If you start recording at a point other than the beginning of your project, set the start position at least one bar earlier than your actual desired starting point. This gives you a few beats to get ready. The pros know this as "pre-roll."

If you have set tempo changes in your ACID project (as discussed in Hour 7, "Constructing Your Musical Arrangement"), you may want to select the Make New Track

Follow Project Tempo (Beatmapped Track) check box. This option ensures that the newly recorded file follows the tempo changes in your project.

By default, ACID records at a 44,100Hz sample rate and at a 16-bit bit depth. Some newer sound cards can record in bit depths as high as 24-bit. You can set ACID to record in 24-bit depth if your sound card supports that bit depth. To change the default settings, click the Change button to open the Project Properties dialog box at the Audio tab. From the Bit-Depth drop-down list, choose 8, 16, or 24. From the Sample Rate(Hz) drop-down list, choose the desired sampling rate. When you're done, click OK.

Don't worry if you aren't familiar with the terms "bit depth" and "sampling rate," You'll learn more about these in Hour 17, "Creating Mixed Audio and Video Files." For now, suffice it to say that CD-quality recordings use 44,100Hz for the sampling rate and 16-bit for bit depth. As you can see, ACID Pro supports better-than-CD-quality recording.

After you have set the options in the ACID Record dialog box, click the Start button and play, sing, speak, or rap...make some noise! As soon as you click the Start button, the button label changes to Stop. When you finish recording, click the Stop button. ACID saves the file to the location you specified and adds it as a new Beatmapper track in your project.

When recording through a microphone, mute the speakers and use headphones to listen to the tracks that already exist in your project. That way, your microphone does not record the sound of previously existing tracks coming through your speakers.

Creating and ACIDizing Loops

You may want to create a loop out of a portion of a file that you recorded into ACID. To ensure that the loops you record work like any other loop, adjust the Track Properties and save the results. This process is referred to as "ACIDizing the file." The following sections show you how to create and ACIDize a loop.

Rendering a Loop

Find the portion of the recorded file that you want to turn into a loop. Define a time selection over the desired area.

You may have to zoom in and make fine adjustments to the time selection while you listen to it in Loop Playback mode. Remember, for a loop to work properly, it must be a very "tight" loop.

Split the event at the beginning and at the end of the desired area. With the Time Selection tool, double-click the event that represents the desired area to make an exact time selection over it. Solo the track that contains the event and choose File, Render As. In the Render As dialog box, enable the Render Loop Region Only check box and make any other appropriate choices. Click OK to render a new file containing only the material within the time selection on the soloed track. This is your new loop.

ACIDizing a Loop

The basics of ACIDizing a file are relatively easy. Add the file you created in the preceding section to your project and open the Track Properties window for that track. This is where you ACIDize the loop. On the General tab, choose Loop from the Track Type field to define the file as a loop.

Click the Stretch tab. If your loop is melodic or harmonic, choose the key in which the loop was recorded from the Root Note drop-down list. Selecting a specific key here enables ACID to adjust the pitch of the loop to match the project key. Choose Don't Transpose for non-pitched loops such as drum or percussion loops.

In the Number of Beats field, enter the total number of beats in the loop. For instance, if the loop is one measure long, enter **4** for the number of beats. If the loop is two measures long, enter **8**, and so on.

Advanced ACIDizing

Extreme changes in project tempo may cause artifacts or distortion of the sound in some of your loops. This often happens when you work with loops that you have created using the techniques described in this hour. In such cases, you may have to adjust the stretch properties of your loops.

The stretch properties determine how ACID deals with time compression and expansion. Stretch markers tell ACID where transients occur. ACID then uses this information to work its magic and play the loop at any tempo you set. Sometimes you have to add, remove, or relocate these stretch markers to maximize their benefit to ACID.

To optimize a track's stretch properties, double-click the Track Header to open the Track Properties dialog box for that track. Click the Stretch tab. The Stretch tab has two components, as shown in Figure 15.4. On the left, you find the tools you used a few minutes ago to set the root note and the total number of beats in the file. The rest of the controls aid you in fine-tuning the stretch markers.

FIGURE 15.4

Adjust the stretch markers to optimize the file's tempo-changing capabilities.

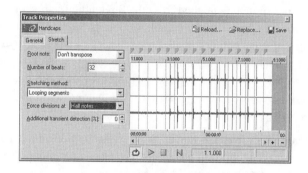

On the right, you see a waveform display with stretch markers that identify the beats and transients in the waveform. These markers correspond to the subdivision of the beat as detected by ACID. The success of advanced ACIDizing rests on proper placement of these markers.

There are three buttons in the upper-right corner of the Track Properties dialog box, two of which play a part in ACIDizing your loops. In Hour 14, "Uncovering Tips and Techniques," you learned how to use the Replace button to swap the file on a track. We'll focus on the other two buttons now.

The Reload button resets all the stretch markers to their last saved position. This feature allows you to experiment, and if all goes awry, to get back to a good starting point.

The Save button saves the loop file with the new settings you have created. The next time you use the file in a project (the same project or a different project), you will not have to ACIDize it again. If you don't save the file with the new stretch properties, this information will still be saved with the current project. But because the loop file itself has not been saved with the new stretch information, you'll have to set the stretch properties again if you use the loop in another project.

If you open the file in an audio editor after ACIDizing it, the file will work fine and show no signs of being changed. However, if you further edit the file in the other application, it may (in some cases) lose the information you added when ACIDizing the file. If this happens, just bring the file back into ACID and reset the properties.

As noted, the waveform display contains a series of stretch markers. These markers correspond to subdivisions of the beats. The biggest cause of audio artifacts is when ACID does not recognize the beats properly. In some cases, you might have to adjust the markers manually. Tweak the loop for its best performance by removing, adjusting, and adding markers.

Select the proper stretching method from the Stretching Method drop-down list in the Track Properties window. Use the default—Looping Segments—for most loops. Use the Non-looping Segments option for sustaining material, such as a keyboard pad. Use the Pitch Shift Segments option to turn off the main feature of ACID—changing tempo without changing pitch. This option can cause problems with loops that have a specific pitch (such as horns, keyboards, guitars, and so forth), but it often works great on non-pitched instruments such as drums.

The option you select from the Force Divisions At drop-down list places markers at different note values ranging from whole notes to 64th notes. Smaller divisions of the beat work well for rapid note rhythms. Use larger division of the beat for less busy rhythms.

The Additional Transient Detection (%) field works in conjunction with the Force Divisions At field. The setting you specify here adjusts the amount of extra beat detection ACID does based on the subdivision set in the Force Divisions At setting.

The main strategy is to align the markers with the beats/transients in the waveform display. In some cases, you may have to add markers. To do so, double-click in the marker bar where you want to place a marker. Notice that the markers you add manually are easy to identify because they are lighter in color than the markers automatically placed by ACID. Click and drag the marker to refine its placement. Use the same zoom-in and zoom-out techniques you use in the Track View area to zoom in and out of the stretch properties waveform to help you place the markers accurately. Place a marker anywhere ACID has failed to place one on a pronounced beat.

You can disable any of the markers that ACID has placed, which is helpful if you want to hear what the loop sounds like without a marker. To disable a marker, double-click it. Alternatively, right-click the marker and choose Disable from the shortcut menu. Note that disabled markers appear as very light gray. Double-click a disabled marker to re-enable it. If you decide you can do without the marker, right-click it and choose Delete from the shortcut menu.

To delete one of the stretch markers that ACID places automatically, you must first disable it.

You can delete the markers you have placed manually at any time. Right-click the marker and choose either Disable (to keep the marker in the project but temporarily disable it) or Delete (to remove it completely). Another method is to double-click the marker to disable it. Double-click a disabled (manually placed) marker to delete it. To re-enable a marker that you have placed and then disabled, right-click the marker and choose Enable from the shortcut menu.

Task: ACIDizing a Bass Loop

This task shows you how to use the Stretch settings in the Track Properties window to perform advanced ACIDization functions on one of the most difficult types of loop to ACIDize—a bass loop.

1. To a new project, add eight bars of `4-4 Loop 33-07.wav` from the Hour 15 Samples folder on the CD-ROM that accompanies this book. This drum loop has been ACIDized. Play the loop and adjust the tempo. The loop sounds good even when taken to extreme tempos.

2. Add eight bars of `Bass loop.wav`. This loop has not been fully ACIDized. Set the project tempo to match the tempo of the bass loop track. (Hint: Right-click the bass loop track icon and choose Use Original Tempo.) Now click the Play From Start button. The bass track sounds okay at this tempo, but if you listen closely, you can hear a bit of warbling. When you slow the tempo down to 85bpm, or speed it up to 135bpm, you really start to hear artifacts in the bass. Try it.

3. Set the tempo back to 109bmp, double-click the track icon to open the Track Properties window for the bass track, and click the Stretch tab. Notice that there are many markers, some of which align with transients and some of which don't (see Figure 15.5). Click the Play button at the bottom of the Track Properties window. Again, note the warble in the bass loop.

FIGURE 15.5

Several of the stretch markers don't align with the transients.

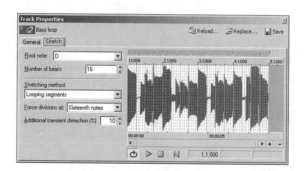

4. Change the Force Division At setting to Quarter Notes. Now the markers align more closely with the transients. Give the file another listen and notice the improvement.

5. Move any markers that do not line up exactly with the beats/transients. Use the zoom-in time controls if you need a closer look. Add or disable markers if they are not needed. Play the file as you make adjustments to monitor the results.

6. After you've made your adjustments, click the Stop button in the Stretch tab and play the project. (Hint: It might help to move the Track Properties window to the Window Docking area so that you can see the Transport toolbar.) Change the tempo and key. Notice that the bass sounds much better, even when you take it far away from its original tempo and key.

7. Click the Save button in the Track Properties window to save the `bass loop.wav` file with its new stretch properties settings. Now—thanks to your ACIDizing efforts—the file works great with any project into which you place it.

Summary

In this hour, you learned how to connect your hardware to your computer sound card so that you can record in ACID. You also learned how to create an original loop and how to ACIDize the file. Now you'll never run out of new loops, and you can customize your projects with your own original loop material.

Q&A

Q. When I record my loop, the other tracks in the project are recorded as well. What causes this?

A. There may be two causes for this. First, check to see how you have your hardware set up. If you use the main mixer outputs to go to your sound card rather than to the aux sends as described earlier in this hour, you send the new material plus the prerecorded tracks back into the sound card.

Another cause may be that your microphone is picking up the other tracks as they play through your speakers. Mute the speakers and monitor your existing tracks with headphones while recording.

Q. Why is there a difference between line-in and mic-in?

A. Microphones output a weaker signal than other devices such as electronic keyboards. Consequently, they need amplification at the input stage. Mic-ins supply that amplification. Line-level devices provide a strong-enough signal on their own and do not require amplification at the input stage. Your sound card needs both types of inputs to accommodate recording from either type of device.

Workshop

This hour's workshop focuses on your hardware setup and on recording loops in ACID. The workshop reinforces what you learned this hour and suggests a couple of activities for further study.

15

Quiz

1. There are normally two kinds of audio inputs on a sound card. Line-in is one type. What is the other?

2. How do you activate the record level meters in the ACID Record dialog box?

3. What is it called when you add important information to a file so that ACID can use it most efficiently?

Quiz Answers

1. The other common input type on most sound cards is mic-in.

2. Enable the Monitor check box to activate the record-level meters.

3. The process of adding important information to a file so that ACID can use it more efficiently is referred to as ACIDizing the file.

Activities

1. Find a percussion instrument (such as a shaker, tambourine, or wood block) and record your own unique percussion loop. Then ACIDize the loop and use it in a project.

2. Find a crash cymbal, gong, or pan lid. Record one hit on the object. Open the Track Properties window for the new track and set the Track Type field to One-Shot. Congratulations! You've made your first one-shot.

HOUR 16

Adding Vocals

- Choosing the Optimal Track Type
- Task: Creating a Rhythm Track for the Vocals
- Recording Vocals
- Task: Adding the Vocals
- Recording Multiple Takes in ACID
- Task: Recording Multiple Takes
- Adding Harmony Tracks and Mixing
- Task: Creating Harmony Background Vocals

So far, we've made a lot of music, and hopefully you are already working on creations of your own. But not everyone wants to make strictly instrumental music. How do you get vocals into your project? ACID makes it easy, and this hour shows you just how easy it is.

In this hour, you will:

- Record a lead vocal track
- Record and manage multiple takes
- Create harmony background vocals with track duplication and event pitch shifting

Choosing the Optimal Track Type

As you've seen, ACID uses three audio track types in addition to MIDI tracks: loops, one-shots, and Beatmapper tracks. Each track type has certain characteristics you can take advantage of when working with lead and background vocals.

Tracks Over 30 Seconds Long

Most lead vocal tracks last for more than 30 seconds. So, how do you decide whether to add your vocals as a one-shot or to Beatmap the track? If the project tempo is set, add the lead vocal as a one-shot. However, if you think the tempo might change as you work on the project, Beatmap the lead vocal to give yourself the flexibility to make tempo changes, knowing that the lead vocal will automatically adjust.

Tracks Under 30 Seconds Long

Background vocals are often short phrases that repeat throughout the project. You can often set their track type to loop so that you can quickly paint them in as you do with other loops throughout the project.

In other cases, saving the short vocal files as one-shots makes perfect sense. In the end, you simply have to experiment to see which track type works best for the material. Because you can change the track type at any time (see Hour 15, "Recording and Creating Your Own Loops," for a refresher on ACIDizing files), you can experiment to find the best setting. The trick is to use these file type attributes to your advantage and get the most mileage out of your vocal tracks.

Task: Creating a Rhythm Track for the Vocals

Before you record the vocals, you need a track to sing along with. It's been said that, "anyone can sing the blues," so we'll start by putting together a simple 12-bar blues tune. All the loops for this task can be found in the Hour 16 Samples folder on the CD-ROM that accompanies this book. The loops are part of a collection from Sonic Foundry called *Paul Black's Whiskey, Cigarettes, and Gumbo* by blues guitarist Paul Black.

1. Open a new ACID project; set the tempo to 120bpm and the project key to E. Add 12 bars of `Drum Tools Promo 01.wav`.

2. Add four bars of `Vibey Shuffle I 01.wav`, starting at bar 1.

3. Starting at bar 5, add two bars of `Vibey Shuffle IV 01.wav`.

4. Add two more bars of `Vibey Shuffle I 01.wav` starting at bar 7.

5. Add `Vibey Shuffle V 01.wav` to the project, and paint in one bar starting at bar 9.

6. Add one bar of `Vibey Shuffle IV 01.wav` at bar 10, and one bar of `Vibey Shuffle I 01.wav` at bar 11.

7. Finally, add one bar of `Vibey Shuffle V 01.wav` at the last bar, bar 12. You have now created the standard 12-bar blues pattern. Click the Play From Start button and check it out.

8. Now for some spice. Add `Drum tools Promo 02.wav` and draw in one bar each at bars 4, 8, and 12.

9. Click anywhere in the timeline and press Ctrl+A to select all the events in the project. Click the Copy button in the ACID toolbar. Place the cursor at bar 13 and click the Paste button. You now have 24 bars of blues.

10. Press Ctrl+A again to select all events, then click and drag the entire project one bar to the right. This action opens up the first bar for a drum intro.

11. Add one bar of `Drum tools Promo 02.wav` to the very beginning of the project. Your project should look like the one in Figure 16.1.

FIGURE 16.1

When you've completed this task, your project should look like the one in this figure.

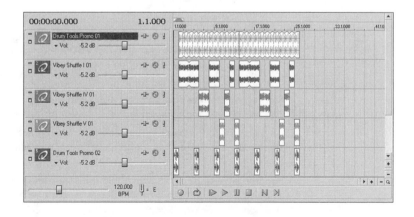

12. Save the project as `Blue Cheese Blues`, and play it to hear your 24-bars blues tune.

Recording Vocals

Now it's time to record your own vocals. If you need help configuring your system for recording, look back at Hour 15, where we fully explain how to set up your "recording studio." After you're set up, take on the next task.

ACID was not designed to function as multitrack recording software (such as Pro Tools from Digidesign or Vegas Audio from Sonic Foundry). A true multi-track application can record multiple tracks simultaneously while playing back multiple tracks. With ACID, you can play back multiple tracks simultaneously, but you can record only one stereo track at a time. Record the lead vocalist first, and go back to record the backup singers. Of course, if you're doing all the vocals yourself, you don't have any other option!

In the next task, you'll add the lead and background vocals. You can find the musical score for this simple blues tune in three PDF files in the Hour 16 Samples folder on the CD-ROM (BCBLUES1.pdf, BCBLUES2.pdf, BCBLUES3.pdf).

If you don't read music, you can call up the previously recorded vocals, learn the part, and then record your own versions of this hit tune. To hear the previously recorded vocals, open Blue Cheese BluesComplete.acd from the Hour 16 Samples folder on the CD-ROM that accompanies this book.

Earlier, we stated that "anyone can sing the blues." However, some folks disagree. For instance, some people say that you can't sing the blues if you drive a Volvo, BMW, or sport utility vehicle. Go buy an old Chevy, a '56 Cadillac rust bucket, or a beat up 'ol truck.

You probably can't sing the blues in the shopping mall or the office. The lighting is just all wrong. Move to a shotgun shack, or at least go out to the parking lot next to the dumpster.

It's hard to sing the blues in Hawaii, Hilton Head Island, and parts of Ft. Lauderdale and Miami. You're better off moving to Memphis, Chicago, or St. Louie.

You also have to be careful what you drink. Sparkling water, diet soda, and spiced tea just don't cut it. You're better off with beverages that start with the word *Jack* or *Southern*.

16

Most of all, you have to have the right name. You'll notice that a lot of the first names of blues singers start with a physical infirmity such as *blind*, or *lame*. A fruit such as *lemon* or *lime* usually follows this adjective. The singer's last name probably belonged to a dead American president such as *Jefferson* or *Johnson*. A perfect example of this is the famous blues man, Blind Lemon Jefferson. If you have a name like *Autumn*, or if people call you *Chipper*, forget it.

For instance, take the ol' gent we got to sing lead vocal on the sample. We found him 'long side the tracks, drinkin' day-old joe from a paper cup. We knew we had our man when we heard his name—Deaf Kiwi Madison. The first part of his name may explain his performance. Further, everyone knows that Madison was the fourth President of the United States and the Father of the American Constitution. And we're pretty sure he's dead. The jury is still out on whether Kiwi qualifies as a true "blues fruit," but as Deaf Kiwi would say, "Two outta three ain't bad."

So, please keep these guidelines in mind when you sing the lead vocal in the next section. And remember, the authors of this book are in no way responsible for the longevity of your marriage or your employment status!

Task: Adding the Vocals

Start your blues career by singing a lead vocal over the entire Blue Cheese Blues project.

1. Click the Record button in the ACID toolbar. In the Record dialog box that opens, use the following settings (see Figure 16.2):

    - Record Type: Audio.
    - File Name: Lead Vocal.
    - Record Folder: use the My Documents folder on your C:\ drive, or specify any other folder in which you'd rather store your work.
    - Record From: Start of Project.
    - Enable the Make New Track Follow Project Tempo (Beatmapped Track) check box.
    - Pick your sound card from the Record Device drop-down list.
    - Enable the Monitor check box.

2. Sing into the mic, and adjust the record level using the Windows Volume Control and the ACID record meters. Refer to Hour 15 for more information about preparing to record.

FIGURE 16.2

Set your Record dialog box to match the settings in this figure.

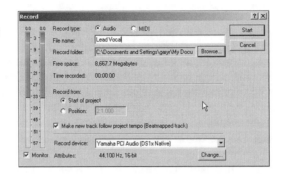

3. Open the PDF file BCBLUES1.pdf from the Hour 16 Sample folder on the companion CD to find the sheet music for the lead vocal part. Click the Start button. After the drum intro, start singing in bar 2. Click Stop when you finish.

4. ACID creates a new Beatmapper track called Lead Vocal. Click the Play From Start button to hear the song complete with your new vocal track.

5. As the song plays, change the tempo to 100. Notice that the pitch of the lead vocal drops. Speed the tempo up, and the pitch of the vocal rises.

6. Double-click the track icon for the Lead Vocal track to open the Track Properties dialog box shown in Figure 16.3. On the General tab, enable the Preserve Pitch when Stretching check box. Adjust the tempo again. The vocal still changes tempo with the project, but now it does not change pitch. Leave this project open; you'll continue with it in the next task.

FIGURE 16.3

Enable the Preserve Pitch When Stretching check box so that you can adjust the tempo without affecting the pitch of your vocal track.

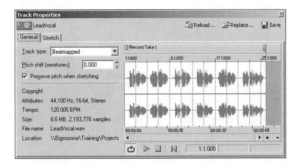

Recording Multiple Takes in ACID

You may have to try several times before you get your vocal right. ACID allows you to try as many *takes* as you need until you're happy with one. Create a loop region encompassing the section where you want to record the takes. Click the Loop Playback button. Now when you start recording, ACID continually loops the defined section of the project until you click Stop in the Record dialog box. Keep recording until you get a take you like.

Takes

The word *take* refers to a single pass at recording something. For instance, a lead guitar player might try several takes before achieving the perfect solo. Or a vocalist might try recording the first verse several times (several takes) before conveying the desired feeling. You might want to record multiple takes of the same passage so that you have several to choose from later.

When you click Stop, ACID creates a new track containing all your takes as one long file. This, of course, means that only one of the takes lines up exactly with the selected loop region. You can now listen to the various takes and find one you like.

When you find the perfect take, create a loop region the length of the take. Solo the track containing your multiple takes and choose Tools, Render to New Track. The Render to New Track dialog box opens as shown in Figure 16.4 where you can name the file, choose a file type, and decide where to save the take. Be sure to enable the Render Loop Region Only check box at the bottom of the dialog box. When you click Save, ACID creates a new file containing only the material within the loop region on the soloed track and creates a new track in your project to hold this file. Unsolo the original takes track, draw an event into the new track, and synchronize the background vocal with the other tracks.

FIGURE 16.4

Make sure that you enable the Render Loop Region Only check box to render just the take you want.

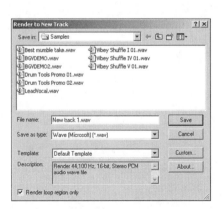

Notice that when you render the take you want to a new track, the track created is a loop track because the background vocal take is less than 30 seconds long.

In the task that follows, you get a chance to record multiple takes by recording some colorful *blues mumbles* to add interest to your composition. You can pick from the following *blues mumble starter kit,* or come up with some of your own. You'll need at least three.

Blues Mumble

A *blues mumble* is created when someone in the band mumbles something in response to what is being played or sung. It may or may not have any direct relation to the subject. Slang terms and ethnic phrases are often used. See the definition for Blues Mumble Starter Kit that follows for examples.

Blues Mumble Starter Kit

A *blues mumble starter kit* contains common blues mumbles to help newcomers to the blues get started in the art. Hopefully, you can then branch out and come up with mumbles of your own. The effectiveness of a blues mumble relates directly to the amount of personal heart and soul supplied by the mumbler—and often the mumbler's financial situation.

For starters, try the blues mumbles listed here (along with their translations), all of which were taken with permission from the official Deaf Kiwi Madison blues mumble starter kit (which you can purchase by sending a large check made payable to Gary Rebholz and Michael Bryant):

- Hab-Moysea (Have mercy)
- Yo, pickmeah messit (Attention, please pick some up for me)
- Hummm, pickit Weason (Say, Wilson, how about playing a little bit of guitar?)
- Yhuno whadi mayynn (do you know what I mean)

Task: Recording Multiple Takes

Follow the steps in this task to learn how to record multiple takes.

1. Set the Blue Cheese blues project that you constructed during the previous task into Loop Playback mode. Drag the left edge of the loop region all the way to the left edge of the timeline; drag the right edge of the region to the 7.1 mark in the

Beat ruler. You have now established a loop region that includes the first six bars of the project.

2. Click the Record button and check your levels using the Windows Volume Control and the ACID record meters while practicing a blues mumble into the mic.

3. Name the file **mumble multi-take** and choose the Start of Project option in the Record From section of the Record dialog box.

4. Click Start to begin recording. ACID continues to record as the project continually loops the first six bars. Mumble each time the loop reaches beat 2 of measure 4. Record at least four different takes of blues mumbles.

5. Click Stop. ACID creates a new track that includes an event containing all four takes of your performance. Only one of the takes fits exactly at bar 4 beat 2.

6. Disengage Loop Playback mode, solo the track, and listen to your performance. Find a good take other than the first take (for this example, assume that take 3 is your best take).

7. Find the measure that contains your best take. If all went well and you chose take 3, the mumble you want should be in measures 16 and 17.

8. Click and drag the Loop Region Indicator bar to position the loop region around the take you want to keep. Your project should look like the one in Figure 16.5.

FIGURE 16.5

Place your best blues mumble take at bar 4.

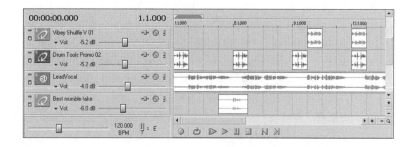

9. Make sure that the track containing your multiple takes is still soloed; choose Tools, Render to New Track. Name the file GoodBluesMumble.wav and enable the Render Loop Region Only check box. ACID saves the part of the soloed track that falls within the loop region to a new file, and creates a new loop track.

10. Draw a loop into the new track at bar 4 and listen to your best take playing at the right measure. Save this file; you'll use it in the next task.

All those multiple takes can add up to very large files. After you have mixed your best take to a new track, you no longer need the multiple-take file. Delete that track from the project. However, that large file is still taking up precious space on your hard drive.

Browse to the folder you designated as the record folder. (If you've forgotten the path, open the Record dialog box and look in the Record Folder field.) Find and delete the multiple-take file.

Adding Harmony Tracks and Mixing

You can sometimes create harmony background vocals from a single take. Record several background vocal takes until you find one you like. Pull out the good take and render it to a new track. Then duplicate the track.

Now you have two tracks of background vocals, both containing the same file. Pitch-shift the second track to create harmony.

Task: Creating Harmony Background Vocals

In this task, you'll record a single background track and use some ACID tricks to turn it into two-part harmony.

1. In the Blue Cheese Blues ACID project you created earlier, establish a loop region from bar 14 to bar 19. Place the cursor at bar 14, set ACID into Loop Playback mode, and click the Record button. Name the track Background Vocals. Notice that under the Record From option, ACID selects the Position radio button by default and specifies the Record From position as measure 14 beat 1 (14.1.000) because the cursor rests at that position.

2. Use the sheet music for the background vocals in the PDF file BCBLUES2.pdf found in the Hour 16 Samples folder on the companion CD. Click the Start button. Record several takes until you find one you like. When you're finished recording, click Stop.

3. Select your favorite take and create a new track from it. Name the new track, BGV, which stands for Background Vocals.

4. Delete the original background vocals track from the project and delete the file from your hard drive.

5. In the new BGV track, draw in three events: the first from bar 16 to 18, the second from bar 20 to 22, and one more from bar 24 to 26.

6. Right-click the BGV track icon and choose Duplicate Track from the shortcut menu. Now you have two tracks of the background vocal.

7. Close the Track Properties dialog box. Select the first two of the three events in the new duplicate track, and press the − key on your computer's number pad twice. This action lowers the pitch of these events one full step. Harmony!

Remember that pressing the + or − key on your numeric keypad raises or lowers the pitch of the selected event or events by one half step. To pitch-shift a whole step, press the appropriate key twice.

16

8. Select the third event on both the original BGV track and its duplicate. Place your cursor at bar 25 and press the S key on your keyboard. This action splits both events at bar 25 so that you now have four events on both tracks.

9. Select the third event of the duplicate track and press the − key twice to lower the pitch a whole step. Select the fourth event and lower it a half step.

10. Select the fourth event in the original BGV track and press the + key twice to raise its pitch a whole step. Click the Play From Start button and check out the harmony background vocals. Figure 16.6 shows how your project should look when you're done.

FIGURE 16.6

Duplicate the background vocals and shift the pitch of the events on the duplicate track to create a harmony vocal arrangement.

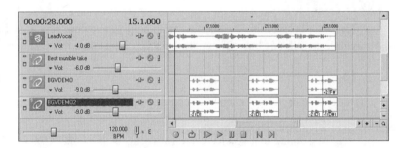

Summary

In this hour, you learned how to record vocals. You learned that the tracks you record are added as Beatmapper tracks, and that in the Track Properties dialog box you can decide whether the new track should change or maintain pitch when the tempo of the project changes. You recorded multiple takes and created a new track out of the best take. You also reviewed how to duplicate a track and created harmony by using the + and − keys to raise or lower the pitch of a single event. You done Deaf Kiwi Madison proud!

Q&A

Q. **How do I change the pitch of a single event if my computer keyboard does not have a number pad with + and − keys?**

A. If you don't have a number pad on your keyboard, right-click the event and choose Properties from the shortcut menu. This opens the Event Properties dialog box. Specify a pitch shift amount in the Pitch Shift (Semitones) field.

Q. **Can the method described in this hour for creating harmony be used with track types other than loop tracks?**

A. Yes. You can use this technique with any track type.

Q. **Why is the Blues Mumble always placed on the end of a musical phrase?**

A. This goes back to the tradition of call and response found in the music of the slaves in early American history. To ease the burden of their backbreaking work, slaves would often sing. Usually a leader would sing out a phrase (the call), which would be answered or echoed by the rest of the group (the response.) This tradition was carried forward into the blues. The first part of the phrase is the call, and the end (in this case, the mumble) is the response.

Workshop

The activities in this workshop serve to help you review, retain, and use the information you leaned in this hour. They also help you have more fun with the ACID software.

Quiz

1. True or False: When you record multiple takes, a new file and a new track are created for each take.

2. Assuming that you have several vocalists, how many tracks of vocals can you record simultaneously in ACID?

3. Imagine that you record a long vocal and then speed up the project tempo. When you play the project back, your vocal track suddenly sounds like it was recorded by Alvin and the Chipmunks on helium. How can you fix the problem?

4. True or False: It's easy to sing the blues while sipping on a peach-flavored iced tea drink.

Quiz Answers

1. False. The takes are all recorded sequentially to the same file and are added to your project on the same track. You'll have to isolate the take you want and move it into synchronization with the rest of the project.

2. One. ACID is not designed to function as a true multitrack recording application.

3. Double-click the track icon for your vocal track to open the Track Properties dialog box. On the General tab, enable the Preserve Pitch When Stretching check box. Now play your project at the faster speed; although you're singing faster, you're still singing in your regular voice.

4. Most folks would say that any flavored iced tea beverage is just too happy a drink to go with the blues.

16

Activities

1. Copy and paste another 12 bars of blues into the Blue Cheese Blues project. Make up a rhymed couplet (or borrow one from Shakespeare) and use these lyrics to sing another verse of the blues.

2. Using the techniques you learned in the "Creating Multiple Takes" section, come up with three new blues mumbles and record them against the new verse you recorded in the first activity. Pick the best of the three and create a new track from it.

PART VI

Delivering Your Creations

Hour

HOUR 17

Creating Mixed Audio and Video Files

- Saving Mixed AIFF or WAV Files
- Comparing Bit Depths and Sampling Rates
- Considering the Major Video Formats
- Creating Compressed Audio Formats
- Task: Encoding an MP3 Version of a Song
- Encoding for Streaming Over the Internet
- Task: Rendering a Streaming Media File with Embedded Metadata

When you have created, edited, enhanced, and mixed your audio and video project, you're ready to deliver the finished product in a mixed file format. As you learned in Hour 4, "Saving Your Work," ACID gives you several delivery options. How do you decide which to use? First, you should learn the strengths and weakness of each option. Then you can decide how to deliver your project to your target audience—CD, the Internet, company intranet, personal MP3 player…. Because you can create several different mixed files of various formats from the same project, you can take advantage of all these delivery technologies.

We'll address these issues, and many more, during the course of this hour. In this hour, you will:

- Save your ACID projects as mixed files
- Set the sample rate and bit depth for your project
- Learn concepts to keep in mind when saving video projects
- Encode your ACID projects to MP3 and other Internet delivery formats

Before we talk about formats and options, you might want to review the differences among the Save, Save As, and Render As commands. Remember that the Save As command allows you to save your project in one of the ACID project file formats. The Render As command is the subject of this hour. The Render As command allows you to save your project in a mixed file format that can be played in many applications other than ACID. Look back at Hour 4 to review the concepts that are a critical foundation to what we talk about here. Hour 4 also explains the process of saving and rendering your files, and gives you several definitions you might need as you work your way through this hour.

Saving Mixed AIFF or WAV Files

ACID supports two uncompressed audio file formats: AIFF (for Macintosh) and WAV (for Windows PCs). Uncompressed files require large amounts of storage space—it takes about 10 megabytes of hard disk space to store one minute of CD-quality stereo audio.

Advantages

AIFF and WAV files boast a couple of key advantages. First, these high-fidelity formats maintain their original audio quality when you render them. If you need the highest quality audio possible, choose one of these formats.

Second, the AIFF and WAV file formats are compatible with the greatest number of media players and audio software programs. As a result, you can open and play them easily on the platform of your choice, or use them in conjunction with a wide variety of MIDI, presentation, or multimedia-related software programs.

Project Properties

ACID renders a mixed AIFF or WAV file using the sample rate and bit-depth settings you have chosen on the Audio tab of the Project Properties dialog box (we'll talk in more detail about sample rate and bit depth in a couple of minutes). Choose File, Properties, Audio if you want to change those settings.

If you want to render with settings that are different than your current project properties, override these settings in the Render As dialog box. There are two ways to do so. Choose File, Render to open the Render As dialog box. Choose Wave (Microsoft) (*.wav) or Macintosh AIFF (*.aif) from the Save As Type drop-down list. Choose a template from the Template drop-down list. Alternatively, click the Custom button and choose your desired parameters from the Custom Settings dialog box. In addition to the bit depth and sample rate, notice that you also can choose between a stereo and mono file by selecting the appropriate option from the Channels drop-down list. Click OK when you've made your choices.

Sample Rates

The sample rate (or sampling rate) describes how often the computer looks at and records the current state of the waveform over a certain period of time—that is, how many samples it takes of the waveform. The sample rate is usually measured in samples per second. The sampling rate for CD quality audio is 44,100 samples per second.

The sampling rate is directly related to *frequency*. Higher sampling rates make it possible to record higher frequencies. To get an accurate recording of a frequency, the sampling rate must be at least two times that frequency. Theoretically, if you want to accurately reproduce the frequency of middle A on the piano—which is 440Hz (440 cycles per second)—you must use, at minimum, a sampling rate of 880 samples per second.

Frequency

Frequency relates to pitch. Higher frequency equals higher pitch, lower frequency equals lower pitch. Frequency is measured in Hertz (Hz) or cycles per second. Think of a guitar string as you pluck it. The string moves above and below its center point as it vibrates. How fast the string vibrates is described as frequency, and we hear it as pitch.

The human ear can hear a range of approximately 20Hz to 20KHz. That's why 44,100 samples per second was chosen as the specified sample rate for CD-quality audio. This sampling rate guarantees that all audible frequencies are accurately recorded and reproduced.

Bit Depth

When the computer takes a sample of the waveform, it describes the sample using binary code (1s and 0s). The term "bit depth" describes the number of bits (the 1s and 0s) that make up a single sample. ACID supports 8-bit, 16-bit, and 24-bit sound files. Higher bit depths make higher-quality sound possible. CD-quality audio uses 16-bit samples.

Bit-depth and sampling rate not only affect the quality of the audio, but also the size of the file. If you're trying to keep the file size small, choose a lower bit depth and/or a lower sampling rate. But be prepared to sacrifice quality. For instance, if you drop the sampling rate from 44,100Hz to 22,050Hz, you'll cut the file size in half. But you will only be able to accurately reproduce frequencies up to 11KHz. As we pointed out, humans can hear up to 20KHz, so some audible frequencies will be lost.

An analogy might help you understand the significance of bit depth. If you were asked to describe this book using only 256 words (an 8-bit sample), you could do it. But think how much more accurately you could describe it if you could use 65,536 words (a 16-bit sample). You could be very accurate with your description. But as you can imagine, the file size is much larger for 16-bit files.

Comparing Bit Depths and Sampling Rates

It might be helpful for you to hear the difference that various bit depth and sample rates make on the audio quality of a file. The following sections helps you make that comparison.

Sampling Rate Comparison

Four of the `.wav` files in the Hour 17 Samples folder show how various sample rates affect sound quality and file size. Each has been saved at a bit depth of 16, but with a different sample rate, as indicated by their filenames. Notice how the lower sample rates affect file size. Listen to these files and hear how the lower sample rate affects the audio quality of each file. The following list gives a summary of what to listen for in each of the four files:

- **`curtsjam-48kHz.wav`**—This sampling rate is better-than-CD quality. Unless you are in a fantastic professional-level listening environment using extremely high-end audio monitoring equipment, you probably won't be able to tell the difference between a 48KHz file and a 44KHz file.

- **`curtsjam-44kHz.wav`**—This rate gives the best sound quality that most people will be able to hear. This is CD quality. Notice in particular how bright and crisp the cymbals sound.

- **`curtsjam-22kHz.wav`**—The sound quality suffers noticeably, although it is still acceptable in some cases. Notice that the cymbals are less crisp and bright than they are in the 44KHz example.

- **curtsjam-11kHz.wav**—At this sample rate, the sound is considerably degraded. This rate works much better for voice than music. Notice that the cymbals are nearly indistinguishable, especially as compared to the CD-quality example.

Listen to these files in your media player or in ACID. In ACID, navigate to and preview the files in the Explorer window, or add them to a project. Click the Views button in the Explorer window and choose Details to compare file sizes.

Bit Depth Comparison

Three of the WAV files have been saved at a sample rate of 44,100Hz, but at various bit depths, as indicated by their filenames. Compare their file sizes and listen to the difference in audio quality from one file to the next. The following list gives you an idea of what to listen for when previewing these files:

- **curtsjam-24bit.wav**—This is better-than-CD quality. Again, most people don't have the equipment or listening environment to hear the difference between this bit rate and a 16-bit file. Your equipment may not even support this bit depth.

- **curtsjam-16bit.wav**—This is CD quality. Notice the brightness of the sound. Also, notice the lack of static or hiss in the background.

- **curtsjam-8bit.wav**—You should be able to hear more background noise such as static or a hissing sound in this file. Using only 8 bits, this file cannot reproduce the sound as accurately as a 16-bit file can.

> Many audio cards do not support 24-bit audio. When you attempt to listen to the 24-bit audio file, you might receive a message that it is an unsupported class or file format. If so, you'll know that your sound card does not support 24-bit files.

Bit Depth and Sampling Rate Summary

Here are some guidelines for the quality you can expect from various sampling rates and bit depths:

- **48,000Hz**—Higher-than-CD-quality audio. Generally used with professional-grade audio cards and hardware. You're not likely to hear the difference between this file and a 44,100Hz file.

- **44,100Hz**—CD-quality audio.

- **22,050Hz**—Comparable to the audio quality of FM radio.

- **11,025Hz**—Comparable to telephone-quality audio.
- **24-bit**—Higher-than-CD-quality audio.
- **16-bit**—CD-quality audio.
- **8-bit**—Generally very noisy, but frequently used for sound effects in game and multimedia applications. 8-bit files may be suitable for voice.

> When you must save your files to either the WAV or AIFF format, but you need to keep the file size as small as possible, save the file as mono. A mono file is half as large as the same file saved in stereo. A mono 16-bit file sounds better than a stereo 8-bit file, even though they are both the same file size.

Considering the Major Video Formats

After you have added music, sound FX, and dialog to a video file, you can render it to a mixed format that includes the video and audio in a single file. You must make the same choices about the audio sampling rate and bit depth that you have to make for audio-only files, as described in the preceding sections. In addition, you must make choices related to the video format.

As is true for audio, certain video formats are more suitable for a particular type of delivery than others. For instance, if you are not concerned about file size, the AVI or MOV formats can yield high-quality video and audio when the proper options are chosen. On the other hand, to stream the file over the Internet (which we'll discuss shortly), a specialized, highly compressed format such as RM or WMV is necessary.

> This section uses a number of terms that were first introduced in Hour 10, "Scoring to a Video." If any of the terms, phrases, or concepts in this hour seem unfamiliar, it would be a good idea for you to go back and review Hour 10.

AVI

The Audio Video Interleave (AVI) file format is the high-quality video format for the Windows platform. ACID offers several templates from which you can choose, and each of these templates can be customized. The default template creates CD-quality audio and uncompressed video.

Rendering uncompressed video makes a very large file. For instance, one minute of uncompressed video creates a file about 35MB in size. Therefore, there are a variety of AVI codecs that can render compressed files of various quality. (You might want to review the discussion on video codecs in Hour 10.) However, the file size of any AVI is still too large for streaming delivery over the Internet.

DV

Digital Video (DV) is an AVI file format that uses a digital video codec to compress the data. DV is a great format to use in ACID because you can take full advantage of the external monitor support discussed in Hour 10. Although DV is a compressed format, it is still too large for streaming delivery. Choose the DV format if you plan to print the project back to DV tape or deliver it on a CD-ROM.

MOV

QuickTime files use the extension .mov. The MOV format is the Apple equivalent of an AVI file. It can be used to create high-quality uncompressed or compressed files. Some MOV files can be streamed over the Internet.

17

Creating Compressed Audio Formats

Developers are constantly looking for ways to create smaller file sizes without sacrificing quality. Many different file compression techniques are available for both audio and video. Some are considered lossless, while others are considered lossy. Lossy techniques can create much smaller file sizes, but result in loss of quality as well. Lossless techniques reduce the file size, but retain the quality. In audio, the MP3 format is an example of a file type that uses a lossy audio compression technique. Sonic Foundry Perfect Clarity Audio (PCA) is an example of a lossless audio compression scheme. A PCA file sounds better than an MP3 file, but also has a larger file size. The following sections look at the various compression formats available for saving audio.

MP3

MP3 files are compressed so that their file sizes are much smaller than WAV files, yet much (although not all) of the original quality of the audio is retained. Because an acceptable-sounding MP3 file can be as much as one-tenth the size of the same file as a CD-quality WAV file, MP3 is a great choice when you want to transfer and download audio files over the Internet.

As shown in Figure 17.1, there are several templates to choose from when rendering (or encoding) a file as MP3. The template options run the spectrum of those that drastically reduce the file size at the expense of quality, to those that strive to maintain original audio quality even though it means larger file sizes. The template names give you an indication of the audio quality you can expect from each, and the Description field gives you even more details.

FIGURE 17.1

Choose an MP3 template and read the description to decide whether that format is the one you want.

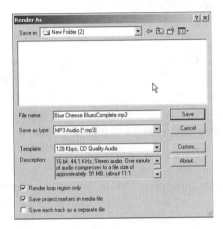

In the Render As dialog box, click the Custom button to choose your own settings. The Custom Settings dialog box opens as shown in Figure 17.2.

FIGURE 17.2

Customize your settings in the Customize Settings dialog box.

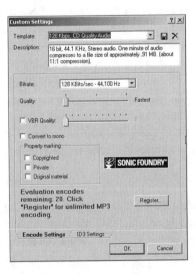

Let's look at a few of the controls on the Encode Settings tab of the Custom Settings dialog box for MP3 encoding:

- The Bit Rate drop-down list allows you to specify the number of bits of information delivered by the file each second. Higher bit rates result in better-quality sound and larger file sizes.

- The Quality slider controls the speed at which ACID encodes your file. To achieve better quality (at the expense of encoding speed), move the slider to the right.

- The VBR Quality setting allows you to adjust the way ACID performs *Variable Bit Rate encoding*. Enable the VBR Quality check box and move the slider to the right to achieve higher quality (at the expense of encoding speed).

NEW TERM

Variable Bit Rate Encoding

Variable Bit Rate encoding allows ACID to automatically adjust the bit rate to achieve higher quality and smaller file sizes. Generally, ACID raises the bit rate for complex passages and lowers the bit rate for simpler or quieter passages.

17

- By default, the MP3 plug-in creates a stereo file. Enable the Convert to Mono check box to create a mono file and cut the file size in half.

In the Custom Settings dialog box, you can also enter *ID3 information*. Click the ID3 Settings tab at the bottom of the Custom Settings dialog box. Enable the Save ID3 Tag to File check box and fill in the various fields to supply ID3 information with your MP3 file. Select an ID3 option; choices are ID3 version 1 (which does not include copyright information), ID3 version 2 (which does include copyright information), or both.

NEW TERM

ID3 Information

ID3 information includes data such as artist, album, song title, and more. MP3 players can display this information, so you might want to provide these details to the people who download and listen to your music. Many media players also use this information to help listeners manage the music collections on their computers.

You can create custom templates using the settings you establish in the Custom Settings dialog box. When you have specified the settings you want, give the template a name and click the Save Template button at the top of the dialog box. The template now appears in the Template drop-down list so that you can use it again in the future. To delete a custom template, choose it from the list and click the Delete Template button.

The technique described here for creating and saving custom templates works in the Custom Settings dialog box regardless of what file format you choose.

Task: Encoding an MP3 Version of a Song

To create an MP3 version of your song (a process referred to as "encoding your ACID project as an MP3 file"), follow these steps:

1. Open an ACID project from a previous hour's Samples folder. `Blue Cheese BluesComplete.acd` from Hour 16 would be a good project to use. Choose File, Render As to open the Render As dialog box. Specify the location in which you want to save the file and give it a new name if you want.

2. From the Save As Type drop-down list, choose MP3 Audio (`*.mp3`).

3. Choose your desired template from the Template drop-down list.

4. Click the Custom button and then click the ID3 Settings tab in the Custom Setting dialog box that opens. Enter information about your song in the Title, Artist, Album, Copyright, Comments, Year, and Genre fields.

5. Click OK to encode your file.

6. Listen to your new MP3 file in your favorite MP3 player. The Windows Media Player and Siren Jukebox from Sonic Foundry are two examples of media players you can use to listen to (and organize) your MP3 files.

MP3 technology is not free. The developers of MP3 charge companies a fee to integrate the technology into their software. Sonic Foundry provides you with 20 encodes so that you can evaluate the results of rendering MP3 files from ACID. After you've used your 20 free encodes, you can register your MP3 usage with Sonic Foundry to enable unlimited MP3 encodes. To do so, click the Register button in the Custom Settings dialog box when rendering an MP3 file, and follow the Registration Wizard. Registration for unlimited MP3 encodes is free if you own ACID Pro, and costs around $20 for the other versions of ACID.

OggVorbis

Because there is a charge for companies (such as Sonic Foundry) to integrate MP3 technology into their software (which is why ACID supplies only 20 evaluation encodes), the industry has been searching for an alternative to the MP3 format. Enter OggVorbis (.ogg). This open-source, patent-free technology is compatible with several operating systems including Windows and Macintosh. ACID offers three templates, ranging from 96Kbps to 320Kbps. With ACID, you have an unlimited number of OggVorbis encodes. Although MP3 still rules, OggVorbis is coming on strong.

Sonic Foundry Perfect Clarity Audio

MP3 and OggVorbis are both lossy codecs. Sonic Foundry Perfect Clarity Audio (PCA) is a completely lossless audio codec. PCA can reduce file size by as much as 50 percent compared to the original WAV file with no loss of quality. PCA is a great way to conserve space on your disk drives, but this relatively new format is not widely supported by products other than those made by Sonic Foundry. It's a good choice if you use Sonic Foundry software for all your audio projects, but note that PCA may not work if you use software from other manufacturers. PCA files are also too large to stream over the Internet.

17

Encoding for Streaming Over the Internet

The Internet is becoming a very popular and powerful medium through which you can share and promote your music and videos. ACID can encode in several different formats that allow you to prepare your files for *streaming* over the Internet. It's important to pick the file format and codec that best fit your target *bandwidth;* ACID gives you many options.

New Term

Streaming

Streaming is a technique for transferring data over the Internet. A streaming file begins playing in the browser or media player even as the remainder of the file is being downloaded. Streaming allows people to listen to or watch the file without having to wait for it to download in its entirety. Ideally, the downloading file always keeps ahead of playback so that the information is buffered until needed. If this is not the case, you will experience pauses in the playback while the download "catches up" to the playback.

Bandwidth

Bandwidth is the amount of data that a given Internet connection speed can handle in a fixed amount of time. See the following coffee break entitled, "It's All About Bandwidth—and Pea Gravel" for a discussion of bandwidth.

It's All About Bandwidth—and Pea Gravel

Pushing audio and video files through the Internet can be likened to pouring pea gravel out of a bucket, through a hose, and into a jar. Think of a 56K dial-up modem as a garden hose, and a cable modem as a fire hose.

The fire hose has a lot higher bandwidth capability than does the garden hose. If you pour the gravel through the fire hose, it will flow fairly well and fairly quickly into the jar. But if you try to pour the gravel through the garden hose, you're looking at a much slower process.

However, if you reduce the size of the gravel by crushing it into sand (using a codec), you can pour it through the garden hose much faster. Unfortunately, just as making the gravel small enough to fit through the garden hose compromises the quality of the pea gravel, making a file small enough to fit through a 56K connection compromises the quality of your audio/video files. Therefore, you don't want to crush the gravel (or compress the audio/video) any more than you have to.

The moral of this fable is: Know your target bandwidth so that you can pick the appropriate compression settings.

Some streaming formats enable you to embed additional data, called metadata, into the file. Metadata can contain commands that manipulate the browser and media player at specific times during the playback of the audio or video. One example is a *URL* flip. When the streaming media file issues a URL flip, the browser opens a specified Web page. If you want to take listeners to a Web page where they can order your CD, embed a URL flip at the end of the song.

URL

URL stands for Uniform Resource Locator. A URL is the global address of documents and resources on the World Wide Web. For example, `http://www.ACIDPlanet.com` is the URL for the ACIDplanet Web site. You'll also hear a URL referred to as the Web address.

Embedding Metadata

You've learned about several different types of markers that you can use in your projects. One more type of marker—the command marker—enables you to embed metadata into your ACID projects. To add a command marker, place your timeline cursor at the point in your project where you want to embed the metadata and choose Insert, Command. This action opens the Command dialog box.

There are several types of metadata commands from which you can choose. By default, the URL option is chosen from the Command drop-down list. This option creates the type of URL flip mentioned in the previous section. In the Parameter field, type the information you want to add as metadata. In the case of a URL flip, type the Web address (URL) of the Web page you want to launch in the user's browser. The Parameter field is mandatory. The Comment field is optional; it gives you a space in which to leave a short note about the purpose of this particular URL flip. The audience will never see what you enter into the Comment field. Both the Windows Media Player and the RealMedia Player support the URL command. The URL command is the easiest to understand and use, and is probably the command you'll use most often if you use any at all.

You can add many other types of metadata with a command marker. Click the arrow for the Command drop-down list to see the various options. The first several options are text options and are only supported in the Windows Media Player. Basically, they allow you to attach text messages to your ACID composition. The first of these messages (Text) creates text that appears in the captioning area of the Windows Media Player (just below the video display area). The other three text options create text that appears on the HTML page in which the streaming media is embedded. You'll need to know something about Hypertext Markup Language (HTML) to understand how to incorporate these commands on your Web pages.

The next three options are Title, Author, and Copyright. These options allow you to embed identification information into your project. The user's media player will display these commands. Both the Windows Media Player and the RealMedia Player support these three commands.

Only the RealMedia Player supports the options that begin with "HotSpot." These options allow you to create clickable areas on your streaming video, which can provide a bit of interactivity. HotSpotPlay enables you to specify a new RealMedia file that will be launched when the hotspot is clicked. HotSpotBrowse enables you to specify a new Web page that will be launched when the hotspot is clicked. HotSpotSeek enables you to specify a specific point in the current RealMedia file to which the player will jump when the hotspot is clicked.

The last two options are specialized options for use in very specific broadcast situations. If you don't know what they are, you probably don't need to worry about them!

Popular Streaming Formats

ACID can render to several different streaming formats. Some are specifically designed for video, some for audio, and some work for both. Each has several different templates from which you can choose to create a file that is optimized for a particular target bandwidth. Table 17.1 describes the various streaming media formats available in ACID.

TABLE 17.1 Streaming Media Formats

Extension	Description	General Uses
.mov	QuickTime	For delivery of audio and video files. Compatible with QuickTime players.
.rm	RealMedia	For delivery of audio and video files. Compatible with Real Networks players such as RealPlayer and RealMedia Jukebox.
.wmv	Windows Media Video	For delivery of video files. Compatible with the Windows Media Player.
.wma	Windows Media Audio	For delivery of audio files. Compatible with Windows Media Player.

The following list gives a little bit of additional information for each of these file formats:

- **QuickTime Codecs.** The QuickTime format was developed by Apple Computers. QuickTime files can contain both audio and video. This format enables you to create everything from uncompressed high-quality audio/video files (not suitable for streaming), to highly compressed files specifically for streaming.

- **RealMedia Codec.** Most people agree that the inventive minds at RealNetworks are the folks who put streaming media technology on the map. The RealPlayer (and the associated file type RM) are widely used on the Internet. RealMedia files can contain both audio and video. It is also possible to embed metadata into RealMedia files.

- **Microsoft Codecs.** Microsoft offers the WMA and WMV formats. Although WMA is strictly an audio format, WMV can include both audio and video content. Both file types support metadata.

Task: Rendering a Streaming Media File with Embedded Metadata

In this task, you'll create a .wma file with a URL flip that takes listeners to ACIDplanet.com (you might want to use the URL for your own Web page) where they can search for—and listen to—more of your ACID compositions.

1. By this point in the book, you've probably created an ACID project or two of your own. If so, open one of your projects now. If you don't have one of your own, open one of the projects from one of the other hours on the companion CD. You might try the project from Hour 13 for instance. Place the cursor in the last measure of an ACID project and press the C key on your computer keyboard. (Alternatively, choose Insert, Command.) This action opens the Command Properties dialog box.

2. By default, the URL command is selected. Open the Command drop-down list to see the other commands you can embed. Close the list, making sure that the URL option is still selected.

3. Type **http://www.ACIDplanet.com** in the Parameter field as shown in Figure 17.3. Write a note to yourself about the command you are using in the Comment field. The Position field reflects the current command marker location. Click OK to place the marker.

17

FIGURE 17.3

Drop a command marker to cause a URL flip in your streaming file.

4. The Commands bar opens at the top of your project and a command marker is placed at the cursor location. The information attached to the marker shows the command and the specific parameters that will be embedded as metadata.

5. Choose File, Render As. In the Render As dialog box, navigate to the location where you want to save the file. Select Windows Media Audio 7 (*.wma) from the Save As Type drop-down list. Select 56Kbps Stereo from the Template drop-down list and read the information in the Description field. Name the file **URLDemo.wma** and click Save.

6. Make sure that your Internet connection is active. In Windows Explorer, navigate to and double-click the file you created in the previous step. This launches the Windows Media Player, which plays the file. (Notice that at the 56Kbps encoding setting, sound quality suffers quite a bit.) When the file reaches the point where you placed the command marker, your browser launches and opens the ACIDplanet home page. Fun!

Summary

In this hour, you learned how ACID allows you to save your media files in several different formats. You learned some basics about the quality of digital audio files and about the factors that go into striking a balance between file size and audio fidelity. Now you know how to save your file into the most popular formats, including those that help you deliver your songs on the Internet. You know when and why you have to shrink your files down for Internet delivery, and how far you have to shrink them.

Q&A

Q. Why is it so important to learn about sample rates and bit depths?

A. When it comes to distributing your audio files, you want to distribute the best-quality audio you can, given the method of delivery you choose. As you learned in this hour, sample rates and bit depths affect the fidelity and size of the audio file. Familiarizing yourself with the differences can help you determine the best settings for each file you prepare.

Q. Why do we spend so much time worrying about bandwidth?

A. Bandwidth is the critical factor in determining the quality settings for streaming media. The higher the quality of the audio file, the larger the file itself, and the higher the data transfer rate requirements for Internet streaming. If you don't have an understanding of your target audience's bandwidth limitations, you can't choose the proper streaming media templates with which to encode your songs.

Q. How can I quickly find out more about streaming media so that I can fully use the advanced features ACID supplies for saving Windows Media and RealMedia files?

A. A wealth of information regarding streaming media exists on the Internet itself. Three great places to start are the help files of the RealPlayer, Windows Media Player, and Apple's QuickTime player. You can also access a huge amount of information on the Web sites for Microsoft (`http://www.microsoft.com/ms.htm`), Real Networks (`http://www.real.com/`), and Apple Computers (`http://www.apple.com/`). Finally, a search for "streaming media" on your favorite Internet search engine should come up with more information than you can handle!

Workshop

The following quiz and activities will help you review some important information about saving audio files and the various properties that can affect file size and download speed.

Quiz

1. What two uncompressed audio formats does ACID support, and which operating systems are they compatible with?

2. True or False: Providing that all else is equal, a 44,100Hz audio file is twice as large as a 22,050Hz audio file.

3. True or False: Providing that all else is equal, a mono 44,100Hz audio file is twice as large as a stereo 22,050Hz audio file.

4. What is bandwidth and how does it relate to the quality of a sound file?

Quiz Answers

1. ACID supports WAV and AIFF file formats. They are compatible with Windows and Macintosh systems, respectively (although these days, both systems can typically play both formats).

2. True. A 16-bit stereo audio file consumes about 10MB per minute at 44,100Hz, and about 5MB per minute at 22,050Hz.

3. False. Actually, they are the same size. A 44,100Hz file is twice as large as a 22,050Hz file, and a stereo file is twice as large as a mono file. Therefore, a mono 44,100Hz file is the same size as a 22,050Hz stereo audio file.

4. Bandwidth is the amount of data a specific connection speed can handle. Although it does not directly affect the quality of a sound file, bandwidth does affect the properties you must select to encode a file that can stream effectively. You must reduce the size of a file to play properly over low-bandwidth connections. Reducing the size of the file typically reduces the quality of the file.

Activities

1. Select one of your favorite ACID projects and save it as a WAV file using the following three setting configurations. Even though all these files will be roughly the same size, notice how different they sound:

    - 22,050Hz, 16-bit, Stereo. Use the filename `22-16-S.wav`.
    - 44,100Hz, 16-bit, Mono. Use the filename `44-16-M.wav`.
    - 44,100Hz, 8-bit, Stereo. Use the filename `44-8-S.wav`.

2. Encode the same project you used in the first activity to your choice of Windows Media, RealMedia, or both. Experiment with the various templates to learn how each setting affects the audio quality of the file.

Hour 18

Burning to a CD

Have you always dreamed of releasing your own CD of original music? Now you can. It's easy to create an audio CD of your compositions without ever leaving ACID.

ACID enables you to create a CD that conforms to the Red Book CD standards, which means that you can play the CD you create on any audio CD player. Play it in your car, your home stereo, or your little brother's boom box. It's easy to create—or "burn"—your own CDs with ACID. We'll show you how.

In this hour, you will:

- Configure preferences for CD recording
- Burn your ACID tunes to CD, one track at a time
- Close the CD project so that it can play on any standard CD player

Creating CDs

To burn the project you currently have open in ACID to a *Red Book standard* stereo *PCM* audio file, make sure that you have a blank (or unclosed, which we'll explain in a few minutes) recordable CD (CD-R) in your CD burner, and choose Tools, Create CD from the ACID menu bar.

New Term

Red Book Standard

Phillips and Sony (the companies that developed CD technology) created the *Red Book* standard as a way to ensure the universality in audio CD production. Among other things, the Red Book standard (so named because the binder that contained the original document had a red cover) specifies the total number of minutes' worth of digital audio that can be included on a CD (74), the data transfer rate that must be supported (150Kbps), the sampling rate that must be used (44,100Hz), and the audio bit depth (16-bit).

PCM

PCM, which stands for Pulse Code Modulation, is a technique for digitizing analog signals. It is used on all audio CDs.

Using the *track at once* method of burning audio files, you can create CDs of your original music without ever leaving ACID. The prices of blank CD-Rs and CD recorders (or burners) are dropping all the time. Burning your own CDs is a great way to capture even a rough mix that you can then take to a listening environment you're used to (such as your car or living room) and compare your mix to that of a major label release. This is a valuable exercise because it can give you a perspective you might not be able to obtain sitting at your PC. Burning a CD also provides a high-quality way to share your music with others. Taking a CD over to a friend's house is a lot easier than lugging your PC across town!

New Term

Track At Once

With *track at once* CD burning, your burner's recording laser turns off at the end of every track. This capability allows you to save your songs to CD one track at a time, so that you can add your current song to the disc and put the CD aside until you have another song to add later.

Always remember to save the project before burning it to CD. Saving the project as an .acd or .acd-zip file makes it easy to recall the project if you ever want to edit or remix the composition.

Of course, to take advantage of the Create CD feature, you must have a *CD-R* (Compact Disc-Recordable) or *CD-RW* (CD-ReWritable) drive installed in your PC. Many PCs come with this option. Check the documentation that came with your PC to verify that your CD-ROM drive is a CD-R or CD-RW. If it's not, these drives are relatively inexpensive and not that hard to install. Trust us, once you hear your own music playing out of your CD player, you'll be glad you've got the ability to burn your own.

NEW TERM

CD-R and CD-RW Drives

A CD-R drive can create data CDs or audio CDs. It uses a special type of CD (also called a CD-R). CD-R drives are capable of multisession recording, which means that you can add data to the CD at different times rather than all in a single session. After you've burned a song to a CD-R disc, you cannot remove that song from the disc.

CD-RW drives use a different type of CD-ROM disc called CD-RW. These discs and drives are slightly more expensive than CD-R discs and drives. The advantage is that you can treat these discs much like a floppy disk in that you can store and remove files to and from the disc. A new standard developed by Philips and Hewlett-Packard enables CD-ROM players to read discs created by CD-RW drives.

18

Some home and car CD players will not play audio CDs created on CD-RW discs. Check your CD player's documentation or check with the manufacturer to see whether your player supports these discs.

Setting Preferences for CD Recording

Before you burn your first track, set the Create CD preferences to match the type of burner you have in your PC; you must also set the write speed. Choose Options, Preferences, CD to open the Preferences dialog box shown in Figure 18.1. From the Write Drive drop-down list, choose your CD-R drive. From the Write Speed drop-down list, pick the default recording speed for your CD recorder. If you choose Max, ACID uses the fastest speed your CD-R drive supports.

FIGURE **18.1**

The CD tab of the
Preferences dialog
box.

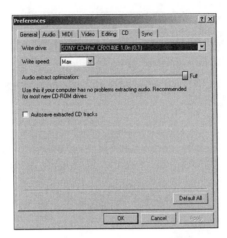

 The highest write speed is not always the best choice. Other factors (such as hard drive access speed) come into play. Opinions vary concerning the optimum speed settings. Some suggest that you should never exceed 2X; others suggest that you set the speed setting at half the amount that your CD-ROM burner supports. Ultimately, trial and error teach you the optimal speed for your system. You might have to sacrifice a CD or two (a process also known as "creating coasters"...great Mother's Day gift idea!) before you find the right speed for your configuration.

Burning a Track to a CD

Choose Tools, Create CD to open the Create CD dialog box shown in Figure 18.2. To burn a track to CD, you must have a project open and a CD-R disc in your CD-R drive. If you don't, the Add Audio button in the Create CD dialog box is unavailable. The time needed for audio (this value is slightly more than the length of your ACID song) and the time available on the disc are listed at the bottom of the dialog box. If you have previously added tracks to the CD, compare the two values to verify that you have enough time remaining on the disc to accommodate the current project.

 In this discussion, the word "track" is used in the context of a song on the CD you are burning. This is not to be confused with the individual tracks that make up your ACID project. In other words, you are burning your ACID project (which happens to contain several tracks) to a single track on your CD.

FIGURE 18.2

To open the Create CD dialog box, choose Tools, Create CD.

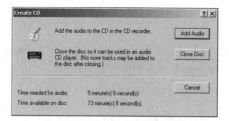

Remember that the Red Book standard dictates that CDs must be recorded at a sample rate of 44,100Hz. If you create your ACID projects at a different sample rate, your song lengths may be miscalculated. Before you burn your song to CD, set the sample rate of your ACID project to 44,100Hz and the bit-depth to 16-bit. Choose File, Properties, Audio to open the Audio tab of the Project Properties dialog box. Choose 44,100 in the Sample Rate (Hz) drop-down list and 16 from the Bit-Depth drop-down list.

Click the Add Audio button to start recording the project to the CD-R disc in the drive. A progress bar at the bottom of the dialog box shows the progress of the recording process. When the recording is complete, the Create CD dialog box closes, and the CD Operation box dialog shown in Figure 18.3 opens to convey information about the success or failure of the recording process.

18

FIGURE 18.3

The CD Operation dialog box reports the success or failure of the recording operation.

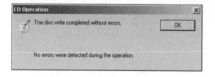

Unless absolutely necessary, do not click the Cancel button in the Create CD dialog box once the disc-writing process has begun. Interrupting the writing process makes the entire disc unusable.

Task: Adding a Track to a CD-R Disc

This task takes you through the steps of adding a track to a CD-R disc.

1. Create or open an existing project. If you create a project, be sure that you save the project as an `.acd` or `.acd-zip` file before continuing.

2. Choose Project, Properties to open the Properties dialog box. Click the Audio tab and set the Sample Rate (Hz) field to 44,100 and the Bit-Depth field to 16. Click OK.

3. Insert a blank or partially-filled (but not closed, as discussed in the next section) recordable CD-R disc into your CD-ROM recorder.

4. Choose Tools, Create CD. Compare the time needed for audio with the time available on the CD to verify that you have enough room to burn your project.

5. Click the Add Audio button in the Create CD dialog box.

6. At the end of the recording process, the CD Operation dialog box reports whether or not errors occurred when writing the disc. Rarely should you experience any problem burning your discs—especially if you ran the experiments we suggested earlier to find the optimal burning speed for your system. If the dialog box reports an error, revisit the discussion on finding the right burning speed and try again. Click OK.

Closing the CD

Even though you've burned your song to the CD, you still cannot listen to it in your home or car stereo at this point. You must first *close* the CD. Because, in most cases, you want to add more than one song to the CD, be sure to handle the disc carefully and keep it in a safe place to prevent dust and scratches from damaging the disc's surface. As you complete more ACID projects, continue to burn them one track at a time until you fill the CD or complete the project. When you've recorded everything you want to the CD, close the CD so that you can play it on your home or car stereo systems. You can close the CD only once, so don't close your CD until you finish burning all the songs planned for the disc.

NEW TERM

Close the CD

When you *close* a CD, ACID writes a table of contents to the disc. This table of contents provides the CD player with the information it needs to recognize the start and end of distinct tracks on the disc. Without the table of contents, the CD player cannot play the disc because it has no way to find the tracks.

Task: Closing Your CD Project

Closing a disc is easy to do. Simply follow these steps.

1. Insert the CD you want to close into your CD-ROM burner.

2. Choose Tools, Create CD. The Create CD dialog box opens.

 If the Close Disc button is disabled, it means that no tracks exist on the CD in the CD-Recorder drive.

3. Click the Close Disc button. A progress bar keeps you informed of the time that remains until completion of the process.

4. When ACID finishes closing the disc, the CD Operation dialog box presents information about the success of the operation. Click OK to close the dialog box.

5. Remove the CD from your CD recorder and insert it into a standard audio CD player or into the CD-ROM drive on your computer. Test the CD to verify that all tracks play properly.

18

Summary

ACID Pro enables you to burn your songs to CD quickly and easily. After you configure your CD recording preferences, it is a simple process to insert a CD-R into your burner and choose Create CD from the Tools menu. You create your own original CDs by recording each project, one track at a time, to the CD-R disc.

Q&A

Q. I started a CD and have recorded several tracks to it successfully. I used that CD when I burned another track that didn't complete successfully. Can I copy the successful tracks to another CD and try again?

A. You can't copy CD audio files in the same manner that you copy computer data files. But you do have two options, one of which uses the files you successfully burned to the CD. First, use ACID to close the CD that contains the successful and unsuccessful tracks. Then choose Tools, Extract Audio from CD to extract the good tracks from the CD. ACID extracts the tracks as .wav files. Open the first .wav file into a new ACID project as a one-shot. Place a new CD-R in the CD burner and choose Tools, Create CD. Burn the other recovered tracks to the CD in the same manner.

Alternatively, use ACID to reburn all the original projects onto a different CD. To avoid a similar problem happening again, keep a "scratch CD" open so that you can test how a track burns before you add it to your final CD project. If it has been a while since you tested your CD Preference settings, test-burn a track on the scratch CD. If the test burn succeeds, repeat the process on the final destination CD. If the test proves unsuccessful, adjust the CD Preferences as described earlier this hour.

Q. **Is there an easy way (without listening to all the tracks) to tell whether all the tracks were recorded correctly?**

A. ACID notifies you that it burned a track successfully when it completes the track. You can also compare the length of each track to the length of your ACID projects. If they are the same, the track likely burned successfully.

Q. **How can I burn songs to CD if I'm not using one of the versions of ACID that has the CD-burning capability?**

A. Save your project as a .wav file. Then use the CD authoring software that came with your CD-R drive, or some other third-party software that accomplishes the same task. One popular CD authoring program is Adaptec Easy CD Creator.

Workshop

As always, we have a workshop at the end of the hour that helps you retain what you've learned. The workshop for this hour focuses on burning projects to CD.

Quiz

1. What is meant by track at once burning?

2. Why can't you listen to your CD in your home stereo as soon as you finish burning your new song to it?

3. How do you know whether or not you have enough room on the CD for your latest song?

Quiz Answers

1. Track at once burning means that you can add a track to the CD-R without closing the disc and then add more tracks later until you have filled the disc. When you have added to the disc all the tracks you desire, you close the disc so that you can play it on any audio CD player.

2. For a CD to be recognizable to your home stereo CD player, it must first be closed. The closing process creates the table of contents information that your home stereo CD player needs to recognize the new CD.

3. ACID knows the length of the audio you are trying to add to the CD, as well as the amount of space remaining on the CD. ACID displays this information for you at the bottom of the Create CD dialog box. Compare the Time Needed for Audio value with the Time Available on Disc value to see whether enough space exists for your song.

Activities

1. Now that you've learned how to burn songs to CD, the activity for this hour is obvious! Burn one or more tracks to CD. Don't forget to close the CD before you pass it along to your friends.

18

HOUR 19

Publishing to ACIDplanet.com

ACIDplanet.com is a free online community of ACID composers who publish original ACID creations on the site so that other "citizens" of the planet can listen to and rate their music. You, too, can become a citizen and can publish your ACID songs for others to hear.

This hour focuses on ACIDplanet.com and how you can publish your songs there.

In this hour, you will:

- Register yourself as an ACIDplanet.com citizen
- Publish an ACID song to ACIDplanet.com
- Explore publishing in various formats

Introducing ACIDplanet.com

With your Internet connection active, open ACID and choose Help, ACIDplanet.com. The ACIDplanet home page opens as shown in Figure 19.1.

Click the buttons in the navigation bar just below the ACIDplanet.com logo to explore
the following key areas of the site:

FIGURE 19.1

*Get familiar with the
ACIDplanet.com home
page.*

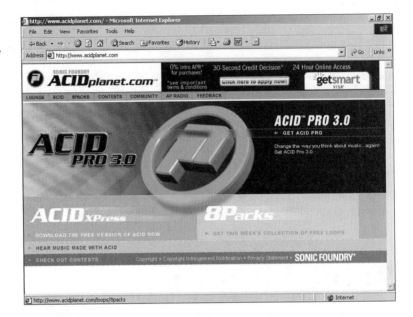

- **Lounge:** Upload your songs, play or download music created by other citizens,
  rate and review songs, and create your own personal playlist.

- **ACID:** Download the free version of ACID (ACID Xpress) and learn more about
  the for-sale versions. You can also follow links to obtain information about Sonic
  Foundry loop libraries and other ACID-related tools.

- **8Packs:** Download a new (free) ACID project and an "8-pack" of loops each week.
  Learn how the project was constructed along with a few of the tips and tricks used
  in production.

- **Contests:** Learn about and participate in remixes and other events that often
  involve major artists. Artists who have been featured on ACIDplanet in the past
  include the Beastie Boys, Garbage, Beck, and Depeche Mode.

- **Community:** Participate in user-based bulletin boards, where citizens announce
  their new songs, share tips and tricks, ask questions, solve problems, and voice
  their opinions about and experiences with ACID.

- **AP Radio:** Listen to a playlist of songs from ACIDplanet.com in your default
  media player.

- **Feedback:** Share your thoughts with the people who created and maintain
  ACIDplanet.com.

Because ACIDplanet.com continually evolves, we can only tell you what the site looks like and how it functions today, as we write this hour. Things may look or behave differently by the time you read this, but regardless, ACIDplanet.com will continue to function as a valuable resource and community of people who love to make music with ACID!

Becoming an ACIDplanet Citizen

Citizenship to ACIDplanet.com is free. Although you don't have to become a citizen, some areas and features of the site are available only to citizens. To become a citizen, click the Lounge button. From the Lounge submenu, choose My Planet. In the menu of choices on the left side of the screen, click the Become A Citizen button. Complete and submit the registration form.

Task: Registering for ACIDplanet.com Citizenship

Follow the steps in this task to become an ACIDplanet citizen.

1. Enter your Profile Name. This is the name you will be known by on the planet.

2. Enter and validate your e-mail address.

When you submit your registration (as explained in step 7), ACIDplanet.com sends your password to the e-mail address you enter here. Make sure that you enter a valid e-mail address, or you won't receive your password to the planet!

19

3. Select a Maximum Content Rating. Figure 19.2 shows the options available for this setting.

Because a wide variety of citizens inhabit ACIDplanet, song content ranges from "squeaky clean" (G) to "#@%# YOU" (R). Select your rating limit from the Maximum Content Rating list to weed out content that you may find objectionable. Any content with a rating higher than the rating you select does not appear in the list of songs that ACIDplanet.com provides for you.

Be careful not to prevent yourself from listening to your own songs. If you set your Maximum Content Rating to PG for example, and then later upload a song that you give a PG-13 rating, you will not be able to see or hear your own song on the site!

You can always change your rating to a different setting later if you want to. See the tip on page 313 to learn how to edit your ACIDplanet citizenship information (including the maximum rating).

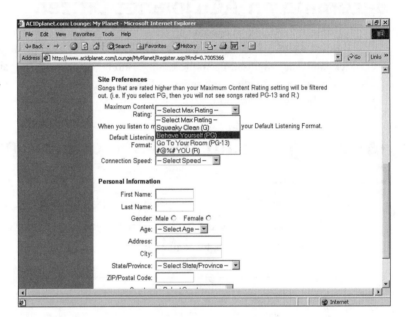

FIGURE 19.2

When you set the Maximum Content rating, select an option that allows you to hear your own recordings.

4. From the Default Listening Format list, set the desired format to Windows Media or Real Media.

5. Choose the connection speed that most closely matches your own from the Connection Speed list.

6. The remainder of the fields seek more personal information. Enter your name, gender, age, and address information. This information is strictly optional, so you can register without supplying it and still receive full citizenship benefits. If you'd like to read the ACIDplanet privacy statement before supplying this information, click the Privacy Statement link at the bottom of the ACIDplanet home page.

7. Click the Register button. A dialog box asks you to confirm the e-mail address you entered in step 2. Click OK to confirm that the address is valid.

8. Within a few moments, ACIDplanet.com sends e-mail confirmation of your citizenship, along with your computer-generated password. Make a note of the password in a safe place, because you'll need it when you log on to the ACIDplanet.com site.

9. Click the Login button in the navigation area on the left side of the My Planet section of the Lounge. Type your e-mail address and the password you received by e-mail. Click the Log In button. Now you have full access to all areas of ACIDplanet.

> Click the Edit/Delete Profiles button to edit your ACIDplanet citizenship information at any time. We strongly suggest that you immediately do so, so that you can change your personal password to one you can more easily remember and feel more secure using.

Posting Your Songs to ACIDplanet.com

Now that you're a citizen of ACIDplanet, you can post your songs to the site from within ACID. As we discussed in Hour 17, "Creating Mixed Audio and Video Files," ACID allows you to publish your song to file formats that stream over the Internet. You can also publish a higher-quality version of the song that visitors can download and listen to offline.

ACID provides two methods for publishing your songs to ACIDplanet.com. You can publish the project you currently have open, or you can publish existing files (as long as those files have already been saved in a streaming format).

Publishing the Current Song

When you choose to publish the project you currently have open, ACID makes nearly all the encoding decisions for you. Make sure that your Internet connection is active and click the Publish to ACIDplanet.com button in the ACID toolbar to launch the Publish to ACIDplanet.com Wizard shown in Figure 19.3.

19

FIGURE 19.3

Use the Publish to ACIDplanet.com Wizard to publish your music.

Make sure that you register yourself as an ACIDplanet.com citizen as discussed a few minutes ago before you attempt to publish your songs. Unfortunately, the ACIDplanet team has experienced abuses of the publishing features in the past and must now require registration before publishing so that future abuses can hopefully be avoided.

On the first page of the wizard, notice that the Publish Your Current ACID Song (Choose a Streaming Format) radio button is selected by default. In the drop-down list for this option are options for Good and Best quality for Windows Media, Real Media, and MP3 files. Choose the format you want to use to publish the song. Click the Next button to continue.

The Publish to ACIDplanet.com Wizard enables you to hear what your file sounds like in the selected file format before you publish it. This is a great time saver because you don't have to complete the process only to discover that the sound quality is unacceptable, making it necessary to republish the song. To preview the song in the streaming format you selected, click the Preview Now button before you click the Next button on the first page of the wizard.

ACID encodes the project and opens a special Upload page at ACIDplanet.com (see Figure 19.4). Select the profile name you want to use for the song from the Profile Name drop-down list. Enter the song title and description, and give the song a rating. You can assign up to three genres to your song to help other citizens find it when they are searching for the genre (style) of music they like. Supply any copyright information you want to attach to the song and enable the I Agree check box to indicate that you have read and agree to the terms of material submission.

It is important that you read and understand the ACIDplanet.com User Material Submission Agreement. If you have not read it, click the Submission Agreement link in the upper-left corner of the window to review it. This link opens the agreement in a separate window, so it won't disrupt the register-and-upload process.

FIGURE 19.4

Provide information about the song you're uploading to ACIDplanet.com.

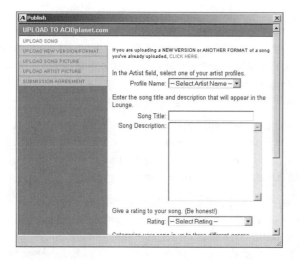

Click the Upload Now! button. A dialog box gives you another chance to confirm that you've read the submission agreement (and points out why it's important). Click OK to continue. The file begins to upload to ACIDplanet.com, and a progress bar tracks the upload status. When the upload is complete, click OK. The next screen indicates that your song is now available in the ACIDplanet Lounge. Click the `in the Lounge` link to navigate to the Lounge, where your song is now available for everyone to hear. Congratulations; you've just published your first song!

ACID not only publishes the song to ACIDplanet, but also saves it in the ACID program folder on your hard drive. The next time you use this method to publish a song, ACID saves the new song to the ACID program folder as well. Here's where you need to be careful.

Every song you encode using this method of publishing to ACIDplanet.com is saved to the same file in your ACID program folder. In other words, when you publish the second song, it replaces the first song, and it does so without giving you any notice. The first song no longer exists on your hard drive unless you've saved it elsewhere!

The reason for this is that ACID passes that filename to ACIDplanet.com so that you can easily publish the song without having to browse for the file. If you want fast and easy, this method works great. If you want more control, use the method described in the next section.

19

Publishing an Existing File

The second method of publishing a song directly from ACID requires a bit more work, but pays off in the added control you get over the publishing process. We suggest that after you become familiar with how ACIDplanet.com works, you should use this second method to publish your ACID songs most of the time.

Before publishing a song with this method, you must render the file in a streaming format. Follow the procedures for doing so outlined in Hour 17. When the song exists on your computer's hard disk in a streaming format, choose File, Publish or click the Publish to ACIDplanet.com button in the ACID toolbar.

On the first page of the Publish to ACIDplanet.com Wizard, enable the Publish a Different Song (Must Be in a Streaming Format) radio button and browse to the location of the file you want to publish. (Make sure that you choose the appropriate file type from the Files of Type drop-down list at the bottom of the Browse for File dialog box.) When you've located the file you want to publish, click the Next button in the wizard.

From this point on, the process is the same as the one described in the previous section. Note that this method is not subject to the caution about overwriting filenames. Because you first encoded and saved your file to your hard drive, you don't have to worry that it will be replaced by the next publish operation you undertake.

Publishing Multiple File Formats

Keep in mind that users connect to the Internet at various speeds, and that people have different preferences when it comes to the file format they like to listen to. Some users prefer to listen to songs using Windows Media Player, while others prefer RealPlayer G2. Yet other visitors prefer to download higher-quality files so that they can listen to music offline.

To accommodate these various preferences, publish your songs in multiple file formats. This way, you can satisfy the listening preferences of a wider range of listeners. We encourage you to take the time to publish your songs in each of the file formats ACIDplanet.com supports (.mp3, .wma, and .rm).

After you render your song to each of these three formats, navigate to the ACIDplanet.com Lounge and click the Upload link. Click the Upload New Version/Format link. To fill in the File Name field, browse to the file you want to upload. Select the previously uploaded version of the same song from the Song Title drop-down list. Accept the Material Submission terms and click the Upload Now! button.

This process allows you to publish the same song in multiple formats. ACIDplanet.com knows which version to stream to the listener based on the default media player settings in the listener's My Planet profile.

The ACIDplanet.com Community Area

The Community area of the ACIDplanet.com site hosts several conferences to which you can post questions, answers, opinions, and so on. This section takes a few minutes to explore the ACIDplanet Community area of the site.

To get to the Community area from anywhere else in the ACIDplanet site, click the Community button in the main navigation bar. The conferences you can join cover several different categories, including the following:

- **Newbies:** Introduce yourself to the community and meet and greet new citizens.
- **ACIDplanet Main:** This conference is sort of a catch-all for general topics.
- **Artist and Song Plug Page:** Let others know you've posted a new song, or promote someone else's song.
- **Tips N Tricks:** Post "how-to" questions or share your cool ACID tips and tricks with your fellow citizens.
- **A.P. Suggestions and Complaints:** Speak your piece directly to the design and tech teams at ACIDplanet.
- **ACID Products:** Ask questions about the ACID product line.

Temporary conferences come and go in the ACIDplanet Community area, so you might see a conference that's not listed here[md]or you might not see one that *is* listed (although those we've listed are probably here to stay).

19

Each conference has a corresponding chat room where you can meet for "real-time" chats with others. Click the Chat button in the Community submenu to go to the Chat area for that conference. You can also see who else is currently visiting the planet and page someone you want to talk to directly. Click the Page button and then click the bell icon next to the name of the person you want to contact (see Figure 19.5). Type your message and click Send.

FIGURE **19.5**

Send a private message to anyone currently visiting the planet.

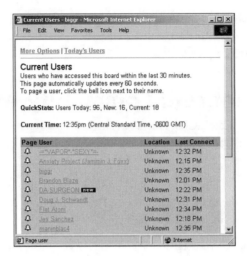

Building Community

The ACIDplanet community includes many thousands of people such as yourself. Most people who post their songs want to know what others think. They also want to know what they can do to improve their compositions.

There is something to be said about community participation. In general, the more you give, the more you get. Take the time to listen to the material other members create. Then send them a brief, honest, and courteous review of what you liked and what (in your opinion) needs improvement. Most people appreciate that you took the time, and they often return the favor. Soon, you'll build a network of friends who help one another improve and promote their music. It isn't long before the word starts to get out, and everybody wins.

Using the ACIDplanet Conferences

After you register yourself as a member, observe the conference area until you become familiar with each conference and the topics each addresses. You'll need to have a feel for the conferences and how to use them to your advantage.

When you're ready to dive in, post a message to the Newbies conference. Introduce yourself. Tell people a bit about who you are, and see who you can get to know. As you become more comfortable, branch out into the specific conference that addresses a topic in which you're interested. You'll be surprised at how quickly you become an old pro of the conferences. And don't be shy; most of the people who participate really want to help you!

Task: Posting a Message to the Newbies Conference

There's no real mystery to posting a message to any of the ACIDplanet conferences. In this task, you'll post your first message to the Newbies conference.

1. Navigate to the ACIDplanet.com home page and click the Community link to enter to the Community area of the site.

2. In the Conferences area on the left side of the screen, click the link to the Newbies conference.

3. Click the Post button in the Community submenu (just above the Conferences list). This action opens the Post a New Topic in "Newbies" form on the right half of the page.

4. In the Topic field, type the topic of your message.

5. Type the text of your message in the large text area field.

6. Click either of the Post buttons to post your message to the conference.

7. Check back later to see whether anyone has responded to your message.

Receiving and Giving Ratings and Reviews

If you posted a message to the Newbies conference, hopefully your brief introduction generates some interest. Now it's time to let folks know about your music. Post a message to the Artist and Song Plug Page. You'll likely pick up a few reviews of your work.

19

> ### C'mon, I Can Take It!
>
> Keep in mind that people (thankfully!) have different tastes in music. Not everyone will consider your compositions to be the best on the planet. Try to develop a thick skin. Even negative feedback can help you improve, and most citizens intend their negative feedback to be constructive. Take all advice—the good, the bad, and...well, you can ignore the ugly—as constructive criticism that can help you create even better music. Remember, if everyone says that they love your music, but you're not yet rich and famous, someone is not telling the truth!

If someone takes the time to give *you* an honest review, they will likely appreciate a review in return. If they don't ask, return the favor anyway. Be honest, but constructive and helpful in your review. Ask yourself questions about your own music, and then see whether or not the song you're reviewing shares the same problems, strengths, or opportunities. What kind of feedback do you want to get? What questions remain unanswered about your songs? These issues are probably on the minds of other composers as well, so if you can, address them in your reviews.

It's not always easy to review other people's music—especially people who, like you, are learning. Some pointers might help you give well-received and appreciated reviews:

- Tell others what you like about their music.
- Tactfully point out the areas you think need a little more work.
- Try to put a positive spin on your suggestions for improvement. For example, instead of saying, "That bass track is too loud and it sounds really bad," try something like, "If you cut back on the bass a little bit, everything will blend better." Another effective method of criticism is to frame your comments as a question. For example, "Do you think you would showcase that cool guitar lick more effectively if you cut the bass a little?"

Task: Reviewing a Song

If someone wants you to review a specific song, they generally provide a link you can follow to get to it. You can also use ACIDplanet.com's Search feature to search for a specific user or song title.

When you first enter the Lounge, the top song of the day appears at the upper portion of the page. By default, the top songs in all categories appear in a list beneath the number one song. The right side of the page lists artists who have recently uploaded songs.

This task shows you how to complete the review form for a song.

1. Click the Rate button that appears next to the song you want to review (the button contains a star icon). The Rate/Review form opens.

2. Click the appropriate radio button to rate the song from 10 stars to 1 star (10 being the best).

3. Type a one-line summary of your review in the small text field. Usually, the entries in this field contain 10 words or less and summarize the "feel" of the song. You might use a phrase such as "smooth as silk," or "a rough ride" to describe the song.

4. In the large text area, type your extended comments about the song.

5. Click the Post button when you are ready to send the review. The review is posted to ACIDplanet.

To read the reviews for any song, including your own, click a song title in list at the Lounge.

Summary

ACIDplanet.com gives you a way to share your ACID creations with thousands of people. Publish your songs to the planet, get feedback and reviews from other users, and help make your music even better. Part of the fun of making music is getting together with other musicians. Building a community of musicians and friends is what ACIDplanet is all about. Develop your own network of friends and colleagues at ACIDplanet.com.

Q&A

Q. Why do I have to register to become a citizen of ACIDplanet? Isn't it free?

A. You don't *have* to register, but you'll get more out of ACIDplanet if you do. Citizenship allows you to perform various tasks at ACIDplanet—among them, uploading songs, creating playlists, submitting ratings and reviews, and participating in the conferences. It also allows ACIDplanet.com to deliver content specifically targeted to your listening preferences. Finally, it protects you and other citizens from abuse that might occur if everyone were allowed to be totally anonymous.

Q. What happens if I change my song after I publish it to ACIDplanet.com? Can I update the song?

A. Of course you can. In the Lounge, click the Upload button. One of the upload options is to upload a new version or format of a song. This option allows you to either replace the same format of a previously uploaded song with a new version in the same format, or to upload the same song in a different format.

Q. What advantages does publishing an existing file have over publishing the current song?

A. When you choose to publish the current song (the song currently open in ACID) in the Publish to ACIDplanet.com Wizard, ACID makes most of the important decisions related to encoding the file for you. When you choose to publish an existing file, you gain more control over the encoding settings (such as format, bit rate, and where the encoded file is saved on your disk).

19

Workshop

So you want to publish your songs to ACIDplanet. This workshop jogs your memory to see whether you remember the most important steps.

Quiz

1. What area in ACIDplanet allows you to upload, download, and review songs?

2. True or false: Anyone can upload songs to ACIDplanet.com.

3. Can you upload multiple versions of the same song?

Quiz Answers

1. The Lounge.

2. False...and true. Only registered citizens of ACIDplanet.com can upload songs to the planet. However, anyone can register as a citizen so, in essence, the statement is true...with just a little work.

3. Yes, you can. In fact, it's encouraged. When you upload your songs in the MP3, RealMedia, and Windows Media formats, you increase the chances of people listening to them.

Activities

1. Go to http://www.acidplanet.com and explore the music others have already posted before you upload your first song. Doing a bit of exploring first helps you get a feel for the types of music people listen to, how to categorize your songs, and much more.

2. Publish a song to ACIDplanet in three formats: MP3, RealMedia, and Windows Media Audio. Listen to each version of the song.

HOUR **20**

Creating Music for Flash Movies

All the ACID techniques we've talked about so far have shown you how to use ACID to make amazing music. In this hour, you'll make the leap from creating music in ACID to shaping that exciting, original, royalty-free music specifically for use in your Flash projects.

You can easily spend a lot of money buying a few loops and maybe a song or two that is supposedly specially constructed for use in your Flash projects. Or you can use ACID to create an infinite number of high-quality, original compositions. You don't have to pay anything extra to use the music you create because you wrote it and you own it.

Throughout this hour, we give you only the steps in Flash that are important to understanding the process of using Flash in conjunction with ACID.

If you would like to learn more about Flash, Sams' Publishing has a number of good books to help. Among these is Sams' *How to Use Macromedia Flash 5* co-written by Gary Rebholz (yes, the same guy who co-authored this book) and Denise Tyler. This graphical approach to learning Flash can get you up and running fast.

In this hour, you will:

- Incorporate your ACID tunes into a Flash project
- Score music to your Flash animation
- Create blocks of music to use in your Flash projects
- Create a family of loops that work together in Flash

Adding Audio to Flash

Let's take the simplest case first. You've just finished creating your Flash animation, and now you want to add a bit of audio to it. Here's how you do it.

Preparing the Audio

First you have to create the audio. Use all the techniques you've learned so far in this book to create the audio you want to add to your Flash project. You can create everything ranging from short event sounds (such as sounds that play when the user clicks a button) to full-length sound tracks that play while the Flash movie rolls by.

Next you have to save your ACID project as a mixed file, which you learned to do in Hour 17, "Creating Mixed Audio and Video Files." In its basic configuration, Flash can import WAV, AIFF, and MP3 files. As explained in the tip below, we suggest that you use full-quality WAV files in your Flash projects. Later, when you save your Flash movie, you'll make some decisions on how to compress your audio. For now, start out with the highest quality you can.

We suggest that you save your loops at 44,100Hz and 16-bit depth. Generally, we advocate bringing the highest-quality audio possible into Flash. However, we do honor one exception: Because stereo files are twice as large as mono files, consider bringing all your Flash audio in as mono to ease the file size burden in your final project. Choose Mono, 44,100Hz, 16-bit PCM from the Template drop-down list to render these loops as mono files.

Adding the Audio to your Flash Movie

Then you must import the audio into your Flash Library. In Flash, choose File, New to start a new project or choose File, Open to open an existing project. Choose File, Import and navigate to the audio file you want to add to your project. Click Open to complete the operation.

After the audio file is imported into Flash, it appears in your Flash Library. To access the Flash Library, choose Window, Library. The Library contains any sounds you have imported, as well as all the other objects and symbols you've added in the course of building your Flash project. To preview the sound, click its filename in the Library and click the Play button at the top of the Library window (where you see the waveform representation of the sound).

Click the Insert Layer button to create a new layer in the Flash Timeline to hold the sound. Give the new layer a descriptive name so that you can easily identify it later. In the new layer, click the frame at which you want the sound to start and choose Insert, Keyframe. Click and drag the waveform from the Library window onto the stage. Nothing appears on the stage (after all, sound is invisible!), but a waveform representation of the sound appears in timeline of the chosen layer.

Setting the Flash Sound Export Settings

You'll want to pay some attention to how you deliver the audio from your Flash movie. This is particularly important if you intend to deliver your Flash animation on a Web page over the Internet. In this case, large file sizes create slow-loading Web pages. Because audio files are so large, you'll want to compress your audio for delivery over the Web.

In the Library, right-click the sound you just added to your project. Choose Export Settings from the shortcut menu. From the Compression drop-down list, choose MP3. Now the Bit Rate and Quality drop-down lists appear. Choose your desired bit rate. Higher bit rates result in higher sound quality and larger file sizes (which means longer download times). You'll have to find a compromise with which you can be happy. We usually settle between 20–32Kbps to keep the files size small.

From the Quality drop-down list, choose a quality setting. The Fast option gives you faster compression but lower quality; the Slow option gives you the best quality at the expense of compression speed.

20

Scoring Audio to Your Flash Movie

To move a step beyond simply importing your existing ACID compositions into the timeline of your Flash movie, use the ACID video track to help you compose music specifically for the Flash movie you've created.

Preparing Your Flash Movie

First you must create your Flash movie. Of course, this step is much more involved than the space we can give it here, but it wouldn't make sense not to mention it as the first step in this process. If you're familiar with Flash, you know that there are a lot of possibilities here. For the sake of this discussion, assume that you have created a scene in Flash that runs for a couple of minutes. Now you want some music to go along with the scene.

When your Flash movie is complete, export the movie as an AVI file. To do this, choose File, Export Movie. In the Export Movie dialog box, specify where to save the file, give the file a name, and choose Windows AVI (`*.avi`) from the Save As Type drop-down list. Click the Save button to begin the export.

The Export Windows AVI dialog box opens as shown in Figure 20.1. Here you specify some of the properties of the movie. Choose whatever settings are appropriate for your movie. Choose Disable from the Sound Format drop-down list if your movie does not yet have any audio. Choose the desired sound format if the movie does contain other audio that you want to import into your ACID project along with the video. Click OK to continue.

If you chose to compress the video, the Video Compression dialog box opens next. The Compressor drop-down list shows all the video codecs installed on your computer. If you are not familiar with compression and video codecs, Hour 10, "Scoring to a Video," contains a discussion on the subject. Choose the desired codec from the list and click OK. Flash exports the movie.

Scoring Music to the Movie in ACID

The next step is to add the AVI movie to your ACID project. Because you exported your Flash movie as an AVI file, ACID treats it exactly the same as other AVI movies. Refer back to Hour 10 if you need a refresher on how to work with video in ACID.

Now that your Flash movie is in the video track of ACID, you can watch the movie for important points where you want to create musical emphasis. Use the techniques you've learned in previous hours to score music to your video. All the techniques we discussed in Hour 10 to synchronize your music to your video work with the AVI file you exported from Flash, so you can truly create original (royalty-free) music that works with your Flash animation!

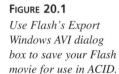

FIGURE 20.1

Use Flash's Export Windows AVI dialog box to save your Flash movie for use in ACID.

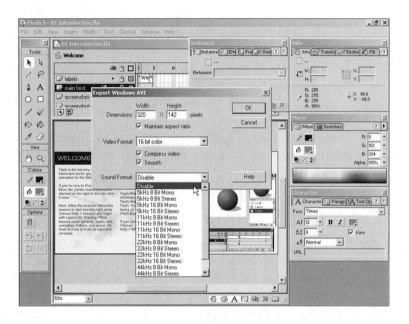

When you have completed the audio bed in ACID, render the project as a mixed audio file. Remember that later, you'll use the Flash Export settings to compress the audio portion of your Flash movie, so for now, we suggest rendering the mixed audio from ACID in a high-quality format such as WAV or AIFF at a sampling rate of 44,100 Hz, and a bit depth of 16. If you need help rendering a mixed audio file, Hour 17, "Creating Mixed Audio and Video Files," is devoted to the techniques and definitions you need.

Notice that here you render the audio out as a mixed audio file (such as WAV or AIFF). Do not render the ACID project out as a movie file (such as AVI). You don't need (or want) the video from the ACID project because the original exists in your Flash project. You simply want the audio so that you can add it to your Flash project.

20

Adding the Audio to Your Flash Project

Now import the mixed audio file into your Flash project. Create a new layer for the audio, add a keyframe at the desired starting point for the audio, and drag the audio from the Library to the stage.

If you spent time in ACID synchronizing the music to events in the movie, make sure that you set the audio's Sync Setting to Stream in Flash. This is the only way to preserve the synchronization. By default, Flash sees the audio as an Event sound, which is not synchronized to the playback of the visual portion of the movie.

To set the sound to streaming so that it synchronizes properly with the movie, choose Window, Panels, Sound. the Sound panel opens. In the timeline, click the keyframe that contains your audio file. The Sound panel now displays the name of the audio file in the Sound drop-down list. Choose Stream from the Sync drop-down list. Now, if the movie cannot stream (or play back) fast enough to keep up with the audio, Flash drops frames from the movie so that the music plays uninterrupted and always remains in synchronization with the movie.

Creating Submixes

So far, we've talked about the simplest cases for creating custom music in ACID for your Flash animations. In the second scenario (in which you score the music to the Flash movie rather than just importing an ACID audio file into the Flash timeline), a two-minute audio track means a fairly large file size. This could be a problem, particularly if you're delivering the Flash movie over the Web. Now, let's get a bit more sophisticated in our approach. We can take advantage of how Flash uses the Library to reference video and audio objects for use on the stage to make more efficient use of the music we create in ACID. In this section, you'll learn how to make submixes of your ACID composition and incorporate those submixes into your Flash project.

> In Hour 13, "Using the Mixer," we talked about making submixes in the context of mixing your ACID compositions. The concept is basically the same one we'll use here. You'll take certain sections of your project and render them as individual pieces of your song that you can later string together in Flash to re-create an arrangement. In the following sections, you'll learn a couple different approaches to creating submixes for use in your Flash projects.

Building an ACID Composition

Create the music you want to use in your Flash project. As you'll see later in the hour, it is helpful to pay close attention to the organization of your project. Suppose that your composition has an introduction, an A section, a B section, a C section, and a distinct ending section. The introduction is different from any other part of your project. The ending is probably also different from any other section. But the A section could be a verse, the B section the chorus or refrain, and the C section a recurring bridge. Therefore, each of these sections might be repeated numerous times throughout the composition. In other words, the structure of your composition might look like this: intro, A, A, B, A, B, C, B, C, A, B, ending. Use region markers to clearly and exactly identify each individual section. Hour 7, "Constructing Your Musical Arrangement," contains a discussion on how to use region markers to define your project sections.

> In a regular composition, you might want to slightly change each recurrence of a specific section. For instance, you might want the second verse to sound a little different than the first verse to build a bit of interest into the arrangement. For use in Flash however, it will be very helpful for all A sections to be exactly the same, all B sections to be exactly the same, and so on. Feel free to create variations on the sections in your ACID project if you're using the project for something else in addition to using it as an audio bed for your Flash animation; you might want to use the region name to identify the one variation you want to use in your Flash movie. Later, you'll see why this matters.

Rendering Horizontal Mixes

The first way to create submixes for your Flash project involves what we call "horizontal" mixes. If you've taken our advice and clearly identified the distinct sections of your ACID composition, you already have a good start on creating horizontal mixes. A horizontal mix is really just a section of your composition. Consider the sample structure we mentioned in the previous section: intro, A, A, B, A, B, C, B, C, A, B, ending. As you scan from left to right along the ACID timeline (that is, as you are moving horizontally across the project), you see the introduction section, the A section, the B section, and so on. In other words, you see all the regions you created as you constructed your composition.

Now render each subsection (or submix) out as an individual mixed file. To do this, double-click one of the region markers for the region you want to render (remember, each region represents a separate section of your composition). This action sets the loop region to exactly the length of the region.

Choose File, Render As to open the Render As dialog box. In the Save As Type drop-down list, choose Wave (Microsoft)(*.wav). Enable the Render Loop Region Only check box and click the Save button. ACID renders only the section of the song that falls within the loop region.

Repeat this process for every other section of the ACID composition that you want to use in your Flash movie. Now you have several pieces of your song in separate WAV files.

20

Before we talk about strategies for adding the submixes to your Flash movie, let's take a look at another type of submix.

Rendering Vertical Mixes

Whereas you create horizontal submixes by choosing sections of your project horizontally along the timeline, there is another way to look at submixing. We call this alternative approach "vertical" mixes, and they are more closely related to the submixes discussed back in Hour 13, "Using the Mixer."

First create the horizontal mixes we talked about in the preceding section. Then think about ways to break those submixes down vertically. What we mean is this: You can look at your ACID project horizontally as you did when you defined the various sections of the composition. You can also look at your project vertically. Think about the A section. This section is made up of several tracks—drums, bass, guitars, horns, keyboards, and so on.

To create vertical mixes, use different combinations of these tracks. For example, you might first make a mix containing only the drums from section A. You've already created a region to identify section A. Double-click one of the region markers for that section to set the loop region so that it exactly covers the section. Select all the drum tracks that have events in section A, and click the Solo button on any one of them. Because they are all selected, soloing one solos all of them. If any track is soloed, ACID renders only the soloed track (or in this case, all the soloed tracks). Choose File, Render As and save the file as a WAV. Make sure that you enable the Render Loop Region Only check box and then click Save. You now have a vertical submix of your horizontal submix of section A.

Create another mix of the same horizontal region, but this time solo the drums, bass, and rhythm section tracks. Finally, render one last mix with all the tracks from the region. Creating these vertical mixes within the horizontal mixes can help you get even more mileage out of your ACID composition.

In the sample arrangement we mentioned earlier, the A section of the song plays a number of times, but not necessarily consecutively. By creating a submix of the A section, you don't have to import it into Flash several times (which is, in effect, what you do if you import the entire song). You can import the submix once and then play it in your Flash project however many times you want. We'll show you just how to do this shortly.

Creating a Family of Compatible Loops

Before we talk about reassembling your song in Flash, let's look at one more way to break your ACID project down: by individual loops. If you really need to keep the file size of your Flash project low, this method might be your best option. In this section, you'll reassemble individual loops in Flash to re-create the composition. In a way, you'll use Flash a bit like you use ACID in that you'll add loops and arrange them on the timeline to create your song.

The problem is that Flash cannot automatically match the tempos and keys of the various loops like ACID can. So you could get some pretty bad-sounding, out-of-sync music. You need ACID to create a "family" of loops in the same key and tempo that will work well together when you bring them into Flash to assemble the arrangement.

Composing Your Music

In ACID, create the song you want to use with the Flash movie. It's best to keep the song simple because Flash's ability to mimic ACID goes only so far—and not really very far, at that! For example, you might not want more than three different keys or tempos in the ACID project.

Every time you have a key or tempo change, create a new region to cover it. For instance, if you have four bars in the key of A, create a region over those four bars. If the next four bars switch to E, create a region over those four bars as well. And don't bother getting too elaborate with instrumentation either. Flash supports only eight layers of audio and, as you'll see shortly, those eight layers are eaten up very quickly when you start reassembling your composition.

Figure 20.2 shows an example of a simple project with a couple of key and tempo changes (notice the key and tempo markers at the top of the ACID window, and the green region markers directly below them). In the next section, you'll export the loops used in this song to create the following family of loops:

- Region 1 creates loops in the key of A at a tempo of 120bpm.
- Region 2 creates loops in the key of A at a tempo of 140bpm.
- Region 3 creates loops in the key G at a tempo of 140bpm (the tempo carries over from the tempo change in region 2).
- Region 4 creates loops in the key of E and sets the tempo back to the original tempo of 120bpm.

20

Figure 20.2

Place key and tempo changes for each region.

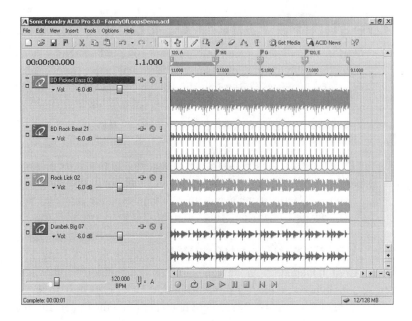

The ACID project you create does not really have to be a complete musical composition. Although the selection and combination of loops should make musical sense (that is, they should obviously sound nice together), you don't have to spend time mixing the project unless you plan to use it for something else in addition to your Flash soundtrack. In fact, track volume, panning, envelopes, and so on have no effect when the loops are exported; you'll simply be exporting the raw loops with their new key and tempo settings.

Exporting the Loops

Open the `FamilyOfLoopsDemo.acd` file from the Hour 20 Samples folder on the CD-ROM that accompanies this book. Choose File, Export Loops to open the Export Loops dialog box. Choose a folder into which to save the loops from the Save In drop-down list. ACID names the files automatically so that you don't have to type a name. Choose Wave (Microsoft) (`*.wav`) from the Save As Type drop-down list. Click Save to export the loops.

ACID exports the loops and appends the name of the original loops with a tempo and key. Figure 20.3 shows the family of loops created from the project shown in Figure 20.2. This list should match the loops you just exported. Notice that 12 loops are created. At first glance, it seems like some loops are missing. After all, there are 4 tracks and 4 key/tempo combinations for each track, so there should be 16 loops. However, two of the tracks (`BD Rock Beat 21.wav` and `Dumbek Big 07.wav`) are percussion tracks. A quick look at the track properties for these tracks in ACID shows that both are set to Don't Transpose. Because these loops don't change key with the project, it isn't necessary to create new loops for them at the key-change points.

FIGURE 20.3

The File, Export command creates a family of files.

Reassembling Your Song in Flash

We've looked at three general ways to prepare your music for importing into Flash. Now it's time to reassemble your composition. In the following sections, you'll use the loop family you created in the last section, import those loops into your Flash project, and build your music sound track. Because Flash supports only eight channels of audio, you're somewhat limited here, and you won't be able to re-create your ACID project exactly. But you can come close. Use the same methods discussed here to reassemble the horizontal and vertical mixes you created earlier.

In the following sections, everything we tell you to do is done in Flash—unless we specifically say to do it in ACID.

Task: Adding the Loops to the Timeline

20

In this task, you'll reconstruct your song in Flash using the family of loops you created in ACID.

1. Open an existing Flash project or create a new one.

2. Choose File, Import and navigate to the folder that contains the loops you want to use. In the Import dialog box, select all the loops that have a tempo of 120bpm. Some of these loops are in the key of A, some are in E, and some (the percussion loops) do not transpose. There are six loop files all together. Click Open to import the selected loop files.

3. Create five new layers in your Flash project (you should now have six layers). Give the layers the following labels:

   - Drum Beat
   - Percussion
   - Bass in A
   - Guitar in A
   - Bass in E
   - Guitar in E

4. Add 20 or 25 frames to each layer so that you can see more of the waveforms you're going to place in the layers. Adding frames to the layers also allows you to play and hear the audio.

5. Choose Window, Library to open the Flash Library. The loops you imported in step 2 appear in the Library.

6. Click the frame in the Drum Beat layer where you want the music to start. Choose Insert, Blank Keyframe (if it is the first frame of the scene, you don't have to insert a blank keyframe because there is already a keyframe there).

7. Drag BD Rock Beat 21 120.000 BPM.wav from the Library to the Flash stage. The waveform for the audio file appears in the Drum Beat layer of the timeline.

8. Repeat this process for each of the other files that you imported into your Flash project in step 2, putting each of them on the appropriate layer. Make sure that all the audio files start at the same frame, or your music tracks will not be in sync.

9. Now let's build 12 bars of music using these loops. First, figure out how many times you'll need to loop each file to make it last for 12 bars: Switch back to ACID. Double-click the Track Header icon for the BD Rock Beat 21 track to open the Track Properties dialog box. Click the Stretch tab, and look at the value in the Number of Beats field. This value tells you how many beats long this loop is. Because the loop is one beat long, it must play four times to make up one measure, and 48 times to last for 12 measures (12 measures times 4 beats per measure).

10. In Flash, choose Windows, Panels, Sound to open the Sound panel. Click the keyframe that holds the audio in the Drum Beat layer to select it, and type **48** in the Loops field of the Sound panel. This setting instructs Flash to repeat the Drum Beat loop 48 times (12 measures). Press the Tab key.

11. Repeat this process for the other loop files. Don't forget to check the number of beats for each loop in ACID because this number determines how many times you must repeat each loop in Flash to make it last for 12 bars (which is the number you must enter in the Loops field of the Sound panel). A four-beat loop must repeat only 12 times; an eight-beat loop must repeat 6 times, and so on.

The technique we show you here for building your soundtrack in Flash is fairly basic, although it's still somewhat complicated. Essentially, we're bringing the loops in as event sounds. Therefore, they must all start on the same frame of your movie so that they play in sync.

There are many techniques for using streaming sounds to build much more sophisticated compositions in Flash, but explaining these techniques would go well beyond the space we have available here. If you have the patience, desire, and Flash know-how, you can learn these more sophisticated methods.

We suggest that you become involved with a good Flash users group—and start asking a lot of questions! Your fellow Flash users should be happy to help you figure it all out, especially when you turn them on to how they can make royalty-free music for their own Flash movies using ACID! (And don't forget to tell them about this great book you read....)

Building the Arrangement

If you were to play your Flash project at this point, you'd hear that you have a real problem. Because all six layers of audio play at the same time in the timeline, you have a bass and guitar playing in A, and another playing in E. It sounds awful. We'll use the Flash Sound panel again to solve the problem.

The first two layers (Drum Beat and Percussion) don't transpose, so they can play straight through the full 12 bars. But for the bass and guitar, we'll start out with four bars in the key of A, switch to four bars in the key of E, and switch back to the key of A for the last four bars.

Select the keyframe that holds the audio in the Bass in A layer. In the Sound panel, click the Edit button to open the Edit Envelope dialog box. Click the button with the magnifying glass and a minus sign to zoom out the waveform display. Click the button until you can see all the loop repetitions (a vertical line running from top to bottom of the channel represents the end of one repetition and the beginning of another).

Click the Envelope line (the horizontal line at the top of the waveform) to add an envelope point. Adjust the point so that it sits on the line between the fourth and fifth loop repetition. Add another point just to the right of the one you just added. Drag the second point all the way to the bottom of the waveform, directly under the previous point you added (do this for both channels). This action drops the volume for this sound to zero after the fourth repetition. Add two more points, and raise the volume back up full between the eighth and ninth repetitions. Figure 20.4 shows what the Edit Envelope dialog box looks like after you've made your adjustments to the volume envelopes. Click

20

the Play button at the bottom of the Edit Envelope dialog box and notice that the bass plays for four bars, drops out, and comes back in for the last four bars.

FIGURE 20.4

Use the Edit Envelope dialog box to raise and lower the volume of your individual layers and create an arrangement.

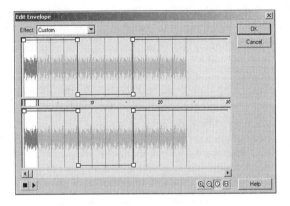

Use this technique in the other bass layer and the two guitar layers. Set your envelopes up so that the bass/guitar in the key of E are silent when the bass/guitar in the key of A are audible, and vice versa. You now have an arrangement, which is made up of very small loops that help you keep the file size of your Flash projects down.

Using a Combination Approach

As mentioned, creating a family of loops helps you keep the file size requirements of your Flash audio as small as possible. If you followed the example in the preceding sections, you are probably a bit disappointed in the limitations of having only eight Flash audio layers to work with. Okay, so we only used six layers in the preceding task. But in previous hours, you've worked with ACID projects that have many more than eight tracks. You've probably already begun to create your own projects that have many more than eight layers. You can see that the eight-layer limitation in Flash is going to be a problem. With just a bit more work, ACID can help.

To build more complex arrangements, combine the ideas of submixes with the concept of a loop family. Here's a simple example. In the project we use in this hour, there is a drum loop and a percussion loop. As you saw, these loops each took up a valuable audio layer in Flash. You can "buy" yourself an audio layer by combining these two loops as a vertical submix in ACID.

To do this, solo both percussion tracks in ACID. Create a loop region that encompasses just one measure. Choose Tools, Render to New Track. Give the file you are about to create a name and choose the save location on your hard disk. Make sure that you enable the

Render Loop Region Only check box. Click the Save button. ACID combines the portion of the soloed tracks that fall within the loop region, and creates a new loop and a new track to hold it.

Mute the original drum and percussion tracks, and draw in an event on the new track (the one holding the combined drum/percussion loop). Now, when you export your loops and import them into your Flash project, you have to sacrifice only one Flash audio layer to the drum and percussion tracks. With a little creative thinking, and this combination approach, you can actually build very sophisticated and intricate sound tracks for your Flash movies that you don't have to pay for in terms of hefty file sizes.

Summary

In this hour, we explored several different strategies for using ACID to create original music for your Flash projects. Those strategies included creating a complete musical arrangement for your Flash movie, creating horizontal and vertical submixes, creating a family of compatible files, and using a combination approach. You also learned how to add your audio to Flash and how to use the Flash Sound panel to reconstruct your musical arrangement. By using the techniques and tools discussed in this hour, you can take your Flash audio to an entirely new level.

Use the following workshop questions and activities to test your knowledge and use your new skills to make some music for Flash movies.

Q&A

Q. Can I put more than one sound on the same Flash layer?

A. Yes. Just add a new keyframe and add the new sound. If you're headed where we think you are with this question, read on to the next question.

Q. Rather than using the envelopes in Flash to raise and lower the volume of a loop, can't I just place the loops on the Flash timeline where I want them to start playing?

A. You can do that, but to achieve flawless transitions from one loop to the next, you're talking about much more advanced techniques than we have room to discuss here. To do it right, you'd have to calculate the mathematical relationship between the Flash frame rate, the tempo of your ACID song, and the length of the musical phrases you're trying to match up. You might also run into problems using event sounds in this scenario, and will have to know quite a bit about how Flash handles streaming sounds. It gets quite complicated, and you have to start asking whether or not it's worth the effort. If it is, start asking questions in the Flash users groups!

20

Q. If I use the family-of-loops method, how do I adjust layer volumes to create a pleasing mix?

A. In this hour, you used the Flash sound envelopes to set the sound to either full volume or no volume. You can also set the envelopes to any volume in between to attain the proper mix.

Workshop

Here are a few questions to test your new knowledge, and an activity to sharpen your new skills.

Quiz

1. You can bring your Flash movie into ACID and create music for it. How?

2. What is a horizontal submix?

3. If you have a track that has one key change and one tempo change, how many loops will be created if you use the Export Loops command?

Quiz Answers

1. Save your Flash movie as an AVI file and then open the AVI in the ACID video track.

2. A horizontal submix is when you break an ACID project into musical sections (for example, verses and chorus).

3. Assuming that the ACID Track Properties settings for this track are not set to Don't Transpose, three loops will be created: one for the original key and tempo, a second for the key change, and a third for the tempo change.

Activities

1. Create a project with four tracks. Draw in six bars of each track. Create a key change at bar 3 and a tempo change at bar 5. Use the Export Loops command to create a family of loops to use in a Flash project.

2. Create an ACID project with an A section and a B section. Create a horizontal submix for section A and another for section B. Create a vertical submix (for example, render just the percussion and bass tracks in section A). Use these mixes in a Flash project.

PART VII

Using the Companion Software

Hour

HOUR 21

Introducing Sound Forge XP Studio

The ACID Pro package includes several additional pieces of software from Sonic Foundry. One of these programs is Sound Forge XP Studio (XP for short). Sound Forge XP Studio is the XPress version of Sound Forge 5.0, Sonic Foundry's award-winning digital audio-editing tool. Sound Forge has often been referred to as the Swiss Army knife of digital audio editors, and XP gives you many of the same capabilities for your ACID project.

XP Studio is the perfect tool for recording and creating your own loops. It's also great for recording and editing dialog, sound effects, and music. The combination of ACID Pro and Sound Forge XP Studio creates a very powerful editing suite.

This hour serves as an overview of some of the key ACID-related features inside Sound Forge XP Studio.

In this hour, you will:

- Familiarize yourself with the Sound Forge XP Studio interface
- Discover Sound Forge XP Studio processes
- Work with Sound Forge XP Studio effects

Sound Forge XP Studio Interface

To write about all the features included in Sound Forge XP Studio would fill yet another book. Therefore, in this hour and Hour 22, we'll focus on the features that provide the most immediate benefit to ACID users. In this hour, we'll begin the overview by giving you a quick tour of the Sound Forge XP Studio workspace and menus. We'll pay special attention to those features that are most helpful to you when you're creating ACID projects.

Launch Sound Forge XP Studio. Open any audio file from the Hour 21 Samples folder on the CD-ROM that accompanies this book and take a look around. The XP workspace is where you open windows containing the files you want to edit. Although you can open more than one file in the XP at a time, you can play or edit just one file at a time. The title bar of each file window displays the filename, which makes it easy to keep track of the currently active file. Click a window to make it the active window. Any commands issued affect the file in the active window.

As you have learned, ACID is a nondestructive editor. You can edit all you want without changing the original source material. On the other hand, XP is a destructive editor. After you save the file, any changes you have made in XP become permanent. There are occasions for both styles of editing.

The Menus

Let's take a look at the menus in Sound Forge XP Studio. The **File menu** provides commands that relate to opening, saving, and assigning properties to your audio files.

If you do not have a data file open in Sound Forge XP Studio, not all options are available under the File menu. After you open a file, all options become available.

Sound Forge XP Studio opens and saves to a wide variety of popular audio formats. You can use XP to convert your ACID songs to just about any audio file format you can imagine.

The **Edit menu** contains commands that allow you to select and edit portions of an audio file. Some of these commands are not available until you select the sound file or change it in some way.

Among the key options in the Edit menu are Undo/Redo, Paste Special (which allows you to crossfade, mix, overwrite, or replicate a portion of your audio file with another segment of audio from the Windows Clipboard), and Trim/Crop (which deletes everything from your file except the selected portion).

The **View menu** provides commands that let you zoom into or out from your audio file. These commands allow you to zoom way in to your waveform and precisely edit or enhance your audio files.

Of particular interest is the Zoom Time command. This command provides quick ways to zoom in to extreme close-up views and zoom out to full views of the waveform display.

Another handy command found in the View menu is the Toolbars command. Choose this command to open the Preferences dialog box and select the toolbars you want to display. We recommend that you select the ACID Loop Creation Tools toolbar and dock it next to the buttons in the regular toolbars. This set of tools is a big help when you begin to create your own loops for use in ACID.

The **Special menu** provides commands that perform a variety of functions. Of special interest to ACID users are the markers and regions which you can use to mark portions of an audio file that work as loops. Use the ACID Looping tools to halve or double the selection area or to move the selection area forward or backward through the song (without moving the audio) to find other good loops. Finally, use the Edit ACID Properties command to ACIDize your loops in Sound Forge XP Studio. You'll learn more about these commands in Hour 22, "Improving and Editing Recordings."

The **Process menu** contains commands that allow you to improve or enhance the qualities of an audio file. Options worth pointing out are the EQ, Fade, and Normalize commands.

The **Effects menu** contains the basic effects included with Sound Forge XP Studio. Generally these effects are not as full-featured as the DirectX plug-in FX that we talked about in Hour 12, "Using Audio FX," but they are still very useful for shaping the sound of your files. Like all the processes already mentioned, effects are destructive edits in Sound Forge XP Studio.

The **Tools menu** enables you to rip songs from, and burn songs to, CD. The Tools menu also contains some interesting synthesis tools that can be fun to explore.

21

The **Options menu** allows you to set program options and preferences to customize certain XP behaviors to match your working style.

 The **Window menu** and **Help menu** are very similar to those you find in most other Windows programs. Use the commands in the Window menu to arrange the display of multiple windows you have opened in Sound Forge XP Studio. Use the commands in the Help menu to search through online help or to access additional information on the Sonic Foundry Web site.

The XP Transport Tools

Sound Forge XP Studio has two sets of transport controls. The main controls are located at the top of the XP window just below the toolbar. These buttons look similar to, and have the same function as, the transport buttons in ACID, so you should feel right at home already. If you have more than one file open, these buttons control the currently selected (active) window.

Another set of transport buttons appears at the bottom of each individual file window; this set of buttons (shown in Figure 21.1) controls the playback of the file in the window with which they are associated. Two buttons control file playback. The first, the Play button, has the same function as the Play button in the main Transport toolbar (and the Play button in ACID). The Play button plays the file starting at the current cursor position. The second playback button is the Play Looped button. This button plays the file or selection in loop playback mode (which again, you are familiar with from your experience with ACID).

Editing an Audio File

To edit an audio file in XP, select the portion of the file you want to edit and apply one of the edit commands or functions. When making a selection in a stereo file, make sure that you click and drag across the horizontal line separating the two stereo channels (the left channel is on the top, the right channel is on the bottom). This ensures that your selection includes both channels. If you want to select material in just one channel, click and drag at the top of the left channel or the bottom of the right channel.

Deleting material from a file may be the most basic edit you can perform in Sound Forge XP Studio. To delete a portion of a file, click and drag across the waveform to make a selection. Click the Play button to listen to the selected material and to confirm that you have selected only what you want to delete. Press the Delete key on your keyboard to delete the selected material.

FIGURE 21.1

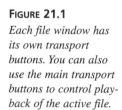

FIGURE 21.1

Each file window has its own transport buttons. You can also use the main transport buttons to control play-back of the active file.

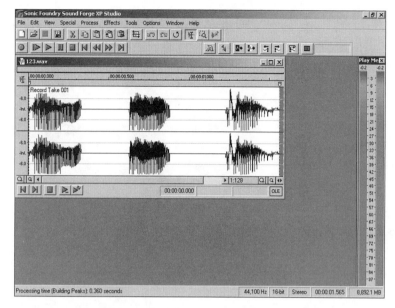

Combining Information from Multiple Files

The ability to have multiple files open in the XP workspace at the same time makes it easy to copy information from one file and add it to another file. You can mix the two files together, create a crossfade from the information in the original file to the newly added information and back, or move the information in the original file out of the way far enough to insert the new information. The default behavior is to create a mix between the two files. To mix information from one file with information in another file, select the information in the first file and then drag and drop it into the second file. As you drag the information into the second file, a shaded area (representing the length of the data you selected in the first file) follows the mouse. Position the mouse where you want to add the data and release the mouse button.

The Mix dialog box (shown in Figure 21.2) opens after you drop the data. The Mix dialog box enables you to adjust the mix between the source file (the file you dragged the information from) and the destination file (the file to which you are adding the new information). Click the Preview button to listen to the mix. Adjust the volumes of the source and destination files until you are happy with the mix between the two. There are also a number of preset options from which you can choose. Click OK to finish the operation.

21

FIGURE 21.2

The Mix dialog box enables you to adjust the mix between the source and destination files.

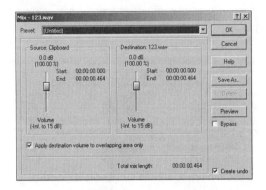

You have two other choices when combining files in this manner: Paste and Crossfade. Pasting the information insets the audio at the mouse position while moving the original audio later in time, making room for the newly pasted material. Crossfade is like a mix. The difference is that in a crossfade, the mix changes over time. The source file gradually fades in as the destination fades out.

To access these alternate methods, click and drag the selection from the source file into the destination file, but don't release the mouse button yet. While still holding down the left mouse button, click the right mouse button. Each time you click the right mouse button, you toggle through the three options—Mix, Paste, and Crossfade modes. The icon next to the mouse pointer changes to reflect the mode you're in, as does the shaded area attached to the mouse.

Task: Copying and Pasting Audio Between Files

In this task, you will copy audio from one file and paste it into another.

1. Open 123.wav and ABC.wav from the Hour 21 Sample folder on the CD-ROM that accompanies this book and position them on the XP workspace so that you can see both files simultaneously. Play the files. When playing the 123.wav file, watch the cursor as it moves through the waveform and make a mental note of where the speaker says "B."

2. Make a selection over the word "B" in 123.wav. Click the Play button (or press the spacebar on your keyboard) to listen to the selection. If you didn't accurately select the desired area, click and drag the edges of the selection to expand or contract it.

3. With the word "B" still selected, press the Delete key on your keyboard. This action deletes the selected information from the file. The cursor is now between the

words "one" and "three". Just as in ACID, press M on your keyboard to place a marker at the current cursor position.

4. Make a selection over the word "two" in ABC.wav. Preview your selection as you did with the first file to ensure that you've selected the correct word.

5. Click and drag the selection from ABC.wav onto the marker you placed in 123.wav.

6. Continue to hold the left mouse button and click the right mouse button one time to toggle to Paste mode.

7. Release the mouse button to finish the paste. Click the Go to Start button, and then click the Play button to evaluate your edit.

8. Save your edits by choosing File, Save As. Choose a file type from the Save As Type drop-down list. Other options, such as Format and Attributes, change depending on the file type you select.

Remember that if you're planning to use the file you create using XP in an ACID project, you'll have to save it as a WAV, AIF, MP3, PCA, or OGG file. For each of these file types, you'll find the same Save As options as those you find in ACID. See Hour 17, "Creating Mixed Audio and Video Files," for details.

Unlike ACID, the edits you perform in Sound Forge XP Studio are destructive. This means that you are permanently changing the original source file when you make an edit and save the file. Make sure that you have a backup of the original file if you don't want to lose it!

Creating ACID Loops

Sound Forge XP Studio is a great tool for creating loops for use in ACID (which explains why it's included with ACID Pro!). Whether you record your own loops or extract them from prerecorded sources, XP makes it easy to edit and ACIDize them. If you prepare them properly, the loops you create in XP work perfectly in your ACID projects. In fact, XP has several built-in tools specifically for ACIDizing loops.

In the following sections, you explore how to record audio in XP and turn that audio into an ACID loop. Later, you'll learn how to extract the exact loop you want from existing audio files for use in ACID (the existing file could be one you just recorded or one that someone else has previously recorded). Then you'll select a loop, and ACIDize it.

21

The process of creating an original loop can be divided into the following six steps:

1. Record some music—an instrument, a voice, or whatever you want.

2. Edit the recording to eliminate unwanted portions.

3. Search for a phrase or a sound that makes a good loop, and select it. Use markers and regions to mark multiple loops in one file.

4. Make a new file from the selected material.

5. ACIDize the new file and save it.

6. Open the new loop in ACID and test it.

Recording in XP works much the same as recording in ACID. Both of these programs contain features that the other one does not offer. You may find that you prefer creating your loops in the XP environment because of its more robust audio-editing features. As we discussed in Hour 15, "Recording and Creating Your Own Loops," you can record from any source such as a keyboard, guitar, or microphone. You can connect your instrument or microphone directly into your sound card, or connect these devices to a mixer and then connect the mixer to the sound card. Take a look back at Hours 15 and 16 if you need help configuring your system for recording.

After you have set up the hardware, choose Options, Preferences to open the Preferences dialog box. Click the Wave tab. You should be on somewhat familiar ground now (see Figure 21.3). From the Record drop-down list, choose the desired input for your sound card, or choose Microsoft Sound Mapper if you want XP to choose the correct settings for you.

FIGURE 21.3

Choose the Wave tab in the Preferences dia-log box to select a sound card for record and playback.

After you have made your sound card selection, click the Perform tab in the Preferences dialog box to view the Perform page. The Temporary Storage Folder field, located at the top of the Perform page, allows you to choose the folder into which XP stores temporary files while you edit them. This also becomes the default folder into which you save files with the File, Save command.

> Create a separate folder just for your audio files rather than mixing them in with other application files. Use the Browse button in the Perform page to browse to and select a different temporary storage folder.

Recording in Sound Forge XP Studio

Now that you have your hardware and preferences set, you are ready to record. The Record button in Sound Forge XP Studio looks exactly like the one in ACID. Close all the files you have open in the workspace and click the Record button. A new data window opens, as does the Record dialog box shown in Figure 21.4.

The Record dialog box in XP is a bit more complicated than the one in ACID because it offers more options (which is one reason you may prefer to record in XP). The Mode drop-down list offers three choices for the recording mode: Automatic Retake (Automatically Rewind); Multiple Takes; and Punch-In (Record a Specific Length).

FIGURE 21.4

Click the Record button to open the Record dialog box.

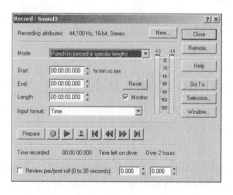

- **Automatic Retake (Automatically Rewind).** The Automatic Retake option is similar to the auto-rewind feature on some tape recorders. Each time you click the Record button in the Record dialog box, XP starts recording at the specified start position. When you click the Stop button to stop recording, XP automatically "rewinds" to the original starting position. This allows you to record a new take

21

that replaces the last take. Select this option when you want to keep trying for that "perfect take," and don't want to save any of the previous takes. Because you record over the old information, you don't waste valuable disk space.

- **Multiple Takes.** In this mode, XP records successive takes in the same file each time you click the Record button in the Record dialog box. XP adds each successive take to the end of the file. This method works well for the times when you want to stop recording for a moment and then later continue recording where you left off.

- **Punch-In (Record a Specific Length).** When you select Punch-In mode, the End and Length fields become active. Punch-In mode allows you to set a Start position and End position for your recording. When you click the Record button in the Record dialog box, XP starts recording at the Start time you specify, and automatically stops recording at the end time. XP replaces only the portion of the file between the Start and End points with newly recorded material. This option allows you to fix a problem area without having to re-record the entire file.

Monitoring the Record Levels

Enable the Monitor check box in the Record dialog box to monitor your record levels. Follow the same rules for setting recording levels as those you learned for ACID. Shoot for an average level around –6dB so that you don't run the risk of clipping.

 Just as you do in ACID, use the Windows Record Control to adjust record levels. See Hour 15 if you need to review this process.

Using the Record Control Buttons

Several buttons near the bottom of the Record dialog box control recording, playback, and navigation through the file. The following list shows the functions of each button in the Record dialog box:

- **Prepare:** Prepares the system so that it goes into record mode as quickly as possible after you click the Record button. If you notice that you're missing the first few notes each time you record, click the Prepare button before you start recording.

- **Record:** Starts recording. Changes to the Stop button after it's clicked. The Stop button ends recording.

- **Play:** Allows you to hear the section of data you just recorded, or the section of data you are about to record over.

- **Drop Marker:** Allows you to drop markers in the file as you record. Use them to mark specific sections of your file or to mark mistakes as you record. The markers make it easy to go back and locate the sections or mistakes later. You can also use the familiar M key command to drop markers.

- **Go to Start:** Goes back to the beginning of the file.

- **Rewind:** Moves back through the file take by take. Use this button to review takes or locate a position for re-recording.

- **Forward:** Similar to the Rewind button, moves forward through the file take by take.

- **Go to End:** Quickly goes to the end of the current file.

Under the row of buttons in the Record dialog box are two time indications. The Time Recorded readout tells you how long you have been recording. The Time Left on Drive readout tells you how much recording time you have left on the hard drive to which you are recording the file.

The Pre-Roll and Post-Roll fields allow you to set the amount of time before and after the Punch-In section. Use these fields when listening to a Punch-In section so that you can hear the transition between the Punch-In region and the audio before and after the region.

The New button opens the New Window dialog box shown in Figure 21.5. The New Window dialog box enables you to set the record properties. You can select number of channels (stereo or mono), sampling rate (from 2000 to 96000 samples per second) and sample size (8-bit or 16-bit).

FIGURE 21.5

The New Window dialog box allows you to set the parameters for the file you are about to record.

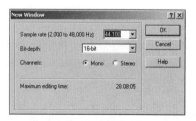

The Close button closes the Record dialog box.

Click the Remote button in the Record dialog box to shrink the Record window down to just the meters, transport controls, and record time fields and to hide the rest of the XP screen as shown in Figure 21.6. This space-saving feature works great when you want to view other controls or text on your computer screen while you record.

21

FIGURE 21.6

The Remote button reduces the XP window and the Record dialog box down to the bare essentials for recording.

The Help button opens the Help window, which contains information about the controls in the Record dialog box. The Go To button is available only in Automatic Retake and Multiple Take modes. When clicked, the Go To button opens a dialog box that helps you locate the beginning or end of the file or any markers in the file. The Selection button is available only in Punch-In mode and assists you in setting the in and out points where you want to punch-in to the existing audio. The Window button allows you to switch between any of the windows you have open in XP.

Task: Recording

Because an ACID loop is usually very short (one or two bars long), you can sometimes get several loops out of a single recording. In this task, you'll record a bass part and then extract two different loops.

If you don't have a bass, or don't know a bass player, you can use a keyboard. If all else fails, record any other instrument or vocal and substitute that recording whenever the bass file is referred to in this discussion.

1. With your hardware properly connected and the Windows Recording Control open, start Sound Forge XP Studio and click the Record button. Enable the Monitor check box in the Record dialog box.

2. Click the Remote button to reduce the Record dialog box down to just the record controls. Arrange the XP record controls and the Windows Volume Control so that you can see both windows onscreen.

3. Start playing or singing. Adjust the input level using the Windows Volume Control while viewing the XP meters.

4. Click the red Record button and play (or sing). The Record button turns into the Stop button, and you see the word Recording flashing in red.

5. Click the Stop button when you finish playing. Then click the Back button to return to the full XP window. You should see the file you recorded behind the Record

dialog box. Click Close to close the Record dialog box. Save the file into your My Documents folder as My_Raw_Bass loop.wav. You'll use this file again later in this hour.

6. Rarely can you start recording and playing instantly. Invariably, you'll have to clean up the beginning and end of your recorded file. In the file you created in the previous task, select the portion from just before the music starts to just after it ends. Choose Edit, Trim/Crop to delete all the unselected material in the file.

Using the ACID Looping Tools

If you didn't do so earlier, make the ACID toolbar visible: Choose View, Toolbars. In the Toolbars tab of the Preferences dialog box, select ACID Loop Creation Tools and click OK. Initially, the toolbar may be free-floating in the XP workspace. To dock the toolbar, drag it up next to the other toolbars and drop it there. Figure 21.7 shows the ACID toolbar.

FIGURE 21.7

The ACID toolbar in Sound Forge XP Studio.

To select a loop, select a segment of the file that represents a musical phrase. For instance, in the file you recorded in the last task, select the first measure of music. Click the Play Looped button so that you can listen to the selected area as you adjust the edges of the selection until you have a perfect loop.

It may be difficult to achieve perfect results with the mouse, so hold down the Shift key while you press the left-arrow or right-arrow key to make the selection longer or shorter. The cursor position determines which side of the selection moves. To change the position of the cursor from the left side of the selection to the right, or from the right to the left, press the 5 key on your computer's number keypad or the tilde key (typically found directly to the left of the number 1 at the top of your keyboard).

When adjusting the selection length using the Shift+arrow-key technique, you may find that each press of the arrow adjusts the length of the selection too much. To solve this problem, use the up-arrow key to zoom into your file. Now each time you press the left-arrow or right-arrow key, you get a finer adjustment. Zoom far enough into your file, and each press of an arrow key results in a very fine adjustment, indeed!

21

The following list summarizes the function of each of the ACID toolbar buttons.

- **Edit ACID Properties:** Define the loop type for the loop you are creating and add ACIDization information. See the following section for more details on using this button.

- **Edit Tempo:** Define important ACIDization parameters for the loop. See the following section for more details on using this button.

- **Double Selection:** Extend the selection to twice the length of the original selection.

- **Halve Selection:** Cut the selection in half.

- **Shift Selection Left:** Move the selection to the left, while keeping the selection at the same length. This button is great for finding other areas of the file that qualify as loops.

- **Shift Selection Right:** Move the selection to the right, while keeping the selection at the same length. This button is great for finding other areas of the file that qualify as loops.

- **Rotate Audio:** Rearrange the audio in the file. If you have nothing selected, this button takes the first quarter of the file and moves it to the end. If you have made a selection at the beginning of the file, the Rotate Audio button shifts the selected area to the end of the file. If you have selected the end of the file, this button shifts the selection to the beginning of the file.

- **Selection Grid Lines:** Toggle grid lines on and off within the selected area. Sometimes it is helpful to line up these grid lines with transients in the waveform when selecting a loop.

ACIDizing Your Loops in Sound Forge XP Studio

The following sections describe the functions of the Edit Tempo and Edit ACID Properties buttons that appear in the ACID toolbar.

Choosing the Loop Type

Now that you have a solid loop, click and drag the highlighted section to a blank area of the XP workspace. This action creates a new data window that contains a copy of the selected portion of the original file. In other words, the new window contains only the loop you created.

With the new data window selected, click the Edit Tempo button in the ACID toolbar. The Edit Tempo dialog box opens. In the Selection Length in Beats field, type the total number of beats in the loop. When you press the Tab key, XP calculates the tempo for you. Click OK to close the dialog box.

Entering Loop Properties

Click the Edit ACID Properties button in the ACID toolbar to open the Edit ACID Properties dialog box. Enable the Loop radio button to designate this file as a loop. In the Root Note for Transposing drop-down list, select the key in which the loop was recorded. Now ACID has the information it needs to transpose this loop and make it match the project key. Type the total number of beats in the loop in the Number of Beats (1 to 10,000) field. This value should be the same as the number you typed in the Edit Tempo dialog box in the previous section. Click the Save button to save the file with the new ACID information.

Task: Finishing and Using Your ACIDized Loop

This task describes how you complete the process of ACIDizing a loop in Sound Forge XP Studio. Continue with the loop you started to create earlier in this hour.

1. Select the first four beats of actual music in the file you created in the previous task. If you didn't record a bass loop, use the Raw_Bass_Part_Hour_21.wav file from the Hour 21 Samples folder on the companion CD and select the region labeled Loop 1 as shown in Figure 21.8. Click and drag the selection to a blank spot on the XP workspace. This action creates a new data window.

FIGURE 21.8

Select the region labeled Loop 1 in the Raw_BassPart_Hour_21 .wav *file.*

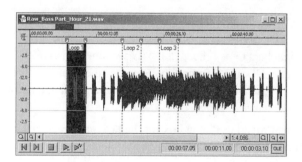

2. Click the Edit Tempo button in the ACID toolbar and type **4** in the Selection Length in Beats field. Click OK.

21

3. Click the Edit ACID Properties button in the ACID toolbar. Make sure that the Loop radio button is enabled. If you're using the first four beats of Raw_Bass_Part_Hour_21.wav, type **4** in the Number of Beats field and type **D** in the Root Note for Transposing field (since the bass in this file was recorded in the key of D). If you recorded your own bass part, type the root note that is appropriate for your recording. Click OK.

4. Save the file into your My Documents folder as BL1.wav.

5. After you save the file, a dialog box asks whether you want to reopen the file in Direct mode. Choose No so that the file opens in a new temporary file. Working in a temporary file is safer; if your computer should crash for some reason and the temporary file you're working on should be damaged, you will still have the original file intact.

6. Click the Raw_Bass_Part_Hour_21.wav data window to make it the active window.

7. Click the Shift Selection Right button three times. Now your selection is a four-beat selection over the region labeled Loop 2.

8. Click the Double Selection button. Now you have an eight-beat selection, which includes the region labeled Loop 2 and the unlabeled region directly following it.

9. Drag the selection to a blank spot on the XP workspace to create a new data window.

10. Click the Edit Tempo button and type **8** in the Selection Length in Beats field. Click OK to close the dialog box.

11. Click the Edit ACID Properties button. Select Loop as the file type. Type **8** in the Number of Beats field and set the Root Note for Transposing to **D**. Click OK.

12. Save the new loop into your My Documents folder as BL2.wav. Choose No to open the file in a new temporary file.

13. Open ACID and start a new ACID project. Set the tempo to 80bpm and the key to D.

14. Add eight bars of 4-4 Loop 33-07.wav from the Hour 21 Samples folder on the companion CD. (This drum loop is part of the Drum Tools loop library from Sonic Foundry.) Add four bars of BL1.wav at the beginning, and four bars of BL2.wav starting at bar 5.

15. Open the Properties dialog box for the BL1.wav track and click the Stretch tab. Set the Force Divisions At option to quarter notes.

16. Open the Properties dialog box for the BL2.wav track and click the Stretch tab. Set the Force Division At option to eighth notes.

17. Click the Play From Start button and listen to your new ACID project constructed from your custom loops.

Summary

In this hour, you learned how to use Sonic Foundry's Sound Forge XP Studio to record audio, do some basic editing, and then ACIDize the file for use as a loop in ACID. You learned how to open and use the ACID toolbar in XP to quickly move around in a file and find additional loop material. Finally, you learned how to save this additional information with the file for use in ACID.

Q&A

Q. If I ACIDize my loops, will I be able to use these WAV files in other applications?

A. No problem. Even though ACIDizing a loop changes the file a little, only ACID reads the additional information; nothing keeps you from using the file in another application such as Vegas Audio or your sampler.

Q. Why do I need Sound Forge XP Studio when I already know how to make and ACIDize loops right in ACID?

A. Some people prefer to use Sound Forge XP because the editing tools are much more refined than those in ACID. ACID is not really intended to do the kind of super-fine detailed audio editing you can do in XP. Sure, there will be times when you can do the job in ACID. But when you have to zoom way into the waveform to edit in minute detail, Sound Forge XP Studio is a better tool for the job. In addition, XP is capable of much, much more than we can cover in two short hours. Take the time to explore the features of XP, and we're sure you'll come up with a number of answers to this question!

Workshop

Using Sound Forge XP Studio to create your own custom loops is easy to do and is a fun way to build up your personal loop library. The following workshop helps you remember some of the tools and techniques you leaned about in this hour.

Quiz

1. What recording mode would you use to replace a section of audio in the middle of an existing recording?
2. How do you access the ACID toolbar in Sound Forge XP Studio?
3. When the ACID Properties dialog box asks for number of beats, does it want the beats in a measure or the beats in the loop?

21

4. How do you quickly clean up the beginning and end of a file leaving only the usable material?

Quiz Answers

1. Use the Punch-In mode for this type of recording task. Set the punch-in and punch-out points using the Start and End fields in the Record dialog box.

2. Choose View, Toolbars. Select ACID Loop Creation Tools and click OK.

3. The number of beats in the loop is the important factor. A loop may be made up of several measures, so you must type the total number of beats, not just the beats in a single measure. Typing the wrong number here causes the loop to play back incorrectly in ACID.

4. Select the audio you want to keep and then choose Edit, Trim/Crop.

Activities

1. Insert an audio CD into your CD-ROM drive. In XP, choose Tools, Extract Audio from CD. Choose a song from the list of songs on the CD and click OK to extract that song from the disc and open it in Sound Forge XP Studio. Find a one- or two-bar section of the song that sounds like it would make a good loop. Select it and drag the selected area to the XP workspace to open it in a separate file. Use the tools in the ACID toolbar to ACIDize two different loops from the file.

HOUR 22

Improving and Editing Recordings

- Using Fades
- Task: Creating a Graphical Fade
- Using Sound Forge XP Studio to Rearrange Audio
- Task: Creating a New File from Regions

Sound Forge XP Studio is perfect for making loops for ACID, and you'll also find that it's a great tool for putting the finishing touches on your music. In fact, certain tweaks and edits are best done on the finished mixed file rather than on the multitrack arrangement. After you have created and saved your music in ACID as a mixed file, open it in XP and tweak the EQ, create fade-ins and fade-outs, and use some XP tricks to create alternative arrangements of the piece.

In this hour, you will:

- Add fades to the final mix
- Create regions
- Create alternative arrangements

Using Fades

We've all heard the fade effect. Usually it occurs at the end of a song that slowly fades to lower volume until you can't hear it anymore. This effect is called a fade-out. Occasionally, the beginning of a song contains a fade-in effect. Sometimes you'll want to fade your compositions out, too.

In ACID, you can use envelopes to control volume and to create the fades for each track individually. But in a large project with several tracks, using envelopes can be time consuming and not very convenient. Sound Forge XP solves the problem perfectly. You can render the project as a mixed file in ACID and then open the file in XP. In XP, you can apply one fade that affects the entire mixed file.

XP offers three fade options. You can create a simple fade-in, a simple fade-out, or more complex fades. The following sections show you how to create each of these types of fades.

Adding a Fade-In or Fade-Out

XP makes creating a fade-in extremely easy. Make a selection at the beginning of your file, the length of which equals the length of the fade-in you want. The Selection Left, Selection Right, and Selection Length fields in the bottom right of the data window (shown in Figure 22.1) update as you drag to aid you in selecting an exact length. If you want the fade-in to be 3 seconds, for instance, drag until the Selection Length field reads 00:00:03.000.

Choose Process, Fade, In. XP creates a smooth fade over the length of the selection; the fade transitions from complete silence up to the file's original volume.

> The Selection Length field, shown in Figure 22.1, serves as more than just an information source. It also provides the fastest way to make a selection of an exact length. Double-click the Selection Length field to open the Set Selection dialog box. Type the desired length into the Length field and click OK. You can also enter exact times for the start and end of the selection in the Set Selection dialog box.

Adding a fade-out works the same way as adding a fade-in. With your mouse at the end of the file, click and drag to the left until you have highlighted the portion of the file over which you want the fade to occur. Choose Process, Fade, Out. XP creates a fade-out that goes from full volume down to no volume over the length of the selection.

Figure 22.1

The Selection Length field tells you the length of the current selection.

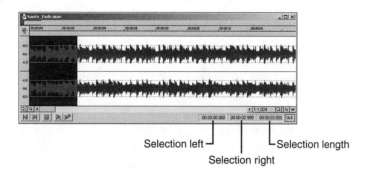

Selection left ⌐
Selection right
⌐ Selection length

22

Adding Graphical Fades

If you want to get more fancy than the simple fades XP provides, you can apply graphical fades for both fade-in and fade-out. A graphical fade allows you to control the fade over time using an envelope so that the fade is not necessarily an even fade from start to end. For example, you can create a fade-out that starts out slow, then fades faster toward the end. Or you can create a fade-in that fades fast at first, slows down in the middle, and then finishes fast again. You can create any type of fade you want.

Start out the same way you create every fade: Make a selection over the intended fade area. Choose Process, Fade, Graphic to open the Graphic Fade dialog box as shown in Figure 22.2.

Figure 22.2

The Graphic Fade option allows you to design a custom fade envelope.

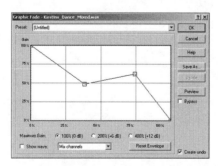

The Graphic Fade dialog box shows a graph with a line representing the envelope. The first time you open this dialog box, the envelope line may be at the very top of the window (indicating that the volume of the selection is constant at full) and may be difficult to see. Pull the drag points (the small square boxes at the beginning and end of the envelope line) up or down to draw a custom fade. Left-click anywhere on the envelope line to add up to 16 additional drag points. Double-click a drag point to delete that point. When you have finished designing your custom graphical fade, click OK to close the dialog box and apply it to the selection.

Task: Creating a Graphical Fade

In this task, you create a fade-out using the Graphic Fade dialog box.

1. In ACID, open the ACID project Original.acd, found in the Hour 22 Samples folder on the CD-ROM that accompanies this book. Click the Play From Start button to listen to the project.

2. Choose File, Render As to open the Render As dialog box. From the Save In drop-down list, choose the My Documents folder (or specify a new folder). Name the file Mixed, and choose Wave (Microsoft)(*.wav) from the Save as Type drop-down list. Click OK to save the file.

3. Open the mixed file you rendered in Step 2 (Mixed.wav) in Sound Forge XP Studio. Click the Play button to hear how the file sounds, and notice that it sounds identical to the ACID project you listened to in Step 1 (as long as you followed the instructions in Step 2).

4. Place the cursor at the end of the file. Click and drag to highlight approximately the last eight seconds of the file (watch the Selection Length field as you make the selection). Choose Process, Fade, Graphic to open the Graphic Fade dialog box.

5. From the Preset drop-down list at the top of the dialog box, choose some of the different fade-out options and look at the various fade shapes available as presets. When you're done looking around, select the –6dB Exponential Fade Out option from the drop-down list.

6. Double-click all but four of the drag points on the envelope line to remove them (leave the first and last points and two in between). Position the remaining points to create a fade envelope that looks like the one in Figure 22.2 (shown earlier in this hour). Click OK to close the dialog box.

7. Click the Play All button and listen to the file with its new fade-out ending. Save the file as a wave file called Fade.wav. Close the file.

Using Sound Forge XP Studio to Rearrange Audio

Imagine that you've worked hard on your composition. You mixed it down while thinking, "That's it, it's done." The next day you decide that, in addition to the mix you created, you want to create a mix with an alternative arrangement. Going back to ACID and creating the alternative mix could be a lot of work. Sound Forge XP Studio gives you another way to solve the problem.

You can use XP to change and rearrange your song even after it is mixed. One way to accomplish this is to place markers at the beginning and end of sections. Convert those sections into regions. Then mix and match the regions in a new data window to create the new arrangement. It's a lot of fun to invent alternative arrangements and, more often than not, the process provides some interesting results.

22

Adding Markers

You already know how to add markers to your XP file. Recall that we added a marker to a file in Hour 21 when you were introduced to XP. Even if you didn't read Hour 21, you know how to add markers in XP because the technique is exactly the same as adding a beat marker in ACID. To add markers in ACID or XP, place the cursor where you want to drop the marker and press the M key. Just as you can in ACID, you can drop markers in XP on the fly: Start playback and, as the file plays, press the M key anywhere you want to drop a marker.

You might want to use a combination of these two techniques. First, you can drop the marker on the fly, then you can stop playback and drag the marker (by clicking and dragging the marker tab) to place it more accurately. Another technique for repositioning an existing marker is to position the cursor where you want the marker, right-click the existing marker you want to move, and choose Update from the shortcut menu. The marker jumps to match the position of the cursor.

There are many reasons you might want to use markers. You can use them to mark the beginnings of musical sections (such as verses, choruses, or bridges in your composition). Or you can place them where you want to add information from another file (as you did in Hour 21). You can also use markers as navigational tools. Press Ctrl+right-arrow or left-arrow to move the cursor from one marker to another. Using markers to navigate the file in this manner enables you to quickly locate specific places in the file.

Creating Regions

You can also create regions in your audio file. Regions designate sections of the file that have a specific start, end, and length.

To create a region, click and drag to highlight a portion of the file. Then press the R key to open the Add Marker/Region dialog box. Enable the Region radio button to add a region; enable the Marker radio button to add a new marker. When you choose the Region radio button, the dialog box displays the start, end, and length of the current selection. You can edit any of these values. By default, XP names the region using the values in the Start and End fields. You can change the name of the region by typing a new name in the Name field.

> Double-click between two markers to select the portion of the file between them. Press R to quickly establish a region over the space between the markers.

Creating the New Arrangement

Now that you have defined regions in your song, select each region, one by one, and drag it to a new file to create a new arrangement. Use the method of dragging audio from one file to another described in Hour 21 to build the arrangement.

Task: Creating a New File from Regions

In this task, you'll add markers to the Mixed.wav file you created earlier in this hour. Next you'll use the markers to create regions. Then you'll mix and match the regions in a new data window to create a new arrangement of the final mix.

1. Start XP and open the Mixed.wav file you created earlier.

2. Right-click the Selection Left, Selection Right, or Selection Length field and choose Measures & Beats from the shortcut menu. Notice that this command not only changes the format of the values in the selection fields, but also changes the format of the Time ruler toward the top of the data window.

3. Double-click the Selection Left field to open the Go To dialog box. In the Position field, type **5:1.0** and click OK. This action moves the cursor to the downbeat of measure 5 (5:1.0). Press M on your keyboard to place a marker there. Use the same technique to place markers at 9:1.0, 13:1.0, 15:1.0, 25:1.0, and 29:1.0.

> Syntax is important here. Be sure to type the measure and beat locations exactly as they are written here.

4. Choose View, Regions List to open the Regions window. The Regions list shows all the markers and regions you've added to your project. Notice that all the markers you placed in step 3 are listed here. Save the file as Markers.wav.

> If you need help with the placement of the markers, open the file Markers.wav from the Hour 22 Samples folder on the CD-ROM and compare your work to this file.

5. Double-click between the beginning of the file and the first marker to select the material between those two points. Don't forget to double-click the horizontal line between the left and right channels so that you select both channels.

6. Press the R key to create a region over the selected area; name the region **1**. Notice that a region called 1 now appears in the list in the Regions window. At the very top of the data window, notice that there is a white region marker containing the region name 1. As is true in ACID, regions in XP have both a beginning marker and an ending marker. In this case, however, you do not see the white region marker that indicates the end of region 1 because the marker you placed back in step 3 at measure 5, beat 1 covers it. See the following note for further explanation.

> As you can see from the results of step 6, when a regular marker and a region marker occupy the same space in the data window, the regular marker covers the region marker. The same is true for the names. In other words, when you add additional regions in the next step, you won't see the white region markers or the region names because the red markers and names cover them. You can verify that you are adding the regions correctly by keeping your eye on the Regions window and making sure that the new regions appear in the Regions list.

7. Double-click between the first and second marker, and create a region called **2**. Create regions between each set of markers until you have created seven regions in all.

8. Your Regions list should now look like the list shown in Figure 22.3. Compare your list of markers and regions to those shown in the figure.

FIGURE 22.3

After adding the markers and regions, your Regions list should match the one in this figure.

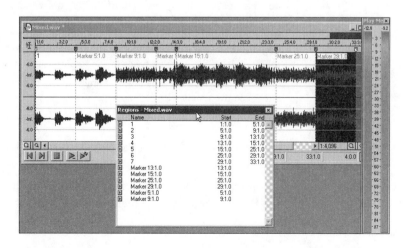

9. Select the first regular marker in the Regions window and press the Delete key to remove the marker from the project. Delete the rest of the regular markers, leaving only the regions.

> Step 9 is not absolutely necessary. However, deleting the markers makes it easier to work with the regions in the following steps because you can now see all the region names and markers.

10. In the Regions window, click the arrow to the left of a region to audition it.

11. Click and drag region 1 from the Regions window to an empty spot in the XP workspace. This action creates a new data window with the material from region 1. The Regions list now reflects the regions in this new data window (there is currently only one region) because the new window currently has focus.

12. Save the new file as `Remix.wav`.

13. Click the `Markers.wav` window to make it the active window. Click and drag region 2 from `Markers.wav` to the end of `Remix.wav`. Notice that the mouse has the letter M next to it, indicating that it is in Mix mode. While still holding the left mouse button, click the right mouse button. The M changes to a P indicating that you are now in Paste mode. Release the mouse button to paste region 2 onto the end of region 1.

14. Repeat step 13 to paste another occurrence of region 2 at the end of `Remix.wav`.

> Don't get confused by the Regions window when the `Remix.wav` data window has focus. In the Name field of the Regions window, the regions are listed just as you have added them to your new file. As you drag a region from `Markers.wav` to the `Remix.wav`, the region's name is added to the Regions list in the Regions window. Because you added two repetitions of region 2, its name appears twice in the Regions list for `Remix.wav`.
>
> The Regions list is sorted by region name, not by the order in which regions appear in the timeline.

15. Use this system of click-and-drag in Paste mode to paste 2 occurrences of region 4 followed by two occurrences of region 3 into `Remix.wav`.

16. Paste a copy of region 5, then a copy of region 4, then another copy of region 5 to the end of the file. Paste region 6 to the end and then add two occurrences of region 7.

17. Now drag region 1 from `Markers.wav` right over the top of the last occurrence of region 7 in `Remix.wav`. While still holding the left mouse button, click the right mouse button until the P changes to an M.

18. Make sure that the shaded area (which represents region 1 from `Markers.wav`) aligns with and completely covers region 7 in `Remix.wav`. Release the left mouse button. The Mix dialog box opens.

19. Make sure that the volume of both the source and destination files are set to 0dB (100%) and click OK. This action mixes the two regions together.

20. Paste region 1 from `Markers.wav` to the end of `Remix.wav`.

21. Select the last region in `Remix.wav` and choose Process, Fade, Out to create a fade-out effect at the end of the file.

22. Now for the surprise ending. Paste region 5, and then region 6 (both from `Markers.wav`) to the end of `Remix.wav`.

23. Double-click region 6 at the end and choose Process, Fade, Out.

24. Click the Play All button and listen to your new arrangement.

An example of the finished project as it should sound at the end of this task can be found in the Hour 22 Samples folder. The file is named `Remix.wav`.

Summary

In this hour, you learned how to add both fade-ins and fade-outs to a WAV file. You also learned how to create envelope-controlled fades by using the Graphic Fade dialog box. You learned how to place markers, how to create regions, and how to use regions to create new arrangements.

Q&A

Q. Is there a fast way to get rid of all the markers so that I can start over?

A. Yes: Choose Special, Regions List, Clear. This command deletes all the markers and regions in the file.

Q. Can I label a marker?

A. Yes. Point to the marker tab, right-click, and choose Edit. This command opens the Edit Marker/Region dialog box. Enter a new name (label) in the Name field and click OK.

Workshop

The questions and activities in this hour's workshop help you solidify the concepts of fades, markers, regions, and paste modes.

Quiz

1. What key do you press to place a marker on the XP timeline?
2. How do you create additional drag points in the graphic fade envelope?
3. How do you switch between Mix mode and Paste mode when you drag a region from one data window to another?
4. How can you create a selection at the beginning of a file that you can turn into a fade-in effect?

Quiz Answers

1. Just as you do in ACID, to place a marker in XP, position the cursor at the desired spot and press the M key.
2. Click the envelope with the left mouse button to create additional drag points.
3. While holding down the left mouse button, click the right mouse button to cycle through Mix mode, Crossfade mode, and Paste mode.
4. There are several ways to create a selection. One way is to click at the beginning of the file and drag to the right. You can also place the cursor at the beginning of the file, double-click the Selection Length field, and type the desired length in the Length field of the Set Selection dialog box. A third way is to place the cursor at the point where the fade-in will be complete, press and hold the Shift key, and press the Home key.

Activities

1. Open an ACID project and save it as a mixed WAV file. Then open the mixed WAV file in XP. Create a simple fade-in of four seconds and a fade-out of any length you want. Use a graphic fade for the fade-out effect.
2. Open (or create) another ACID project and save it as a mixed WAV file. Open the mixed WAV file in XP. Divide the file into regions of musical phrases. Drag the various regions into a new data window to create a new arrangement.

Hour 23

Vegas Audio LE Basics

Vegas Audio LE (the Limited Edition version of the Vegas Audio application from Sonic Foundry) is a multitrack recorder and editor. "Multitrack" means that you can record multiple tracks while simultaneously playing back multiple tracks. Vegas Audio LE allows for one video track and eight audio tracks. Editing in Vegas Audio LE, like editing in ACID, is nondestructive. Because Vegas Audio LE shares many of the same user interface features as ACID, learning it will be a snap.

Vegas Audio LE can be used for music production, broadcast production, film scoring, and streaming media creation. The combined power of Vegas Audio LE and ACID opens a world of possibilities for creating, editing, and finishing your projects.

In this hour, you will:

- Become familiar with the Vegas Audio LE interface
- Add media to the timeline
- Learn basic audio-editing techniques
- Navigate through a project

- Discover several approaches to recording
- Save and render projects
- Learn how to combine ACID and Vegas Audio LE

Comparing Vegas Audio LE to ACID

Even though they are fundamentally different programs, each designed for a different purpose, many of the features found in ACID can also be found in Vegas Audio LE. These similarities make it easy to switch between applications. Many of the concepts, commands, and shortcuts you've learned for ACID are exactly the same in Vegas Audio LE, including media management, project navigation, and saving/rendering. The programs are also similar in how they deal with video. Being aware of the programs' similarities—as well as their differences—will help you get the most out of these two products.

Multitrack Recording

One major difference between the two products is how they work with multiple tracks of audio. At first, it appears that ACID is a *multitrack application* because you can add an unlimited number of tracks to your project. But a closer look reveals that ACID lacks at least one feature that really separates ACID from Vegas Audio LE (which is a true multitrack application): the ability to record multiple tracks simultaneously.

Multitrack Application

A multitrack application is one that (among other things) allows you to record one or more tracks of audio simultaneously, while also listening to one or more tracks of previously recorded audio. Multitrack tape decks have been in use at professional recording studios for many years. Multitrack software packages (such as Vegas Audio LE and Vegas Audio from Sonic Foundry, as well as Digidesign's Pro Tools, and Syntrillium's CoolEdit) bring the power of professional multitrack capabilities to your computer.

Even though you can record a stereo track in ACID, the program was never intended to be a true multitrack application. In ACID, you can record only one stereo track at a time. In Vegas Audio LE, you can record up to eight tracks simultaneously. In Vegas Audio

LE, you could (for example) add a couple of horn, string, or background vocal tracks while listening to the playback of the rhythm tracks you've already recorded.

Working with Loops

Another difference between ACID and Vegas Audio LE is how the two programs work with loops. This is ACID's strength, and what it was designed to do. Throughout this book, you've seen how ACID works its magic on the loops you add to your project. Vegas Audio LE does not automatically pitch and tempo match like ACID does. Although you can cause audio to loop in Vegas Audio LE (and it is often useful to do so), the loop will remain at the original pitch and tempo.

Exploring the Interface

Now that you have been working in ACID, the Vegas Audio LE interface should look very familiar. As shown in Figure 23.1, the screen is divided into two basic areas much like the ACID screen. The top half holds the title bar, menu bar, toolbar, Track List, and Track View areas.

FIGURE 23.1

The Vegas Audio LE screen looks much like the ACID screen.

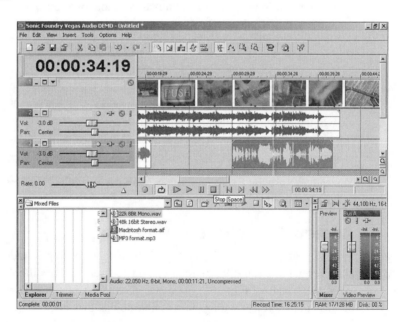

As is true in the ACID screen, the bottom half of the Vegas Audio LE display is the Window Docking area. The Vegas Audio LE windows you can display in this area include the following:

- **Explorer:** Like the Explorer window in ACID, this window is used for file and folder navigation and maintenance.
- **Trimmer:** Much like the ACID Chopper, the Vegas Trimmer enables you to select a portion of a file and add it to the Track View.
- **Media Pool:** Use this window to easily organize the media files in your project.
- **Video Preview:** Just as you can in ACID, use this window to view the video playback of the project at the current cursor position.
- **Mixer:** This window enables you to add buses and monitor and control the volume of the buses and the preview control. Unlike ACID, the Vegas Audio LE Mixer window does not contain a Master control.
- **Edit Details:** Use this window to edit the start, end, and duration times for all the events in each track.
- **Plug-ins:** Manage and maintain all the audio plug-ins you have installed on your PC in this window.

All these windows can be opened and closed from the View menu.

Finding Media

Choose View, Explorer to open the Explorer window if it is not already open. The default view of the Explorer window shows the Tree view on the left and the List view on the right. Click a folder in the Tree view to display the contents of the folder in the List view. Just as you can in ACID, you can audition files before adding them to the project.

You can also use the Explorer window to create new folders and move, rename, and delete files.

Adding Tracks to the Timeline

In ACID, each track is dedicated to a single media file. Vegas Audio LE enables you to place several different files on the same track. Even files of different types—such as WAV, MP3, and AIFF files—can be placed on the same track. Vegas Audio LE resamples the files to the project settings in real time so that they all work seamlessly. This keeps you from having to prerender the files before using them in the project.

Click and drag a file from the Explorer window to the timeline to add it to the project. Alternatively, double-click the file, or select it and press Enter.

Different from what you're used to in ACID is the Vegas Audio LE right-mouse-button method of adding files. When you click and drag files from the Explorer window using the right mouse button, a shortcut menu appears when you release the mouse button. As shown in Figure 23.2 you have several choices:

- **Add Across Time:** If more than one file is selected in the Explorer window, all the files will be added to the same track and arranged one after the other.

- **Add Across Tracks:** If more than one file is selected, all the files will be added one under the other in different tracks (up to eight tracks).

- **Add as Takes:** If more than one file is selected, all the files will be added in a single event on the same track. Only one take can play at a time, but you can choose which take you want to be the active take.

- **Video Only:** In video files, add the video portion of each file only, then choose from the preceding three options.

- **Audio Only:** In video files, add the audio portion of each file only, then choose from the first three options in this list.

- **Cancel:** End the operation without adding the selected file or files.

FIGURE 23.2

You have a variety of choices when adding files to the timeline.

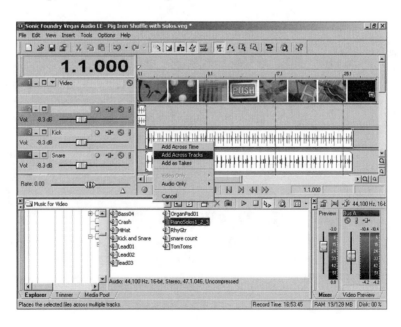

Task: Adding Multiple Files on One Track

In this task, you'll add four files to a single track in a Vegas Audio LE project. Notice that even though you're using a variety of file formats, you can still add the files to the same track. Vegas Audio LE matches each of them to the project properties so that they work seamlessly together.

1. In Vegas Audio LE, start a new project. Navigate to the Hour 23 Samples folder on the CD-ROM that accompanies this book. This folder contains files of different file types, bit-depth, and sampling rates.

2. Select these four files: `22k 8Bit Mono.wav`, `48k 16Bit Stereo.wav`, `Macintosh format.aif`, and `MP3 format.mp3`.

3. Point to any of the selected files. With the right mouse button, click and drag them onto one of the tracks labeled Audio in the timeline. (Tracks 2 through 9 are all audio tracks. Track 1 is the video track; you cannot drop audio files onto it.)

4. Release the mouse button and choose Add Across Time from the shortcut menu. All four files are added, each in its own event, one after another, to the same track.

5. Click the Play From Start button (which looks just like the Play From Start button in ACID) to listen to the project. The music in each file is unrelated to the others, but the point is to notice that the project plays each file, even though one of the files is a mono file, three of the files are stereo, and all the files have various bit depths, sampling rates, and file formats.

Using the Trimmer

If you want to add only a portion of the file to the timeline, use the Trimmer, which is similar to the Chopper in ACID. Right-click a file in the Explorer window and choose Open in Trimmer from the shortcut menu. This command shifts focus to the Trimmer window and displays the selected file. Select the portion of the file you want to use and drag and drop it on the timeline. Add markers and create regions to help identify portions of the file to be used later in the project.

Editing Audio Events

Editing audio events in Vegas Audio LE is very similar to editing in ACID. Basic editing functions include move, edge edit, split, cut, copy, and paste. The Cut, Copy, and Paste commands work exactly like they do in ACID, as do the Paste Insert and Paste Repeat commands. See Hour 7, "Constructing Your Musical Arrangement," for complete details. The slip and slide features you learned about in ACID also work on both the video and audio tracks in Vegas Audio LE.

Basic Editing

Click an event to select it. Hold the Ctrl key as you click additional events to add those events to the selection. Alternatively, click the Selection Edit tool and click and drag across the events you want to select. Click and drag an event to move it to another position on the timeline or to a different track. Note that you cannot move an event from one track to another in ACID. As you saw in the previous task, this is another big difference between the two programs. Vegas Audio LE allows you to put more than one file on the same track.

It is sometimes helpful to group individual events in the timeline. To do so, select two or more events (even if they're on different tracks), and choose Edit, Group, Create New. Now when you move any of the events in the group, all the events in the group move. To remove an event from the group, right-click the event and choose Group, Remove From. To ungroup the events in a group, right-click any event in the group and choose Group, Clear.

Splitting events works exactly the same in Vegas Audio LE as it does in ACID. In the easiest case, select an event and press S on the keyboard. See Hour 6, "Shaping Your Project," for a full discussion of splitting events.

Using Switches

Switches in Vegas Audio LE enable you to modify the behavior of events in a number of ways. Right-click an event to access the Switches menu show in Figure 23.3. These switches have the following functions:

- **Mute:** Mutes the selected event without affecting other events in the same track.

- **Lock:** Makes it impossible to move, edit, or delete the event.

- **Loop:** Causes the event to repeat when you drag the right edge beyond the natural length of the event.

- **Normalize:** Raises the volume so that the highest-level sample in the file reaches a user-defined level. This switch enables you to use the full dynamic range available. To define the normalization level, choose Options, Preferences, Audio, and change the value of the Normalize Peak Level (dB) field.

23

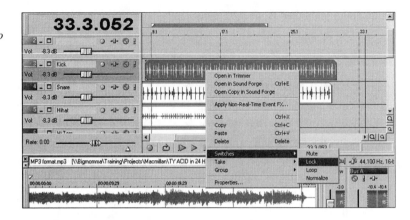

FIGURE 23.3

Right-click an event to access the Switches submenu.

Playback and Navigation

In the previous task, you saw that the Play From Start button In Vegas Audio LE looks and operates just like the Play From Start button in ACID. In fact, all the playback and navigation functions are almost identical to those in ACID. The first eight buttons on the Transport toolbar have the same function in both ACID and Vegas Audio LE. Two additional buttons on the Vegas Audio LE Transport toolbar (Skip Backward and Skip Forward) move the cursor forward or backward through the project in large increments (which are determined by the zoom level). Figure 23.4 shows the Vegas Audio LE Transport toolbar.

FIGURE 23.4

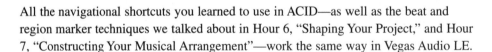

The Transport toolbar in Vegas Audio LE is almost identical to the one in ACID.

All the navigational shortcuts you learned to use in ACID—as well as the beat and region marker techniques we talked about in Hour 6, "Shaping Your Project," and Hour 7, "Constructing Your Musical Arrangement"—work the same way in Vegas Audio LE.

Recording

As mentioned earlier, Vegas Audio LE enables you to record multiple tracks while simultaneously playing back multiple tracks. The following sections discuss a few different techniques for recording.

Basic Recording

Each Track Header has an Arm For Record button as shown in Figure 23.5

Arm for Record

FIGURE 23.5

*Each Track Header
has an Arm For
Record button.*

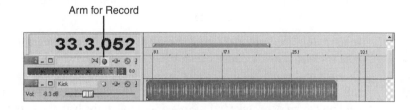

23

After properly configuring your computer to record (as described in Hour 15, "Recording and Creating Your Own Loops"), click the Arm For Record button on all the tracks to which you want to record. A record meter appears that allows you to check the record level before recording. With some sound cards, you can control the record level right in Vegas Audio LE. If this is the case with your sound card, a Record Level fader appears directly below the Record Level meter. If you do not see this fader, use the Windows Recording Control to set the proper record level. Position the cursor where you want the recording to begin, and click the Record button on the Transport toolbar. Vegas Audio LE draws the waveform in real time as you record. Click the Stop button to end the recording. In the Recorded Files dialog box that opens, choose whether you want to Delete or Rename the recording. Click Done when finished.

Punch-In

Sometimes you'll want to *punch-in* a recording. To do so, you'll use the punch-in method of recording.

NEW TERM

Punch-In

The term "punch-in" refers to the process of recording over a portion of an already-existing event, without affecting different portions of the same event. For example, if your guitarist plays a spectacular solo, but plays one bad note in the middle, you don't have to re-record the whole solo. You can set Vegas up so that it plays the solo, keeps the good parts, and instantly kicks into record mode when it reaches the bad note so that your guitarist can play the right note without recording over any of the material you want to keep from the first take.

Split the event where you want to start recording. Split the event again where you want the recording to stop. Select the middle event (the one over which you want to record).

Make a time selection starting a few seconds before the split and lasting a few seconds after the second split. This creates some pre-roll so that you can get ready to record, and a little post-roll after you stop recording so that you can see how it will fit. Arm the track(s) for recording, and click the Record button on the Transport toolbar. The new material records over the selected event.

In the case of our guitarist trying to replace one bad note, create the splits so that the bad note is isolated in a separate event. Click the event containing the bad note to select it. Create a time selection that covers the selected event as well as providing adequate pre-roll and post-roll. Click the Record button. The guitarist can play through the pre-roll to get into the groove, and continue playing through the bad note—but playing the correct note, of course! Even though the guitarist plays during the pre-roll and maybe the post-roll, only the selected event is replaced with the new take.

Multiple Takes

Sometimes you need to try several times before you get the recording you want. In these cases, set Vegas up to record multiple takes. Click the Loop Playback button and then follow the directions for punch-in recording given in the last section. Vegas loops the time selection (that is, it plays it back continually), and records a new take each time the cursor reaches the selected event.

After you've finished recording, right-click the event and choose Take from the shortcut menu to access any of the takes (they'll be listed at the bottom of the shortcut submenu as shown in Figure 23.6).

FIGURE 23.6

Access additional takes from the Take shortcut submenu.

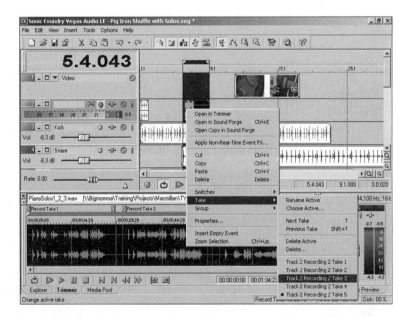

Saving and Rendering

The saving and rendering processes in Vegas Audio LE are essentially the same as those in ACID. Refer to Hour 4, "Saving Your Work," and Hour 17, "Creating Mixed Audio and Video Files," for details.

Task: Building a Project Using ACID and Vegas Audio LE

23

In this task, you will create a drum tack in ACID, render it to a WAV file, bring it into Vegas Audio LE, add additional tracks (both audio and video), and render the project to a WMV file.

1. Add `Snare Count2.wav` from the Hour 23 Samples folder on the companion CD to a new ACID project. Draw an event that covers the first measure.

2. Add the loops `Kick and Snare.wav` and `HiHat.wav` and draw in events from bar 2 to bar 26 for each.

3. Add one loop of the file `TomToms.wav` at bars 5, 9, 13, 17, 21, and 25.

4. Add the one-shot `Crash.wav` at bars 2, 14, and 26.

5. Pan the `HiHat` track 30% to the left; pan the `Crash` track 30% to the right. Now, as they say on the cooking channel, mix to taste. Watch your levels and remember not to let the meters go into the red.

6. Make sure that the project tempo is set to 120bpm and save the project. Choose File, Render As. Choose My Documents from the Save In drop-down list (or navigate to your desired folder), name the file **DrumTrack.wav**, choose Wave (Microsoft) (*.wav) from the Save As Type drop-down list, and use the default template. Make sure that all the check boxes are disabled. Click Save to render the file to the My Documents folder (or whatever folder you specified).

7. Start Vegas Audio LE. In the Explorer window, navigate to the Hour 23 Samples folder on the companion CD. Using your right mouse button, drag the file `MusicVideo.avi` to the beginning of the project. Choose Video Only, Add Video Across Time from the shortcut menu that opens when you release the mouse button.

8. Navigate to the My Documents folder (or wherever you saved it) and add the `DrumTrack.wav` file you created in ACID in steps 1 through 6 to the first audio track at the beginning of the Vegas Audio LE project.

9. Navigate to the Hour 23 Samples folder on the CD-ROM. Click the `Bass04.wav` file to select it. Hold the Ctrl key and add the `OrganPad01.wav` and `RhyGtr.wav`

files to the selection. Using the right mouse button, drag these three files to track 2 at the beginning of the project; choose Add Across Tracks from the shortcut menu.

10. Click the drop-down arrow next to the View button in the Explorer window and choose Region View.

11. Select the `PianoSolos1_2_3.wav`. Notice that there are three regions associated with this file. Using the right mouse button, select and drag all three regions to the beginning of the project in track 6. Add them as takes.

12. Choose Options, Ruler Format, Measures and Beats to display measures and beats on the Time ruler.

13. Select all three files—`Lead01`, `Lead02`, and `Lead03.wav`—and add them as takes at bar 13 in Track 7.

14. Play the project. Experiment with the different lead and solo piano takes until you find a combination you like. To choose a different take, right-click the event in track 6 or 7 and choose Take from the shortcut menu. From the bottom of the cascading menu, choose the take.

15. Mix your project to taste by adjusting volumes and pan settings and adding FX. Save the project and then render it as a WMV file using the 1Mbps template.

> We shot the footage for this video in and around the Foundry one evening. We edited it in Vegas Video. The drum loops were created by Rick Hoefling and Mark Siegenthaler. Rick also played the guitar parts. Mark played all the keyboard parts. We recorded the tracks in Gary's office using Vegas. The project was simple and lots of fun!

Summary

This hour was a whirlwind overview of Vegas Audio LE. You learned the differences and similarities between the ACID and Vegas Audio LE music-creation tools. You explored the interface for Vegas, learned about the various recording techniques, and used a combination of ACID and Vegas Audio LE to create, edit, and deliver a music video.

Q&A

Q. Can I use files from the ACID loop libraries in Vegas Audio LE?

A. Yes. In fact, any file you can open in ACID can also be opened in Vegas Audio LE. However, Vegas Audio LE is not designed to automatically match tempo and key. That's a job for ACID!

Q. Vegas Audio LE can open still-frame files such as bitmaps, TARGAs, and JPEGs. How can I make use of these types of files?

A. Even though these file types are for static images, they still might be useful for branding your projects. If you encode your file for streaming over the Internet, you can encode it as in a video format such as WMV or RM and use a bitmap of the CD (or some other) artwork for people to look at as they listen to the music.

Workshop

The following quiz and activity test your knowledge of Vegas Audio LE, and give you another opportunity to work with the application.

Quiz

1. Which product enables you to record multiple tracks simultaneously—ACID or Vegas Audio LE?

2. What is the best way to add a portion of a file to the Vegas Audio LE timeline rather than the entire file?

3. How do you split an event in Vegas Audio LE?

Quiz Answers

1. Vegas Audio LE enables you to record multiple audio tracks while simultaneously playing back multiple tracks.

2. The best way to add just a portion of a file to the Vegas timeline is to open it in the Trimmer, select the portion of the file you want to use, and drag it onto the timeline.

3. Just as you do in ACID! In the most simple case, place the cursor where you want the split to occur and press S on the computer keyboard.

Activities

1. When you finished the last task in this hour, one of the eight audio tracks remained free. If you have to, reconstruct the project. Then record a vocal part onto track 8.

23

HOUR 24

Using the Sonic Foundry Virtual MIDI Router

With a little help from a free software utility from Sonic Foundry called the Virtual MIDI Router (VMR), you can synchronize the playback of your ACID project with another software program running on the same PC (such as a MIDI sequencer or a multitrack audio program). What this means is that when you click the Play button in ACID, your ACID project begins to play back—and so will the other software that is synchronized to ACID. All this is explained in this hour, where you will:

- Learn about the SMPTE timecode, MIDI timecode, and MIDI clock
- Install and use the Sonic Foundry Virtual MIDI Router
- Set ACID to generate or receive a MIDI timecode
- Synchronize one application to another

Understanding MIDI Synchronization

In addition to all the synthesizer performance information presented in Hour 8, "Working with MIDI Tracks," a MIDI signal may contain two types of timing information called MIDI timecode and MIDI clock. This information can be used to synchronize two MIDI devices so that they play in unison.

MIDI timecode holds *SMPTE timecode information.* You can configure ACID to generate MIDI timecode (in this scenario, ACID acts as the "master" device), or to be triggered by the timecode generated sent by another MIDI device (in this case, ACID acts as a "slave" device).

SMPTE Timecode Information

SMPTE stands for the Society of Motion Picture and Television Engineers. This group standardized a timing and synchronization signal that enables various hardware and software devices to stay synchronized. The timecode is displayed in Hours:Minutes:Seconds:Frames format. This information can be conveyed in MIDI timecode.

Another part of the MIDI signal carries MIDI clock, which contains time data. MIDI clock advances one step (called a tick) each 1/24 of a beat (24 ticks per quarter note) from the beginning of the project, and is most commonly used to synchronize two sequencers. ACID can generate MIDI clock to synchronize the playback of an ACID project and a MIDI sequencer.

Setting MIDI Synchronization Options

In ACID, choose Options, Timecode to set up MIDI synchronization. Choose Generate MIDI Timecode to generate MIDI timecode from ACID. Choose Generate MIDI Clock to generate MIDI clock information from ACID. Or, choose Trigger from MIDI Timecode if you want ACID to follow the MIDI timecode generated by another device.

Choosing an Input/Output Device

The master device generates the MIDI information that the slave device follows. But there's one more step: An input/output device must be in place to allow the master and slave to communicate.

It's All About Communication

The master device has to communicate with the slave device through an input/output device—huh? Sounds confusing, but it's not really. Here's an analogy.

On your home stereo system, you have a CD player, and you have speakers. Both work just fine. Still, you won't hear any sound unless you run the signal from the CD player into an amplifier before it goes to the speakers.

Think of the CD player as the master device (the device generating the signal), and the speakers as the slave device (the device receiving the signal). You need the amplifier (the input/output device) so that the master and slave can communicate.

The input/output device you use can be hardware or software. The Sync page in the Preferences dialog box, (choose Options, Preferences, and click the Sync tab) allows you to select the hardware or software device that transmits or receives the timecode. Figure 24.1 shows the Sync tab of the Preferences dialog box. Note that you can choose an output device for MIDI timecode and for MIDI clock. This is because ACID can generate both MIDI timecode and MIDI clock. But remember that ACID does not receive MIDI clock from another device. Therefore, you can only choose an input device for MIDI timecode (which ACID *can* receive from another device).

FIGURE 24.1

The Sync tab of the Preferences dialog box enables you to customize your sync settings.

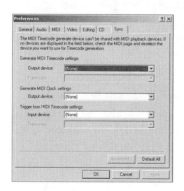

If you don't have any input or output devices on your system, no options appear in either of the Output Device drop-down lists or the Input Device drop-down list. In addition, both of the Frame Rate fields are unavailable. Before you can synchronize MIDI devices, you'll have to install an input/output device on your system. Here's where the Sonic Foundry Virtual MIDI Router comes in.

The Sonic Foundry Virtual MIDI Router

The Sonic Foundry Virtual MIDI Router (VMR) utility allows two software programs on the same PC to share MIDI timecode and MIDI time clock information. VMR is included free with ACID Pro and several other professional-level products from Sonic Foundry.

The steps you need to follow to install the VMR depend on the operating system installed on your PC. Step-by-step instructions for installation on Windows 98, Windows Me, and Windows 2000 are included in the ACID Online Help files.

To access these instructions, launch ACID and choose Help, Contents and Index. Click the Index tab. In the Type In The Keyword To Find field, type **Virtual MIDI Router**. The Virtual MIDI Router entry is highlighted in the index list. Just below it are two sub-sections: Configuring and Installing. Double-click the Installing entry.

In the right pane of the ACID Online Help window, select your operating system from the list. The entry expands to show you the step-by-step instructions you have to follow to install the Virtual MIDI Router on that system.

Configuring Your Sync Preferences

After you have installed the VMR, ACID can communicate with other software using MIDI timecode and MIDI time clock. The following sections explain how to set ACID to generate MIDI timecode and MIDI time clock information. Then you'll learn how to set the playback of ACID to be triggered by MIDI timecode generated by another device.

Generating MIDI Timecode

To set ACID up as the master device, you must first specify the output device that will transmit the MIDI data. Choose Options, Preferences to open the Preferences dialog box and click the Sync tab. In the Generate MIDI Timecode Settings section, the Output Device drop-down list displays every output device currently installed on your system. The Sonic Foundry Virtual MIDI Router is listed here. Choose a device (such as VMR) from the list.

Make sure that you set all your slave devices to receive from the same master device (the device you select from the Output Device drop-down list in the Generate MIDI Timecode Settings section.

As soon as you choose an output device, the Frame Rate drop-down list becomes available. Choose a frame rate from the list. In most cases, it probably won't matter what you choose here. What does matter is that you make sure that all your slave devices use the same frame rate as the one you choose here for the master. Keeping the frame rates the same ensures that the master and all the slaves use the same unit of time measurement.

Frame Rate? Isn't That a Film Thing?

Choosing a "frame rate" implies that you're somehow dealing with film or video, but that's not really the case here. And what's with all the choices in the Frame Rate drop-down list?

A frame rate is really just a way to measure time. The term did spring from film, where it represents how many frames display per second. Notice that all the choices in the list begin with SMPTE. The Society of Motion Picture and Television Engineers were concerned with time as it related to frames of film or video per second. Several SMPTE standards for measuring frame rate exist because film, U.S. video, and European video all display different numbers of frames per second and therefore require different time measurement.

You don't have to be dealing with film or video to make use of the SMPTE timecode standards. What really matters is that the frame rate you choose for each slave device matches the frame rate you choose for the master device. You just want to make sure that all your devices are "speaking the same language" and talking at the same pace.

24

Generating MIDI Clock

To set ACID to generate MIDI clock information, you essentially follow the same steps for generating MIDI timecode (as described in the preceding section). But first, you must enable a MIDI port that will carry the MIDI clock information. To do this, click the MIDI tab in the Preferences dialog box. Select the desired device from the Make These Devices Available for MIDI Track Playback and Generate MIDI Clock checklist.

Now click the Sync tab in the Preferences dialog box. The Output Device drop-down list in the Generate MIDI Clock Settings section displays all the MIDI devices you enabled back on the MIDI tab. Pick a device from the list, and then set all your slave devices to receive from the same device.

Chasing to MIDI Timecode

When you set ACID to trigger from MIDI timecode, you make ACID the slave, and ACID "listens" for and reacts to the incoming timecode (this process is referred to as "chasing" timecode). When the master device generates a message to play, ACID begins playing from the position indicated by the timecode.

To make ACID a slave, choose an input device from the Input Device drop-down list on the Sync tab of the Preference dialog box. Either a hardware device (such as a synthesizer or tape machine) or a virtual device (such as software like the VMR) that reads the timecode from another device can act as the input device. The Input Device drop-down list displays all the hardware or virtual input devices installed on your system. Choose a device from the list that matches the output device used by the master device.

The Frame Rate drop-down list in the section becomes active. From the list, choose the same frame rate that the master generates.

Specifying Offset

Sometimes it is useful to create a timecode offset so that the `0:00` time on your Time ruler does not actually correspond to the beginning of your ACID project.

To specify an offset, choose View, Time Ruler, Show Time Ruler to make the Time ruler visible. Click in your project timeline at the point where you want to make the new `0:00` point. Right-click the Time ruler and choose Set Time at Cursor. A text field appears below the cursor. In this text field, type the time you want at this point in the timeline. For instance, if you want this to be the `0:00` point, type `0:00` into the text field. Press the Tab key to enter the new offset. Notice that the `0:00` point in your Time ruler no longer corresponds to the beginning of the timeline.

Why Offset?

You might have a number of reasons for creating an offset like this. Here's one example: Suppose that you're scoring music for a film. The film is on an external video machine that you want to sync to your ACID project using the sync techniques you've learned in this hour.

The film has several scenes, and you want to create the music for each scene in its own ACID project. Right now you're working on the music for scene 3. Obviously, scene 3 starts several minutes into the film. For our example, assume that scene 3 starts at 15 minutes, 30 seconds. In SMPTE timecode lingo, that's `00:15:30:00`, which is the timecode generated by the video machine.

To make your life easier, create an offset in your ACID project so that the first measure of the project starts at `00:15:30.00` instead of at `00:00:00:00`. Now you don't have to build 15 minutes and 30 seconds of empty measures into the beginning of your project to sync up with the video.

Establishing the Master/Slave Relationship

Now that the hard part is done, all that remains is to specify which device will be the master, and which will be the slave. To make this choice for your current ACID project, choose Options, Timecode. You are presented with three options:

- Generate MIDI Timecode
- Generate MIDI Clock
- Trigger From MIDI Timecode

Those should look familiar! They match the preferences we've been discussing throughout this hour. Choose the appropriate one from the list depending upon the role you want ACID to play in the sync relationship.

Task: Use the Virtual MIDI Router to Sync Two Applications

For this task, you'll sync two instances of ACID. The same steps can be used to sync ACID to other software (including non-Sonic Foundry software) or to hardware devices. Before you begin, make sure that you have installed the VMR as described earlier this hour.

> Because ACID allows for an unlimited number of tracks, you can accomplish all you need to do in a normal project with only one instance of the program running. Therefore, in practice, you'd probably never have a reason to link two instances of the program together. But because we don't know what additional MIDI software you have on your PC, using two instances of ACID effectively demonstrates the procedures for syncing two devices.

1. In a new project, create two tracks using Mid Tempo Ballad Drums A 04.wav and Maria Bass A 01 I.wav. Draw in 16 bars of each file.

> All the loops used in this example can be found in the Chapter 24 Samples folder on the CD-ROM included with this book. These loops are from the *ACID Latin* loop library from Sonic Foundry.

24

2. Click the Save button and name the project **Master**.

3. From the Windows Start menu, open a second instance of ACID.

4. In the new project, create two tracks using `Maria Perc Mix A 03.wav` and `Maria Guitar A 01 1.wav`. Draw in 16 bars of each file. Click the Save button, and name the project **Slave**.

5. Back in the `Master` project, choose Options, Preferences to open the Preferences dialog box. Click the Sync tab.

6. In the Generate MIDI Timecode Settings section, choose Sonic Foundry MIDI Router from the Output Device drop-down list. Choose SMPTE Non-drop 30(30fps) from the Frame Rate drop-down list. Click OK.

7. Choose Options, Timecode, Generate MIDI Timecode. The master is now set to generate MIDI Timecode.

8. In the `Slave` project, choose Options, Preferences to open the Preferences dialog box. Click the Sync tab.

9. In the Trigger From MIDI Timecode Settings section, choose Sonic Foundry MIDI Router from the Input Device drop-down list. Choose SMPTE Non-drop 30(30fps) from the Frame Rate drop-down list. Click OK.

10. Choose Options, Timecode, Trigger From MIDI Timecode. The slave is now set to chase MIDI timecode generated from the master.

11. Click the Play From Start button in the `Master` project. Notice that the `Master` and the `Slave` projects begin to play simultaneously.

12. Stop playback and place the cursor in measure 4 of the `Master` project.

13. Click the Play button in the `Master` project and notice that the `Slave` project also starts to play back from measure 4. You've successfully synchronized the two projects using MIDI!

> Some sound cards may require you to route the output from the two ACID projects to separate outputs for this experiment to work.

Summary

In this hour, you learned the meaning of SMPTE timecode, MIDI timecode, and MIDI clock. You also learned how to install and use the Sonic Foundry Virtual MIDI router to send timecode from one application to another and to sync two MIDI applications or devices together.

Q&A

Q. How do I get a SMPTE timecode from an external device into my PC?

A. You have to purchase a specific hardware device that connects to your PC. This device must accept SMPTE timecode and convert it to MIDI timecode.

Q. When would I use MIDI clock?

A. MIDI clock is best used when you are syncing to a sequencer. MIDI clock contains tempo as well as positional information. If your ACID project contains tempo changes, MIDI clock will send the tempo change information to the slave application. MIDI timecode is the best choice for syncing to an external hardware device such as a video tape machine that will lock to SMPTE timecode.

Workshop

The following quiz and activity will help you put the information you have learned in this hour to use.

Quiz

1. What does SMPTE stand for?

2. What do you call a device that chases or is triggered by timecode?

3. In SMPTE timecode, what do the last two digits represent?

Quiz Answers

1. SMPTE stands for the Society of Motion Picture and Television Engineers.

2. When a device chases or is triggered by timecode, it is called the slave device.

3. SMPTE timecode breaks time into Hours:Minutes:Seconds:Frames. The last two digits in SMPTE timecode represent frames.

Activities

1. Open ACID and any other application that can sync to SMPTE or MIDI timecode. Set ACID as the master device and the other application as the slave. Use the Virtual MIDI Router to sync the two together.

2. You're now armed with a huge amount of valuable information on how to use ACID to create your own royalty-free music. Undoubtedly, you've got countless ideas running around in your head. Use the knowledge you now have to "go out there" and turn those ideas into great music! Have fun, and thanks for reading!

24

GLOSSARY

.aif   Mixed AIFF file. Uncompressed file format, compatible with Macintosh computers.

.asf   Mixed Windows Media file. Highly compressed file format, suitable for streaming over the Internet. Compatible with Windows Media Player. *See also* .wma.

.mp3   MPEG Layer 3 file. Highly compressed file format, suitable for playback in portable players. Requires a media player that supports .mp3 file playback.

.rm   RealMedia file. Highly compressed file format, suitable for streaming over the Internet. Compatible with Real Networks players, such as RealPlayer and RealMedia Jukebox.

.wav   Mixed WAV file. Uncompressed file format, compatible with PCs running Microsoft Windows operating system.

.wma   Mixed Windows Media file. Highly compressed file format, suitable for streaming over the Internet. Compatible with Windows Media Player. *See also* .asf.

accelerando   To speed up the music over time.

amplitude modulation   Periodic gain adjustment or change in volume over time.

analog   With regard to audio recording: a method that uses continually changing voltage or current to represent a signal. The electrical signal can be thought of as being analogous to the original signal.

ASR   A type of audio envelop available in ACID and Vegas events with attack, sustain, and release parameters.

attack   The attack is the initial portion of the sound wave. A drum would have a fast attack since its peak (maximum amplitude) occurs early in the waveform. A violin would have a slow attack because its peak occurs relatively later in the waveform.

attenuate   To make the volume lower in level.

bandwidth   The amount of data that a given device can handle in a fixed amount of time. In this book, the term is used in the context of an Internet connection. Usually expressed in bits per second.

beats per measure   Signifies how many beats occur in one bar or measure of music. By default, ACID assumes 4 beats per measure.

beats per minute (bpm)   The tempo of a piece of music is indicated by how many beats occur in one minute. If the tempo is 60bpm, a single beat occurs once every second. A lower bpm is a slower tempo. A higher bpm is a faster tempo.

bit   The most elementary unit in digital systems. Its value can only be 1 or 0. Bits are used to represent values in the binary numbering system. For instance, the 8-bit binary number 00000110 is equal to the number 6 in the decimal system.

bit-depth   The number of bits that represent a single sample. Also referred to as word length. The bit-depth for CD quality audio is 16-bits.

blues mumble   When someone in the band mumbles something in response to what is being played or sung. It may or may not have any direct relation to the subject. Slang terms and ethnic phrases are often used.

buffering   When you send signal from a track to an effects plug-in, ACID actually loads a certain amount of the signal into RAM before it sends any signal to the plug-in. This process—called buffering—helps provide a steady stream of data to the effect. The more signal ACID buffers, the greater the latency you experience.

bus   The electrical signal path along which signals travel. In the Mixer window of ACID, there may be up to 26 stereo buses in addition to the Master bus and the Preview bus.

byte   Eight bits equal a byte. A 16-bit CD-quality recording requires 2 bytes of memory to store a single sample.

channel   In the context of MIDI, channel refers to one of 16 possible data channels over which MIDI data may be sent.

chase   The process whereby a slave device attempts to synchronize itself with a master device.

clipping   When the amplitude (volume) of a sound is above the maximum allowed recording level, clipping occurs. In digital systems, clipping is seen as a clamping of the data to a maximum value, such as 32,767 in 16-bit data. Clipping causes sound to distort.

codec (*co*der/*dec*oder)   An algorithm that compresses the data in the file and reduces the file size considerably.

crossfade   When two audio (or video) events overlap a crossfade is created by fading the end of the first event out as the beginning of the second events fades in. During the crossfade the two signals are mixed together.

DC   Direct Current.

DC offset   Sometimes the PC soundcard adds DC current to the audio signal as it is recorded. This current causes the audio signal to alternate around a point other than the normal centerline in the sound file. ACID, Sound Forge, and Vegas enable you to adjust for DC offset, returning the signal to its normal centerline.

decibel   Audio volume and changes in audio volume are represented by decibels (dB). Engineers use this logarithmic representation of volume change because it most accurately represents how the human ear perceives changes in volume. Sounds of the same volume have a value of 0dB. If you want to make a sound twice as loud as its current volume, you apply a 6dB gain. Likewise, to reduce the volume of a sound to half its current volume, apply a gain of –6dB. The equation used to calculate dB is dB = 20 X log (V1/V2).

destructive edits   When an edit you make to a file permanently changes the source data this is referred to as a destructive edit. Sound Forge XP is a destructive editor.

DirectX plug-in   Software that conforms to the DirectX plug-in architecture allows for the best possible performance of multimedia in the Windows environment.

dry   A signal to which no FX have been added. Conversely, a signal to which FX have been added is referred to as *wet*.

dynamic range   The difference between the maximum and minimum signal levels. Music that has very quiet sections as well as very loud sections is said to have a wide dynamic range.

envelopes   As used by ACID, a way of automating the change of a certain parameter over time. Envelopes can be used to change volume, panning, FX, and bus sends over time.

equalization   The selective attenuation (cutting) and boosting of different frequencies in the audio signal. You will usually hear EQ discussed in terms of low, mid-range, and high frequencies.

event   In ACID (and Vegas), a placeholder on the Track View timeline that contains all or a portion of a media file. When you drag a media file (or portion of a media file) into the Track View, you create an event. By editing an event, you are editing pointers to the media file rather than editing the actual media file itself.

frame rate (video/film)   The speed (or rate) at which individual frames (images) of the video or film are displayed. A faster frame rate results in smoother motion. The human eye perceives 24 frames per second as full motion.

frequency   Description of how many cycles of a repetitive waveform occur in one second. A waveform that completes one cycle in one second has a frequency of 1Hz.

gain   The amount by which a signal is amplified.

Hertz (Hz)   Hertz represents cycles per second; in audio, Hertz is used as a unit of measurement for frequency. The note Concert A on a piano has a frequency of 440Hz. In other words, it vibrates at 440 cycles per second.

ID3 information   ID3 information includes data such as artist, album, song title, and more. This information can be added to your MP3 files and displayed by MP3 players. ID3 information allows you to provide these details to the people who download and listen to your music.

latency   The amount of time it takes for your computer to respond to and let you see or hear a change you make in a program's controls.

master   The device that generates MIDI Timecode for other devices or applications to chase to.

media file   Where a data file represents a document or spreadsheet, a media file represents an image, audio, or video file. ACID (as well as Sound Forge and Vegas) can accommodate both audio and video media files. When you drag a media file into the Track View, an event is created.

MIDI (Musical Instrument Digital Interface) Pronounced "middy." A digital signal system used to communicate performance information to and from musical instruments such as synthesizers and computer sound cards. MIDI is not audio. It simply contains performance information concerning a note's pitch, length, volume, attack, delay time, and so forth. MIDI does not make a sound. It simply tells the synthesizer, sampler, or sound card how to perform.

MIDI clock Part of the MIDI signal that contains time data. It advances one step each 1/24 of a beat and is most commonly used to sync two sequencers together. ACID can generate MIDI clock for syncing ACID and a MIDI sequencer.

MIDI port The physical MIDI connection on a piece of MIDI gear. This port can be a MIDI in, out, or thru. Your computer must have a MIDI port to use MIDI playback to an external device such as a synthesizer, or to output MIDI Timecode to an external device.

MIDI Timecode All the SMPTE timecode information that has been converted into part of a MIDI signal. Used as a standardized timing and sync signal that enables various hardware and software devices to stay synchronized (playing at the same time).

mix A function in ACID that allows multiple sound files to be blended into one file at user-defined relative levels. Multiple tracks can be mixed together to create a single stereo file.

mixed audio file In this type of file, multiple tracks of audio are combined into a single mono or stereo file. To listen to your ACID compositions outside of ACID (for example, with a CD player or media player), you must create a mixed audio file.

non-destructive When any edits preformed do not alter or "destroy" the original media file in any way, it is termed a non-destructive edit.

normalize To raise a file's volume so that the highest-level sample in the file reaches a user-defined level. Use this function to make sure that you are fully using the dynamic range available to you.

octave A full set of eight musical notes where the frequency (which determines the pitch) of the last note is exactly double the frequency of the first note.

pan To place a mono or stereo sound source perceptually between two or more speakers. ACID enables you to place a track 100% in the right speaker or 100% in the left—or anywhere in between—by using the pan fader in the Track Headers.

Peak file (*.sfk)   ACID displays the waveform of audio files graphically on a computer monitor. This visual information must be generated by ACID when the audio file is opened and can take a few seconds. ACID then saves this information as a Peak file (*.sfk). This file stores the information for displaying waveform information, so that opening a file is almost instantaneous. The Peak data file is stored in the directory in which the file resides and has a `*.sfk` extension. If the Peak data file is not in the same directory as the file or is deleted, it will be recalculated the next time you open the file.

plug-in   An applet that can be added to a software product to enhance the feature set. ACID supports DirectX-compatible plug-ins.

plug-in chain   Plug-ins, such as Sonic Foundry DirectX FX, can be strung together into a chain so that the output of one effect feeds into the input of another. ACID enables you to chain up to 32 effects in a single FX chain.

pre-roll/post-roll   Pre-roll is the amount of time elapsed before an event occurs. Post-roll is the amount of time after the event. When performing a punch-in style of recording, the pre-roll determines the amount of time before the punch-in occurs and the post-roll determines the amount of time the project will continue to play after the recording has ended.

preset   A snapshot of the current settings in a plug-in. Presets are created and named so that you can easily get back to a group of settings that you have previously created. All presets can be accessed from the combo box on the top of most plug-in dialog boxes.

punch-in   To record over an isolated portion of existing audio to add audio or to fix a mistake in the original audio.

RAM   Random Access Memory.

real time   In ACID, edits and FX are applied in real time, meaning that you do not have to stop and render the file to hear the FX or edits.

Red Book standard   Phillips and Sony (the companies that developed CD technology) developed the *Red Book* standard as a way to ensure universality in audio CD production. Among other things, the Red Book standard (so named because the binder that contained the original document had a red cover) specifies the total number of minutes worth of digital audio that can be included on a CD (74), the data transfer rate that must be supported (150Kbps), the sampling rate that must be used (44,100Hz), and the audio bit depth (16-bit).

region   A subsection of a sound file denoted by a start and end point. You can define any number of regions in a sound file.

ripple editing A type of editing in which events are moved later in time to make room for newly inserted events or moved earlier in time to replace events that are deleted. When a one-minute event is ripple-inserted into a project, the duration of the project lengthens by one minute. If one minute is ripple-deleted from the project, the project length is reduced by one minute. If ripple editing is turned off, the same operation does not affect the overall duration of the project.

ritardando (ritard) To slow down the music over time.

sample A discrete point of a sound signal in time. When you digitize a sound (by recording it onto your computer), you break the sound signal into discrete points, or samples.

sample rate The number of samples per second used to digitally store a sound. (Also referred to as the sampling rate, or sampling frequency.)

shortcut menu A context-sensitive menu, sometimes called a pop-up menu, which appears when you right-click certain areas of the screen. The functions available in the shortcut menu depend on the object being clicked as well as on the state of the program. As with any menu, you can select an item from the shortcut menu to perform an operation.

SMPTE Timecode A standard of time display and synchronization developed by the Society of Motion Picture and Television Engineers. SMPTE timecode is used to synchronize time between two applications or hardware devices. The timecode is calculated in Hours:Minutes:Second:Frames, where Frames are fractions of a second based on the frame rate. Frame rates for SMPTE timecode are 24, 25, 29.97 and 30 frames per second.

sound card The audio interface between your computer and the outside world. It is responsible for converting analog signals to digital and vice versa. ACID, Sound Forge, and Vegas Audio LE work with any Windows-compatible sound card.

streaming media Multimedia files that have been compressed to a small enough size that that they can be simultaneously downloaded and listened to or viewed over the Internet.

take A single pass at recording something. For instance, a lead guitar player might try several takes before achieving the perfect solo. A vocalist might try recording a verse several times (several takes) before conveying the desired feeling.

tempo The rate of the beat of a musical composition, usually specified in beats per minute (bpm).

track   A discrete timeline for audio or video data. Events are placed on tracks and determine when sound or images start and stop. Multiple audio tracks are mixed together to give you the composite sound that you hear.

track-atonce   With track-at-once CD burning, your burner's recording laser turns off at the end of every track. This capability allows you to save your songs to CD, one track at a time, so that you can add your current song and then put the CD aside until you have another song to add later.

transient   The initial peak at the beginning of a waveform. For instance, the moment at which the hammer strikes the string of the piano, it creates a transient.

Trim/Crop   A function that deletes all data in a sound file outside of the current selection.

triplet   Where three notes are performed in the time it usually takes to perform two. In standard 4/4 musical time, there are 4 beats per measure. A whole note lasts for the whole measure, a half note for half the measure, and a quarter note for a quarter of the measure. A quarter note can further be divided into two 8th notes. An 8th note triplet occurs when a group of three 8th notes are performed in the time of two 8th notes.

variable bit rate encoding   Automatically adjusting the bit rate to achieve higher quality and smaller file size. Generally, ACID raises the bit rate for complex passages and lowers the bit rate for simpler or quieter passages.

Virtual MIDI Router (VMR)   A software-only router for MIDI data between programs. No MIDI hardware or cables are required for a VMR, so routing can only be performed between programs running on the same PC. A VMR is normally used to synchronize two MIDI-capable programs (for example, a VMR allows ACID to drive a sequencer with SMPTE/MTC). Sonic Foundry supplies a VMR with Sound Forge, ACID, and Vegas called the Sonic Foundry Virtual MIDI Router.

volume envelopes   Volume envelopes vary the volume of an event or track across time.

waveform display   The part of the data window that shows a graph of the sound data waveform. The vertical axis corresponds to the amplitude of the wave. The horizontal axis corresponds to time, with the left-most point being the start of the waveform.

INDEX

C

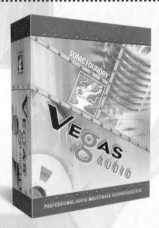

SAMS
Teach Yourself
in 24 Hours

When you only have time for the answers™

Sams Teach Yourself in 24 Hours *gets you the results you want—fast! Work through 24 proven 1-hour lessons and learn everything you need to know to get up to speed quickly. It has the answers you need at the price you can afford.*

Sams Teach Yourself Flash 5 in 24 Hours

Phillip Kerman
  ISBN 0-672-32892-x
  $24.99 US/$37.95 CAN

Other *Sams Teach Yourself in 24 Hours* Titles

Photoshop 6
  Carla Rose
  ISBN 0-672-31955-1
  $24.99 US/$37.95 CAN

LiveMotion
  Molly Holzschlag
  ISBN 0-672-31916-0
  $24.99 US/$37.95 CAN

GoLive 5
  Adam Pratt
  ISBN 0-672-31900-4
  $24.99 US/$37.95 CAN

Paint Shop Pro 7
  T. Michael Clark
  ISBN 0-672-32030-4
  $19.99 US/$29.95 CAN

HTML
  Dick Oliver
  ISBN 0-672-31724-9
  $19.99 US/$29.95 CAN

Macromedia Dreamweaver 4
  Betsy Bruce
  ISBN 0-672-32042-8
  $24.99 US/$37.95 CAN

JavaScript
  Michael Moncur
  ISBN 0-672-32025-8
  $24.99 US/$37.95 CAN

All prices are subject to change.

SAMS

www.samspublishing.com

Hey, you've got enough worries.

Don't let IT training be one of them.

Get on the fast track to IT training at InformIT,
your total Information Technology training network.

 | **www.informit.com** | **SAMS**

■ Hundreds of timely articles on dozens of topics ■ Discounts on IT books from all our publishing partners, including Sams Publishing ■ Free, unabridged books from the InformIT Free Library ■ "Expert Q&A"—our live, online chat with IT experts ■ Faster, easier certification and training from our Web- or classroom-based training programs ■ Current IT news ■ Software downloads ■ Career-enhancing resources

What's on the CD-ROM

The companion CD-ROM contains all the project files used in the book and several evaluation versions of software products from Sonic Foundry, including ACID, ACID loops, Sound Forge, Vegas Audio, Vegas Video, VideoFactory, and Viscosity.

Windows 95, Windows 98, Windows Me, Windows NT, Windows 2000 Installation Instructions

1. Insert the disc into your CD-ROM drive.
2. From the Windows desktop, double-click the My Computer icon.
3. Double-click the icon representing your CD-ROM drive.
4. Double-click on `default.htm`. All the CD-ROM files can be accessed by the HTML interface.

If you have the AutoPlay feature enabled, `default.htm` will be launched automatically whenever you insert the disc into your CD-ROM drive.

By opening this package, you are also agreeing to be bound by the following agreement:

You may not copy or redistribute the entire CD-ROM as a whole. Copying and redistribution of individual software programs on the CD-ROM is governed by terms set by individual copyright holders.

The installer and code from the authors are copyrighted by the publisher and the authors. Individual programs and other items on the CD-ROM are copyrighted by their various authors or other copyright holders.

This software is sold as-is without warranty of any kind, either expressed or implied, including but not limited to the implied warranties of merchantability and fitness for a particular purpose. Neither the publisher nor its dealers or distributors assumes any liability for any alleged or actual damages arising from the use of this program. (Some states do not allow for the exclusion of implied warranties, so the exclusion may not apply to you.)

This CD-ROM uses long and mixed-case filenames requiring the use of a protected-mode CD-ROM driver.